HISTORY OF
United States Naval Operations
IN WORLD WAR II

★

VOLUME FIVE
The Struggle for Guadalcanal
August 1942–*February* 1943

Admiral William F. Halsey USN

HISTORY OF UNITED STATES NAVAL
OPERATIONS IN WORLD WAR II

VOLUME V

The Struggle for Guadalcanal

August 1942–*February* 1943

BY SAMUEL ELIOT MORISON

WITH AN INTRODUCTION BY

John B. Lundstrom

NAVAL INSTITUTE PRESS
Annapolis, Maryland

This book was brought to publication with the generous assistance of Marguerite and Gerry Lenfest.

Naval Institute Press
291 Wood Road
Annapolis, MD 21402

This edition published by arrangement with Little, Brown and Company, New York, NY. All rights reserved.
First Naval Institute Press paperback edition published 2010.
New Introduction © 2010 by United States Naval Institute.

Library of Congress Cataloging-in-Publication Data
Morison, Samuel Eliot, 1887–1976.
    History of United States naval operations in World War II / Samuel Eliot Morison.
        v.   cm.
    Originally published: Boston : Little, Brown, 1947–62.
    Includes bibliographical references and index.
    Contents: v. 1. The Battle of the Atlantic, 1939–1943 — v. 2. Operations in North African waters, October 1942–June 1943 — v. 3. The Rising Sun in the Pacific, 1931–April 1942 — v. 4. Coral Sea, Midway and Submarine Actions, May 1942–August 1942 — v. 5. The Struggle for Guadalcanal, August 1942–February 1943 — v. 6. Breaking the Bismarcks Barrier, 22 July 1942–1 May 1944.
    ISBN 978-1-59114-547-9 (v. 1 : alk. paper) — ISBN 978-1-59114-548-6 (v. 2 : alk. paper) — ISBN 978-1-59114-549-3 (v. 3 : alk. paper) — ISBN 978-1-59114-550-9 (v. 4 : alk. paper) — ISBN 978-1-59114-551-6 (v. 5 : alk. paper) — ISBN 978-1-59114-552-3 (v. 6 : alk. paper) 1. World War, 1939–1945—Naval operations, American. I. Title.
    D773.M6 2010
    940.54'5973—dc22   2009052288

Printed in the United States of America on acid-free paper

27 26 25 24 23 22   15 14 13 12 11 10

To

The Memory of

WILLIS AUGUSTUS LEE

1888–1945

Vice Admiral, United States Navy

In 201 B.C. *Philip of Macedon defeated Rhodes in the naval battle of Lade, sinking two quinquiremes, forcing the other ships to flee, and occupying their base. Nevertheless, the Rhodian writers Zeno and Antisthenes claimed a victory for their fleet.* POLYBIUS, *writing the 16th book of his* HISTORIES *about fifty years later, has this to say about them:—*

That historians should give their own country a break, I grant you; but not so as to state things contrary to fact. For there are plenty of mistakes made by writers out of ignorance, and which any man finds it difficult to avoid. But if we knowingly write what is false, whether for sake of our country or our friends or just to be pleasant, what difference is there between us and hack-writers? Readers should be very attentive to and critical of historians, and they in turn should be constantly on their guard.

Preface

DURING the six months covered by this volume, the United States Navy fought six major engagements in waters adjacent to Guadalcanal, more bitter and bloody than any naval battle in American history since 1814. Four of them were night gunfire actions of a kind that we may never see again; two were carrier-air battles of the pattern set at Coral Sea; all are highly interesting and significant in the history of war. In addition, there were a score of naval actions involving destroyers and motor torpedo boats which never attained the dignity of names; fights almost daily between the Imperial Japanese Air Force and American fliers; some thirty occasions when land-based airplanes attacked ships; a fair number of submarine battles; and almost continual ground fighting by United States Marines and Army against Japanese troops, including the Battles of the Tenaru River, the Matanikau River, the Bloody Ridge, Henderson Field, Point Cruz, the Gifu and the Galloping Horse, which are worthy to figure in any military history. The Guadalcanal campaign is unique for variety and multiplicity of weapons employed and for coördination between sea power, ground power and air power. And certainly no campaign in modern history is more fraught with ferocity and misery; none has blazed more brightly with heroism and self-sacrifice. So, although this story is one primarily of naval operations, we have endeavored to describe the struggle for Guadalcanal as a whole, subject to the limitations of space, time and imperfect human knowledge.

We cannot pretend to write of that stinking island with the detachment and objectivity expected of trained historians, for both Commander Shaw and I had a part in the torment and the passion; and we sometimes feel that we are writing not for the present or for posterity but for ghosts, like that of Private First

Class Cammeron of the Marine Corps whose rude epitaph I copied from one of the long rows of crosses and stars in the Lunga Point Cemetery:—

> And when he goes to Heaven
> To Saint Peter he will tell:
> Another Marine reporting, Sir;
> I've served my time in hell!

I visited Guadalcanal shortly after the island was secured, obtained many data which otherwise would have been lost, and served for a time in U.S.S. *Washington*. Commander James C. Shaw, who took part in the campaign as gunnery plotting room officer of *Atlanta*, did part of the basic research. Lieutenant Roger Pineau USNR helped in the research; Mr. Donald R. Martin drew up the Task Organizations. Information and expert advice on ground fighting have been furnished by Lieutenant Colonel Robert D. Heinl USMC and Major John L. Zimmerman USMCR of the Marine Historical Section, by Colonel Samuel B. Griffith USMC and Lieutenant Colonel John Howland USMCR, and by Colonel Kent Roberts Greenfield and several members of his staff in the Army historical Section, especially Dr. John Miller. Commodore R. W. Bates of the War College Analysis Section kindly made available the preliminary findings of his exhaustive study of the Battle of Savo Island. Most of the charts and maps were executed by Mr. Charles H. Ward and Miss Isabel J. Gatzenmeier of the Naval War College staff.

All dates in this volume for events in and around Guadalcanal are East Longitude dates, and all times are those of Zone "Love," which is Greenwich time minus eleven hours. The Japanese coming from the west, and Americans coming from the east, often used other zone times, but an effort has been made to transpose everything into that of Zone minus Eleven.

During the period when this volume was under preparation, Rear Admiral John B. Heffernan was Director of Naval History, Rear Admiral Felix Johnson and Rear Admiral Edward C. Ewen,

Chiefs of Public Relations; Rear Admiral Thomas B. Inglis, Director of Naval Intelligence; Admiral Raymond A. Spruance, Rear
Admiral Allan E. Smith and Vice Admiral Donald B. Beary, Presi-
dents of the Naval War College; Honorable John L. Sullivan, Secretary of the Navy; Honorable James Forrestal, Secretary of National
Defense. As our former Commander in Chief, President Franklin
D. Roosevelt, named the destination, so these officers furnished the
provisions, sea letters, clearance and pratique. But, in good naval
tradition, they have allowed the captain to sail his own ship. So he,
and he alone, is to be held accountable for errors in navigation.

SAMUEL ELIOT MORISON

HARVARD UNIVERSITY
10 February 1949

During the four years since the first edition of this volume appeared, all Guadalcanal survivors have had a chance to read it, and
very many have sent in corrections, most of them minor. But I am
proud to say that my narratives and conclusions on highly controversial actions like Savo Island, Tassafaronga, and Rennell Island
have remained virtually unchallenged. Captain John W. McElroy
USNR has had charge of investigating complaints and incorporating
corrections.

S.E.M.

NORTHEAST HARBOR, MAINE
August 1953

Contents

List of Illustrations

(All photographs not otherwise desribed are official United States Navy)

List of Charts

Abbreviations

Officers' ranks and bluejackets' ratings are those contemporaneous with the event. Officers and men named will be presumed to be of the United States Navy unless it is otherwise stated; officers of the Naval Reserve are designated USNR. Other service abbreviations are: —

RAN, Royal Australian Navy
RN, Royal Navy
USA, United States Army
USMC, United States Marine Corps; USMCR, Reserve of same

Other abbreviations used in this volume: —
A.A.F. — United States Army Air Force
Anzac — Australian-New Zealand Area Command
ATIS — Allied Translator and Interpreter Section, General MacArthur's
     command
BB — Battleship
Buships — Bureau of Ships
CA — Heavy Cruiser
Cardiv — Carrier Division
C. in C. — Commander in Chief
Cincpac — Commander in Chief, United States Pacific Fleet
Cincpoa — Commander in Chief, Pacific Ocean Areas
CL — Light Cruiser
C.N.O. — Chief of Naval Operations
C.O. — Commanding Officer
Com — as prefix means Commander. Examples: Comairsopac — Com-
     mander Aircraft South Pacific; Comcrudiv — Commander Cruiser
     Division; Cominch — Commander in Chief United States Fleet;
     Comsopac — Commander South Pacific Force and Area
CTF — Commander Task Force; CTG — Commander Task Group
CV — Aircraft Carrier
CVE — Escort Carrier
DD — Destroyer
Desdiv — Destroyer Division; Desron — Destroyer Squadron
H.M.A.S. — His Majesty's Australian Ship
H.M.N.Z.S. — His Majesty's New Zealand Ship
IFF — Identification, Friend or Foe (a radio device)
Inter. Jap. Off. — USSBS *Interrogations of Japanese Officials* 2 vols., 1946

JANAC — Joint Army-Navy Assessment Committee *Japanese Naval and Merchant Shipping Losses World War II* (1947)
LCT — Landing Craft tank
MTB — Motor torpedo boat
O.N.I. — Office of Naval Intelligence
Op — Operation
PT — Motor Torpedo Boat
R.A.A.F. — Royal Australian Air Force
Sonar— Echo-ranging sound gear
Sopac — South Pacific
TBS (Talk Between Ships) — Voice radio
TF — Task Force; TG — Task Group
USSBS — United States Strategic Bombing Survey
VB — Bomber plane or squadron
VF — Fighter plane or squadron
VMF — Marine fighter squadrom
VMSB — Marine scout or dive-bombing squadron
VP — Patrol plane or squadron
VS — Scout plane or squadron
VT — Torpedo-bomber or squadron
WDC — Washington Document Center
YP — Patrol Vessel

Aircraft designations (numerals in parentheses indicate number of engines)

United States

B-17 — Flying Fortress, Army (4) heavy bomber, land-based
B-26 — Marauder, Army (2) medium bomber, land-based
F4F — Wildcat, Navy (1) fighter, land- or carrier-based (F4F-3P, photo)
OS2U — Kingfisher, Navy (1) scout-observation seaplane
P-38— Lightning, Army (2) pursuit (fighter) plane, land-based
P-39, P-40 — Army (1) pursuit (fighter) planes, land-based
PBY — Catalina, Navy (2) patrol seaplane; PBY-5A, amphibian
SB2U-3 — Vindicator, Navy (1) scout bomber, land- or carrier-based
SBD — Dauntless, Navy (1) scout or dive-bomber, land- or carrier-based
TBD, TBF — Devastator, Avenger, Navy (1) torpedo-bomber, carrier-based

Japanese

"Betty" — Mitsubishi Zero-1 (2) medium bomber
"Emily" — Kawanishi Zero-2 (4) bomber (flying boat)
"Kate" — Nakajima 97-2 (1) high-level or torpedo-bomber
"Mavis" — Kawanishi 97 (4) patrol bomber (flying boat)
"Val" — Aichi 99-1 (1) dive-bomber
"Zeke" (called "Zero" in 1942–43) — Zero-3 (1) fighter plane

Introduction

THE STRUGGLE for Guadalcanal, August 1942–February 1943, is the fifth volume of Rear Admiral Samuel Eliot Morison's magisterial *History of United States Naval Operations in World War II.* The large tropical island of Guadalcanal, situated near the southern end of the Solomon chain in the southwest Pacific Ocean, fell to Imperial Japan in May 1942 during the Battle of the Coral Sea. Soon afterward it became strategically significant because of the airfield the Japanese were constructing to extend their reach deep behind Allied lines. In August 1942 Guadalcanal was the main objective of the first amphibious offensive launched by the United States in the Pacific War. Morison's Volume IV, *Coral Sea, Midway and Submarine Actions, May 1942– August 1942*, ends on the second day of the invasion, 8 August, when the successful landing on Guadalcanal led to the swift capture of the vital airfield. The next day, 9 August, as Volume V begins, the Allies suffered in the Battle of Savo Island what was, aside from the attack on Pearl Harbor, their worst naval defeat of the entire Pacific War. The balance of Volume V deals with the incredibly difficult task of holding and expanding the Guadalcanal beachhead against the savage Japanese counteroffensive on sea, air, and land. The issue of who would dominate was in doubt many times that summer and fall. Only on 15 November 1942, after a dizzying succession of bloody battles on, around, and over Guadalcanal, did Japan finally relent.

Nonetheless, as Volume V explains, nearly three more months of hard fighting were required before 9 February 1943, when the last Japanese position on Guadalcanal was finally taken. The naval battles for Guadalcanal were rarely equaled during the war for ferocity and valor. The final tally of warship losses, as Morison notes in this volume (p. 372), was "surprisingly even" between both sides, but the final tally of men and aircraft losses was not: the campaign cost Japan far more. Even worse, Japanese losses were far more difficult for the Empire to replace, while American mobilization was truly just beginning. More than the epic victory at Midway, the long, bitter, and costly naval campaign to secure Guadalcanal constituted the turning point of the Pacific War. Never again would Japan meet the Allies on more or less equal terms in the Pacific, and never again would a Japanese victory have the potential to affect the outcome of the war.

Morison's Volume V first appeared in November 1949, barely four years after the signing of the surrender on board the U.S.S. *Missouri* in Tokyo Bay. That brief interval between the end of the conflict and publication compares to a history of the American Civil War published in 1869. Today, very few Civil War books from as early as 1869 are regularly consulted by general readers. The same is true for most World War II histories that originated so near to its end. Granted, Volume V is part of the U.S. Navy's de facto official history of World War II, but it is fair to ask after so many years whether advancing scholarship has passed it by. Most certainly, one of its strongest assets is the author's superb writing style. Like the rest of Morison's large body of work, Volume V sparkles and flows with a clarity and turn of phrase few histories can match. The question becomes whether it should be on the shelf alongside the works of other superb stylists like Edward Gibbon and William H. Prescott, whose brilliant histories, though outdated, are now treasured mainly because they are such delightful reading.

The answer to that question is decidedly "no," this work should not stay on the shelf. Far from being rendered obsolete, Volume V remains important for the history of the Pacific War precisely because nothing has superseded it as the indispensable one-volume account of the naval campaign of Guadalcanal. Morison took full advantage of being on the scene shortly after the campaign ended. He examined the island and the surrounding waters where the battles took place and came to know many of the participants, including senior commanders. That invaluable perspective brought an immediacy and a passion to his treatment that no one today could duplicate. In the long run, however, its early compilation also represents a weakness that Morison fully understood. The preface he wrote in 1947 for the first volume of the series observed, "No history written during or shortly after the event it describes can pretend to be completely objective or even reasonably definitive. Facts that I know not will come to light; others that I discarded will be brought out and incorporated in new patterns of interpretation."[1] Morison's emotional involvement inevitably included certain judgments and prejudices that, if he had had more time to reflect and more access to additional sources, he might have modified. Moreover, unlike other "official histories," there was very little vetting of the manuscripts by others who might have tempered some of his more controversial assessments. Except for matters of national security, such as communications intelligence, he was given free rein to write what he wished.

The best and most comprehensive study of the entire campaign by land, sea, and air is Richard B. Frank's *Guadalcanal: The Definitive History of the Landmark Battle* (New York: Random House, 1990), a tour de force that is based on Japanese as well as extensive Allied sources. Another basic account with a heavy emphasis on naval operations is the trilogy by Eric Hammel: *Guadalcanal: Starvation Island* (New York: Crown, 1987), *Guadalcanal: The Carrier Battles* (New York: Crown, 1987), and *Decision at Sea* (New York: Crown, 1988). Certain naval battles have received treatments in more detail. Two books by Australian authors analyze Savo Island: Denis and Peggy Warner, with Sadao Seno, *Disaster in the Pacific: New Light on the Battle of Savo Island* (Annapolis, MD: Naval Institute Press, 1992), and Bruce Loxton with Chris Coulthard-Clark, *The Shame of Savo: Anatomy of a Naval Disaster* (Annapolis, MD: Naval Institute Press, 1994). Other fine battle studies include Charles Cook, *The Battle of Cape Esperance* (New York: Crowell, 1968), James W. Grace, *The Naval*

---

[1] Samuel Eliot Morison, *History of United States Naval Operations in World War II*, vol. I, *The Battle of the Atlantic, September, 1939–May 1943*, vii.

Battle of Guadalcanal: Night Action 13 November 1942 (Annapolis, MD: Naval Institute Press, 1999), and Russell S. Crenshaw, *Battle of Tassafaronga* (Annapolis, MD: Naval Institute Press, 2010). The air campaign for Guadalcanal is ably addressed in Thomas G. Miller Jr., *The Cactus Air Force* (New York: Harper & Row, 1969). This author's *The First Team and the Guadalcanal Campaign: Naval Fighter Combat from August to November 1942* (Annapolis, MD: Naval Institute Press, 1994) likewise discusses the air fighting over Guadalcanal and reconstructs the carrier battles of the Eastern Solomons (24–25 August 1942) and Santa Cruz (26 October 1942).

It is necessary to note some areas where subsequent scholarship on the naval campaign of Guadalcanal has contributed to "new patterns of interpretation" that go beyond Volume V. Morison based his battle accounts largely on the wartime Office of Naval Intelligence *Combat Narratives*, a preliminary effort based on action reports and war diaries. Only with the Battle of Savo Island did he have the benefit of a more comprehensive (if not totally objective) analysis by the U.S. Naval War College, an analysis, however, that was based only on official U.S. naval sources. Given the tight constraints of his publication schedule, Morison had little opportunity to avail himself of detailed interviews of participants (a real shame in the case of senior officers, from whom in many instances few personal insights have been preserved) or access to other important sources, especially detailed message files and collections of personal papers. Nor did he have extensive access to Australian and other Allied sources. For example, in their book on Savo the Warners explain that Morison wrongly blamed Sergeant William J. Stutt (the Royal Australian Air Force search pilot who spotted the Japanese cruiser force on the morning of 8 August) for supposedly delaying his report, thus contributing to the ambush of the Allied cruisers. Another mistake by Morison with regard to Australian naval forces was unintentionally omitting the participation of its cruisers in the Battle of the Eastern Solomons.

Probably the greatest area where new facts have come to light on Guadalcanal concern the Japanese side. Morison had to depend on a patchy collection of captured enemy documents and postwar summaries and interrogations that proved totally inadequate. The War History Office of the Japan Self-Defense Forces subsequently published a 102-volume official history, *Senshi Sosho*, of which Volume 49, *Nantohomen Kaigun Sakusen 1, Gato Dakkai Sakusen Kaishimade* [Southeast Area Naval Operations 1, To the Beginning of Operations to Recapture Guadalcanal] (Tokyo: Asagumo Shimbunsha, 1971) and Volume 83, *Nantohomen Kaigun Sakusen 2, Gato Tesshumade* [Southeast Area Naval Operations 2, To the Withdrawal from Guadalcanal] (Tokyo: Asagumo Shimbunsha, 1975) cover the Guadalcanal naval campaign in great detail. Richard Frank was the first Guadalcanal historian to use the *Senshi Sosho* volumes to his enormous benefit. Since then, an increasing number of Japanese sources are utilized in the West.

The second vast new resource of World War II history that was unavailable to Morison is communications intelligence, the Ultra decryption of Axis radio messages that the Allies used with great success throughout the war. Oddly enough, Morison's ignorance of Ultra was not a significant factor in his treatment of most of the Guadalcanal campaign because, unlike at Coral Sea and Midway, Japanese naval messages, with very few exceptions, could not be deciphered until early November 1942. Thus on 24 August naval intelligence failed to predict the early arrival of three Japanese carriers during the Battle of the Eastern Solomons, and in October of that same year it missed the deployment of two more carriers from Japan prior to the Battle of Santa Cruz. Only by the middle of November did the regular code breaking of Japanese messages resume in time to help the Americans fight and win the decisive Naval Battle of Guadalcanal.

Newer publications on some of the key admirals at Guadalcanal include George C. Dyer, *The Amphibians Came To Conquer: The Story of Admiral Richmond Kelly Turner*, 2 vols. (Washington, DC: U.S. Government Printing Office, 1971), E. B.

Potter, *Bull Halsey* (Annapolis, MD: Naval Institute Press, 1985), Gerald E. Wheeler, *Kinkaid of the Seventh Fleet: A Biography of Admiral Thomas C. Kinkaid, U.S. Navy* (Washington, DC: Naval Historical Center, 1995), and this author's *Black Shoe Carrier Admiral: Frank Jack Fletcher at Coral Sea, Midway and Guadalcanal* (Annapolis, MD: Naval Institute Press, 2006). Some of Morison's judgments regarding naval commanders can be questioned. He singled out Vice Admiral Frank Jack Fletcher, in charge of the carriers at the beginning of the Guadalcanal Campaign, for special criticism, especially Fletcher's recommendation to withdraw the carriers on 8 August, an act Morison indirectly blamed for the crushing defeat at Savo. Based on important new sources, including the personal papers of a marine colonel who was on Fletcher's staff, *Black Shoe Carrier Admiral* lays out the case in support of Fletcher's actions on 8–9 August 1942.

Any shortcomings of Samuel Eliot Morison's Volume V, *The Struggle for Guadalcanal*, do not overshadow its enduring historical value, particularly as a wonderfully vivid introduction to the topic. In the past sixty years, it has helped inspire many budding historians, including this author, to devote themselves to the history of the Pacific War. No doubt, *The Struggle for Guadalcanal* will continue to inspire historians for many years to come.

JOHN B. LUNDSTROM

The Struggle for Guadalcanal
August 1942–*February* 1943

CHAPTER I

King Solomon's Isles [1]

1567–1942

ON 8 August 1942 the American public, who had been starved
for good war news for two months, read in their morning
papers that United States Marines had landed on Guadalcanal and
Tulagi, islands in the South Pacific of which few had ever heard.
For the next year, hardly a day passed when Guadalcanal was not
in the news. That mountainous island of the Solomons group —
only ninety miles long by twenty-five wide, inhabited by a few
thousand wooly-haired Melanesians and offering no natural resources but mud, coconuts and malarial mosquitoes — was bitterly
contested by the naval, air and ground forces of the United States
and Japan for almost six months. In the Pacific war, Leyte and
Okinawa may have been as stubbornly fought for as Guadalcanal;
but this Solomon Island has had the distinction of being the scene
of numerous pitched battles and the occasion for six major naval
engagements within a space of four months.[2] In addition, there were
some half a hundred ship-to-ship and air-sea fights, only one of
which, in this superabundance of heavy slugging, attained the dignity of a battle name.[3] Costly they were, too, both in ships and in
men. You may search the seven seas in vain for an ocean graveyard with the bones of so many ships and sailors as that body of

[1] *The Discovery of the Solomon Islands by Alvaro de Mendaña in 1568*, ed. by
Lord Amherst and Basil Thomson, a Hakluyt Society Publication of 1901, contains
the best account of the early history of these Islands.
[2] (1) Savo Island, 9 Aug.; (2) Eastern Solomons, 23–25 Aug.; (3) Cape
Esperance, 11–12 Oct.; (4) Santa Cruz Islands, 26 Oct.; (5) Guadalcanal, 13–15
Nov.; (6) Tassafaronga, 30 Nov. 1942.
[3] The Battle of Rennell Island, 29–30 Jan. 1943 (chap. xv).

water between Guadalcanal, Savo and Florida Islands which our bluejackets named Ironbottom Sound.

Six weeks before the operation began, the United States Navy knew little more of the Solomons than did the public. If Admiral Turner's task force had been embarked on a voyage to the moon, the junior officers and bluejackets would have been only a little more ignorant of their destination than they were of Guadalcanal and the Solomons. These islands had never figured in the prewar plans of the United States Navy. The Marines, usually prepared to land anywhere at any time, possessed information on almost every group of Pacific islands except the Solomons. A hasty search for more data in Australia had yielded little, and knowledge of that was confined to the top echelons of command. The few Australian pilots on board were glum and close-mouthed; or, if asked by someone in the know, described Guadalcanal as a "bloody, stinking hole," which is exactly what it was. For six months after D-day the enemy made things so lively for all hands that opportunities to delve into the background were few, although contact with the Solomons' scenery was all too close.

Much as the Lesser Antilles tail off from Puerto Rico, so the Solomon Islands stream southeasterly from Rabaul, for about 600 miles. The seven big ones on the map look like a two-column task force being led by fiddle-shaped Bougainville toward Rabaul, with a wide, deep-water channel between columns which American sailors called "the Slot." The northeasterly column consists of Choiseul, Santa Isabel and Malaita; the southwesterly one of New Georgia, Guadalcanal and San Cristobal. There are plenty of medium-sized and small islands, too, that we shall be familiar with in due course — Tulagi, Russell, Rendova, Kolombangara, Vella Lavella, Treasury, Shortland, and finally Buka, which makes the head of the Bougainville fiddle.

Situated right under the Line, between latitudes 5° and 11° S, the Solomons are wet, hot and steamy. There is no difference between seasons except that more rain falls from November to March, when the northwest tradewinds blow, than during the rest of the year. The islands are jagged, lofty and volcanic; on Guadalcanal the mountains, rising to 8000 feet above the sea, are clothed with a dense tropical rain forest through which white cockatoos, minah birds and a variety of other bright and raucous wild fowl flit and scream. They are happy hunting grounds of the malaria-carrying mosquito. Parts of the northern plain and of the adjacent foothills which were so bitterly contested are covered with kunai grass which at a distance looks like that of a green New England pasture. But the blades of the kunai grass run up to seven feet tall; they are stiff, edged like a bandsaw and almost as bad for soldiers to work through as the jungle. The grass is shorter on the ridges, and the effect of these light green patches on the dark green jungle gives the islands a strange, leprous appearance. Smooth coral beaches, common in other parts of the Pacific, are rare here; but there is compensation in the lack of coral heads and reefs that bedevil landing operations. The only cultivation is on selected coastal plains, where during the last fifty years the jungle and kunai grass have given way to extensive coconut plantations owned by Europeans but tended by Melanesian natives. These fine, upstanding "blackfellows" have resisted the impact of European civilization far better than their gentler Micronesian and Polynesian cousins.

Don Alvaro Mendaña was responsible for the discovery and naming of the Solomons. Like Columbus he was looking for gold, and like many other explorers he endeavored to conceal his failure under a delusive name. A young Spanish soldier, favorite nephew of the Viceroy of Peru, Don Alvaro persuaded his uncle to give him two well found ships, in order to find King Solomon's Ophir and the lost continent of Terra Australis. They sailed from Callao on 19 November 1567, passed between the Marquesas and Tuamotus without sighting either, made first landfall in the Ellices, narrowly escaped shipwreck at Ontong Java, and on 7 February 1568 sighted a high island that Mendaña named "Santa Isabel." An unusual daytime appearance of Venus led the ships into a bay that they called after her, Estrella.

While Hernan Gallego, an ancient mariner among the officers,

set the sailors to felling trees and building a small vessel, Pedro de
Ortega with soldiers in armor hacked a jungle trail up to the jagged crest of Santa Isabel, hoping to be the Balboa of Terra Australis. By the time they returned, *Santiago*, the new vessel, was
ready to set forth on an exploring expedition under Ortega's command. Sailing through the strait later named Indispensable after a
British frigate, they discovered and named Florida Island on Easter
Sunday,[4] doubled back through Sealark Channel and named the
great high island on their port hand Guadalcanal,[5] after Ortega's
home town in far-off Valencia. *Santiago* anchored in Lunga Roads,
her company went ashore, met an unfriendly reception from the
natives, promptly set sail and steered toward a small jagged island
looking like a blue cockscomb rising from the sea. Its name, they
ascertained from the natives, was Sabo; and Savo Island it still is,
a name not likely to be forgotten. "This island is high and round
and contains much food, yams, honeycombs, roots and pigs," reported Ortega. "In the middle is a volcano" — which last erupted
in 1850. After satisfying their curiosity about Savo, the Spaniards
rejoined their fleet at Estrella Bay.

Santiago then piloted the other two ships back to Guadalcanal.
Mendaña landed west of Point Cruz, which he so named; he intended to prospect for gold, but the warlike natives objected violently. So, after calling at Malaita and San Cristobal, taking on board
a few samples of what passed for gold, and a flock of white cockatoos which had to be eaten on the homeward passage, Mendaña's
fleet made sail on 18 August 1568. The commander wished to steer
southeasterly, counting on an equinoctial change in the tradewind;
but Gallego, remarking "The landsman reasons but the seaman
navigates," insisted on standing north to catch the westerlies. They
discovered Wake Island on this route and finally, after terrible
sufferings and the loss of one third of the men, arrived at Callao on
11 September of the following year.

[4] *Pascua florida* in Spanish; the American Florida was so named by Ponce de
León for the same reason.
[5] The spelling "Guadalcanar," found in several books and old charts, is a cor-
ruption.

Although Mendaña was eager to colonize the Solomon Islands, he was unable to organize another expedition until 1595. On that voyage he was unable to find anything nearer to the Solomons than the Santa Cruz Islands, and there he died. The survivors promptly returned to Peru.

For almost two centuries the Solomon Islands were forgotten. Royal hydrographers assumed that they had never existed — how pleased the United States Navy would have been, were that true! — and removed them from the charts. Not until 1767 was Guadalcanal rediscovered, by a great French navigator, the Sieur de Bougainville, for whom the big northern island is named. Lieutenant Shortland RN followed in 1788 and named a small island after himself and a big one after his king, New Georgia.

By that time nobody wanted the Solomons. There was not enough gold to attract prospectors, and the islands were too remote, sinister and devoid of game to attract pleasure seekers. "Blackbirders" seeking slave labor for the Queensland sugar plantations made an occasional raid; but the Melanesians were usually able to fight them off, and a good part of their time and energy was consumed in fighting one another. Unlike the Polynesians, the Solomon Islanders had no political sense. Each island contained several tribes with no common loyalty and often no common language.

During the last two decades of the nineteenth century, when European powers divided up the Pacific islands, Germany annexed Bougainville along with the Bismarcks and Papua,[6] while Great Britain took the rest of the Solomons and the Santa Cruz group, which together were organized as the Solomon Islands Protectorate.

Pax Britannica settled down over the islands where internecine wars and ceremonial head-hunting had been the rule. Missionaries, both Catholic and Protestant, had already made good progress. Australian pioneers, in order to profit by the world demand for copra, planted coconut palms at favored spots, and most of them eventually sold out to Lever Brothers subsidiary or Burns Philp

[6] These were mandated to Australia after World War I.

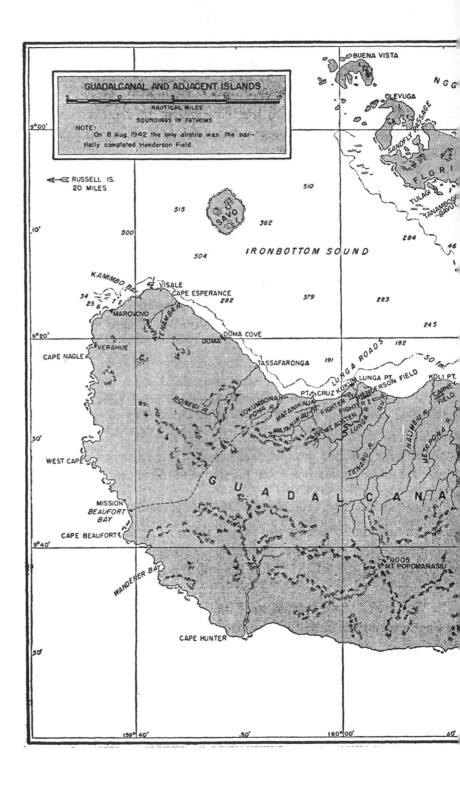

BUENA VISTA

N G G

OLEVUGA

SANDFLY PASSAGE

F L O R I

TULAGI
TANAMBOGO
GAVUTU

GUADALCANAL AND ADJACENT ISLANDS

NAUTICAL MILES

SOUNDINGS IN FATHOMS

NOTE: On 8 Aug. 1942 the only airstrip was the partially completed Henderson Field.

9°00'

RUSSELL IS.
20 MILES

510

515

SAVO

362

500

10°

504

IRONBOTTOM SOUND

284

46

KAMIMBO BAY

VISALE
CAPE ESPERANCE

282

379

283

34

25 6

MAROVOVO

TENAMBA R.

245

9°20'

DOMA

DOMA COVE

VERAHUE

CAPE NAGLE

TASSAFARONGA

191

LUNGA ROADS

182

50 fm.

BONEGI R.

KOKUMBONA
POMA R.

MATANIKAU R.

PT. CRUZ KUKUM LUNGA PT.

LUNGA PT.
HENDERSON FIELD

KOLI PT.

CARNEY
FIELD

FIGHTER 1

FIGHTER 1

MT AUSTEN

LUNGA R.

ILU R.

MATANIKAU R.

NALIMBIU R.

METAPONA R.

30°

WEST CAPE

TENARU R.

G U A D A L C A N T A L

MISSION
BEAUFORT
BAY

CAPE BEAUFORT

9°40'

BOOS
MT POPOMANASIU

WANDERER BAY

CAPE HUNTER

50'

159° 40'

50'

160° 00'

10'

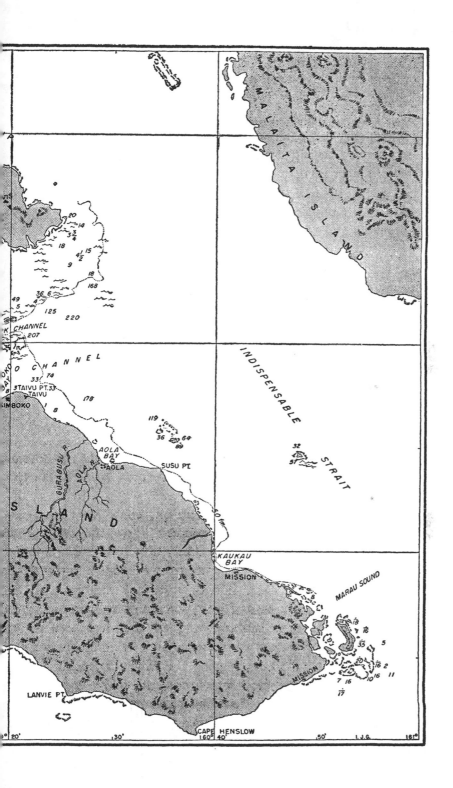

of Sydney. The colonial capital was established on a comparative healthy island, Tulagi, close to Florida; and in nearby Purvis Bay the Anglican Bishop of Melanesia, assisted by an old trader who had experienced religion, presided over a palm-leaf cathedral, a neat native village and a few score of his many thousand catechumens. Tulagi in 1939 was a one-street town with Chinese shops and a small hotel, a wireless station and neat bungalows on the hill for the British officials. On Guadalcanal there were two or three Christian missions and at Aola a Burns Philp trading station. Business was fair for the planters and encouraging for the missionaries. Every once in a while the natives murdered an overseer, burned property and made off to the jungle. Planters lived on canned food drenched with chutney and Worcestershire sauce, grumbled over the price of copra and the unreliability of native labor, and hoped to sell out and retire to Sydney. Missionaries came full of apostolic fervor and retired after a few years, full of malaria. Nobody expected anything to happen in the Solomons, and nothing usually did. The government did not even take the trouble to survey them properly. Extant maps were very imperfect, showing only dotted lines for estimated courses of rivers.

According to American and Australian standards, the Solomon Islands were almost pure "bush" or wilderness. None of the apparatus of civilized life was present; there was no lively colonial capital like Suva or Nouméa, where one could have relief from savage nature. No "white man's country" these; they lay too near the steaming Line ever to be so. Only at a few points along the edges had the European stolen space from the jungle to plant coconut groves and build copra houses, stores and missions. Only foot trails led inland to clusters of filthy huts in dismal and odoriferous clearings which let in sunlight to a soil that had been in rain-drenched shadow since time immemorial. The Solomons were still a region of uncharted seas, laving the edges of trackless forests.

At the time the Pacific war broke, the native population of Guadalcanal was between 8000 and 10,000, with over 40,000 more in Malaita. The Australian Air Force stationed a squadron of Cata-

linas in Gavutu Harbor near Tulagi and assigned 20 infantrymen
to help the "Gilbert and Sullivan Army" of 15 whites, 5 Chinese
and 130 native police in defending their base. Japanese planes began making bombing runs on Tulagi and Gavutu in January 1942,
after which Europeans and Chinese shopkeepers began to get out.
When the Japanese task force, part of the Coral Sea operation,
approached on 1 May, the Australian government saw that defense
was hopeless and ordered Tulagi to be evacuated.

The Japanese promised great benefits to the Melanesians, now
that they were in the "Co-prosperity Sphere," and handled very
roughly those who refused to accept paper "occupation shillings"
for labor, or who otherwise failed to show proper gratitude for
liberation from white imperialism. The effect was to make most
of the natives eager to have the white men back.[7]

One important institution outlasted the Japanese invasion — the
Australian "coastwatchers." They were a network of small radio
stations through the Bismarcks and Solomons, established several
years earlier and taken over by the Australian Navy in 1939. Only
eight or nine coastwatchers remained in all the Solomons after the
evacuation of Tulagi, but many others were brought back by
American boats or planes. These coastwatchers, whom the natives generally aided and abetted, were of inestimable value
throughout the Solomons campaign. They relayed to Allied headquarters the movements of enemy ships, planes and ground forces.
At a time when American air power was worn thin, their reports
of southward-flying enemy aircraft, received as much as fifty
minutes in advance, made it possible for American planes to take
off and gain altitude in time to swoop down on the enemy. And,
in less than a year, coastwatchers succored 120 crashed Allied airmen.[8]

[7] Winston Turner "The Singapore of the Solomons," *Sydney Sun and Guardian*
28 Mar. 1943; conversations with Lt. F. A. Rhodes (former manager of Burns
Philp's Lavoro plantation) when Australian liaison officer on Admiral Turner's
staff.

[8] Information from Lt. Rhodes and from Mr. W. H. Brocklebank, who originated the system at the R.A.N. office, Melbourne, in June 1943; Cdr. Eric A.
Feldt RAN *The Coastwatchers* (1946).

For some time after their occupation of Tulagi on 2 May, the Japanese paid no attention to Guadalcanal except to send over parties to round up and kill the wild cattle. But before the end of June a convoy of 13 ships put in, bringing a substantial force of labor troops, engineers and heavy equipment to build the landing field. It was the discovery of this by an Allied reconnaissance plane on 4 July that put the heat on Operation "Watchtower."

That operation had been conceived by Admiral King as early as February 1942. He wanted Tulagi partly as an additional bastion to the America–Australia lifeline, partly as the starting point for a drive up the line of the Solomons into Rabaul, and as a deterrent to any further expansion by the Japanese. General MacArthur, too, liked the idea, since Japanese possession of Rabaul blocked his eventual return to the Philippines. The first leg-up toward Guadalcanal was made in March — the occupation of Efate in the New Hebrides, by elements of General Patch's Americal Division, followed by the quick development of an airfield there.

On 1 April 1942 the Pacific had been divided into two great Allied commands, the Southwest Pacific Area under General MacArthur, and the Pacific Area under Admiral Nimitz; as a subordinate part of the latter, the South Pacific Area was set up, east of long. 160° E and south of the Equator. Vice Admiral Robert L. Ghormley, appointed Commander South Pacific Force and Area on 17 May, set up his command at Nouméa, New Caledonia, but soon moved to Auckland, New Zealand. The 1st Marine Division, commanded by Major General Alexander A. Vandegrift, was already on its way thither, in order to spearhead the first Allied offensive in the Pacific.

This first offensive, Operation "Watchtower," was ordered by the Joint Chiefs of Staff at Washington on 2 July 1942. The ultimate objective was defined as "seizure and occupation of the New Britain–New Ireland–New Guinea area," including the principal enemy base at Rabaul. Task No. 1, with target date 1 August, was to be seizure of "the Santa Cruz Islands, Tulagi and adjacent positions." But on 4 July an Allied reconnaissance plane reported that

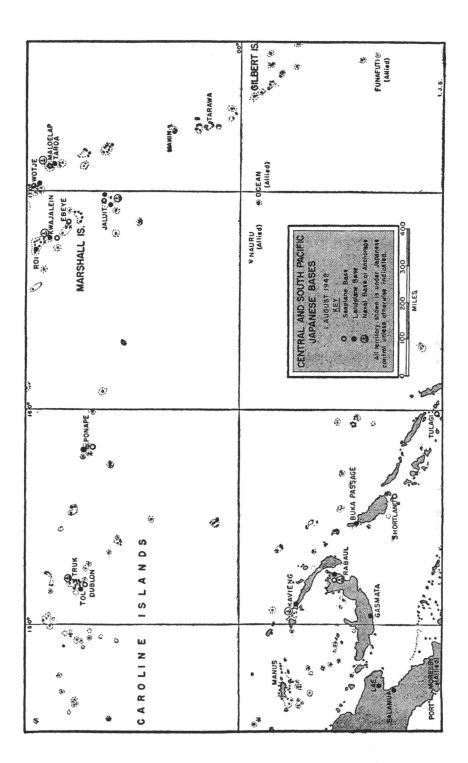

CENTRAL AND SOUTH PACIFIC
JAPANESE BASES
1 AUGUST 1942
KEY

○ Seaplane Base
● Landplane Base
⊕ Naval Base or Anchorage

All territory shown is under Japanese
control unless otherwise indicated.

0   100   200   300   400
MILES

GILBERT IS.

FUNAFUTI
(Allied)

I.J.G.

MALOELAP
TAROA
WOTJE

TARAWA

MAKIN

OCEAN
(Allied)

ROI
KWAJALEIN
EBEYE

MARSHALL IS.

JALUIT

NAURU
(Allied)

PONAPE

CAROLINE ISLANDS

TRUK
TOL
DUBLON

TULAGI

BUKA PASSAGE

SHORTLAND

KAVIENG

RABAUL

GASMATA

MANUS

LAE

SALAMAUA

PORT MORESBY
(Allied)

the Japanese were starting work on an airfield — the future Henderson Field — near Lunga Point, Guadalcanal. That is why this large and fecaloid island became the immediate and urgent Allied objective. For, if the enemy were allowed to complete the Lunga field and to base planes there, he might be able to knock out Espiritu Santo, Efate or even Kumac, the northern airfield on New Caledonia.

On 10 July Comsopac (Ghormley) received the operation order of Cincpac (Nimitz) for the seizure of Tulagi and Guadalcanal. The assault troops, mostly of the 1st Marine Division, were already being gathered from New Zealand and San Diego. With July almost half gone, it was impossible to meet the target date of 1 August, and Ghormley postponed D-day to the 7th.

Rear Admiral Richmond Kelly Turner, whose grizzled head, beetling black brows, tireless energy and ferocious language were to become almost legendary in the Pacific,[9] was given command of the Amphibious Force South Pacific and on 18 July raised his two-star flag at Wellington, New Zealand, in transport *McCawley*, the famous "Wacky Mac" which remained his flagship until sunk under him off Rendova a year later.

Above Turner in the chain of command was Vice Admiral Frank Jack Fletcher, veteran of Coral Sea and Midway, who flew his flag in carrier *Saratoga*. Rear Admiral Leigh Noyes had immediate command of the Air Support Force, which included old "Sara," *Wasp, Enterprise*, battleship *North Carolina*, five heavy cruisers, one light cruiser, 16 destroyers and three oilers. Escorting the Amphibious Force were eight cruisers (three of them Aus-

---

[9] Richmond Kelly Turner, b. Portland, Ore., 1885, Naval Academy '08 (5th in class); attained his first command, of a destroyer, in 1913 and served in *Pennsylvania, Michigan* and *Mississippi* as gunnery officer during World War I. Ordnance duty ashore for 3 years, gunnery officer on staff of Commander Scouting Fleet 1923, C.O. *Mervine* 1924–25, trained as a naval aviator, commanded aircraft squadrons Asiatic Fleet 1928 and headed plans section Buaer 1929–31. Technical adviser on naval aviation to American delegation at Geneva Disarmament Conference. "Exec." of *Saratoga* and chief of staff to Commander Aircraft Battle Force 1933–35. Took senior course at War College and served on staff. C.O. *Astoria* 1938–40. Director War Plans Division C.N.O. 1940–42, also assistant chief of staff to Admiral King 1941–42 when appointed Commander Amphibious Force South Pacific Force.

tralian) and a destroyer screen under Rear Admiral V. A. C. Crutchley RN — most of them destined to take a terrible beating on 9 August.

There was little time for planning this important operation, and little enough to do with — South Pacific sailors nicknamed it Operation "Shoestring" — but almost the entire Expeditionary Force managed to assemble at a mid-ocean rendezvous on 26 July, at a point about 400 miles south of the Fijis. Some 75 ships were there, "loaded with rude humanity, trained only for fighting and destruction," as Parkman said of Wolfe's force that captured Quebec in 1759. What better phrase for United States bluejackets and Marines! Lucky indeed for America that in this theater and at that juncture she depended not on boys drafted or cajoled into fighting but on "tough guys" who had volunteered to fight and who asked for nothing better than to come to grips with the sneaking enemy who had aroused all their primitive instincts. Fortunate, too, that they had a commander of the Stonewall Jackson breed; a quiet, unassuming man who had learned the fighting trade in the hard Marine school, who had a paternal regard for his troops, but never forgot what they were there for — Major General Alexander A. Vandegrift USMC.[10]

Before dawn on 7 August, while Turner's Expeditionary Force rounded Cape Esperance, Guadalcanal, Fletcher's carrier group maneuvered restlessly south of the island and prepared to furnish air support for the landings. These landings were the least part of the long-drawn-out Guadalcanal operation. The first amphibious operation undertaken by the United States since 1898 went off fairly smoothly because the enemy was taken completely by surprise and overwhelmed. Landing craft from 15 transports took 11,000 Marines ashore on a beach at Guadalcanal, about four miles east of Lunga Point, by nightfall. By the following afternoon the

[10] Born Virginia 1887; after 2 years in the University, commissioned 2nd Lt. USMC; fought in Nicaragua, at Vera Cruz and in Haiti; assistant chief of staff, Fleet Marine Force, 1933–35; commanded Marine Embassy Guard, Pekin, two years; assistant to Commandant 1937–41; C.O. 1st Marine Div., 1 Apr. 1942; C.O. Marine Amphibious Corps with rank of Lieut. Gen., 10 July 1943; Commandant Marine Corps, 1944–47.

Marines were in possession of the partially completed airstrip and of the principal Japanese encampment at Kukum on the west side of Lunga Point. The enemy, not more than 2000 in number and mostly labor troops, retired after only token resistance.

During the afternoon of 8 August, Lieutenant Commander Dwight H. Dexter USCG and 25 coastguardsmen were set ashore from *Hunter Liggett* with their landing craft, as nucleus of a naval operating base on Lunga Point, and Dexter assumed the duties of beachmaster.[11] These men proved both courageous and resourceful; indispensable in moving small bodies of Marines along the coast.

On the Tulagi side, where the lesser part of the troops were discharged, the Marines ran into stout opposition. Tulagi was not secured until the afternoon of 8 August, nor did the Japanese seaplane base on the small islands of Gavutu and Tanambogo fall into American possession until just before midnight of the same day. In the meantime, the transports and their escorting destroyers, with effective aid by fighter planes from the three carriers, beat off several heavy attacks by Japanese bombing and torpedo planes that flew down from Rabaul. Transport *George F. Elliott* and, indirectly, destroyer *Jarvis*, were lost as a result of these air attacks; but on the whole the landings at Tulagi and Guadalcanal were very successful. Not the most pessimistic old chief petty officer in the Expeditionary Force could have predicted that it would take twenty-six weeks' hard fighting by Navy, Marine Corps, Army and Air Forces to secure what had been occupied in little more than that number of hours.[12]

[11] *The Coast Guard at War, the Pacific Landings*, VI (15 Mar. 1946); information from Mr. Frank R. Eldridge. Nineteen of the 23 transports and APDs in the landing force carried coastguardsmen, and several of their surfmen and coxswains distinguished themselves handling landing craft.

[12] In Vol. IV of this History, chaps. xii-xiv, will be found a more detailed account of the planning of Operation "Watchtower" and of the landings and other events of 7–8 August. The complete task organization will be found on pp. 270–75.

CHAPTER II

The Battle of Savo Island[1]

9 August 1942

1. The Setup, 7–8 August

FROM NOUMÉA, on 8 August, Admiral Ghormley greeted all hands in and around Guadalcanal, declaring that the "results so far achieved make every officer and man in the South Pacific area proud of the task forces." Yet, even before the sun dropped behind Cape Esperance, the enemy was setting the stage for an outstanding victory. The Battle of Savo Island placed the occupation of Guadalcanal in jeopardy and delayed the completion of Operation "Watchtower" for several months. It was one of the worst defeats ever inflicted on the United States Navy.

---

[1] Every ship in this battle excepting *Jarvis* submitted an Action Report. Admiral Turner made none, but early in 1943 Admiral A. J. Hepburn conducted for Cominch an investigation of the facts. His "Report of Informal Inquiry into Circumstances Attending Loss of U.S.S. *Vincennes* . . . on Aug. 9, 1942 in the Vicinity of Savo Island" 13 May 1943 is brief; but is accompanied by a valuable Appendix, a collection of statements by about 100 officers and men. This Appendix is wanting in all but two existing copies of the Report, one of which I have used. Beginning in April 1943, I have frequently discussed the battle with key officers who participated. After the war the usual interrogations of Japanese officers were made and appear in *Inter. Jap. Off.* The Japanese after the war prepared, for ATIS, "Historical Reports, Naval Operations" 15 Mar. 1946, which include one on this battle (ATIS 15685). Several War Diaries of enemy ships are in the Washington Document Center. Concurrently with the research on this chapter, Commo. R. W. Bates and Cdr. W. D. Innis were making the *War College Analysis* for the Naval War College. It is a far more thorough investigation than Admiral Hepburn could or did make in 1943, and I am more indebted to it than to any other source, although it was still incomplete when this volume went to press. Finally, in June 1949, Lt. Roger Pineau USNR of my staff went over this chapter with Admiral Mikawa, Capt. T. Omae, his chief of staff in the Battle, and Capt. Watanabe of Yamamoto's staff, who had gone to Rabaul immediately after the Battle to investigate. They made sundry suggestions which, if accepted, are incorporated here.

Early in the morning of 7 August news of the American landings reached Vice Admiral Gunichi Mikawa, Commander Eighth Fleet and Outer South Seas Force, at Rabaul. Shortly after 0800 came the last message from his countrymen in Tulagi, "We pray for enduring fortunes of war," promising resistance "to the last man." The Japanese Admiral had already decided to supplement prayer by gun power. His first effort was unsuccessful. Troops were hastily collected at Rabaul and embarked in six transports to reinforce the garrison at Guadalcanal. While one of these transports, the 5600-ton *Meiyo Maru,* with an escorting destroyer, was steaming about 14 miles west of Cape St. George at midnight August 8, she encountered U.S. submarine *S–38* (Lieutenant Commander H. G. Munson), a veteran of the Asiatic Fleet.[2] Munson submerged, closed to 1000 yards, and, using sound tracking instead of periscope sight, fired two torpedoes. Both hit and the transport sank with a loss of 14 officers and 328 men.[3] *S–38* evaded the destroyer's depth-charge attack as well as other attacks on subsequent days and reached Brisbane on 22 August. It is a pity the crew could not know the magnitude of their achievement after this hot, uncomfortable voyage in their nineteen-year-old boat; for she had sunk *Meiyo Maru,* a key vessel of the expedition, whose loss caused Admiral Mikawa to recall the other five transports to Rabaul, hoping for a more auspicious moment to reinforce Guadalcanal.

Owing to Mikawa's gun-power reaction to the American landings, that auspicious moment arrived very shortly. When the bad news started to come in from Tulagi around 0700 August 7, it happened that five heavy cruisers had just departed Kavieng, three of them bound for the Admiralties, two for Rabaul. In accordance with an urgent message from Mikawa at 0800, all five headed for Rabaul at top speed. In the early afternoon *Chokai* and destroyer

[2] For her penetration of Lingayen Gulf early in the war, see Vol. III of this History p. 179. At Brisbane before leaving for this, her seventh war patrol, her crew had worked day and night to put her back in shape and had enjoyed no liberty.

[3] Eighth Fleet War Diary; *S–38* Patrol Report.

Yunagi peeled off to enter Simpson Harbor for orders, while the rest steamed at reduced speed toward a rendezvous in St. George Channel.

Admiral Mikawa broke his red and white striped flag in *Chokai* and at 1628 August 7, led out light cruisers *Tenryu* and *Yubari*, already under his command, to join the four heavies. By the end of the second dogwatch, his task force of seven cruisers and one destroyer had taken departure from Cape St. George; course E by N to pass to the northward of Buka Island.[4]

These ships did not pass unobserved. The first six were reported by B–17s of the MacArthur command [5] when south of New Ireland before reaching Rabaul. All eight, as they debouched from St. George Channel around 2000 August 7, were sighted by submarine *S–38*. (This was the day before she sank *Meiyo Maru*.) The Japanese force passed so close that *S–38* was unable to fire torpedoes and felt the wash from the big ships; Lieutenant Commander Munson radioed a contact report of "two destroyers and three larger ships of unknown type" moving southeasterly at "high speed."

While United States Marines were spending the first of many uneasy nights ashore in the Solomons, and Admiral Turner's ships were patrolling off shore, Admiral Mikawa and staff considered how to deal with the invaders. The attack must be delivered by stealth if possible, by night for certain; for the Emperor's sailors had been well trained in night gunfire and torpedo action, and they knew that few American aviators were trained for night flying. So the plan was made to strike into the Sound in the small hours of 9 August. But the 8th would have to be passed mostly in the open, where search planes might rob them of surprise.

Sure enough, at 1026 August 8 a Hudson plane of the Royal Australian Air Force located the cruisers and trailed them briefly.

[4] At this time numerous troop and supply convoys were making heavy demands on Japanese destroyers. On such short notice it was impossible for Mikawa to round up more than the single destroyer. Lack of an adequate anti-submarine screen was to cost him a heavy cruiser.

[5] Dispatch from MacArthur at 2319 Aug. 7: "Six unidentified ships sighted by Forts in St. George Channel, Course SE."

Mikawa ordered evasive courses, to deceive the pilot. He was not deceived but anti-aircraft fire kept him at a distance that prevented accurate identification. He reported the force as consisting of "three cruisers, three destroyers, two seaplane tenders or gunboats, at lat. 5°49′ S, long. 156°07′ E, course 120°, speed 15." At 1101 a second Australian Hudson sighted the Japanese still milling about in the same location north of the strait between Bougainville and Choiseul. The pilot reported two heavy cruisers, two light cruisers and one unidentified vessel.

Mikawa, eager for latest information of his enemy, had already ordered one float plane from each of his five heavy cruisers to search ahead fan-wise for 250 miles. Two of these, catapulted at 0625 August 8, made an excellent reconnaissance of Tulagi in the face of fighter-plane and anti-aircraft opposition and returned at noon with a mouth-watering report of one battleship, 6 cruisers, 19 destroyers and 18 transports in the waters around Tulagi and Guadalcanal. Mikawa, who had been waiting for this information near the place where the Hudsons had seen him, decided at once to make for Turner's force. He headed south at 24 knots through Bougainville Strait and entered New Georgia Sound south of Choiseul at about 1600.

In every Japanese ship sailors busied themselves with preparations for battle. Inflammables and depth charges were stowed below, ordnance and ammunition were inspected. During their cruise down the Slot the only craft they sighted, either air- or waterborne, was seaplane tender *Akitsushima* en route to northern New Georgia.

At 1640 Mikawa drew up a brief battle plan and sent it by signal blinker to every ship. The gist of it was, first, to make a torpedo attack on the United States ships at the Guadalcanal anchorage; then to cross to Tulagi-side and shell and torpedo the enemy there; then to retire north of Savo Island.[6]

---

[6] "On the rush-in we will go from S. of Savo Island and torpedo the enemy main force in front of the Guadalcanal anchorage; after which we will turn toward the Tulagi forward area to shell and torpedo the enemy. We will then withdraw north of Savo I." Lt. Pineau's translation of Mikawa's Signal Order No. 25 in Crudiv 18

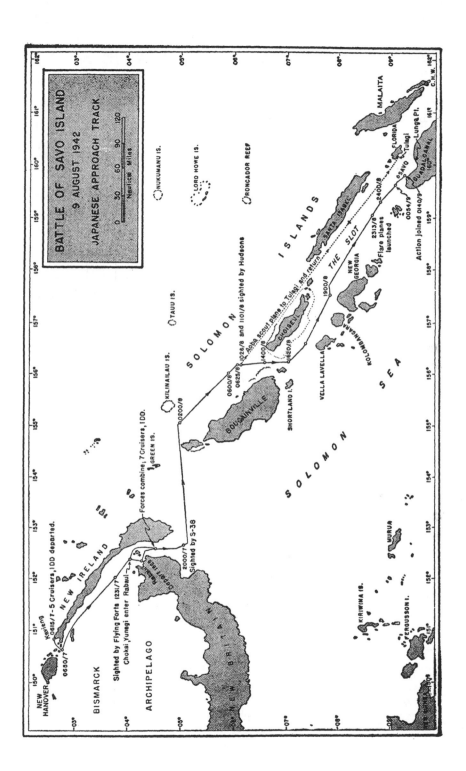

BATTLE OF SAVO ISLAND
9 AUGUST 1942
JAPANESE APPROACH TRACK

Nautical Miles
0 30 60 90 120

As a double check on American shipping, two planes from cruisers *Chokai* and *Aoba* took the air at 1612 for a final daylight look at the enemy.

Satisfied that everything was in readiness, Admiral Mikawa in Nelsonian fashion at 1840 sent a semaphore signal that spelled out to his delighted sailors: —

"Let us attack with certain victory in the traditional night attack of the Imperial Navy. May each one calmly do his utmost!" [7]

While the Japanese were racing toward Savo Island, circumstances conspired to make their mission a brilliant success.

Anyone who expects attack wants an answer to three questions — *Where? When? How?* Admiral Nimitz knew the answer to all three before Midway, but it was very different now. Admiral Turner assumed that his own force, pinned down by the nature of its function to the narrow waters between Guadalcanal, Tulagi and Florida Island, was the target. *How?* could be answered only by good reconnaissance, because the Japanese themselves had no plan until 7 August. They might attack by planes, ships or submarines, alone or in combination, and Turner had to be prepared for all three. He was a master at repelling aircraft, even with little fighter-plane protection. Submarines, on the other hand, were Admiral Crutchley's forte; his experience fighting U-boats in the Atlantic made him very wary, and numerous reported sightings of I-boats justified his concern.

There still remained the big poser. *When* would the enemy attack? Australian coastwatchers could be depended on to give the alarm of a daylight air raid, but they could not see vessels far off shore at night. Long-range detection of an approaching surface force must be done by aircraft and submarines. Half a dozen United

---

War Diary (WDC No. 160,984). By "main force" the Admiral meant all ships of any kind on Guadalcanal side; Crutchley's force had not yet taken up their night dispositions. This interpretation is confirmed by Crudiv 6 Records (WDC No. 160,997).

[7] Mikawa's Action Report, Central Intelligence Group "Solomons Naval Action 7–10 Aug. 1942," 27 June 1947.

States submarines were scattered along the Truk-Solomons seaways and more were lurking around the Bismarcks. The responsibility of air search was shared by Admiral McCain's Catalinas and Flying Forts of the South Pacific Force, General MacArthur's United States and Australian Army planes, and Admiral Fletcher's carrier scout bombers. Search sectors had been established from Allied bases with a view to three possible approaches by the enemy: the Bismarcks, Truk and the Marshalls. MacArthur's planes took care of the Bismarcks, McCain's observed the northern approaches, and the carrier planes were to make short-range substitute searches in sectors where bad weather precluded a flight by land-based fliers — McCain to advise Fletcher when and where. Fletcher's carrier planes were used for short search during the two first crucial days because, having no information to the contrary, the Admiral assumed that all sectors were being properly covered.

Long-range searches were inaugurated several days before the landings. By an ingenious use of seaplane tenders, these were extended as the operation progressed. Lieutenant Commander Alderman brought tender *McFarland* to Ndeni of the Santa Cruz group on 5 August and immediately began providing food, fuel and what were humorously referred to as "all the comforts of home" to five PBYs whose searches could now be extended by about 300 miles. On the day of the Guadalcanal landings, Commander Hitchcock of tender *Mackinac* conned his ship through the little-known entrance to Maramasike Estuary on the southeast coast of Malaita Island and set up a boardinghouse for nine more PBYs. Beginning on 8 August these Catalinas extended the search range nearly 500 miles. They were assigned the sea lane between Truk and Guadalcanal.

MacArthur's planes were responsible for patrolling the enemy-dominated waters on his side of the line of demarcation.

As Admiral Turner studied the air-search plan, he felt uneasy about the Slot, the obvious enemy route from Rabaul to the lower Solomons. Flying Forts based on Espiritu Santo were to cover this vital sea lane, but only up to the southeastern cape of Choiseul.

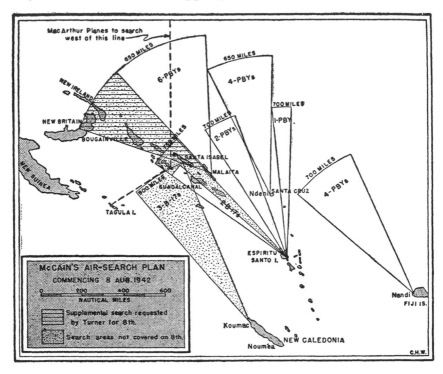

Furthermore, their search would reach its outer limit very early in the morning, leaving undetected any hostile force entering the Slot later in the day. Turner's anxiety, well justified in the light of later events, prompted him on 7 August to urge Admiral McCain to send a Catalina up the Slot from *Mackinac* then at Malaita, even though it would cover part of MacArthur's search area. It seems that two B–17s made only a portion of the requested search, and missed sighting the Japanese by a mere sixty miles. Admiral Turner, in absence of information to the contrary, assumed that the search had been complete.[8]

<hr />

[8] Turner's message to McCain: "The plan of search for 8 August does not cover sector 290° to 318° from Malaita. Southwest Pacific is responsible for this sector but I consider a morning search by you is necessary for adequate cover." Extant records do not indicate whether or not McCain relayed this request to *Mackinac*, whose skipper does not recall being asked to make the search. Because of the early hour of searches from Espiritu Santo and Koumac, only Turner's requested supplemental search could have found Mikawa. A letter of 1948 from Rear Admiral

First air-search contact, as we have seen, was that of MacArthur's Flying Forts on Mikawa's cruisers south of Kavieng on 7 August. Their report reached Admiral Turner before midnight, but the presence of cruisers close to a naval base was no cause for alarm. Second contact was made by submarine *S–38* south of Cape St. George after nightfall on the 7th. The high speed and southeasterly course of the enemy indicated an urgent mission. Admiral Crutchley received this intelligence about breakfast time next morning, but awaited amplification by a nearer contact (the ships were then 550 miles from Guadalcanal) before assuming that they were after him. The third sighting, by the Australian Hudson at 1026 August 8, would have been the tip-off but for several unfortunate circumstances. The pilot of this plane,[9] instead of breaking radio silence to report as he had orders to do in an urgent case, or returning to base which he could have done in two hours, spent most of the afternoon completing his search mission, came down at Milne Bay, had his tea, and then reported the contact. About sundown August 8 this vital information was finally sent to Townsville, which originated a dispatch to General MacArthur's headquarters at Brisbane. From that moment there was prompt action; Radio Canberra at 1817 put the contact report on "Bells," from which Admiral Crutchley got it at 1839; Canberra also sent it to Pearl Harbor, where it was placed on "Fox," from which Admiral Turner got it at 1845.[10] Thus it took over eight hours to pass ultra-hot intelligence only 350 miles from a search plane to the Allied flagship.[11] If the pilot's report had been made by radio, MacArthur

M. B. Gardner, who was chief of staff to Admiral McCain in 1942, is my authority for the B-17s, whose search is not shown on the appended chart. *War College Analysis* accepts it.

[9] An Australian Hudson, on search mission FR-623 originating at Milne Bay, New Guinea.

[10] The message of the second Hudson that sighted Mikawa at 1101 was similarly delayed; it reached Ghormley at 2136 and Turner got it about an hour later. "Bells" was the Australian counterpart to "Fox," for an explanation of which see Vol. I of this History p. 103.

[11] This was the first of several failures of search planes to get their hard-won information promptly to those who needed it. Similar incidents occurred at the Battle of Santa Cruz Islands (see chap. xi) and at the Battle of the Philippine Sea. *Vincennes's* captain later stated that he had a report of the enemy at 1015 Aug. 8.

could have sent out a search mission to track the ships and bombers to harass them. If the aviator had flown back to base immediately and his report had been transmitted promptly, Turner could have requested additional searches from that side. And any such search, despite foul weather in the Slot, might with fair luck have corrected another fatal defect, the unfortunate wording of the Australian pilot's report: "Three cruisers, three destroyers, two seaplane tenders or gunboats, course 120°, speed 15 knots."

Turner and Crutchley, recent recipients of vicious air attacks, are not to blame for pouncing on the "two seaplane tenders" to infer that the enemy planned an air strike tomorrow rather than a surface strike that night. For a surface action more than three cruisers would be wanted, and certainly no seaplane tenders. The report made sense only on the hypothesis that the force sighted was bent on setting up a seaplane base; and that is what MacArthur's headquarters thought too.[12] On the northwestern coast of Santa Isabel, only 155 miles from Savo, lies the protected harbor of Rekata Bay. That is where Admiral Turner expected the enemy to moor his "two seaplane tenders" in order to renew air attacks with seaplanes the following day. Thus, the faulty and long-delayed report of one pilot completely misled both American commands as to Japanese intentions.

Moreover, Turner had the right to assume that the enemy force had sheered left and by evening was concealed behind the mountains of Santa Isabel. For, if it had continued down the Slot, within the supplemental search sector requested of McCain, it should have been spotted and trailed. Here, circumstances again confused the Allies. The foul weather that day had turned back the supplemental search. Even the regularly assigned searches up the Slot were curtailed (although these, because of timing, would

---

Astoria's captain said he had a coastwatcher report early in the day. I believe that these captains were speaking of the submarine's contact on the 7th, which they would have received about 1000 Aug. 8. H.M.A.S. *Australia* was the only Allied ship guarding the coastwatcher radio circuit and she received no coastwatcher report, so no other ship could possibly have got one.

[12] At about 2000 Aug. 8 they sent Turner a message that the force sighted was probably about to establish a seaplane base at Shortland Island.

not have discovered Mikawa anyway). In any such exigency Admiral Fletcher had agreed to assist by a late-evening fan search to 200 miles on a 45-degree arc Northwest of Savo by his carrier planes; and that presumably he would have done, if either he or Turner had known the score. Admiral McCain reported search deficiencies on the 8th, but the message did not leave his headquarters until nearly midnight.

These failures in ship identification and communications are enough to explain why Admiral Mikawa managed to make his approach undetected. Yet there were still other factors to make happy Japs and sorry Allies. One was the complete withdrawal of Fletcher's three carriers from waters where they could be of any help to Turner or Crutchley.

At the ocean conference of 26 July on board *Saratoga*, Admiral Fletcher had announced that he would not remain within supporting distance for more than two days. Admiral Turner protested vehemently, remarking that he could not possibly unload the transports in less than four days, during the whole of which they would need air cover; but he failed to convert Fletcher. Admiral Ghormley, superior to both in chain of command but capable of exercising only a general strategic direction from Nouméa, was in no position to resolve this important difference of opinion.

At 1807 August 8, after recovering all his planes from the day's strikes and patrols, when he had been in the area only thirty-six hours, Fletcher sent this important dispatch to Ghormley: "Fighter-plane strength reduced from 99 to 78. In view of the large number of enemy torpedo planes and bombers in this area, I recommend the immediate withdrawal of my carriers. Request tankers sent forward immediately as fuel running low."

It is easy to understand Turner's consternation when he intercepted this dispatch, even though Fletcher had warned him he would pull out before 10 August. It must have seemed to him then, as it seems to us now, that Fletcher's reasons for withdrawal were flimsy. Supposing his fighter-plane strength had been reduced 21 per cent? His air groups still numbered one more Wildcat than the three American carriers had had before the Battle of Midway. Supposing the Coral Sea to have been infested with Japanese night-flying bombers (which was by no means true) and that they threatened the safety of fast-stepping, well-defended carriers; were not these planes an infinitely greater threat to anchored transports? Turner could not presume to judge the oil situation; but it can now be ascertained from ships' logs that at noon 8 August the destroyers still had enough fuel for several days' operations, and they could have been refueled from the cruisers and carriers, as well as from fleet oilers.[13] No Japanese search plane had yet found the carrier force, and Fletcher had no evidence of having been "snooped"; his force could have remained in the area with no more severe consequences than sunburn. But Fletcher, who had lost *Lexington* at Coral Sea and *Yorktown* at Midway, apparently was determined to take no risks this time. In the carrier task force his retirement request was greeted with dismay by senior officers, especially when they learned that the Australian Hudson's report of Mikawa's force had been received on board before 1900, and guessed that the Japanese Fleet was about to show its hand.

At 1807 when he originated the "recommend withdrawal" dispatch, Fletcher was off the northwestern cape of San Cristobal, about 120 miles from Savo Island. Instead of waiting for a reply, the commander of this powerful, mobile force built around three carriers, changed course to the southeastward, leaving Turner (in his own picturesque phrase) "bare-arse."

While Fletcher was retiring and Mikawa was advancing at 26

[13] From ships' logs of Admiral Fletcher's task force I obtain these figures of gallons fuel oil on hand at 0000 or 1200 Aug. 8 (it is not clear which); they are to the nearest thousand gallons: *Saratoga*, 1,149,000; *Enterprise*, 521,000; *Wasp* records lost; *North Carolina*, 878,000; *Balch*, 73,000; *Maury*, 70,000; *Gwin*, 88,000; *Benham*, 68,000; *Grayson*, 40,000; *Lang*, 72,000; *Sterett*, 59,000; *Stack*, 64,000; *Laffey*, 94,000; *Farenholt*, 68,000. The destroyers' daily expenditures varied from 12,000 to 24,000 and their total capacity from 127,000 to 184,000. In the *Saratoga* group *Dale* had just been topped off and was 97 per cent full; the other five averaged three quarters full. The cruisers with capacity of 618,000 to 839,000 gallons were half full or better. Thus it is idle to pretend that there was any urgent fuel shortage in this force. *War College Analysis* states that Fletcher's real reason for retirement was fear of exposing his carriers to air attack, and severely criticizes him for failure to consult with Turner by radio.

knots, Crutchley's cruisers and destroyers assumed their night dispositions. In order to protect the transports off Tulagi and Guadalcanal, the Sound was divided into three sectors to be patrolled by a Northern, a Southern and an Eastern Force. Crutchley took immediate command of the Southern Force with cruisers *Australia* *Canberra* (Captain H. B. Farncomb RAN), (Captain F. E. Getting RAN) and *Chicago* (Captain Howard D. Bode), and with destroyers *Patterson* (Commander Frank R. Walker) and *Bagley* (Lieutenant Commander George A. Sinclair). These ships had operated together for months in the old Anzac Force and at the Battle of the Coral Sea. They patrolled south of a line running 125° from the center of Savo Island, to block the entrance between it and Cape Esperance. The Northern Force, which covered the area north of that line to block the entrance between Savo and Florida Islands, comprised cruisers *Vincennes, Astoria* (Captain William G. Greenman) and *Quincy* (Captain Samuel N. Moore) with destroyers *Helm* (Lieutenant Commander Chester E. Carroll) and *Wilson* (Lieutenant Commander Walter H. Price), under the tactical command of *Vincennes's* skipper, Captain Frederick L. Riefkohl. For early-warning purposes, destroyers *Blue* (Commander Harold N. Williams) and *Ralph Talbot* (Lieutenant Commander Joseph W. Callahan), which carried SC radar, were assigned patrol lines to the westward of Savo Island, supposedly to cover both western entrances to the Sound. The sector east of the meridian of Lunga Point, covering the eastern approaches by Lengo and Sealark Channels, was covered by Rear Admiral Norman Scott with light cruisers *San Juan* and H.M.A.S. *Hobart* and destroyers *Monssen* and *Buchanan*. Turner had tactical command of all the vessels off Guadalcanal, and Scott of all those off Tulagi. The remaining 18 transports (*Elliott* being then on fire and sinking), intended to continue unloading all night.

This four-way division of forces proved to be very unfortunate, although in view of the Admiral's ignorance of enemy deployment and intentions, it was the natural thing to do. All three passages leading into the Sound had to be defended against submarine as well as surface attack. *San Juan*, the one ship with the new SG surface search radar, would have been more useful elsewhere; but the eastern approaches, where Japanese heavy ships would be unlikely to enter, was the place to post a light-hulled anti-aircraft cruiser. It would have been well to have sent Admiral Scott on board *Vincennes*, but 8 August was a busy day that left Turner no time to shuffle commands and shift flags. The separation of the Northern and Southern Forces, and the disposition of the two radar picket destroyers were both unnecessary and faulty; [14] cruisers in single column would have covered both entrances more effectively and given a better account of themselves if surprised.

Admiral Crutchley led his Southern Force to its station southeast of Savo and commenced a 12-knot patrol along a general northwest-southeast line, reversing course about every hour. Heavy cruisers *Australia, Canberra* and *Chicago* were in column 600 yards apart, with destroyer *Patterson* 1300 yards broad on the port bow of *Australia*, and *Bagley* in a corresponding position on her starboard bow. In the Northern Force Captain Riefkohl employed a box patrol, steaming at 10 knots in a square between Savo and Florida Islands, turning 90 degrees about every half-hour. *Vincennes* led *Quincy* and *Astoria*, spaced 600 yards; while destroyers *Helm* and *Wilson* steamed broad on the leader's bows.

No battle plan or instructions were signaled to either of these two forces. Presumably *Ralph Talbot* and *Blue* would give adequate warning of approaching enemy ships, but as Admiral Crutchley had never found opportunity to confer with the captains of the three northern cruisers, they had no idea how he expected them to fight a battle that might be forced upon them. Their situ-

---

[14] The *War College Analysis* criticizes it on three counts: (1) The picket screen was inadequate both for radar and submarine detection as the two destroyers could be as much as 20 miles apart at the outer ends of their patrol lines, a situation which almost occurred when the enemy struck; and their SC radars were reliable only up to 10 miles under optimum conditions, which (owing to nearby land) did not here obtain. (2) Both destroyers, especially *Talbot*, were too near the cruisers to give adequate warning. (3) The two cruiser groups were too far apart for mutual support in a surface action; in a single column they might have crossed the "T" of an enemy force entering the Sound and evaded torpedoes by individual 90-degree turns.

ation was not improved by the fact that Crutchley, for no fault of his own, was absent during the battle.

At 2032 Admiral Turner urgently summoned Admiral Crutchley, already on patrol, and General Vandegrift, ashore at Guadalcanal, to report on board amphibious force flagship *McCawley*, then lying off Lunga Point. Turner's desire for an immediate conference was prompted by his concern over the departure of Fletcher's carriers and by the information that little or no cargo had yet been unloaded from the transports at Tulagi. He wished to find out from the General whether he could get enough supplies ashore by morning to permit the transports to depart, and from Crutchley whether he thought the fighting ships could stick it out without air protection a day or two longer. Fletcher's retirement placed the amphibious force commander in a distressing dilemma — either to leave the Marines hungry and short of ammunition, or take a beating from enemy air power augmented by big bombers from the assumed seaplane base at Rekata Bay.

Crutchley, upon receipt of the summons, directed Captain Bode of *Chicago* to take charge of his Southern Force, and at once left the formation in cruiser *Australia* to join *McCawley* in Lunga Roads.[15] By 2230 the British Admiral was greeting Turner on board his flagship; but General Vandegrift, absent from his command post when the dispatch came, did not arrive until forty-five minutes later. All three commanders were haggard with fatigue. The General admitted that he was "pretty tired, but as for those other two, I thought they were both ready to pass out."

Turner bluntly proposed that the transports depart next morning. All three agreed they had better do so, although Vandegrift was dismayed at the prospect of his 18,000 Marines being left with inadequate supplies and no naval support. But he could arrange to discharge the most urgently wanted items at Tulagi

[15] Crutchley made the 20-mile trip in his flagship instead of his barge because a barge would have taken several hours, and Turner's summons was urgent. The mystery about this conference is why Turner insisted on seeing Crutchley. He knew as well as the British Admiral the risks of operating combat ships without air protection, and he was not an officer who wanted much advice anyway.

and Guadalcanal during the night. Crutchley took occasion to ask Turner's opinion as to the belated report of an enemy force of cruisers, destroyers and "seaplane tenders or gunboats." Turner reiterated his belief that this force would hole up in Rekata Bay, thence to launch torpedo-carrying float planes against the amphibious force. To anticipate them, McCain's land-based planes had been requested to bomb the shipping in Rekata Bay next morning. Turner admitted the possibility of a surface raid, but was satisfied that all was in readiness to meet it.[16]

While this flag conference was taking place, all ships except *Australia* continued to patrol their assigned areas. Captain Bode of *Chicago*, now commanding the Southern Force, turned in without taking station ahead of *Canberra*, for he expected Crutchley would be back before midnight. To the northward Captain Riefkohl's force continued its monotonous round. Sailors on board the cruisers were still talking of their performance during the two days past. They had helped the Marines to land by chasing Japs into the hills with 8-inch shells; they had protected the transports with anti-aircraft fire. But they were dog-tired after two days of incessant action and excitement. Particularly weary were the commanding officers, holding exacting positions and heavy responsibilities. Condition II, a state of readiness which required only half the crew to be on watch, was set in order to give officers and men a little rest.[17] It was a hot, overcast and oppressive night, "heavy with destiny and doom" as a novelist would say, inviting weary sailors to slackness and to sleep.

At about 2330 a heavy rain squall began making up on the slopes of Savo Island. As it drifted slowly to the southeastward it drew a wet, opaque curtain between the two cruiser groups. At 2345,

[16] Admiral Crutchley's report and Turner's memorandum to Admiral Hepburn.
[17] Admiral Crutchley had ordered Condition I, all stations fully manned and alert, on the evening of Aug. 6th. He had relaxed this condition by signal permitting small groups to leave their stations for meals, thus bringing about a readiness somewhere between Condition I and Condition II. *Astoria's* captain stated positively he never received either the original order or the modification. Admiral Hepburn declared that the relaxation of vigilance by individual captains was their prerogative, and that the crews were not unduly fatigued. Visibility was 4000 to 12,000 yards, wind NE, force 1 or 2; no moon.

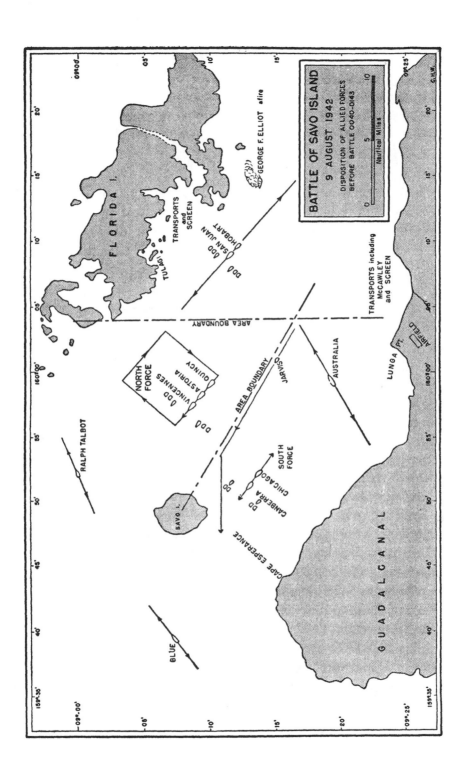

BATTLE OF SAVO ISLAND
9 AUGUST 1942
DISPOSITION OF ALLIED FORCES
BEFORE BATTLE 0040-0143

Nautical Miles
0   5   10

just as the midwatch was gulping down "jamoke" and stumbling up to relieve the "eight to twelvers," came the first disturbance of the night — three reports of one or more unidentified planes. These were two scouts launched from Mikawa's cruisers at 2313 to check upon the night locations of the Allied ships and to illuminate them at the proper time. *Ralph Talbot*, the northern picket, sighted one of them, identified it as a cruiser type and broadcast an alarm: "Warning — Warning: Plane over Savo headed east." Despite numerous repetitions of this report, it failed to reach Admiral Turner's flagship, only 20 miles distant.[18] *Blue*, the southern picket, heard *Ralph Talbot's* call and subsequently picked up a plane on her radar; but the radio warning was received by only a few ships present and those who did get it failed to grasp its significance, even though they sighted the planes themselves. *Quincy*, for example, made radar contact on a plane and several minutes later disregarded it as of no consequence. *Vincennes's* captain was deceived into the belief that the planes were friendly because they showed running lights. Other commanding officers assumed that Turner had received the report and knew the planes to be friendly; otherwise he would have sent out an alarm. So, for the next hour and a half, the Japanese aircraft continued to drone unmolested over the American ships, and to send exact information of their movements that was very interesting to Admiral Mikawa.

The first hour of 9 August was disarmingly quiet. Admiral Crutchley, leaving *McCawley* five minutes before midnight to return to his flagship, could see very little. Low water-burdened clouds hung sullenly overhead, barely drifting in a light air from the northeast. Rain blotted out the western horizon toward Savo. Winking flashes of distant lightning occasionally limned the dark-hulled transports. To the northeast a fitful red glow marked the burning shell of *George F. Elliott*. The Admiral had offered to set General Vandegrift on board minesweeper *Southard* for passage

---

[18] The distance was too great for TBS voice radio, which *McCawley* had, under existing atmospheric conditions. When Lt. Cdr. Callahan of *Ralph Talbot* could get no answer from the flagship his division commander, Cdr. Walker in *Patterson*, assumed the burden of getting the message through, but never could.

to Tulagi; it took time for his barge to find *Southard* and, by the time Crutchley was back on board his flagship and clear of the transport area, only the butt of the night remained. He decided to patrol seven miles west of the Guadalcanal transports, rather than attempt rendezvous with *Canberra* and *Chicago*. By this decision the Southern Force was shy a much-needed heavy cruiser; but that heavy cruiser would probably have arrived at the same time as the enemy and added to the existing confusion.

2. *The Battle South of Savo, 0054–0150*

On the flag bridge of *Chokai* Admiral Mikawa was eagerly assimilating the reports of his scout planes. One American ship burning brightly — a good guide to the location of the others; transports off Tulagi and Guadalcanal — the prime objective; Allied cruisers to the west of the beach area — a hazard to be met and brushed aside before reaching the fat transports. The Admiral had his force in a long column: heavy cruisers *Chokai*, *Aoba*, *Kako*, *Kinugasa* and *Furutaka*; light cruisers *Tenryu* and *Yubari* and destroyer *Yunagi*. Several of these had never operated together before, but with a generous 1300 yards between ships they had ample sea room. Their total armament was 62 torpedo tubes (all but ten of them 24-inch), 34 eight-inch guns, ten 5.5-inch guns and 27 five-inch and 4.7-inch guns. The force had orders to steam single file into the Sound, tackling first the American ships off Guadalcanal, next those off Tulagi; a lightning strike at the enemy and a quick getaway to be beyond carrier-plane range by daybreak.[19] "Battle Warning" was signaled to every ship at 2230; "Three Heavy Cruisers South of Savo" and "Prepare to Fire Torpedoes" at 0025; "Battle Stations Alerted" at 0045.[20]

No Japanese ship mounted radar, but at 0054 *Chokai* sighted

[19] By the time he reached Savo, Mikawa probably had received information, from the plane launched by *Aoba* at 1612, concerning Crutchley's night dispositions; but he made no change of battle plan, only warned his ships what to expect.
[20] *Kako* War Diary (WDC No. 160,143); *War College Analysis*.

destroyer *Blue* on her starboard bow, heading southwesterly. Anxious moments followed. While the force tore by at 24 to 26 knots, some fifty guns were trained on *Blue*, waiting for her to act. But the American destroyer steamed slowly away, giving no indication that she had seen the Japanese; nor had she. Her SC radar was not good enough and her lookouts must have been looking everywhere but astern — a common failing of lookouts.

Nevertheless, Admiral Mikawa feared that *Blue* had reported him and so ordered a small course change left to pass north of Savo Island. Shortly after making the turn, his lookouts reported a destroyer bearing NE by E. *Ralph Talbot* actually was out there but (according to her log) she must have been a good ten miles away — too far to be seen, even by a cat's-eyed Japanese lookout. Mikawa, however, believed the report and returned to his original plan to enter the Sound between Savo and Cape Esperance. At 0105 he ordered course 150° and 26 knots to leave Savo on the port hand. As it rounded the island, the Japanese column swung more to the eastward; at 0132 to course 95°. One minute later, Mikawa spat out his battle order, "All Ships Attack!" It was the time, no doubt about that. At 0134 his port lookouts vaguely discerned the outline of an American destroyer moving slowly westward, only 3000 yards to the northward. Detection seemed inevitable, but this was the damaged destroyer *Jarvis*, who had no means of communication.[21] Two more minutes passed, and the starboard lookouts chimed in, reporting ships ahead. These were *Patterson* and *Bagley* of the Southern Force, then nearing the northwestern extremity of their patrol course, closing the Japanese on a collision heading at 36 knots. Lookouts on other Japanese ships sighted *Jarvis*, mistook her for a cruiser and launched torpedoes, all of which missed; but they did not open gunfire because the flagship did not, and their good discipline served the Emperor

[21] *Jarvis*, badly hit in the air attack of 8 August, departed Lunga Roads at midnight. Her C.O., Lt. Cdr. William W. Graham, a capable and conscientious officer, was eager to get to Sydney where destroyer tender *Dobbin* was stationed in order to obtain immediate repairs and rejoin the Fleet. He had been ordered by Admiral Turner to wait for an escort and depart by an eastern channel, but it is not clear whether he received the orders.

well, as gunfire would have alerted the Southern Force, which was unable to observe the oncoming Japanese ships because a heavy rain cloud to the south of Savo Island blended with their silhouettes.

Japanese lookouts were sending a continuous stream of reports to bridge and gunnery stations; now two destroyers sharp on port and starboard bows respectively; now *Chicago* and *Canberra* in view, distant 12,500 yards, closing fast. The Admiral now ordered speed reduced to 18–20 knots — so he said in 1949; but promptly built up again to 26 knots — as his track chart proves. "Independent Firing!" ordered Mikawa at 0136. Target angles were hastily cranked into torpedo directors and at 0138 hissing "fish" leaped out of their tubes, one salvo bound for *Bagley,* others for the cruisers. *Chokai* was soon a mere two miles from them, still closing, still undetected. Suddenly, at 0143,[22] from the only American ship that was properly awake, came the long-delayed tocsin. *Patterson* sighted the loom of a ship 5000 yards ahead and broadcast a radio alarm: —

WARNING — WARNING: STRANGE SHIPS ENTERING HARBOR!

It was too late. At that very moment — only seconds before or after *Patterson's* warning — Japanese float planes dropped brilliant flares over the transports at Lunga Point which silhouetted *Chicago* and *Canberra;* at that very moment *Chokai,* only 4500 yards away, *Aoba,* 1000 yards farther, and *Furutaka* at 9000 opened fire with main batteries. At that very moment, too, a sharp-eyed lookout on *Canberra's* bridge was trying to point out a strange ship, dead ahead, to the officer of the deck. As the two Australians peered intently into the gloom, torpedoes came slashing in on both sides of the ship. These had been fired five minutes earlier, but the 8-inch and 4.7-inch salvos did not take many seconds to arrive. The fateful minute 0143 had not elapsed, General Alarm was still sounding, and *Canberra's* guns were still trained in, when two

---

[22] The exact minute of *Patterson's* sighting is disputed, but it was undoubtedly within sixty seconds of the flares, and our belief is that it was 0143.

torpedoes sundered her starboard side and the first of 24 shells hit her high hull. Captain Getting was mortally wounded and his gunnery officer killed instantly. The Australian cruiser got off two torpedoes and a few 4-inch shots from her secondary battery before power and propulsion died. Fires spread topside, and a ten-degree starboard list developed. In less than five minutes this fine ship was out of the war.

Patterson, after repeating her radio warning by blinker, commenced a hard left turn to unmask her batteries. Gunners laid a spread of star shell; Commander Walker shouted, "Fire Torpedoes!" The enemy replied in kind. Walker, noting that the Japanese column had come left to a northeasterly heading, conned his destroyer on a high-speed zigzag course and engaged in a vigorous gunfire duel. Yet *Patterson* escaped the usual fate of a David in modern warfare. A shell hit near her No. 4 gun, igniting ready-service powder and putting two guns out of action. She came full circle, parallel to the enemy course, clawing at the aftermost cruisers with her remaining guns until they could no longer be seen. Only then did the captain discover that his order to fire torpedoes had not been heard. So brief and sudden was the action that the executive officer, then off watch, had no time to arrive at his battle station before the shooting stopped. He rallied the crew aft and put out the fire quickly.

Destroyer *Bagley*, screening on *Canberra's* starboard bow, saw the Japanese cruisers only a few seconds after *Patterson* did. A sharp left turn brought her starboard torpedo batteries to bear faster than torpedomen could insert firing primers. Lieutenant Commander Sinclair did not wait for them but made a tight circle to the left until the port torpedoes bore; then he fired.[23] The few moments lost were fatal because the enemy column was disappearing so fast to the northeastward that the best-aimed torpedoes

---

[23] All the American destroyers in this action were of the *Craven* class, which carried 8 torpedo tubes on each side. The Hepburn Report intimates that Bagley's torpedoes may have hit *Vincennes* to the northeast. That is just possible but very improbable, and enemy records show that *Chokai* fired torpedoes at *Vincennes* at 0148, one minute before *Bagley* launched hers.

could not catch up with it. Although Japanese vessels passed within a mile of *Bagley*, they did not fire on her, as their gun sights were already on bigger game.

Chicago's turn came next. She had been favored with three warnings. Orange flashes were seen at 0142,[24] then the aircraft flare over the transports; then a sudden right turn by *Canberra* ahead; but not until two black objects loomed out of the darkness did Captain Bode, just awakened from a sound sleep, direct his 5-inch guns even to prepare to illuminate with star shell. At 0146 a lookout saw a torpedo wake to starboard. Bode gave the order for full right rudder, then shifted helm when he saw torpedoes approaching his port bow. He did his best to comb the bubbling wakes but, at 0147, one of the warheads smacked into *Chicago's* bow and knocked off a part of it. A tall pillar of water rose into the air, then deluged the ship from bow to No. 1 stack. *Chicago's* gunners caught their breath, sputtered and gasped, went into action. Star shell was fired on both bows to spy out the enemy, but as all were duds the gunners groped blindly for targets. A Japanese cruiser made one shell hit of little consequence on her foremast. *Chicago* did not turn away like the destroyers, because at this juncture a vessel to the westward illuminated what appeared to be two targets ahead and gave her something to strike at for two minutes.

Admiral Mikawa, concerned about leaving his rear uncovered to the attention of *Blue* and *Jarvis*, at 0136 had directed his one destroyer, *Yunagi*, to reverse course and block the southwestern entrance to the Sound; she is the ship that attracted *Chicago's* attention. After the cruiser had fired 25 rounds, *Yunagi's* searchlight went out; *Chicago* snapped on her own searchlights at 0151 and swept the water to port and ahead but found nothing. The main battle had moved to the northeast, leaving Captain Bode's bewildered cruiser alone, slowly steaming in the wrong direction.[25] And, what was even worse, the Captain failed to alert the *Vincennes* group.

[24] Those were probably flashes from the firing charge of enemy torpedo tubes.
[25] *Chicago's* story does not check with *Patterson's*, particularly as to who was illuminating what; the *War College Analysis* agrees with my guess.

Hitherto, Mikawa's cruisers had been steaming in a single column. Now, at 0144, probably because he had briefly glimpsed the *Vincennes* group to the northeastward, Mikawa changed course almost 30° left, to 69° (ENE). The other ships were expected to follow *Chokai*, but the maneuver was badly executed. Cruiser *Furutaka*, fifth in column, perhaps to avoid collision with *Kinugasa* ahead, sheered off to starboard and charged directly at the Allied formation; at about 0147, she came hard left to 11° (N by E). Light cruisers *Tenryu* and *Yubari* turned simultaneously and in the same direction as *Furutaka*. Thus Mikawa's force was divided into two separate groups: a western one of three cruisers in line of bearing; an eastern one of four cruisers led by flagship *Chokai*.[26]

At 0146 *Tenryu* sighted the *Vincennes* group bearing 60 degrees, distant over seven miles. Mikawa's ships had fired 17 torpedoes for only three hits, yet by 0149 they had finished the Southern Force as an effective fighting unit, without receiving a single hit. All in six minutes!

Mikawa's swing northward was decisive. It meant three more Allied cruisers in the bag. His column, at this point, resembled a vicious prehistoric monster, deadly at both ends. The battle south of Savo was only a tail-lashing. Now with two heads, hydra-like, the beast would put the bite on the Northern Force.

3. *The Battle East and North of Savo, 0143–0230*

At the very moment (0143) when *Patterson* was broadcasting her "Warning — Warning: Strange ships . . ." Japanese float

[26] Japanese reports of this are contradictory and incomplete. Our sources: *Campaigns of the Pacific War* (USSBS No. 255); *Inter. Jap. Off.*; Cent. Intell. Group Reports No. OOW45 (74633), OOW63 (86297). Both as to times and movements our chart reconciles discrepancies as far as possible. Rear Admiral Matsuyama in *Tenryu*, unaware of the *Furutaka* near collision, was much perplexed by this unscheduled split of forces. In post-battle reports Mikawa, with normal human frailty, wrote that everything went according to plan. That may well be true of the left turn, since his plane spotters had given him American cruiser positions. But the erratic maneuver of *Furutaka* was certainly not in the plan, and it is unlikely that Mikawa would intentionally have divided his forces in the heat of action. Capt. Omae said (1949) *F.* was unmasking torpedo batteries.

planes loosed a string of brilliant and long-burning parachute flares over the two transport areas off Tulagi and Guadalcanal. Flares and warning, seen and heard simultaneously, were the first inkling of danger to Captain Riefkohl's Northern Force. Frequent buzzing overhead from the enemy cruiser planes had been reported and discounted as "friendly." Cruisers *Vincennes*, *Quincy* and *Astoria* with *Helm* and *Wilson* on the flanks were just turning a corner on their box patrol, from SW to NW,[27] steaming quietly at 10 knots.

The action east and north of Savo commenced only five minutes after the action south of Savo began, at 0148, when flagship *Chokai* fired four torpedoes at the Northern Force, then ahead of her and less than 10,000 yards distant. *Astoria*, as the aftermost of the Northern Force was, however, the first to be hit, and by shellfire. This second half of the battle was such a mêlée that we can only clarify it by relating the experience of each American ship in turn.

On *Astoria's* bridge at 0143 the officer of the deck was intent on maintaining station. The quartermaster carefully wrote the course change in his notebook. The damage control officer, Lieutenant Commander Topper, acting as supervisor of the bridge watch, noted gunfire on Florida Island and remarked that the Marines were having no picnic that night at Tulagi. The gunnery officer tested the forward fire control radar, which had been acting cranky; the radar technician had just replaced some defective tubes. Captain Greenman, worn out by the exertions of the past two days, was asleep fully clothed in his emergency cabin, about two jumps from the bridge. Three bells of a quiet "graveyard watch" had passed.

Nobody on board had yet reacted to the flares or to *Patterson's* warning when, about 0145, Topper felt a slight tremor in *Astoria's* hull. Probably a destroyer dropping depth charges, he thought; everyone had been warned repeatedly of submarines. Actually it was *Chokai's* torpedoes exploding after their run past the *Chicago* group. Topper called the damage control watch. Yes, they had felt

---

[27] The turn from the SW to the NW leg had been delayed 20 minutes to 0140 by Capt. Riefkohl in order to bring the patrol closer to Savo.

a slight shake and were very much on the alert. The supervisor turned his attention to another report of aircraft overhead. The ship's blowers made a lot of noise; maybe that was it. Suddenly a shout from the port wing of the bridge — "Star shell on the port quarter!" Topper dashed out on the wing, to see a string of aircraft flares over Guadalcanal casting reflections on clouds and water. What could that mean? Lieutenant Commander Truesdell, the gunnery officer, also saw the bright lights and told the bridge to go to General Quarters. High time, too, for out of the darkness at 0150 came searchlights [28] and, less than a minute later, a salvo of Japanese shells, short and ahead. Main battery spotter announced that there were enemy cruisers on the port quarter. "Guns" ordered Commence Firing, and at about 0152½ six 8-inch guns roared out at Mikawa's flagship.

On the bridge the watch was still puzzling over the flares when the first main battery salvo lashed out. Quartermaster Radke jerked the general alarm lever while the junior officer of the watch called the Captain, who reached the bridge just before the second salvo. It was an awkward position for Greenman, awaking to find his ship in action, with whom and why he knew not. He barked some hurried questions and orders, which were not forgotten: — "Who sounded the general alarm? Who gave the order to commence firing? Topper, I think we are firing on our own ships, let's not get excited and act too hasty. Cease firing!"

This order went to the gunners, but Truesdell was sure his guns were firing at Japs and made an impassioned plea over the telephone, relayed to the Captain as: "Mr. Truesdell said, 'Sir, for God's sake give the word Commence Firing!'" The Captain did so, about 0154, remarking, "Whether our ships or not, we will have to stop them." [29]

Although *Chokai* had fired four salvos at *Astoria*, she had not yet made a hit when *Astoria's* guns were permitted to resume

[28] The first searchlight came from *Chokai*. Admiral Mikawa said in 1949 that he kept it on throughout the action.
[29] Statements of Lt. Cdrs. Truesdell and Topper in *Astoria* Action Report.

firing. But the debate on the bridge gave the Japanese time to find the range and to close. Presently an 8-inch salvo ripped into her superstructure, turning the midships section into a flaming torch. Now the Japanese had a nice point of aim. *Astoria*, blazing in her own consuming fires, was an easy and a close target. Shell after shell, accurate and deadly, plowed into the cruiser from 6000 down to 5300 yards' range. Captain Greenman, in order to unmask what was left of his main battery, altered course slightly to port and rang up full speed, keeping a seaman's eye on *Quincy* next ahead. But loss of communications, destruction of men and material topside, and the effects of choking smoke and blinding flame fatally lowered *Astoria's* battle efficiency. Eleven salvos of varying quantity left her 8-inch guns. One of *Quincy's* burst in Mikawa's staff chart room in *Chokai*. It was easy to keep station on the two cruisers ahead, since both were burning amidships. Captain Greenman maneuvered on a zigzag course, slightly on *Quincy's* port quarter, for several minutes while his ship received a steady rain of blows. Both forward turrets were knocked out, aircraft amidships spouted flame, the 5-inch gun batteries became mangled and useless, the navigator and chief quartermaster were killed. At

KEY TO JAPANESE CHART OF BATTLE OF SAVO ISLAND

From Action Report of *Kako*

Although this chart is far from completely accurate, as the author of it admits, "because records were lost when this ship was sunk," it illustrates vividly the tail-lashing on the Southern Force and the crossfire to which the Northern Force was subjected.

The solid line indicates the track of Mikawa's main force; the broken line, that of *Furutaka* and the light cruisers. Times are of the Tokyo Zone, two hours earlier than the time used in this volume. Allied ships, shown in red in the original, are mostly crossed off as supposedly sunk.

The bracketed key at left reads: C = enemy heavy cruisers; d = enemy destroyers. ①②③④ indicate torpedo or gun firings by *Aoba*, *Kako*, *Kinugasa* and *Furutaka* respectively.

about 0202, when the navigator was struck down, the Captain realized that his ship was in line of fire between *Quincy* and the enemy. To correct this he commenced a right turn just as a shell ground into the starboard side of the bridge. Down in a heap went the signal officer, the helmsman and a boatswain's mate. For perhaps half a minute *Astoria* had no helmsman. Boatswain's Mate J. Young, severely wounded, staggered to his feet from the huddled pile of bodies, clutched the wheel and brought the ship back to a north-westerly heading. But the black gang were being driven from their stations below by the heat and smoke from main deck conflagrations, and *Astoria* slowed down. Her propellers still thrashed the water but gave only a feeble seven knots. Enemy shells sprinkled her with their fragments and ignited fires over her entire length. Proud *Astoria*, who three years before had borne the ashes of Hiroshi Saito to Japan, was becoming little better than a funeral pyre for American sailors. But she was still fighting. Lieutenant Commander Davidson, communications officer, climbed into un-damaged turret No. 2, coached its guns onto a searchlight to the eastward, and this, the twelfth and last salvo, hit a forward turret on *Chokai*.

Quincy, next ahead of *Astoria*, received the worst beating of all on this terrible night. As in other ships, the low-flying Japanese aircraft were heard, reported and discussed on several occasions; but the assertion of a junior officer that they must be enemy was regarded by his seniors as mildly hysterical, so the last two contacts were not even reported to the Captain. Enemy aircraft flares were the first signs accepted as ominous. Immediately after they were seen, *Patterson's* "Warning — Warning . . ." was heard on the bridge. The gunnery control officer, Lieutenant Commander Andrew, was still trying to figure out the flares when the general alarm sounded. The bridge reacted promptly to *Patterson's* warning, calling Captain Moore from his emergency cabin off the chart house, but in the confusion nobody informed the gunners. As the enemy closed from astern, *Aoba* snapped open her searchlight shutters and illuminated *Quincy* so brightly that the Japanese lookouts could see that her guns were trained in, fore and aft. "We continued the battle very easy minded, without any worries," recalled the executive officer of *Chokai*. But Admiral Mikawa snorted at this: "We had plenty of worries; target selection, shortage of time, use of torpedoes, running aground, etc., etc."

The same searchlight beam that proved so soothing to Japanese nerves was a horror to the startled crew in *Quincy*. Lieutenant Commander Heneberger, gunnery officer, arrived in the gun control station just as shells began to fall in the water ahead. Men were still dashing to battle stations when the 8-inch turrets turned to port. "Fire at the ships with the searchlights on!" came from Captain Moore on the bridge. Two quick 9-gun salvos were pumped out at 8000 yards' range, but immediately after these the Captain, who had not seen the dim silhouettes of the enemy cruisers, decided that he was firing on friendly ships and ordered recognition lights turned on. While junior officers were trying to argue him out of it the officer of the deck, fearing a collision with *Vincennes* ahead, ordered a change of course and committed the error of turning right with an enemy shooting at him from the port quarter, which masked the fire of his forward turrets. Before the completion of this turn a Japanese shell touched off a plane resting on the catapult. Thereafter no searchlight was needed to see *Quincy*. Caught in a crossfire between the *Chokai* group and the *Furutaka* group, unable even to see her antagonists, the cruiser was doomed. Turret No. 2 was hit, and exploded. The Captain telephoned to the gunners: "We're going down between them — give them hell!" Immediately after this an enemy shell wounded him fatally and snuffed out almost every life in the pilot-house. A torpedo hit the port side at No. 4 fireroom, bashing it in. Last words from gun plot were a telephoned message giving news of the explosion. The engineer officer, Lieutenant Commander Elmore, sent a messenger to tell Captain Moore that his ship would have to stop — last words again. For the engine rooms, though yet undamaged, had lost communication and become sealed deathtraps. In mess compartments, repair stations and bunk rooms, men struggled hopelessly with fire and explosions. The sick bay was wiped out. On anti-aircraft batteries, guns and men were flattened down, chopped up and blown to bits. At No. 4 five-inch gun a shell neatly removed the bases from several cartridge cases and ignited them, "causing them to burn like a Roman candle and killing all hands on the left side of the gun." [30] There was no doubt now among surviving officers that *Quincy* was doomed; the only question was whether she would succumb to fire or water.

Gunnery officer Heneberger sent his assistant Andrew to the bridge for instructions. Andrew thus described his mission: —

> When I reached the bridge level, I found it a shambles of dead bodies with only three or four people still standing. In the pilothouse itself the only person standing was the signalman at the wheel, who was vainly endeavoring to check the ship's swing to starboard and to bring her to port. On questioning him I found out that the Captain, who was at that time lying near the wheel, had instructed him to beach the ship and he was trying to head the ship for Savo Island, distant some four miles on the port quarter. I stepped to the port side of the pilothouse, looked out to find the island and noted that the ship was heeling rapidly to port, sinking by the bow. At that instant the Captain straightened up and fell back, apparently dead, without having uttered any sound other than a moan. [31]

When Andrew returned to gun control station with his dismal report, Heneberger ordered Abandon Ship. The forecastle was now completely awash with water coming over the gun deck. Life rafts and flotsam were cast overboard in the nick of time; at about 0235 *Quincy* capsized to port, twisted completely around in her agony with stern high in air, and slid under the black waters — first of many fighting ships whose shattered hulls would justify the name "Ironbottom Sound" for that body of water.

There is this consolation for *Quincy* survivors. Admiral Mikawa and his chief of staff recalled in 1949 that the "centre ship of the Northern Group" returned the heaviest fire of any American

[30] Lt. Cdr. Heneberger in *Quincy* Action Report.

[31] Capt. Moore's body was subsequently washed up on Savo Island and interred by the natives, one of whom retained his Annapolis class ring, by which it was later identified.

cruiser, and expressed great admiration for her commanding officer's gallantry.

Leading the northern cruiser column and first to be sighted but last to be engaged was *Vincennes*, "Vinny Maru" as her crew called her.[32] Captain Riefkohl had retired to his emergency cabin on the bridge less than an hour before; Commander Mullan, his executive officer, was on the bridge and Lieutenant Commander Craighill at gun control. These officers had heard *Talbot's* radio warning of the enemy plane sighting at 2345 and had been cautioned in the Captain's night order book to exercise extreme vigilance. Yet *Vincennes* too was not alerted until enemy flares fell on her port quarter. It is not clear whether *Patterson's* "Warning — Warning" of 0143 reached the Captain; he was called to the bridge after the flares were seen but before he reached it General Quarters sounded. Riefkohl and Mullan were still speculating on the significance of the flares when they felt two underwater explosions, heard gunfire and even saw a few gun flashes through the rain squall to the southward; but they assumed that this was the *Chicago* group shooting at planes. Oh the stupendous optimism of that night!

Captain Riefkohl decided to continue on his course after increasing speed to 15 knots. At 0150 searchlights from three ships abaft the port beam fastened each to an American cruiser. The Captain, assuming they came from the Southern Group, sent out a request by voice radio that they be shut off, while his gunnery officer, Lieutenant Commander Adams, as a precaution trained on the nearest one. Doubts were quickly resolved by a salvo from *Kako* that fell 500 yards short of *Vincennes*. She replied at 0153 with a full 8-inch salvo (range about four miles) after her 5-inch had fired star shell for illumination. "Vinny" drew Japanese blood with her second salvo by hitting *Kinugasa* but, simultaneously, enemy shells hit her amidships and planes on the catapults went

---

[32] Lt. (jg) Donald H. Dorris and others *A Log of the Vincennes* (1947) pp. 265–84 has a vivid account of the battle by survivors from this fine cruiser, followed by (pp. 297–373) survivor stories and letters.

up in fire. Japanese searchlights snapped shut, as no longer necessary, and their gunners and torpedomen commenced a methodical
destruction of this easy target.

Captain Riefkohl now decided to close the enemy by turning
left; but more hits on his brightly illuminated ship prevented. One
on the port side of the bridge killed several men. Hits throughout
the superstructure demolished guns, destroyed communications
and kindled blistering fires. Main battery gunfire was resumed in
local control but with little hope of success. The concentrated fire
from both enemy groups was so devastating that Riefkohl turned
his ship hard right in an effort to escape. During this turn, at 0155,
two or three torpedoes from *Chokai* penetrated No. 4 fireroom
on the port side. The eviscerated cruiser shuddered in agony.
Below decks the No. 2 fireroom crew were smothered in smoke
and showered with debris. In the after engine room men watched
with dismay the steady drop in steam pressure and tried in vain
to call the bridge. At 0203½ a torpedo from *Yubari* hit her No. 1
fireroom, killing everyone there. Now *Vincennes* floundered to a
halt, still under concentrated fire. The Captain, deprived of communications, mobility, sight and organization, had only a chaotic
picture of what was happening. A submarine was rumored to be
close aboard. Two enemy searchlights which leisurely inspected
Vincennes were identified as friendly, because they came from her
hitherto unengaged side, so the Captain ordered a large set of
colors raised to the fore. The enemy, mistaking this big battle
ensign for an admiral's flag redoubled his efforts to sink *Vincennes*.[33] Riefkohl ordered funnel smoke to conceal his blazing
hull, but all surviving water tenders and firemen had been driven
from their boilers.

So it went, from one horror to another. The Captain sent a
messenger to the gunnery officer asking for fire on the two searchlights still focused on the ship; "Guns" himself came down to the
bridge to announce that no guns remained. Both forward turrets
had received direct hits and the 5-inch batteries were nothing but

[33] Japanese admirals' flags were striped and rayed with red.

twisted metal and flame. *Vincennes* was now listing heavily to port, with enemy gunfire still aggravating her many grievous wounds. The Captain was seriously considering whether he should order Abandon Ship to save lives when at about 0215 the Japanese guns ceased fire and the searchlights blinked out. The enemy had moved on, leaving *Vincennes* dead in the water, burning and helpless.

Commander Mullan strove to put out fires and jettison ammunition but was shortly felled by an explosion which broke his leg. He and several other wounded were lowered into a life raft. In the coding room Acting Pay Clerk Willess ordered his men to don gas masks as smoke filled the compartment. As minutes went by and no communications could be established, he opened the door to find the ship ablaze. His men jettisoned the coding equipment while he went out on deck with the disbursing records, a paymaster's sacred trust. He was still looking for a floating object on which to stow them when the rising water floated him off the deck, minus his box of records. Captain Riefkohl, his Marine orderly Corporal Patrick, and Chief Yeoman Stucker stayed with the ship to the last; even when in the water the Captain swam from one group to another, rendering what aid and encouragement he could after his ship went down. It was about 0250 when *Vincennes* heeled to her beam-ends, hesitated briefly, capsized and sank. Water and fire mixing in angry swirls of steam and smoke marked her end.

Wilson and *Helm*, screening destroyers of the Northern Force, were eager to help their cruisers, but to them the battle appeared a confused jumble with Japanese ships everywhere you did not want them and nowhere when you did want them. Lieutenant Commander Price of *Wilson* was duly alerted by the aircraft flares and *Patterson's* radio warning. At about 0150 he sighted a three-ship Japanese column illuminating and attacking his cruisers. At once he opened fire, his four 5-inch guns shooting over the Americans at the enemy searchlights some five miles away. At the same time he tried to conform to the cruiser movements, turning first left and then hard right, firing continuously whenever his guns would bear. Fire was interrupted when *Helm* materialized out of the darkness ahead. Price rang up 30 knots, turned hard left and passed clear. *Wilson* continued to toss out 5-inch shells at *Chokai*. The enemy, intent on sinking cruisers, took little notice beyond firing a few salvos at her, all of which missed.

Destroyer *Helm*, on the port bow of *Vincennes*, never did lend a hand. Lieutenant Commander Carroll, alerted by the flares, observed signs of action in the Southern Group but did not realize that his own cruisers were engaged until he saw them plastered with shellfire; the enemy he never did see. He maintained course ahead of the formation, turning south when the cruisers were left behind, blazing. At 0200 *Helm* took off in pursuit of a ship four miles distant on the starboard bow, but ascertained that the stranger was friendly — probably *Bagley*.

Admiral Mikawa and staff had been watching the battle's progress with relish. At 0200, for reasons which to the present writer are inexplicable, the Admiral turned flagship *Chokai* away from the northerly course, whether to port or to starboard cannot now be determined. Apparently he expected the column to follow, but they kept right on to the northward. Mikawa, accordingly, made another quick change, returned to the original course and fell in at the rear of *Kinugasa*. This move was a fortunate break for us. It not only saved the transports, but got *Chokai* into trouble. At 0205 two shells from *Quincy* hit the Japanese flagship. One shell wiped out the Admiral's staff chart room and a second scored near the aviation crane. A third shell hit a forward turret, but inflicted no damage of consequence. At 0220 Mikawa signaled his captains, "All ships withdraw." Still steaming in two columns, they turned westward to leave Savo Island on the port hand. *Chokai* turned left and increased speed to 35 knots and cut the corner to regain the lead position. At the same time the *Furutaka* group ran into destroyer *Ralph Talbot*, who, singlehanded, took on the lot.

Ralph Talbot was the picket destroyer that patrolled the channel between Savo and Florida Islands. *Patterson's* first radio warning had sent her scurrying southwest at 25 knots. Lieutenant Commander Callahan and everyone else topside watched the battle within the Sound, wondering what the score was. At 0215 they began to find out when *Tenryu,* moving westward, focused a searchlight on them and shells began to come their way. *Furutaka, Tenryu* and *Yubari* opened up on *Talbot* from a range between 4500 and 6000 yards, and in about seven salvos scored one hit on her torpedo tubes. Callahan, seeing a single searchlight and colored splashes like those from American shells, thought he was being fired on by friends, flicked on recognition lights and shouted his identification over voice radio. This unexpected procedure appears to have puzzled the enemy, who checked fire momentarily. But *Ralph Talbot* had little respite. *Yubari,* the rear Japanese cruiser, less than two miles away, turned searchlights on the destroyer's bridge and fired several more salvos. Callahan replied, but after his second salvo the enemy got the range. One shot hit the destroyer's charthouse and knocked out part of the automatic gun control system, a second exploded in the wardroom, a third demolished a torpedo tube and a fourth struck the after 5-inch gun. *Talbot* launched four torpedoes at her antagonist without success. *Talbot* entered a rain squall and the battle ended abruptly, leaving the destroyer in flames and listing 20 degrees to starboard. Yet *Ralph Talbot's* plucky fight may have convinced Admiral Mikawa that there were more American ships about than met his eye, and so furthered his decision to retire.

Talbot was not the only destroyer that night to have an individual fight. During the cruiser battle to the eastward of Savo the Japanese destroyer *Yunagi,* which Mikawa had detached to cover the southern entrance to the Sound, was fighting on her own. At 0152 she had a brush with an alleged light cruiser which "went down with a great rumble." [34] *Chicago,* in all probability, was this opponent; but she was not sunk although she rumbled plenty. At 0200 *Yunagi* encountered another "light cruiser," attacked and

[34] Translation of Crudiv 18 War Diary (WDC No. 160,984).

claimed damage. This ship can only have been *Jarvis*, still trying to retire to the westward.[35] *Yunagi* finally fell in astern of cruiser *Yubari* to the northwest of Savo Island shortly after the latter's engagement with *Ralph Talbot*.

While battle raged around Savo Island, American ships in the transport area were baffled but busy. The first enemy parachute flares, expertly placed to silhouette the Guadalcanal transport area, were quickly followed by another cluster over the Tulagi group. Thoroughly alarmed, all ships discontinued unloading, got under way and milled around in uneasy expectation. Admiral Turner from *McCawley's* flag bridge could see occasional gun flashes and the sudden flare of explosive hits. Rain squalls directly in line with Savo Island drew a curtain of uncertainty. The situation was even more obscure to Admiral Scott's *San Juan* force, which continued its routine patrol between Florida Island and Guadalcanal. Admiral Crutchley in *Australia*, patrolling to seaward of the Guadalcanal transports, ordered the seven destroyers he had earlier designated as a striking force [36] to close his flagship if not in contact with the enemy. But this order, too, got fouled up and its only effect was to pull four destroyers out of the battle and send them hot-footing toward their assigned rendezvous five miles northwest of Savo Island. In the amphibious force the situation was touch-and-go.

[35] *Jarvis* was sighted by *Blue* at 0325 still steaming westward, and after daybreak was seen by a scout plane from *Saratoga* at lat. 9°42' S, long. 158°59' E, course SW, down by the bow and trailing oil. Her fate was a mystery until Japanese sources became available. *Yunagi's* War Diary says that on 9 Aug. "our air force was ordered to attack and destroy the damaged destroyer which split and sank." War Diary 25th Air Flotilla (WDC No. 161,730) for 9 Aug. gives the assignment of planes to sink her — 16 VT and 15 VF — and says that she was sunk by torpedoes at 1300. Lt. Cdr. Graham had jettisoned all boats and rafts at Lunga Roads to save weight, and not a man survived.

[36] It was arranged that, if Admiral Crutchley so ordered, Captain Cornelius W. Flynn, Commander Destroyer Squadron 4, was to form a striking force composed of seven destroyers drawn from the other two forces and the transport screen, *Selfridge, Patterson, Mugford, Helm, Henley, Bagley* and *Wilson*. This Striking Force was ordered, when and if formed, to concentrate five miles to the northwest of Savo Island and "In the event of contact with enemy surface units at once attack with full outfit of torpedoes and then maintain touch from the westward. The Striking Force will engage the enemy in gun action when our cruisers engage, provided it is quite clear that our own forces are not in the line of fire, and must be prepared, if ordered, to illuminate the enemy targets for our cruiser gunfire."

Each transport was blacked out, apprehensive, with no guide and in no formation; one overimaginative gunner might have sparked a battle of friend against friend. On the other hand, observing that the battle was moving away, transport sailors were convinced that their side had won. And as far as they were concerned it had; Admiral Mikawa was going home.

After Mikawa had cleared the passage between Florida and Savo Islands, he showed indecision. His flagship, as we have seen, was now at the rear of the heavy-cruiser column. The *Furutaka* group was scattered, out somewhere in the darkness. Mikawa thought three hours would be needed to whip his ships into battle formation again, and by that time it would be almost daybreak. If he then ventured into the Sound with weather clearing, as it always did around sunrise, he would lay himself open to a carrier air attack; Fletcher's departure was unsuspected.

It is always difficult to assign exact motives to a decision like this, where some criticism of the commanding officer is involved. Admiral Kurita's retirement at Leyte Gulf, after his action with the escort carriers, is another case in point. Admiral Yamamoto was displeased with Mikawa for not carrying out his explicit orders to destroy the transports, and his Commander in Chief's displeasure put Mikawa on the defensive. In 1949 both he and his chief of staff insisted that Mikawa personally wished to return to the fray, but that the staff dissuaded him for two reasons: the fact that all torpedoes had been expended, and fear of a daylight carrier air attack.[37] This may well be true; but the present writer suspects that the Admiral and staff simply did not want to go back and tempt luck a second time; felt they had done enough.

By about 0240 all Mikawa's ships had increased speed to 30 knots for a hasty run up the Slot.

[37] The reasons (loss of charts, etc.) given by *Chokai's* exec. in *Inter. Jap. Off.* I 255 are obviously frivolous, and need not be taken seriously. Admiral Mikawa further insisted in 1949 that he did not give the retirement order until 0240; but Crudiv 6 (or 18) Action Report distinctly says 0220.

4. *Picking up the Pieces, 9–10 August*

The tornado-like onslaught on the Southern Force left it shattered. H.M.A.S. *Canberra*, hardest hit, was in dire straits at 0148 when Commander J. A. Walsh RAN, the executive officer, felt his way to the bridge to take over command from the mortally wounded Captain Getting, who died next day. Now that the hard-shooting ships had swept on, the immediate enemy was fire. Bucket brigades were formed, ammunition and gasoline jettisoned, magazines flooded. Explosions of ammunition, want of any kind of light or power, and the presence of wounded throughout the ship impeded the work. It was with great relief that Commander Walsh at 0300 saw *Patterson* coming in out of the darkness. With fire-fighting equipment from the destroyer, the cruiser stood a good chance of survival.

Patterson was closing *Canberra* by order of Captain Bode of *Chicago*. As she came alongside, ammunition was erupting with volcanic violence. This, combined with heavy rain, gusts of high wind and a choppy sea, prevented the destroyer from securing on the port side for nearly an hour. Flames were gaining control in spite of the drenching rainfall. At last, about 0400, *Patterson* passed four hoses and a handy-billy pump to Walsh's crew, who promptly turned them on the fires. An hour later *Canberra* received her death warrant in the form of a dispatch from Admiral Turner. The Australian cruiser must either join him at 0630, to retire from the area, or be abandoned and destroyed. This was Hobson's choice for a ship dead in the water. Commander Walsh reluctantly ordered Abandon Ship and commenced the transfer of his men to the destroyer.[38] Orderly evacuation was interrupted at 0510 by the appearance of a strange vessel some four miles away. *Patterson* challenged her three times; no reply. *Patterson* cast off her lines

---

[38] *Canberra's* damage was so serious that even with more time and destroyers to help she would have been a goner. The R.A.N. board of inquiry found that she was not torpedoed, but we beg to differ.

and illuminated the stranger, who answered with shell fire; *Patterson* returned the compliment. But Commander Walker sensed something familiar about his sparring partner's dim silhouette; could it be *Chicago?* He set off an emergency identification signal[39] and ceased gunfire; the other ship, which really was *Chicago*, promptly knocked off.

During the night that damaged cruiser had steamed to the westward, chasing a ship which can only have been the destroyer *Yunagi*, until Turner ordered her to turn back. It is not surprising that her gunners struck out blindly when *Patterson* turned on the searchlight. The spirited duel fortunately was brief; and as neither hit the other this little exchange provided the only comic interlude to a grisly night.

The only ship within fifteen miles of Savo Island which did not fire a shot during the action was picket destroyer *Blue*, the first ship sighted by Mikawa's force. *Blue's* first alarm was the aircraft flares over Guadalcanal. She watched the battle of the Southern Force until diverted by a sound contact nine miles west of Savo Island which materialized as a Japanese auxiliary schooner. At 0250 she sighted an unidentified vessel rounding Cape Esperance, closed, and identified her as damaged destroyer *Jarvis* retiring painfully at 8 knots, trailing a long slick of oil. *Blue* turned away at 0325 and *Jarvis* passed out of sight and disappeared.[40]

At 0515 *Blue* was directed to assist *Canberra* and at 0622 reached her side. *Patterson* came back to help at 0625, and within fifteen minutes they had taken every living soul off the cruiser. The two destroyers transferred their load of 680 survivors to transports off Guadalcanal. *Canberra* was sunk by a torpedo from *Ellet* at about 0800.

Three American cruisers of the Northern Force were still precariously afloat when Admiral Mikawa bowed out. *Quincy*, as we

[39] The wrong one, said Capt. Bode, but good enough.
[40] It is ironical that *Blue* should have picked up a tiny sailing vessel and a destroyer hugging a mountainous coastline, yet missed seeing any of the seven Japanese ships. There was some discussion to the effect that *Chicago* may have engaged *Jarvis*, but *Chicago* more likely tangled with *Yunagi*. Cf. note 35.

have seen, went down at 0235; about fifteen minutes later *Vincennes* took the awful plunge. Their survivors were picked up after daylight by destroyers. But *Astoria* suffered a lingering death. As Mikawa's cruisers pulled away she slid to a halt, all power of every description gone. Young, the wounded helmsman, collapsed and his place was taken by a quartermaster. It was no use; the ship's nerves and muscles were dead. Gunnery officer Truesdell recommended that the bridge be abandoned because machine-gun ammunition above was exploding. The Captain ordered all wounded men brought to the forecastle.

Lieutenant Commander Topper had made a record dash from the bridge to his damage control station shortly after the Captain appeared in the pilothouse. He did what he could, sending men to fight fires as they were reported, but a hit directly over his head soon filled central station with smoke. Men escaping from other stations crowded into Topper's small space. Finally, with all communications lost, he directed evacuation to the forecastle and reported to the Captain. By that time some 300 men including 70 wounded were gathered in the bow clear of the fires. Bucket brigades were formed but eye-droppers would have done as well against that conflagration. The magazines were ordered to be flooded. Preparations were made to abandon ship if need be.

The engineer officer, Lieutenant Commander Hayes, asleep when the enemy opened up, was called by a petty officer who remarked, "The shells are sure flying up there!" The Chief took his station in the forward engine room and was soon overwhelmed with damage reports, more damage reports, loss of communications, smoke and noxious fumes. As his engines rumbled to a stop for want of steam, Hayes and the surviving engineers made a tortuous progress to the fantail. On the main deck aft they found about 150 men, including the executive officer, Commander Shoup, who was concerned about a possible return of the enemy. For that eventuality *Astoria* still had No. 3 turret ready to shoot 8-inch shells by hand power. With no pressure left in the fire hoses, men fastened lines to empty powder cases and used them to scoop up sea water to fight the smaller fires; they were actually making some progress at 0330 when a rainstorm came to their assistance.[41] Commander Shoup began to believe he might save the ship, for she had only a three-degree list and the sound of a gasoline pump far forward indicated that there was life up there. His hopes were raised still further when destroyer *Bagley* appeared, attracted by the flames; she was the only undamaged ship of the Southern Force.

Captain Greenman, anxious lest a magazine explode and unaware that there was life in the after part of his ship, requested the destroyer to close and remove the crew. *Bagley* made a skillful "Chinese landing," [42] and by 0445 had embarked the forecastle group. Shortly thereafter a flashing light on *Astoria's* stern apprised her of a survivor group on the fantail. At daybreak, when *Bagley* went alongside *Astoria's* quarter to take off Shoup and his companions, Captain Greenman decided to make another attempt to save his ship. For this purpose he transferred himself and a salvage party of 300 able-bodied men to the cruiser. For the next six hours, everything possible was done. Fast minesweeper *Hopkins* took *Astoria* in tow stern-first, destroyer *Wilson* joined the fire-fighting effort, repair parties plugged holes with mattresses and pillows, engineers wrestled with broken machinery. Before noon both destroyers were called away to screen transports after being relieved by *Buchanan*. Fires in the vicinity of the wardroom quickly gained ascendancy, and the list to port increased rapidly as shell holes on that side sucked in water. A magazine exploded at 1100, releasing bubbles of sickly yellow gas that broke surface abreast of it. *Buchanan* made an effort with her pumps to check flooding, supply ship *Alchiba* offered a towline, but they were too late to do any good, except recovering survivors. At noon August 9, with the sea lapping the main deck, the crew and Captain Greenman took

---

[41] While the bucket brigades were inching forward, Shipfitters C. C. Watkins and W. J. Wyatt and Watertender R. R. Touve plunged into the flames to rescue 3 wounded sailors. Cdr. Shoup called this the bravest act of a night when bravery was commonplace.

[42] Landing made by bow-to-bow approach on course reverse to *Astoria's* heading. So called because the fast-moving Whang-Po River at Shanghai often dictated that kind of approach.

to the water. Fifteen minutes later the ship heeled over on her port side and sank.[43]

Scrappy *Ralph Talbot*, on fire, listing badly and without power, was nursed back to ambulatory convalescence by noon; with two boilers alight she crawled into Tulagi.

Carriers *Saratoga, Enterprise* and *Wasp* had almost cleared San Cristobal at 0100 August 9 when Admiral Fletcher, not yet having received permission from Admiral Ghormley to execute the retirement that he had been virtually pursuing for twelve hours, turned back toward Guadalcanal. At 0300 he received a "flash report indicating some type surface action in Tulagi–Guadalcanal area." [44] Captain Forrest Sherman of *Wasp*, whose air group, trained in night operations, was still intact, thrice requested the flag officer on board, Rear Admiral Noyes, to continue northwestward at high speed with a few well-fueled destroyers, and then launch aircraft to chase the Japanese up the Slot and furnish Turner with air support. A glance at the carrier's track chart proves that Sherman's proposal might well have been carried out, but Noyes declined to forward his request to Fletcher. At 0330 Ghormley's permission to retire reached the task force commander who, without seeking more information about the surface action, changed course again to the southeastward and hightailed out of the area.

The 9th of August was a sad Sabbath for the Allies. Overnight the heady wine of victory had soured, leaving a humiliating aftertaste of defeat. And the enemy might return in a daylight surface raid, an intensified air offensive or submarine attack. Turner disregarded every nasty possibility and ordered unloading to be resumed. Chance favored this stalwart choice; for the Japanese air strike that morning never got through.[45] By midafternoon the

---

[43] There is a possibility that *Astoria* might have been beached if destroyers had been sent to the spot immediately when *Bagley* reported her condition at about 0500, and if vigorous fire-fighting and pumping measures had been undertaken continuously.

[44] TF 16 War Diary for 9 Aug. Same diary for 2100 that day contains significant admission: "Prompt report of situation [at Savo] might have permitted aircraft units from TG 61.1 to participate and engage enemy forces present."

[45] The War Diary of 25th Air Flotilla mentions this strike and admits loss of

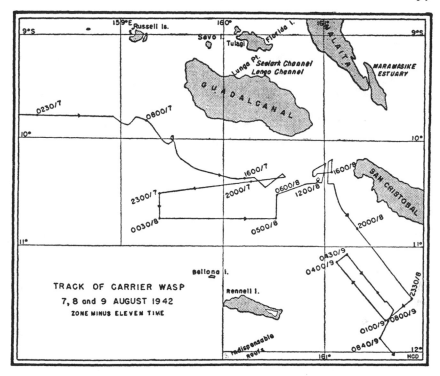

Marines had four units of fire for their weapons [46] and thirty-seven days' supply of food ashore. Shortly before the first dog-watch, the Amphibious Force got under way for Nouméa in two groups, leaving Ironbottom Sound empty of shipping — at least on the surface. The Marines were now on their own.

Admiral Mikawa, anticipating a retaliatory air attack at dawn, ordered anti-aircraft disposition and scanned the skies anxiously, but no Allied planes appeared. After consulting his ship captains he figured out that he had sunk seven cruisers and five destroyers — more than were present. The damage to his own ships was trifling: a torpedo-tube nest in *Aoba* hit and burned, with a fire that took some time to control; a chart room in *Chokai* wiped out;

---

planes, but significantly claims only the sinking of a cruiser (DD *Jarvis*). Probably they were sent to get Fletcher's carriers and searched too long for their gas supply.

[46] A unit of fire is a quantity of ammunition for any given weapon, based on the average daily consumption for that weapon in combat.

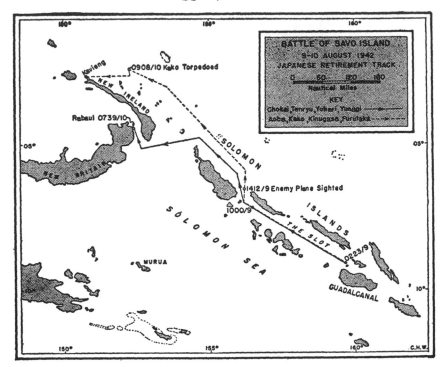

a storeroom in *Kinugasa* flooded by a shell hole; hits in No. 1 engine room, and some damage to port steering control room; one of *Kako's* planes and its crew lost; machine-gun damage to all ships; in all 58 men killed and 53 wounded.[47] No wonder the little people in Japan now believed their Navy to be invincible; nobody had told them the facts of Midway.

Just before reaching Bougainville Strait, Mikawa diverted *Aoba*, *Kako*, *Kinugasa* and *Furutaka* to Kavieng in New Ireland, while he continued with the rest to Rabaul. That afternoon an Australian Hudson patrol plane dogged the four heavy cruisers for nearly an hour but gave them little concern. Next morning, 10 August, the disdainful Nipponese were south of Simbari Island, a scant 70

[47] "Detailed Battle Report 6th Crudiv" (WDC No. 160,997); Crudiv 18 War Diary (WDC No. 160,984). More details in Nos. 160,623 and 161,407, which give following figures of rounds fired by the cruisers only: 1014 eight-inch, 830 five- and 4.7-inch.

miles from Kavieng. The ships were arranged in a rough rectangle, steaming at 16 knots without destroyer escort but with an airplane on patrol. At this juncture the small, seventeen-year-old submarine *S-44* (Lieutenant Commander John R. Moore) happened along, to prove that big things sometimes come in small packages. Shortly before nine o'clock Moore sighted these juicy targets, closed and attacked from a range of 700 yards. Eight minutes later, four American torpedoes exacted the first payment for Savo Island. Cruiser *Kako* sighted the wakes too late, buckled under the impacts and sank within five minutes.[48] The American S-boat escaped easily.

At about the time *Kako* was being eliminated, Admiral Mikawa arrived in Rabaul to be greeted with the *Banzais* of the garrison and a message from Admiral Yamamoto: "Appreciate the courageous and hard fighting of every man of your organization. I expect you to expand your exploits, and you will make every effort to support the land forces of the Imperial Army, which are now engaged in a desperate struggle."

Neither Admiral knew, although Yamamoto probably suspected, how desperate that struggle would be.

Savo Island was the first large surface action since Santiago to be fought by a predominantly United States force. Unlike Java Sea, here the command as well as the major part of the force was American. Unlike Pearl Harbor, here the United States Navy had been at war eight months, operating in a combat area. The enemy was little superior in strength — inferior in destroyers — yet one side was all but annihilated and the other escaped virtually unscathed.

The violent repercussions within the Navy and later among the American people [49] brought about an investigation. In December

---

[48] None of the victor ships of Savo Island survived the war. *Furutaka* was sunk in the Battle of Cape Esperance; *Kinugasa* in the Battle of Guadalcanal; *Tenryu*, *Yubari* and *Yunagi* by U.S. submarines; *Chokai* in the Battle off Samar, and *Aoba* in the carrier raid on Kure.

[49] The Navy concealed its losses in order to keep the enemy guessing until 12 Oct., when it was able at the same time to announce a victory.

1942 the Secretary of the Navy ordered Admiral Arthur J. Hepburn, former Commander in Chief of the Fleet, to conduct an inquiry to determine the "primary and contributing causes of the losses and whether or not culpability attaches to any individual engaged in the operation." The Admiral, with Commander Donald J. Ramsey, traveled all over the Pacific to talk with the principal officers involved and to obtain their statements. He concluded that "the primary cause of this defeat" was "the complete surprise achieved by the enemy." The reasons for this surprise he listed as follows, in order of importance: —

(*a*) Inadequate condition of readiness on all ships to meet sudden night attack.
(*b*) Failure to recognize the implications of the presence of enemy planes in the vicinity previous to attack.
(*c*) Misplaced confidence in the capabilities of radar installations on *Ralph Talbot* and *Blue*.
(*d*) Failure in communications which resulted in lack of timely receipt of vital enemy contact information.
(*e*) Failure in communications to give timely information of the fact that there had been practically no effective reconnaissance covering enemy approach during the day of August 8.
> As a contributory cause . . . must be placed the withdrawal of the carrier groups on the evening before the battle. This was responsible for Admiral Turner's conference . . . [and] for the fact that there was no force available to inflict damage on the withdrawing enemy.[50]

Admiral Nimitz agreed with Admiral Hepburn that complete surprise was responsible, but listed the causes of it in a somewhat different order: communication weaknesses, poor air search, erroneous estimate of enemy intentions, dependence on ineffective radar, disregard of the unidentified planes, want of a flag officer in the Southern Force, and "the probability that our force was not . . . sufficiently 'battle-minded.'" Admiral King, in general, concurred, and all three agreed that blame for the defeat was so evenly dis-

[50] Hepburn Report pp. 52–3; the last paragraph only is direct quotation, the rest a summary.

tributed that it would be unfair to censure any particular officer. That was wise and just. Some of the commanding officers concerned were broken by the defeat, but Admiral Crutchley later made a creditable record in command of Allied forces in the Southwest Pacific, and Admiral Turner went on from Guadalcanal to become a master of amphibious warfare.

The present writer has little to add. Lack of "battle-mindedness," faulty radar and communications, basing decisions on the enemy's probable intentions (as at Pearl Harbor) and premature withdrawal of carrier forces (as at Wake)[51] are painfully evident to anyone who has read the sad story. But let us remember, too, that Luck — the constant and baffling major factor in naval warfare — was with the Rising Sun this time. We may deem it fortunate that the capricious lady smiled once on the Allies at the end, in persuading Mikawa not to come back.

Despite the grievous losses that night,[52] some consolation could be gleaned from the battle. As Admiral Crutchley later declared, "Our forces did achieve our object, which was to prevent the enemy from reaching the transports." Defeat taught the United States Navy many lessons; planners of later operations put them to good advantage. Americans gained a new and healthy respect for Japanese night fighting and would eventually beat the enemy at this game. Important, if minor, technical improvements came about as a result of the battle: the removal from all ships of wooden

[51] See Vol. III of this History pp. 131, 243.
[52] Tabulation by Medical Statistics Division, Bureau of Medicine, Navy Dept.; *Canberra's* from her Action Report: —

	Killed or Died of Wounds	Wounded
CANBERRA	84	55
CHICAGO	2	21
VINCENNES	332	258
QUINCY	370	167
ASTORIA	216	186
RALPH TALBOT	11	11
PATTERSON	8	11
	1023	709

It is not known how many men *Jarvis* lost during the battle, since she went down with all hands — 247 — in an air attack later in the day.

furniture and other inflammable material, such as "battleship lino-leum" and paint, which had burned like dry brush; provision of fireproof covers for bedding; improved fire-fighting equipment such as a fog nozzle, which poured a cooling, quenching mist on flames, far more effective than solid streams of water; a more reasonable battle-readiness condition that relieved sailors from con-tinual tension; improvements in communication methods and equip-ment; the development of adequate air-search systems.[53]

Savo Island was not a decisive battle, although it might have been if the Japanese had followed it up with energy instead of commit-ting forces piecemeal. Savo was the inaugural engagement of a bloody and desperate campaign and the 9th of August was the first of many terrible days when commanders on either side might well have raised their hands to Heaven like the Psalmist, to cry out, "For all the day long have I been plagued, and chastened every morning."

[53] Information about the Battle of Savo Island available during the last six years has been so spotty that a number of myths have grown up, which may be briefly dealt with here. (1) That placing a British admiral in command of U.S. naval ves-sels was responsible. Answer: Turner approved Crutchley's dispositions and C. was absent from the actual battle. (2) That the C.O.'s of *Vincennes, Chicago* and other ships knew by noon of 8 August the Japs were coming but miscalculated their speed, or were improperly informed by Turner. Answer: The information the C.O.'s had was based on the contacts with Mikawa's force on 7 August; Turner sent them the important 8 August contact report as soon as he got it. (3) That Admiral Ghormley was responsible as overall commander and was relieved as a consequence. Answer: Ghormley in Nouméa was able to exercise a general stra-tegic direction only; he was not relieved until mid-October, and then for other reasons. (4) That during the battle *McCawley* warned the Marines ashore that Japs were landing on Beach "Red," Guadalcanal. Answer: No such messages went out or were received; there was a brief alarm of possible enemy landing craft off shore on the night of 7–8 August which probably gave rise to the yarn.

CHAPTER III

Three Weeks on Guadalcanal[1]

9 August–1 September 1942

1. *The Marines' Problem and Initial Skirmishes*

AS the transports that had brought the Marines to this un-pleasant island disappeared over the horizon on the afternoon of 9 August, escorted by all combat ships still afloat, General Vandegrift knew that he was in for a rough, tough time. No ground force, not even United States Marines, can long hold a remote island against an enemy who commands the surrounding seas and the routes to its own bases. Mahan's axiom needed no fresh proof after what had happened at Wake and Corregidor. It is true that Admiral Mikawa had not made a clean sweep; but, by forcing all combat shipping that he did not sink to retire, he had opened the water-gates through which Japan could reinforce her small garrison on Guadalcanal at will. Kelly Turner had made no promise to "return," but Vandegrift knew he would send sup-plies, reinforcements and fighting ships at the earliest possible date and that McCain would fly in planes as soon as an airfield was ready. The only question was whether he could hold out that

[1] Commanding General 1st Marine Division (General Vandegrift) "Final Report on Guadalcanal Operation"; Maj. John L. Zimmerman of Marine Corps Historical Division *The Guadalcanal Campaign* (seen in preliminary draft); Brig. Gen. Pedro del Valle "Marine Artillery on Guadalcanal; The Story of the 11th Marines" *Marine Corps Gazette* XXVII No. 7 (Nov. 1943), XXVIII Nos. 1, 2 (Jan., Feb. 1944) and the Army Historical Division monograph *Guadalcanal: The First Offensive* (also in preparation) by John Miller, a former Marine, are my principal authorities for these and all other ground and land-based air operations described in this volume. Of the non-official works, John A. DeChant *Devilbirds* (1947) is the most useful.

long. While the Marines in general felt that the Navy had let them down badly,[2] Vandegrift, a man of iron, uttered no complaint and let no doubt enter his mind that the Corps would hold Guadalcanal, with or without help from the Navy.

The Marine problem on Guadalcanal was threefold: fending off enemy counterattacks, supplying the garrison and completing the airfield. If one failed, all failed. To meet a possible counterlanding, Vandegrift set up a five-mile defense line from the Ilu (Tenaru) River to Kukum. Since no coast defense guns had been landed, the largest weapons along the waterfront were mobile 75-mm "half tracks," 37-mm field pieces and a captured Japanese 3-inch gun. To the rear and on their inland flanks the Marines maintained separate strong points manned by small security detachments until the enemy commenced night infiltration. After that a thin outpost line was set up. At Tulagi the defense was simplified by quick elimination of the Japanese, but for some time the commanding general, William H. Rupertus USMC, felt he had to be prepared against an amphibious counterlanding on the back of Florida Island.

In addition, there was the constant peril of aërial and naval bombardment. Defense had to be passive until the airfield could be used. The 90-mm anti-aircraft batteries could and did keep enemy planes at a respectful altitude — say 27,000 feet — but even from that height the Japanese high-level bombers, who were unprovided with the Norden bombsight, managed to lay their "eggs" with care and no mean accuracy. The captured 3-inch gun was turned against surfaced submarines; but most of them flaunted the Rising Sun impudently out of gun range, as did the Japanese destroyers whose guns outranged anything the Marines had. One of the submarines, *I-123*, ventured too near the converted minesweeper

---

[2] This feeling appears humorously in an unofficial medal that the 1st Marine Division had struck in Melbourne after their relief. Obverse: an arm bearing rear admiral's stripes dropping a hot potato into the hands of a Marine kneeling on a tropical island; motto FACIAT GEORGIUS (let George do it). Reverse: rear end of a cow standing near an electric fan. Inscription: "In fond remembrance of the happy days spent from August 7th 1942 to January 1943. USMC."

Gamble, which disposed of this boat very neatly in Indispensable Strait on 28 August.

Supplying Guadalcanal was a tough problem. The unloading so rudely interrupted on 9 August had deprived the troops of many coast defense guns, heavy construction equipment and half the required ammunition. Food supplies, husbanded by serving only two meals a day and using Japanese rice, could last but a month. There was not enough aviation material to operate a combat airstrip. Yet the transports and cargo ships, of which the South Pacific Force had few, were too vulnerable and valuable to be risked. Old converted destroyers with high speed and maneuverability were selected to do the job.

On 15 August the first destroyer-transport echelon — *Colhoun, Gregory, Little* and *McKean* — brought in aviation gas, bombs and ammunition, proving that it could be done. Their most important passengers were Major Charles H. Hayes USMC, the first operations officer of Henderson Field, Ensign George W. Polk and 120 men of "Cub One" to service the daily expected planes.[3] Again, on 20 August the first three APDs brought in 120 tons of rations, enough for about three and a half days, and retired safely. Another vessel impressed into the lifeline was not so lucky. This was the old China river boat *Lakatoi,* acquired by the Navy and loaded at Nouméa with 400 tons of rations and ammunition. She might have made it had she not been fitted with a machine gun and a concrete shield to the wheelhouse, which made her topheavy. Three days out, after consuming several tons of the diesel oil that served as ballast, *Lakatoi* "just turned over and sank." Her volunteer naval crew lost one man during two weeks in a lifeboat and rubber rafts.[4]

Putting the airfield into operation was a back- and heartbreaking task for the 1st Marine Engineer Battalion. The Japanese had merely cleared the ground and made a flat surface, which General Vandegrift wished to lengthen by another thousand feet. The

[3] CTF 62 War Diary; Letter of Col. Hayes 8 Feb. 1949. Ensign Polk survived the war but was murdered when serving as a correspondent in Greece in 1948.
[4] Op Order A6–42; TF War Diary; sound recording by survivor M. W. Raderman, Office of Naval Records 24 Aug. 1943.

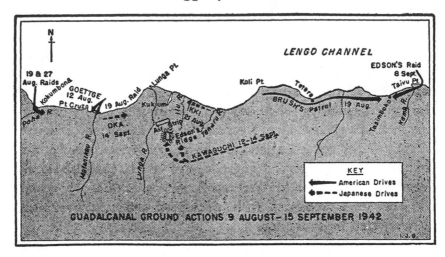

tough, saw-toothed kunai grass resisted burning, and most of it had to be mowed by bayonets. A large hole in the center of the runway had to be filled by hand-loaded Japanese trucks and dump carts. Tropical rainstorms beat the field into a wallow of viscous mud which sucked at men's feet and swallowed up truck wheels. Even so, by 12 August, the first plane, an amphibious Catalina, made a trial landing; and on the 17th Vandegrift informed Ghormley that Henderson Field, named after a Marine hero of Midway, was ready for use in dry weather. Hideouts were ready for the SBDs, an operations station was set up in the Japanese-built control tower known as the "Pagoda," Cub personnel organized fueling details and an air warning system; but barracks, mess halls, fuel tanks and the like were wanting and conditions were still embarrassingly primitive on 20 August when the first flight of Marine Corps planes alighted on Henderson Field.

In preparing his ground defenses, General Vandegrift wished to know where the enemy was concentrated. Patrols threading through the jungle to the west of Lunga River reached the Matanikau on 10 August, where they found the answer from numerous Jap automatic weapons that cut loose. But there was still doubt as to where the main enemy body was encamped. First Sergeant Stephen A. Custer of Division Intelligence proposed that a reconnaissance party be taken by boat to a position west of the Matani-kau River, there to land and thence to probe the interior for enemy spoor.

A Japanese naval warrant officer taken prisoner admitted that the main body of his countrymen lay beyond the Matanikau and, on being pressed, admitted that "perhaps" they might be persuaded to surrender. This tied in neatly with a report of a white flag's being displayed in the vicinity. Colonel Frank B. Goettge, division Intelligence officer, jumped to the conclusion that the enemy was starving and ripe for surrender, and took command of the recon-naissance party, which landed somewhere west of the Matanikau in pitchy darkness during the night of 12 August. Within a few minutes of landing they were ambushed and only three men escaped. Goettge, Custer, and many other valuable men were killed. As for the white flag, it had been an ordinary Japanese banner with the "meat ball" concealed in drooping folds. No treachery had been intended; but from that time on it was hard to persuade Marines to capture live Japanese, who in any case pre-ferred death to capture.

A week later, on 19 August, another jab was made on the Matani-kau sector, to keep the enemy off balance. Three companies of the 5th Marine Regiment, covered by artillery, made a three-pronged assault: from seaward, from the east and from the south. The villages of Kokumbona and Matanikau fell after a brief but spirited skirmish in which 65 Japanese and 4 Marines were killed. But Vandegrift had insufficient troops to extend his lines thither, so the three companies retired to the perimeter.

2. Battle of the Tenaru River, 21 August [5]

There were bigger doings on the Marines' eastern flank, the result of decisions made in Tokyo and Rabaul. Shortly after the

---

[5] Originally so called, then changed to Battle of Ilu River, owing to an original error in identifying the stream; but when this volume was in press the Marine Corps officially renamed it Tenaru. (Cf. Bunker Hill — Breeds Hill.) I hope this

American landings, General Tojo transferred the conduct of ground operations on Guadalcanal from Navy to Army. Lieutenant General Harukichi Hyakutake, commanding the Emperor's Seventeenth Army with headquarters at Rabaul, studied the situation and decided that 6000 troops would be sufficient to recapture the island. And, since that many soldiers were not available, he decided to commit what he had, fewer than 1000; for he estimated that there were only 2000 Americans on Guadalcanal, instead of the 17,000 actually there.

Colonel Kiyonao Ichiki, originally slated to occupy Midway, was given the honor of retaking Guadalcanal. He embarked 916 men at Truk in six destroyers which entered Savo Sound on the night of 18 August and, unseen from the shore, passed eastward of the American perimeter to land unopposed in the vicinity of Taivu Point. His scheme was simply to move westward along the coast and destroy the Americans by flank assault. The day before, units of the Special Naval Landing Force landed at Tassafaronga.

The six destroyers indulged in a brief bombardment of Guadalcanal and Tulagi after landing the troops. They caught and destroyed a Higgins landing boat plying between the two bases, and plopped a few salvos onto the airfield and the Tulagi docks. This gave the Army's Flying Forts based at Espiritu Santo a chance to bomb the enemy in broad daylight. Hitting a squirming destroyer by horizontal bombing methods is a difficult business, and the B–17s did well to lay one egg on the after gun mount of destroyer *Hagikaze*. She got away, but the bomb was a clear warning to the Japanese that daylight operations around Guadalcanal were unhealthy.

The Marines were not completely in the dark about Ichiki. Major Martin Clemens and 60 native troops of the British Solomon Islands Defense Force went scouting to the eastward, as did a

---

may excuse some inconsistencies here, it being too late to alter all the maps. Special sources: Brig. Gen. Clifton B. Cates USMC "Battle of the Tenaru," *Marine Corps Gazette* XXVII (No. 6) Oct. 1943; Capt. John Howland USMC in *Harvard Alumni Bulletin* XLV No. 14 (24 Apr. 1943). The troops engaged belonged to the 1st Regiment 1st Marine Division.

Marine patrol under Captain Charles Brush, on 19 August. Shortly after noon that day, Brush encountered an Ichiki patrol hiking westward and heedless of danger. The Marines neatly ambushed this force and wiped out 31 of the 34 men. A careful examination of the dead revealed that these Japanese were sleek, clean-shaven and well-dressed Army troops. Their pockets and dispatch cases bulged with charts, codes and diaries, which said very clearly that fresh enemy troops were ashore and that an offensive was in preparation on the east flank. They even had accurate maps of the Marines' positions. Fortunately the battalions of the 1st Marine Regiment had dug in on the left bank of the Ilu (Tenaru) River. They now laid wire, spread out a net of listening posts, installed a 37-mm gun and sat back to await developments. Early in the evening of 20 August a white flare seared the dark eastern sky, and individual Marines in listening posts reported Japanese patrols. Ichiki was on the move.

At 0130 on the 21st, the battle broke on a dry sandbar, when the first Japs to arrive encountered the trip wire. Along this narrow 45-yard-long spit at the mouth of the river poured 200 Japanese infantrymen, shouting and screaming, with bayonets fixed, guns blazing and hand grenades popping. Lieutenant Colonel Pollock's battalion, strongly entrenched at the west end of the bar, turned rifles and machine guns against the attackers, while gunners of the Special Weapons Battalion gnawed away with 37-mm canister shot. Saber-waving officers in the van fell, but their men did not falter; some even overran the American positions, throwing giant firecrackers behind the Marines' lines to make them think they were surrounded. The Marines refused to be rattled. Riflemen stood toe-to-toe with the attackers and killed them with rifle butts, bayonets, machetes and knives. One private stripped a jammed machine gun and reassembled it while two pals kept the Japanese out of his emplacement with bayonets. Colonel Pollock brought up the battalion reserve and before daylight every Japanese who had forded the stream was dead.

As immediate victory had been assumed in Ichiki's plan, his men

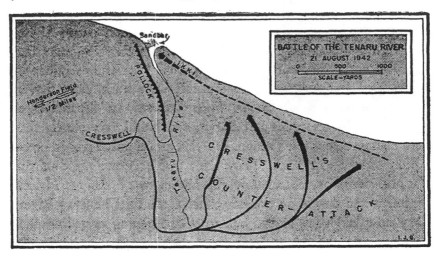

now milled aimlessly around in small groups which made convenient targets for the Marines. The survivors by daybreak were holed up in a coconut grove on the east bank of the river, well defended by water on two sides of a small triangle. Marines smothered the position with all kinds of fire and at the same time started envelopment from the south. Lieutenant Colonel Cresswell led his battalion upstream, crossed the river and by 1400 had the enemy squeezed tightly between the river on the west and the sea on the north.

The Japanese reacted viciously to envelopment by mounting a determined bayonet attack against the Marines on their southwest flank. Captain Stevenson's "C" Company held firm, then closed in with a successful bayonet charge of their own. Cresswell's next move was a full battalion assault which drove the desperate enemy from cover. Flight followed a frantic resistance; many took to the sea and drowned, others tried to slip through to the east. But the majority died from Marine bullets. About four in the afternoon a platoon of light tanks waddled over the stacked-up bodies on the bar and got to work. It was a great sight seeing them weaving through the coconut grove, knocking down snipers from the palms by butting at the trunks, and chasing survivors on the run. By nightfall Ichiki's force was virtually exterminated; the Colonel and some of his officers took leave by the suicide route. Thirty-five Marines lost their lives and 75 were wounded, many of them in the last mop-up — when some of the enemy, who had simulated death by smearing themselves with blood, rose up with gun or grenade for a final effort. But the Marines had sent almost a thousand Sons of Heaven to the wrong address.

This Battle of the Tenaru River, a model of perfectly coördinated effort, fire and movement, freed the eastern flank. And its effects were far reaching. The Marines' first stand-up fight with the much touted jungle-fighting Jap,[6] it proved to the Corps and to their countrymen that the American was the better fighting man, even on the enemy's chosen terrain. From that time on, United States Marines were invincible.

3. *Henderson Field and the Seabees*

An American motorship named *Mormacmail* had plied a drab but respectable trade of cargo and livestock transport between North and South America during the ten months following her completion in May 1940. Then came the national emergency. The Navy could not wait to build aircraft carriers from the keel up, so *Mormacmail* was acquired, a flight deck slapped on her topsides and a few guns mounted, and in June 1941 she was commissioned as the escort carrier *Long Island*, first of her kind in the U.S. Navy. Here she was, on 20 August 1942, carrying 19 Wildcats and 12 Dauntless dive-bombers of two Marine Squadrons,[7] with their crews.

From a position southeast of San Cristobal, *Long Island* catapulted the planes and retired. Coconut palms were pointing long

---

[6] Wake and Corregidor were earlier, but the Marines who fought there were all dead or in captivity, or among the guerillas; and neither on these islands nor Tulagi was there any jungle.

[7] VMF-223 and VMSB-232. For complete list of Marine Corps and other plane squadrons at Guadalcanal, see Appendix.

shadows eastward when Lieutenant Colonel Charles L. Fike, executive officer of Marine Air Group 23, led his planes in for a landing on Henderson Field. The Colonel would have liked another six weeks' training before being turned loose on the Japanese air force, but the very next day his planes were mixing it with the enemy. Major John L. Smith, leader of his fighter squadron, chalked up Henderson Field's first kill, a "Zeke." Eighteen more planes would fall to the Major's guns in days to follow.[8] And on the 25th Lieutenant Colonel Mangrum's SBDs bombed the ships that were hurrying in a second echelon of Ichiki's regiment, and postponed another enemy landing effort. It looked as if command of the sea would go by default if we commanded the air; but one needed both to hold Guadalcanal.

Within five days of their arrival at Guadalcanal, one third of the planes sent in by *Long Island* were washed out for one reason or another, and on 30 August only five of the original 19 Wildcats could fly. But help had come.

On 22 August, Henderson Field welcomed a portion of the Army's 67th Fighter Squadron composed of P–400s, a bastard version of the P–39 originally intended for export. These planes were practically useless as fighters since it was impossible to fly them high enough to catch the Japanese.[9] But, as they were well armed with a 37-mm cannon and six guns each, they afforded the Marines close ground support by strafing enemy positions.

The Naval Air arm was first represented on Henderson Field on 24 August when the *Enterprise* contributed her dive-bombers. From that time on there was an irregular flow of all types of planes from every imaginable source. Nobody cared about lineage. If it had wings it flew; if it flew it fought; and if it fought very long, something was certain to happen to it. The trouble might come from a Japanese plane's machine guns, a concealed rut or bomb hole on the field, an enemy bomb hitting the parked plane, anti-aircraft fire, naval bombardment, bad weather, or just hard usage.

[8] John A. Dechant *Devilbirds* (1947).
[9] They were equipped with a British high-pressure oxygen system, but Guadalcanal had no high-pressure oxygen bottles.

By the end of August, 19 more Wildcats and 12 SBDs had arrived. Colonel Wallace, commander of the group, took over from Colonel Fike while "Scat" (South Pacific Combat Air Transport) brought in a big bear of a Marine major general, Roy S. Geiger, as commander of all Allied planes flying out of Henderson Field.[10] There was nothing formal about command relationships. Marine, Navy and Army fliers flew on missions together, lived through bombing raids together, and many died together aloft or in foxholes.

On 1 September 1942 Marines posted on the Lunga waterfront observed Higgins boats, loaded to the gunwales with men and gear, putting off from transport *Betelgeuse* and heading for the beach. Curious leathernecks strolled to the water's edge, hoping to meet old friends among the newcomers. No such luck; these faces were those of "old men," frequently framed by gray hair. But their owners wore a quiet air of competence, as of men who had confronted life and bested its problems. These were the first Seabees, men of the Naval Construction Battalions, to reach an action area; and their good works would be a vital factor in the Guadalcanal campaign. And they brought six 5-inch coast defense guns.

Rear Admiral Ben Moreell, Chief of the Bureau of Yards and Docks, was responsible for the organization of the Seabees [11] two months before Pearl Harbor. Shortly after, experience of unarmed civilian workers at Wake, Midway and Cavite, inefficient and useless in case of attack, proved that Moreell had the right idea. A large proportion of petty-officer ratings, a special insignia,[12] and, most of all, the promise that they would be an integral part of the

[10] Roy Stanley Geiger, b. Florida 1885; after graduating LL.B. Stetson 1907 enlisted in Marine Corps; 2nd Lt. 1909. One of the earliest Marines to qualify as an aviator, he served as such in World War I and later in Hispaniola and Nicaragua. Command and General Staff School, 1925; Army and Naval War College courses; C.O. 1st Marine Air Wing, 1942; Com. I 'Phib Corps 1943; Com. III 'Phib Corps. 1944; and of Tenth Army at Okinawa, 1945. On active duty as Lt. Gen. USMC at his death, 23 Jan. 1947.

[11] Budocks *Building the Navy's Bases in World War II* (2 vols.); "History of the 6th U.S. Naval Construction Battalion" compiled by Seaman Tom O'Reilly and edited by Ens. R. H. Gedney; Summary of Construction Jobs, 6th Construction Battalion; Lt. (jg) W. B. Huie USNR *Can Do! The Story of the Seabees* (1944).

[12] A flying bee wearing a sailor's cap and carrying a tommygun, a wrench and a hammer.

fighting Navy and provided with weapons, attracted skilled and patriotic artisans. Their officers, largely obtained from the Navy's Civil Engineer Corps or commissioned from the engineering professions, were granted full autonomy, a departure from the peacetime practice of allowing only line officers to command. The result of this effort was a military organization composed of carpenters, plumbers, metalsmiths, surveyors, road builders and the like, solid citizens of the average age of 31; men who could have stayed at home and earned high pay. All received basic military training, and so in case of need could substitute guns for tools, as they later proved both to delighted friend and discomfited foe.

The cadre which landed on Guadalcanal on 1 September consisted of a portion of the 6th Seabee Battalion, 387 men and five officers. Two bulldozers and other equipment came with them, and they promptly took over from the Marine Corps engineers the maintenance and improvement of Henderson Field. In addition they tackled road, wharf and bridge construction, electric power installation, building tank farms and fuel lines, developing camps, base and raid shelters, and they brought in six 5-inch guns.

The Seabees found many enemies besides Japanese. The soil, for instance, was an elastic and unstable muck which stimulated the toughest former road boss to new heights of profanity. Daily tropical rains taxed drainage ditches and kept the mud from drying. Equipment was long in arriving, so Japanese trucks and power rollers were pressed into service along with the American bulldozers, half a dozen dump trucks, a grader and an excavator. But the worst enemy was the almost daily Japanese naval and artillery bombardment. Yet no challenge remained unanswered by the Seabees. The existing portion of Henderson Field was put in shape by adding to the base material quantities of gravel, coral and clay and by raising a crown along the center. An extension was constructed by blasting coconut palms with Japanese powder and surfacing the new runway solid. Then a grid of Marston mat — perforated metal strips or "pierced plank" — was laid over the field to support planes in every kind of weather. A supplementary fighter strip, quickly constructed, handled all air traffic in October when Henderson Field was knocked out. Later, a second fighter strip was built. Work stopped only while bombs or shells were actually falling. Then the Seabees retired to foxholes and waited for the last explosive to "crump" before dashing back to the job. Trucks stood loaded with earth ready to fill new craters, but the Seabees also used their helmets as buckets. Commander Joseph P. Blundon USNR, Seabee skipper, described the task: —

We found that 100 Seabees could repair the damage of a 500-pound bomb hit on an airstrip in forty minutes, including the replacing of the Marston mat. In other words, forty minutes after that bomb exploded, you couldn't tell that the airstrip had ever been hit. But we needed all of this speed and more. In twenty-four hours on October 13 and 14, fifty-three bombs and shells hit the Henderson airstrip! During one hour on the 14th we filled thirteen bomb craters while our planes circled around overhead waiting to land. We got no food during that period because our cooks were all busy passing up the steel plank. There were not enough shovels to go around, so some of our men used their helmets to scoop up earth and carry it to the bomb craters. In the period from September 1 to November 18, we had 140 Jap raids in which the strip was hit at least once.

Our worst moments were when the Jap bomb or shell failed to explode when it hit. It still tore up our mat, and it had to come out. When you see men choke down their fear and dive in after an unexploded bomb so that our planes can land safely, a lump comes in your throat and you know why America wins wars.

Shell craters are more dangerous to work on than bomb craters. You have a feeling that no two bombs ever hit in the same place; but this isn't true of shells. A Jap five-inch gun lobs a shell over on your airstrip and blasts a helluva hole. What are you going to do? You know, just as that Jap artilleryman knows, that if he leaves his gun in the same position and fires another shell, the second shell will hit in almost the same spot as the first one. So a good old Jap trick was to give us just enough time to start repairing the hole and then fire a second shell. All you can do is depend on hearing that second shell coming and hope you can scramble far enough away before it explodes. But this is a gamble which is frowned upon by life insurance companies.[13]

[13] Huie *Can Do!* p. 42. In Oct. 1942 the 1st Marine Aviation Engineer Battalion came up, bringing more much-needed heavy equipment.

Life for sailors and Marines alike on the borders of Henderson Field was a hodgepodge of horror and discomfort. Foremost in nastiness were the constant attentions of the enemy, dropping air bombs day and night, sending naval shells crashing through palms and men and planes, firing field artillery from concealed positions at anything that moved. Marines who had occasion to spend a night at Henderson Field were always glad to get back to the comparative quiet of the front lines. Then there was the business of keeping the "crates" flying. There was never enough of anything — gasoline, starter cartridges, spare parts, tools, men or time. Fliers even borrowed engine starter cartridges from the crews of Marine tank battalions. Rest was impossible. Air raid warning flags on the Pagoda kept men leaping in and out of foxholes at all hours. Just for variety, an earthquake one night helped murder sleep. Rain drenched them every night, and the heat roasted them every day. Anopheles mosquitoes squirted a man full of malaria, while gastroenteritis sneaked into his guts and racked his bowels with enervating dysentery. Officers and men, pilots, ground crews, antiaircraft gunners and Seabees were brothers in misery.

The exploits of the pilots who flew from Henderson Field will appear as the story of Guadalcanal unfolds, but we must also keep in mind the men of courage and good will who defended and developed the field. It was alike the target and the prize of sea battles, jungle assaults and bombardment missions. If we kept Henderson Field we would keep Guadalcanal and, someday, go roaring up the Slot toward Rabaul. If we lost it, our first Pacific offensive would have to be written off as a costly failure.

CHAPTER IV

The Battle of the Eastern Solomons [1]

24 August 1942

1. Storm's Eye

THE American landings in the Solomons had generated a typhoon of enemy reaction. The advance semicircle of this hurricane was the destructive Battle of Savo Island. On it swept, leaving a restless turbulence — the eye of the storm, promising more disaster when the rear and more dangerous half of the tempest broke. On 24 August it came: the Battle of the Eastern Solomons. [2]

Japan had recovered naval initiative with the Battle of Savo Island; there was no doubt about that. The war lords at Tokyo were annoyed by the Marines' hold on Guadalcanal but confident that control of the surrounding waters would give them the island at their convenience. At Rabaul commanders of the Eighth Fleet, the Seventeenth Army and the Eleventh Air Fleet put their heads together to plan a Marine ouster before the end of August.

This Rabaul get-together resulted in the Japanese landings on 18 August which were expected to win the island in three days. As we have seen, the Marines shot this plan and its executors full

---

[1] Sources: *The Campaigns of the Pacific War*, and USSBS *Inter. Jap. Off.*; Cincpac "Solomon Island Campaign-Action of 23–25 August" 24 Oct. 1942; Lt. Cdr. Salomon's notes obtained at Tokyo; action reports of ships in TFs 16 and 17; O.N.I. Combat Narrative No. 3, *Solomon Islands Campaign;* war diaries of enemy fleets and units concerned, and ATIS translation "Southeast Area Operations Part 1 (Navy)."

[2] First called the Battle of the Stewart Islands; the Japanese refer to it as the Second Battle of the Solomons.

of holes at the Ilu River. Another conference must be called; more forces must be brought up.

The conferees decided on a new all-out effort, Operation "KA," [3] commencing 24 August. A reinforcement of only 1500 troops would be supported by the entire Combined Fleet, a flexible organization which Admiral Yamamoto could expand or contract at will. Ships of all types were drawn from far corners of Greater East Asia. In preparation for the big push, planes of the Eleventh Air Fleet would hammer the Marine positions with daily bombings while the Eighth Fleet harassed them nightly with naval bombardment. The planes of two big carriers and one light carrier would dispose of United States surface interference. Finally the troops would be landed under cover of carrier planes and ships. This naval set-up seems elephantine in comparison with the small troop contingent, but it proved to be too little rather than too much. Scheduled operations in New Guinea would go forward as planned; the Japanese still considered Guadalcanal a side show, but not for long.

Mobilization for Operation "KA" was speedy. By 21 August Admiral Yamamoto could place his stubby forefinger on the chart near Truk and cover the position of 3 carriers, 3 battleships, 5 cruisers, 8 destroyers, one seaplane carrier and numerous auxiliaries, all ready to move south at his command. And at Rabaul Admiral Tsukahara had 4 cruisers and 5 destroyers together with 100 planes of the Eleventh Air Fleet.

Japanese preparations did not escape the notice of Australian coastwatchers and American reconnaissance planes. Admiral Ghormley ordered Admiral Fletcher's carrier force (*Enterprise*, *Saratoga*, *Wasp*) to the passive rôle of protecting his sea lanes into the Solomons, keeping well south of Japanese search-plane radius. A fourth carrier, *Hornet*, with supporting cruisers and destroyers, set out from Pearl Harbor for the Coral Sea on 17 August; battleships *Washington* and *South Dakota*, anti-aircraft cruiser *Juneau* and destroyers from the East Coast were ordered through the Pan-

[3] *Ka* is the first syllable of Guadalcanal in Japanese.

ama Canal. Everything was held back to meet the big Japanese push. No serious effort was made to drive off Mikawa's nightly surface raiders, who came so regularly down the Slot as to be named the "Tokyo Express" by disgusted Marines. And on 23 August, by threat alone, the Tokyo Express caused the loss of an American destroyer.

Supply ships *Fomalhaut* and *Alhena* were proceeding to Guadalcanal on 21 August, escorted by destroyers *Blue*, *Henley* and *Helm*. Upon approaching Lengo Channel, *Blue* and *Henley* peeled off to reach Ironbottom Sound in time to thwart an anticipated Japanese landing. By 0330 the two destroyers were near the center of the Sound steaming back and forth at ten knots, radars sniffing for trouble through a moonless night.

Blue, while steaming east and 400 yards ahead of *Henley*, at 0355 made a contact both with radar and sonar on a fairly high-speed vessel only 5000 yards distant on the starboard beam. As she continued on the same course and speed, bringing guns and torpedo tubes to bear, the range closed to 3200 yards. At 0359 the stranger's intent was violently revealed by the orange-red explosion of a torpedo which sliced off several feet of *Blue's* stern, immobilized the propeller shafts, tossed men and gear as much as 50 feet in the air, killed 9 and wounded 21. This was one of many instances early in the war when Japanese eyes were quicker than American radar. The unseen agent was destroyer *Kawakaze*, which had just landed her reinforcements.[4]

Henley stood by *Blue*, and at daylight towed the cripple toward Lunga Roads, then was ordered to take her into Tulagi. *Blue's* twisted and chipped stern made her an irascible tow, and by nightfall 23 August she was still outside Tulagi Harbor. As the enemy was then on his way to Guadalcanal in strength, the destroyer squadron commander recommended scuttling her, and Admiral Turner so ordered.

---

[4] Records of Desron 2 (WDC No. 161,711). At 0750, 100 miles north of Tulagi, Henderson Field fliers caught and strafed *Kawakaze*, wounding one man and inflicting minor damage on the ship.

At daybreak 23 August, when the American carrier force was about 150 miles east of Henderson Field on the other side of Malaita, the Japanese Combined Fleet was advancing from Truk in five main groups. First there was Admiral Nagumo's Carrier Striking Force, now shorn of the four flattops sunk at Midway but still formidable, with two veterans of Pearl Harbor and the Coral Sea — *Zuikaku* and *Shokaku*. Slightly ahead of the carriers, Rear Admiral Abe of Wake fame led the Vanguard Group composed of battleships *Hiei* and *Kirishima* and three heavy cruisers. Ready to be detached from the Striking Force was a Diversionary Group baited with small carrier *Ryujo* under the leadership of Rear Admiral Hara, who must have remembered somewhat uneasily what had happened to *Shoho*, the corresponding Yank-bait at Coral Sea. Vice Admiral Kondo, overall tactical commander of the Supporting Forces, had under his visual control [5] six cruisers and a seaplane carrier, which steamed far in advance of the Striking Force. Six fleet submarines swept ahead of him in line-abreast to act as scouts and weapons of opportunity, while three more took station in the Coral Sea west of the New Hebrides. The troops were carried in *Kinryu Maru* and four old destroyer-transports escorted by the famous Desron 2, Rear Admiral Tanaka commanding in light cruiser *Jintsu*. Yamamoto, unshaken in his basic strategy, intended to pull the old gambit of tempting the enemy to gang up on the insignificant *Ryujo* group, while planes from his big flattops struck the American carriers and Henderson Field was bombarded with heavy gunfire and 1500 troops got ashore.

One of Admiral McCain's patrol planes flying from tender *Mackinac* at Ndeni, Santa Cruz Islands, sighted enemy transports at 0950 on the 23rd and passed the word — two cruisers and three destroyers covering the troop vessels, speeding at 17 knots for

[5] Battleship *Mutsu* and her destroyers were not in company with Kondo, having remained with the force oilers north of the Stewart Islands. According to a translated extract from Admiral Kondo's private diary, recently in hand, the presence of an American task force in the area was reported to Kondo as early as 20 Aug. and he proposed to seek out and attack it on the 23rd; but early that day Yamamoto ordered him to delay his attack until the position of Fletcher's carriers was positively known.

Guadalcanal.[6] This contact caused a flurry of excitement in Admiral Fletcher's task force. Captain DeWitt C. Ramsey passed on Flag's orders to the *Saratoga* air group — Attack with 31 SBDs and 6 TBFs. "Sara's" planes zoomed aloft at 1445, circled to gain height, formed in orderly ranks and sped over the northwest horizon. An hour and a half later, the Guadalcanal Marines launched a 23-plane strike at the same transports.

Saratoga pilots sought earnestly for the enemy through a pall of dirty weather but their search, as well as that of the Marines, was unsuccessful. At dusk the weary fliers of both groups landed on Henderson Field, bombs and torpedoes still unexpended. Also, a night strike of 5 PBYs failed to locate the elusive transports. The enemy had escaped notice for a good reason. Alerted by the McCain patrol plane, foxy Tanaka reversed course to the northwest at 1300, which kept his transports beyond bomber range and deceived the Americans as to his future movements. Kondo's forces followed suit at 1800. Before dawn the "bait" group was detached to take an advanced position to the southward and by 0600 on 24 August every Japanese ship was once more headed toward the Americans.

By the end of the first dogwatch on 23 August, Admiral Fletcher had no positive intelligence of the enemy. "Sara's" planes had brought none; Pacific Fleet Intelligence believed the enemy carriers to be well north of Truk; no word had reached Fletcher of the recent course change of the Japanese transports. He was now beset by two familiar problems: fueling, and finding the enemy. Reasoning that a major clash would not occur for several days, Fletcher sent Noyes' *Wasp* group south to a fueling rendezvous as the destroyers were reported to be running short of oil.[7] This was a bad guess, because Yamamoto had ordered a nonstop run

---

[6] *Enterprise* planes on dawn search the same morning had sighted two of the enemy scout subs moving rapidly southward; such a sighting might or might not mean bigger game at hand.

[7] Once more, the destroyers' logs prove that this anxiety was unwarranted. The fuel on hand in the seven destroyers with *Wasp* at noon 23 August varied from 68,885 gals. to 104,794 gals., the average being 84,824 gals.

to the Solomons, fueling at sea. The American force was thus deprived of one of its three carriers in a crucial battle.

On board *Saratoga* and *Enterprise* the night of 23–24 August passed quietly. The sky was overcast, rain fell occasionally and the weather did not improve until after sunrise. At Guadalcanal the temporarily grounded *Saratoga* airmen were treated in midwatch to a nuisance bombardment by destroyer *Kagero*. It was ineffective, but the guests passed an uncomfortable night, stimulated only by an occasional shot of "jamoke" tendered by the hospitable Marines. The carrier planes were held in readiness pending reports from the dawn search. When Marine scout aircraft reported no contacts, they flew back to *Saratoga*, landing on board at 1100 August 24.

2. *Composition of Forces*

a. Japanese [8]

COMBINED FLEET
Admiral Isoroku Yamamoto in BB *Yamato*

Operating near Truk with CVE TAIYO and DDs AKEBONO, USHIO, and SAZANAMI

GUADALCANAL SUPPORTING FORCES
Vice Admiral Nobutake Kondo (C. in C. Second Fleet)

ADVANCE FORCE, Vice Admiral Kondo

Main Body

Crudiv 4: ATAGO, MAYA, TAKAO
Crudiv 5 (Vice Admiral Takeo Takagi): MYOKO, HAGURO
  Screen: Desron 4, Rear Admiral Tamotsu Takama in Light Cruiser *Yura*
Destroyers ASAGUMO YAMAGUMO, KUROSHIO, OYASHIO, HAYASHIO

Support Group, C.O. of *Mutsu*

Battleship MUTSU, Destroyers MURASAME, HARUSAME, SAMIDARE
  Seaplane Group, Rear Admiral Takaji Joshima (Comcardiv 11)
  Seaplane Carrier CHITOSE (22 VSO), Destroyer NATSUGUMO

STRIKING FORCE, Vice Admiral Chuichi Nagumo (C. in C. Third Fleet)

[8] Compiled by Lieut. Roger Pineau, USNR, and Walton L. Robinson from official Japanese sources.

Carrier Group

SHOKAKU (26 VF, 14 VB, 18 VT, 1 VSO), ZUIKAKU (27 VF, 27 VB, 18 VT)
Screen: DDs AKIGUMO, YUGUMO, MAKIGUMO, KAZAGUMO, SHIKINAMI, URANAMI

Vanguard Group, Rear Admiral Hiroaki Abe (Combatdiv 11)

Battleships HIEI, KIRISHIMA
Crudiv 7 (Rear Admiral Shoji Nishimura): SUZUYA, KUMANO, CHIKUMA
  Screen: Desron 10, Rear Admiral Susumu Kimura in Light Cruiser *Nagara*
Destroyers AKIZUKI, HATSUKAZE, MAIKAZE, NOWAKI, TANIKAZE, YUKIKAZE

Diversionary Group, Rear Admiral Tadaichi Hara (Comcrudiv 8)

Cruiser TONE, CVL * RYUJO (16 VF, 21 VT),⁹ DDs AMATSUKAZE, TOKITSUKAZE

SOUTHEAST AREA FORCES

Vice Admiral Nishizo Tsukahara, at Rabaul

OUTER SOUTH SEAS FORCE, Vice Admiral Gunichi Mikawa (C. in C.
Eighth Fleet)

Reinforcement Group, Rear Admiral Raizo Tanaka (Comdesron 2)
Escort Unit: CL JINTSU; DDs KAGERO, * MUTSUKI, YAYOI, ISOKAZE, KAWAKAZE ¹⁰

SUZUKAZE, UMIKAZE, UZUKI
Transport Unit: Auxiliary Cruiser KINRYU MARU, embarking 5th Yokosuka Special Naval Landing Force, 800 men; Patrol Boats ¹¹ Nos. 1, 2, 34 and 35,
embarking 2nd echelon Army Ichiki Detachment, 700 men

Covering Group, Vice Admiral Mikawa in CA *Chokai*

Crudiv 6 (Rear Admiral Aritomo Goto): AOBA, KINUGASA, FURUTAKA

Submarine Group

I–121, * I–123, RO–34

LAND–BASED AIR FORCE

Vice Admiral Tsukahara (C. in C. Eleventh Air Fleet)
About 100 operational aircraft

ADVANCE EXPEDITIONARY FORCE

Vice Admiral T. Komatsu (C. in C. Sixth Fleet) in Light Cruiser *Katori* at Truk
Submarines I–9, I–11, I–15, I–17, I–19, I–26, I–31, I–174, I–175

* Sunk in this operation; *I–123* by fast minelayer *Gamble* east of Guadalcanal on 28
August.
⁹ June 1942 air complement; August figures not available.
¹⁰ These five destroyers comprised a special Bombardment Unit which shelled Henderson Field the night of 24 August.
¹¹ Former destroyers *Shimakaze, Nadakaze, Suzuki,* and *Tsuta,* converted along lines
similar to U.S. Navy APDs.

b. United States

TASK FORCE 61
Vice Admiral Frank Jack Fletcher

TF 11, Admiral Fletcher

| SARATOGA | Capt. DeWitt C. Ramsey |

Air Group 3: 1 SBD–3 (Dauntless), Cdr. Harry D. Felt

VF–5:	36 F4F–4 (Wildcat)	Lt. Cdr. Leroy C. Simpler
VB–3:	18 SBD–3	Lt. Cdr. Dewitt W. Shumway
VS–3:	18 SBD–3	Lt. Cdr. Louis J. Kirn
VT–8:	15 TBF–1 (Avenger)	Lt. Harold H. Larsen

Rear Admiral Carleton H. Wright

| MINNEAPOLIS | Capt. Frank J. Lowry |
| NEW ORLEANS | Capt. Walter S. DeLany |

Destroyer Screen, Captain Samuel B. Brewer (Comdesron 1)

| PHELPS | Lt. Cdr. Edward L. Beck |

Desdiv 2, Cdr. Francis X. McInerney

FARRAGUT	Cdr. George P. Hunter
WORDEN	Lt. Cdr. William G. Pogue
MACDONOUGH	Lt. Cdr. Eric V. Dennett
DALE	Lt. Cdr. Anthony L. Rorschach

TF 16, Rear Admiral Thomas C. Kinkaid

| ENTERPRISE | Captain Arthur C. Davis |

Air Group 6: 1 SBD–3, Lt. Cdr. Maxwell F. Leslie

VF–6:	36 F4F–4	Lt. Louis H. Bauer
VB–6:	18 SBD–3	Lt. Ray Davis
VS–5:	18 SBD–3	Lt. Stockton B. Strong
VT–3:	15 TBF–1	Lt. Cdr. Charles M. Jett
NORTH CAROLINA	Capt. George H. Fort

Rear Admiral Mahlon S. Tisdale

| PORTLAND | Capt. Laurance T. DuBose |
| ATLANTA | Capt. Samuel F. Jenkins |

Destroyer Screen, Captain Edward P. Sauer (Comdesron 6)

BALCH	Lt. Cdr. Harold H. Tiemroth
MAURY	Lt. Cdr. Gelzer L. Sims
BENHAM	Lt. Cdr. Joseph M. Worthington
ELLET	Lt. Cdr. Francis H. Gardner

Desdiv 22, Cdr. Harold R. Holcomb

| GRAYSON | Lt. Cdr. Frederick J. Bell |
| MONSSEN | Cdr. Roland N. Smoot |

TF 18, Rear Admiral Leigh Noyes

WASP   Capt. Forrest P. Sherman

Air Group 7: 1 F4F–4, Lt. Cdr. Wallace M. Beakley

VF–71:	28 F4F–4	Lt. Cdr. Courtney Shands
VS–71	18 SBD–3	Lt. Cdr. John Eldridge
VS–72:	18 SBD–3	Lt. Cdr. Ernest M. Snowden
VT–7:	15 TBF–1	Lt. Henry A. Romberg

Rear Admiral Norman Scott

SAN JUAN	Capt. James E. Maher
SAN FRANCISCO	Capt. Charles H. McMorris
SALT LAKE CITY	Capt. Ernest G. Small

Destroyer Screen, Captain Robert G. Tobin (Comdesron 12)

FARENHOLT	Lt. Cdr. Eugene T. Seaward
AARON WARD	Lt. Cdr. Orville F. Gregor
BUCHANAN	Cdr. Ralph E. Wilson

Desdiv 15, Captain William W. Warlick

LANG	Lt. Cdr. John L. Wilfong
STACK	Lt. Cdr. Alvord J. Greenacre
STERETT	Cdr. Jesse G. Coward

Desron 4, Captain Cornelius W. Flynn

SELFRIDGE	Cdr. Carroll D. Reynolds

3. *The Battle Joined, 24 August*

While *Saratoga's* planes were coming on board from Guadalcanal, four of her Wildcats led by Lieutenant David C. Richardson were chasing a Japanese snooper located by radar some 20 miles from the carrier; Richardson got the first "Emily" (a four-engine flying boat) to be encountered. There was great jubilation in *Saratoga* over this, the first kill made as a result of her fighter-director crew vectoring out combat air patrol.

At 0905 August 24, one of the flying felines from Ndeni spotted "bait" carrier *Ryujo*, heavy cruiser *Tone* and two destroyers steering south, 220 miles north of Malaita [12] and some 280 miles northwest of Fletcher's force. At 1128 another plane from the same base reported the same group, now 245 miles away on the same bearing. Admiral Fletcher, freshly remembering *Saratoga's* fruit-

[12] Lat. 4° 40' S, long. 161° 15' E.

less search on the 23rd, was still skeptical but ordered *Enterprise* to conduct a 250-mile search between 290° and 90°. Rear Admiral Thomas C. Kinkaid,[13] commanding the *Enterprise* group, swung directly into the 16-knot southeasterly wind and at 1229 twenty-three planes soared away armed with binoculars and bombs. Their valuable discoveries were promptly forgotten when radar screens in the task force showed many "bogies" a hundred miles away, headed for Guadalcanal. This was a flight of 15 fighters and 6 bombers which had left *Ryujo* at 1300 to take a few licks at Henderson Field, and it was joined over Guadalcanal by twin-engine bombers from Rabaul. They were effectively intercepted by Marine Fighter Squadron 223 and lost 21 planes; the airfield suffered only minor damage.

Fletcher now took the initiative. *Saratoga* at 1345 launched 30 scout-bombers and 8 torpedo planes, Commander Felt leading, against the *Ryujo* group. Some 51 bombers and 15 torpedo planes were now aloft, engaged in search, attack and anti-submarine missions; 14 bombers and 12 torpedo planes still remained on the two carrier decks. That was the situation when, at 1400, a PBY reported a carrier 60 miles northeast of *Ryujo*. Shortly after, search planes from *Enterprise* reported several significant contacts: at 1410 *Ryujo*, bearing 317° less than 200 miles distant; at 1430 *Shokaku* and *Zuikaku*, reported 340° distant 198 miles;[14] at 1440 four cruisers and several destroyers, bearing 347° distant 225 miles. These last belonged to Abe's Vanguard Group.

These and several other sightings that we have not mentioned confused the American task commander, very understandably. Fletcher was now experiencing the exercise of command at the point of contact with bad communications. Radio reception was abominable. *Enterprise* failed to pick up her own planes' contact

[13] Thomas Cassin Kinkaid, b. Hanover N.H. 1888, Naval Academy '08, served 5 years in battleships followed by a year ashore qualifying as an ordnance engineer. Gunnery officer *Arizona* 1918–20, ordnance duties ashore, various sea commands and staff duties to 1929. Senior course Naval War College, Sec. General Board, and duty at Geneva Disarmament Conference. "Exec." *Colorado* 1933–4; C.O. *Indianapolis* 1937–8; Naval Attaché, Italy, 1938–41; Comcrudiv 6 at Coral Sea and Midway.
[14] Their actual distance was then about 230 miles.

with *Ryujo* and the two big carriers, although others did. And Fletcher had already committed the majority of his air strength. As soon as he heard from other ships of these contacts, he made an unsuccessful effort to divert Commander Felt's strike to the big carriers. He could not close the enemy to the northwest because the wind blew from the southeast and he had to head up into it for flight operations, which held him back. *Enterprise* readied 7 fighters, 11 bombers and 7 torpedo planes at 1400, but orders to launch this small strike were held up since launching them against targets so far distant would have required night landings upon return. At the same time, Fletcher had to expect an enemy air attack because, in addition to Lieutenant Richardson's morning kill of a curious "Emily," two other snoopers had become Wildcat victims by 1250. So he had to assume that a position report had reached enemy ears from one of these three sacrifices.

Extra combat air patrol was stacked above the carriers while more fighters sat on deck with full tanks and warm engines; if the enemy came, he would have to meet 54 Wildcats. Admiral Fletcher had certainly learned something from the loss of *Yorktown* at Midway.

While the two American carrier groups prepared to repel attack, two search planes from *Enterprise* encountered *Shokaku*, and dove down on her at 1515. They succeeded in making one hit or near-miss, inflicting minor damage and a few casualties. At 1440 two other pilots from *Enterprise* had an unsuccessful try at the Vanguard Group. Of the seven *Enterprise* Avengers in the afternoon search, five made contact with Japanese ships. Two launched torpedoes at *Ryujo* but did not hit her. Two sighted her but were driven off by Nipponese fighters. Two others sighted cruiser *Tone* of her screen but were jumped by fighters before they could attack, and one of them was shot down.

Commander Felt of the *Saratoga* attack group, launched at 1345, found Hara's *Ryujo* force. His SBDs, under Lieutenant Commander Shumway, had helped put flattops under at Midway and knew exactly how to go about it. The first dive-bomber pushed over at 1550 just after *Ryujo* turned into the wind to launch planes. The SBDs whined down from 14,000 feet on the little Japanese flattop, discharged bombs, pulled out with engines scream-ing, passed through heavy gouts of anti-aircraft fire and dodged the low-altitude enemy fighters who swarmed at them greedily. The Commander, unable to spot hits from his high altitude, di-rected his group to concentrate on the carrier, and punctuated this order by tilting his own plane's nose into a dive that scored. *Ryujo* thus became the bull's-eye for 30 thousand-pound bombs. The six Avenger torpedo planes under Lieutenant Bruce L. Harwood can-nily waited for the dive-bombing attack to divert the foe, then glided swiftly down to deliver the Sunday punch. Like the Japa-nese at Coral Sea, the torpedo pilots used "anvil" tactics, coming in on both bows of the target so that a rudder shift either way would still expose the hull to warheads. Opaque sheets of smoke from bomb-smitten *Ryujo* rendered the attack difficult though encouraging. "Fish" were dropped from a height of 200 feet, range less than a half mile; then the planes concentrated on escape.

After the attack Felt retired to broken cloud cover to observe results. *Ryujo* was running in fast circles like a waterbug, cough-ing black smoke from consumptive fires, struggling for life. Her effort was futile; from four to ten bomb hits and one torpedo hit combined to destroy the plucky Yank-bait, which soon listed 20 degrees to starboard, her engines wheezing to a halt. The captain directed his plane strike already sent to Guadalcanal to head for Buka, and ordered Abandon Ship. Flagship *Tone* and the destroy-ers took off all but about 100 of her crew. At 2000 *Ryujo* briefly exposed her punctured bottom and was swallowed by the sea.[15] Unfortunately Fletcher could not be certain of this until next day.

Not one American plane had been lost in sinking this light car-rier. But the Japanese considered that she had served her country well, because in the meantime their main force was employing its full air strength against Fletcher.[16]

[15] Crudiv 8 War Diary.
[16] "Outline of Citations for Naval Units (Airflot 26)" WDC No. 161,709. *Ryujo* sank in lat. 6°10′ S, long. 160°50′ E.

Admiral Nagumo, when he heard of the attack on *Ryujo*, believed that the hour had come to avenge Midway. At 1405 a float plane from cruiser *Chikuma*, just before being downed by Wildcats, had sent him the location of Fletcher's carriers. Here was the heaven-sent opportunity to catch them with planes away, picking on sacrificial *Ryujo*. At 1507 the first attack wave rolled off the decks of *Zuikaku* and *Shokaku*, the former contributing 9 dive-bombers and 6 fighters while *Shokaku* sent torpedo planes as well.[17] And at 1600 a second attack group of about the same composition hustled over the horizon toward the American force.

The Americans had no exact knowledge of what was in store, but every man was prepared for attack. Fighting seamen, whose lives depend upon their commander's decisions, are vociferous amateur strategists, quick to praise or condemn, eager to pick up and chew on the slightest crumb of gossip from flag plot or bridge. The modern task force with widespread communications nets within and without the ships lends itself to the spread of "scuttlebutt." So it was on the afternoon of 24 August. Japanese planes had been shot down close to the task force; American eyes had seen alien carriers; an attack must be on its way. This reasoning, simple but logical, produced an atmosphere of tense expectancy. While gunners and repairmen waited at their stations, imaginations ran riot. For sailors who had already seen action the wait was tolerable since they need only concern themselves with what the enemy would do; but others not yet blooded were anxious about their own reactions as well as the enemy's actions. Every carrier battle hitherto had meant heavy damage and numerous casualties to both sides. We were confident of winning this one, but some of us were going to get hurt in the process.

Poseidon and Æolus had arranged a striking setting for this battle. Towering cumulus clouds, constantly rearranged by the 16-knot SE tradewind in a series of snowy castles and ramparts, blocked off nearly half the depthless dome. The ocean, two miles deep at this point, was topped with merry whitecaps dancing to a

[17] *Shokaku's* exact contribution not now obtainable.

clear horizon, such as navigators love. The scene, with dark shadows turning some ships purple and sun illuminating others in sharp detail, a graceful curl of foam at the bow of each flattop, *North Carolina's* long bow churning spray, *Atlanta* bristling like a porcupine with anti-aircraft guns, heavy cruisers stolid and businesslike and the destroyers thrusting, lunging and throwing spray, was one for a great marine artist to depict. To practical carrier seamen, however, the setup was far from perfect. Those handsome clouds could hide a hundred vengeful aircraft; that high equatorial sun could provide a concealed path for pouncing dive-bombers; that reflected glare of blue, white and gold bothered and even blinded the lookouts and made aircraft identification doubtful. Altogether it was the kind of weather a flattop sailor wants the gods to spread over his enemy's task force, not his own.

As at Midway and Coral Sea, each carrier operated independently of the other as the center of a task group. In a tight circle, two miles in diameter, the *Enterprise* group (*North Carolina*, two cruisers and six destroyers) operated ten miles northwest of *Saratoga* with her two cruisers and five destroyers.

Final preparations were made to repel the expected raid. At 1600 Admiral Fletcher ordered *Enterprise* to take over the duties of fighter-plane direction. Two minutes later, ships' radars picked up "many bogies" 88 miles distant bearing 320°. Wildcats scurried into the air, raising the total combat air patrol to 53 — old *Lexington* and *Yorktown* had never been half so well protected. Flight decks were cleared of all other types, "Big E" dispatching her last eleven bombers and seven torpedo planes to counterattack the enemy ships. On board *Saratoga* five Avenger and two SBD pilots were preparing to taxi their planes forward to clear the afterdeck for the returning strike, when they heard the astounding order: "Take off immediately, join up with *Enterprise* group and strike the enemy!" The planes flew off without flight or navigational gear — only one pilot had a precious chart board — but fortunately they were armed with bombs and torpedoes. Their strike was destined to be remarkable.

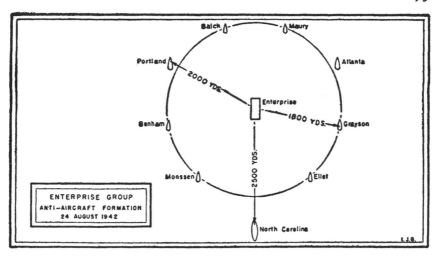

The two *Enterprise* fighter-director officers [18] stacked Wildcats at high altitude over the carriers and along the probable approach of the hostile planes. At 1604 they vectored out another group of fighters to intercept an unidentified "bogie" 42 miles to the WNW. This, unfortunately, proved to be a returning search plane. It was a constant fighter-director problem to separate sheep from goats, friend from foe; for the electronic identification system (IFF) that registered on radar screens was far from perfect in those days. The fighter-director officers sent out an imperative broadcast to all search planes to keep clear. In the meantime the large distant "bogie" indication which had started all this excitement faded from the screens and only guesses could be made as to its progress. One other major problem, radio discipline, beset the harried fighter-directors. Combat air patrol of 53 Wildcats, anti-submarine air patrol of several SBDs and all planes returning to their carriers were crammed into one narrow radio frequency, a circumstance which was to have a marked influence on the outcome of the fight.

The large radar indication, which had faded from the screen almost as soon as detected, did not reappear until 1619. Fighter-

[18] Lt. Cdr. Leonard J. Dow and Lt. Cdr. Henry A. Rowe.

director officers then estimated its altitude at 12,000 feet. At 1615 came visual confirmation of radar accuracy. A fighter-plane section to the northwest shouted a radio warning: 36 bombers at 12,000 feet, with many planes above and below. This was the crucial moment for the sweating fighter-directors; if they acted quickly and intelligently, they might destroy the raid before it split and arrived over the task force. The two officers did their best; but the air radio circuit was so jammed with "Tally-hos" (sightings) and with unnecessary conversation between Wildcat pilots [19] that it was a hopeless task to send out positive directions to the interceptors.

The enemy formation did not wait for our pilots to stop talking. At 1629, when less than 25 miles from *Enterprise*, the Japanese task group commander sighted his target and ordered deployment into several small groups. The radar screen became a confused blur of friendly and unidentified "pips." Fighter-directors could only pray that their initial stationing of interceptors had been correct.

For the next twelve minutes the safety of the task force lay in the trigger fingers of its airmen. The enemy dive-bombers and torpedo-bombers were well protected by "Zekes"; any American flier starting a high-speed approach on a "Val" or "Kate" soon discovered an alert enemy fighter after him; and although in the majority of cases he shot the "Zeke" down, his scrimmage allowed the enemy bombers to proceed unmolested to their targets. Warrant Machinist Donald E. Runyan, leading a fighter section, was one of the few pilots who managed to get at the dive-bombers. Flying at 18,000 feet some five miles northwest of *Enterprise*, Runyan flashed down out of the sun on an unsuspecting "Val," squeezed the joystick trigger button and watched his target explode in mid-

---

[19] Most of the conversation between birdmen was nonessential, much of it frivolous, such as: "Shift to high yaller"; "Look at that one go down"; "You'll get yours yet, Barney. O.K., let's go give them hell"; "Did the belly tank come off yet?" "Just wanted to know if you're still there." Constant, repeated efforts were made during the war to prevent this aimless chatter and by 1944 it was much less frequent, but could never be entirely stopped because the pilot of a combat plane is so isolated that he feels an almost irresistible urge to exchange gossip with his fellows.

air. Turning back into the sun, he placed himself for another shot and came down out of the glare to ignite a second "Val" with a burst of incendiary .50-caliber bullets. But the third time he tried these tactics a Japanese fighter tried it on him. The Jap missed and passed ahead where his unprotected tail was soon lined up in the American pilot's gun sights; another quick burst and the "Zeke" blew up in flames. Machinist Runyan's guns were still hot as he rounded up underneath a fourth plane — a "Val" — whose tender belly was soon engulfed in flames. By this time a second "Zeke" was ready to have a try at the sharpshooting machinist. Runyan's guns stuttered again and drove a smoking, chastened Jap from the scene. Nor was Runyan's action a one-man show; two of his section mates damaged four more Japanese bombers, and apparently so dismayed another pair of "Vals" that they turned and fled.

Not only the Wildcats, whose special business it was, but the Avenger and dive-bomber pilots tangled with enemy planes. These bomber pilots, whose normal targets were the impersonal hulls and decks of enemy ships, seemed to harbor secret longings for the more spectacular plane-to-plane fighter conflict. Lieutenant Commander L. J. Kirn and squadron of ten SBDs, returning from the *Ryujo* strike, at 1710 sighted four enemy "Vals" at the low altitude of 500 feet. This was a chance not to be missed; the Kirn contingent, in parade formation, passed beneath the enemy letting fly with fixed nose-guns followed by continuous salvo fire from the free guns. The attack paid off; three of the enemy planes flopped heavily into the sea and the fourth fluttered painfully away, smoking. There were many other encounters between planes of different types. Ensign Howard R. Burnett USNR, a member of the anti-submarine patrol over the carriers, pressed home a beam attack on a low-flying dive-bomber; his guns started a fire which was quenched only when the Japanese splashed.

All these dogfights were outside the main attack. During the sky battles Kinkaid's *Enterprise* group bent on 27 knots; course 130° was held into the wind. Radars continued to probe the ether for information which could promise gunners an early sighting.

The fighter-director had ordered everyone to look out for low-flying torpedo planes as well as high-altitude dive-bombers. Hundreds of watchers strained their eyes to the far horizon and the high zenith but saw nothing. At 1641 a voice radio warning went out from *Saratoga:* "Warning — torpedo planes bearing 320°, distant 10 miles!" [20] It was maddening that nothing could be seen either low or high. Where the hell were they? Actually the enemy planes were directly overhead at 18,000 feet, their well-camouflaged undersides invisible from the surface. Only a few American fighters had been able to nibble away at this particular group of some 30 dive-bombers. The cold muzzles of scores of 5-inch anti-aircraft guns were ready to reach out eight or ten miles, if only the gunners could see a target. At last, at 1641, the leading Japanese plane commenced his long, whistling drop on the carrier target. There was a scintillating flash of light from bright metal, a brief glimmer against the dazzling sky, as the plane's wing tilted down. That was enough. An alert *Enterprise* battery officer saw it and ordered his 20-mms to designate the target with a stream of tracer bullets. That thin thread of golden tracers was the baton for a cacophony of 5-inch, 1.1-inch and 20-mm gunfire from all ten ships, converging on the tiny silhouette of the Japanese plane leader. *Enterprise* put her rudder over in a series of violent turns, weaving and twisting to dodge the enemy bombs. She was in a tough spot.

In the carrier's gun sponsons and on her island superstructure, men watched with indrawn breath. Sky lookouts and gun pointers craned their necks backward to follow the long lines of darting tracers to the point where they met on the target. Huge blobs of black fragment-filled smoke materialized from 5-inch shell bursts. On and on came the flying Nip. Behind him in a long spiraling column were his fellows, tangling with a few angry American pilots who chanced the anti-aircraft fire for the sake of destroying one more assailant. The leading dive-bomber filled more and more of the gun-sight field. "Val's" distinctive landing-gear "pants" and the dark carcass of the bomb tucked under his fuselage were

[20] Comdesron 6 Action Report p. 4.

now plainly visible. Then plane and bomb separated, the former pulling out, the latter dropping fast toward the target. The bomb loomed larger and larger, seemed aimed at each individual watcher; then it flashed by. A terrific slap in the water alongside proved that the first egg had gone bad.

Hot on the tail of the first bomber came another and another, until more than two dozen had made the plunge. As each plane came in it was forced to pass through the waiting steel curtain. With flames licking around their feet, the resolute Japanese persisted. At least three of them were blown to bits by 5-inch shellbursts. Two or three planes, hopelessly damaged, tried to crash *Enterprise* with no success. About every seven seconds, another came in, giving the gunners no respite. The landing signal officer, Lieutenant R. M. Lindsey, fuming with rage, pulled out his .45-caliber pistol and emptied its magazine at an oncoming foe. The explosion of a near-miss on the port quarter hurled a busy 20-mm gunner from his own gun sponson some 15 feet into another sponson. Photographer's Mate R. F. Read stood stoutly in the after starboard 5-inch gun gallery calmly swinging his camera lens from one bomber to the next.

The first bomb ever to strike "Big E" crashed into a corner of the after flight-deck elevator and bored through the hangar deck into a third deck compartment. There the delayed-action fuse touched off an explosion which started fires, ruptured decks and side-plating, and killed about 35 sailors. It also broke a fire main, whose leaking water served to put out one of the largest fires. Fragments which pierced the ship's side let in the sea and the ship listed three degrees. Thirty seconds after the first explosion a second bomb hit in nearly the same spot, penetrating an ammunition locker in the after starboard 5-inch gun gallery, setting off some 40 rounds of powder. The cumulative effect of bomb and powder explosions wrecked the 5-inch guns and killed the entire gun crew of 38 men and photographer Read. The entire area became a caldron of flames. At 1645, only five minutes after the battle had commenced, a third bomb registered, this time on the flight deck just abaft the island structure. Luckily the explosive in this bomb was defective, its low order detonation inflicting only minor damage. The three bombs took a toll of 74 killed, 95 wounded.

To Lieutenant Commander Orlin L. Livdahl, gunnery officer, the sky now appeared to be drained of enemy planes. Bluejackets and Marines manning the anti-aircraft weapons swapped impressions; bruises and wounds acquired in action were noted for the first time. One gun pointer, a big Negro steward's mate, cackled with glee, "I done got four of them!"

Enterprise had come through the shooting part of the battle in a gallant fashion which justified her proud name. But there remained the job of saving the ship, patching up the flight deck, succoring the wounded. Out from isolated repair stations trooped the damage control parties — carpenters, shipfitters, electricians, machinists and pharmacists, laden with tools, fire hoses, oxygen masks and stretchers. Weary months of monotonous drill by Lieutenant Commander Herschel A. Smith (damage control officer) and Commander Owsley (medical officer) paid off well on that August day.

Battleship *North Carolina*, stationed a mile and a quarter astern of the carrier, also interested the enemy pilots. *North Carolina* had opened fire on the attacking planes at 1641. Two minutes later ten "Vals" peeled off over the ponderous battlewagon, which gave them a tremendous reception; but at least three planes laid their bombs close aboard the ship. Since *Enterprise* had built up her speed to 30 knots during the action, *North Carolina*, with a top speed of 27 knots, gradually fell back until she was a good two miles astern of the carrier. The enemy took advantage of this to pour six more dive-bombers on her; these again missed their mammoth target despite the fact that only 20-mm guns, all others being already engaged, opposed them. Coördinated with this last dive-bombing attack was a high glide-bombing run by eight heavy bombers. The bombs splashed harmlessly in the water between carrier and battleship.[21]

[21] *North Carolina* Action Report. I can find no other evidence from either side that the glide-bombing occurred. Opinion in *Atlanta* regarding the large number of planes attacking *North Carolina* was that several were dive-bombers whose runs against *Enterprise* were completed, and who were interested mainly in es-

Where were enemy torpedo planes during the battle, the vicious "Kates" which had done for *Lexington* at Coral Sea and *Yorktown* at Midway? *North Carolina* reported possible approaches of this type, but no other ship saw a torpedo plane or a torpedo. Wildcats claimed splashing four, but there were others unaccounted for. Some may have been operational casualties, but the rest must have been shot down by combat air patrol.

The few enemy aircraft to survive the blistering anti-aircraft fire were clear of the American formation by 1647, streaking northward in an effort to avoid Wildcat machine guns. *Enterprise* was then brightly aflame, and a thick column of smoke towered over her. The handful of Japanese pilots who successfully returned to their carriers were convinced that the American flattop was mortally gouged. But Captain Arthur C. Davis on her bridge could have told them differently. Reports coming from the fire fighters were most encouraging. Pistol-packing Lieutenant Lindsey discarded his .45 for a fire hose and went after the flames sparked by the second bomb. Ensign Wyrick rushed to the gun-gallery fire, where he and Clapp, Botts, and Pulaski, three brave seamen, piled in to jettison burning ammunition. Below decks, repairmen were crawling through smoke-glutted compartments to stamp out fires. On the flight deck, huge platters of sheet metal were quickly hammered over the bomb holes.

Less than an hour after the last bomb hit, *Enterprise* was making a respectable 24 knots, colors whipping proudly as she turned into the wind to recover aircraft. At 1749 the first plane braked to a stop on the flight deck, followed in rapid succession by two dozen more. Things were indeed looking up for the grimy, sweating carrier sailors; hearty talk and cheerful back-slapping recalling the confidence held by *Lexington* crewmen at Coral Sea. And as with *Lexington*, there was unseen trouble brewing for *Enterprise*.

---

cape. It is possible that the planes were heavy land-based ones, but high-level bombing of ships at sea was never looked upon as profitable by the Japanese Navy. It is possible, too, that some were friendly. The plane piloted by Max Leslie, *Enterprise* air group commander, was hit by *North Carolina* on her first salvo — Leslie congratulated her on good shooting!

Delayed effects of the first two bombs were responsible. The first, striking the starboard side aft, ripped off a ventilating trunkline, allowing black smoke from the second bomb's fire to enter the steering-engine room — an after compartment well below, which houses the engine that operates the rudder on impulses transmitted from the wheel. The men on duty promptly put a cover on the vent and shut off their ventilation system. Eventually the ventilation system had to be reopened to give the watch air; and as soon as it was opened the compartment was flooded with water, smoke and fire-fighting chemicals. A steering-engine motor "grounded," the rudder jammed hard at 20 degrees right, and all the men on watch were knocked out by smoke and fumes before anyone could switch on the stand-by motor. Captain Davis tried to steer his ship with engines alone, but to no avail, and he narrowly avoided a collision with destroyer *Balch*. Her rudder jammed, *Enterprise* could not even be towed successfully.[22] In the bowels of the ship men fought through the smoke toward the steering-engine room. Chief Machinist William A. Smith, although twice overcome, managed to cut in the stand-by motor; and the rudder was brought under bridge control at 1859, exactly 38 minutes after the steering failure. That's the kind of thing that wins battles, no less than good shooting and accurate bombing.

These steering difficulties occurred at the exact moment when Admiral Nagumo's second aërial-attack wave should have come in. This attack group, comprising some 18 dive-bombers, 9 torpedo planes and 3 fighters, had been sighted and reported at 1655 by Lieutenant Commander Kirn of "Sara" about 15 minutes before he tangled with the 4 "Vals." The Nip planes were then steering 140°, a course which should have brought them right onto "Big E's" neck. But they made the mistake of changing course about 40° toward the south, and at 1651 they were detected by radar 50 miles to the westward of the Americans. Finally they gave up, doubtless because gas was running low, and retired to the north-

---

[22] Germany's *Bismarck* and Japan's *Kirishima* were lost partly through casualties to steering control.

westward. Had they then turned due north, they would have brought high-explosive trouble just at the time when *Enterprise* was helpless. "Big E" always carried good luck.

We have not yet accounted for the American attack group of 13 SBDs and 12 TBFs which had been so brusquely ordered into the air before the Japanese planes struck. Confusion incident to the presence of enemy planes prevented their rendezvous. In the twilight at 1835, 20 minutes after sunset, the TBFs mistook surf-lashed Roncador Reef 100 miles north of Santa Isabel Island for a group of high-speed ships. They saw their error before attacking the reef, but by this time gas supply was so low that they jettisoned torpedoes and headed for *Enterprise*, landing about 2000. The SBDs also ran out of luck and gas. For a time they groped for the enemy in the gathering darkness, then jettisoned their explosives, headed southwest and landed safely on Henderson Field, where they were a welcome reinforcement to the Marines.

Saratoga's contribution to this strike — two SBDs and five TBFs — was the only one to flush game. Lieutenant Harold H. Larsen, flying an Avenger, found Admiral Kondo's Advance Force at 1735 about 70 miles north of the Stewart Islands, on an aggressive southeasterly course.[23] The five Avengers circled slowly around to the north, sizing up their targets which were growling with long-range anti-aircraft fire. Taking advantage of cloud cover at 7000 feet on the enemy port quarter, the pilots shoved throttles and sticks forward for a swift power glide into the release point. Admiral Kondo's ships were temptingly disposed in line abreast. Five torpedoes were released half a mile on the port bows of the targets, which by quick wriggling succeeded in dodging them.

In the meantime the two dive-bombers which had missed Kondo's force, Lieutenant (jg) Robert M. Elder usnr and Ensign Robert T. Gordon usnr, flying several thousand feet higher than the Avengers, attacked what they believed to be a battleship surrounded by its cruiser and destroyer screen. At 1740 the two pilots approached the target, and from an altitude of 12,500 feet

[23] Lat. 6° 10′ S, long. 162° 20′ E.

commenced their two-bomb blitz. The battleship, actually sea-plane carrier *Chitose*, expressed resentment by steaming in tight circles and spitting out steel. The two American bombs bracketed the light-hulled vessel, damaging her planes, igniting fires and opening the port engine room to the sea. A seven-degree increasing list, hard steering, topside damage and progressive flooding reduced *Chitose's* effectiveness to zero.

Saratoga's strike, less two Avengers which made emergency landings on San Cristobal,[24] was snugly bedded down on board by 1930 that night. It may sound easy as one reads about it; but consider carefully the gamble these young men took. They left their carrier when she was about to be attacked, in doubt whether she would be there when they came back. Their return would have to be in darkness, and they had no experience in night landings. Like the unfortunate TBDs at Midway, they had no fighter escort. Finally, they numbered but 7 planes on a strike for which 70 would have been considered fair later in the war. Mistake not, reader; theirs were stout spirits.

After *Enterprise* regained steering control, Admiral Fletcher decided to call it quits for the day. He continued a southerly run toward an assigned fueling rendezvous, but left destroyer *Grayson* behind with orders to proceed 40 miles northwest to rescue pilots from fuel-depleted planes. It was then suspected that *Ryujo* was probably on the bottom, that some damage had been inflicted on other ships and that, by mere count of planes shot down, enemy air power was leaning on the ropes. On the American side, *Enterprise* was not fully effective — but the loss of only 17 planes from all causes left the two air groups close to full strength. Furthermore, Admiral Noyes's *Wasp* task group, which had intercepted news of the battle, was pounding northward at best speed. It was not known whether the Japanese had had enough, but it was clear that their available gunfire power was much greater than Fletcher's, and night was no time to test the truth of this estimate. Comparing this night retirement with that of Spruance after the carrier

[24] The crews were later rescued.

battle at Midway, and considering what happened next, Fletcher's move was amply justified.

Admiral Kondo still had the initiative and was eager to exploit it. If, as returning pilots assured him, two American carriers and one battleship had been damaged, it was time to close in for the kill. His first impulse was to send out on night attack the planes of his abortive second strike, but that seemed too risky with weather making up. So he prepared for a night search and gun-fire battle. At 1630, joined by the Vanguard Group, he set course for Fletcher's 1700 position — 23 miles southeast of the Stewart Islands — at high speed. This sea-going cavalry force totaled 2 battleships, 10 cruisers and screening destroyers. A scouting line abreast was formed with ships 10 kilometers apart, and cruiser float planes were sent ahead, all depending on visual sighting since none of the force mounted radar.

The only contact actually made was by one of these planes, which sighted by moonlight an enemy "cruiser" making high speed to the south. This was destroyer *Grayson* returning from her pilot rescue mission.[25] The plane, burning running lights, circled *Grayson* and, when challenged, blacked out and beat a retreat. This contact did not particularly interest Admiral Kondo, who at 2330 indicated that he had gone about as far south as he cared or dared. If nobody saw anything significant in the next half hour, course would be reversed. And as no sightings did occur before the midnight deadline, Kondo turned due north and retired at 28 knots. He believed that by so doing he escaped "much damage,"[26] but actually, if he had continued, no contact would have been made as the Americans were long since gone.

Kondo's retirement marked the end of aggressive action by Japanese carrier planes and heavy ships. The next day they spent between Ontong Java and Truk, cruiser and battleship planes searching for an enemy that was far beyond their range, ships low in fuel taking on oil from tankers. By 28 August Kondo's

[25] Lat. 7°59′ S, long. 163°21′ E.
[26] Rear Admiral Komura in *Inter. Jap. Off.* II 461.

force was back in Truk. Hull-wrinkled *Chitose*, having recovered from a nearly fatal 30-degree list, entered the lagoon at a spanking 16 knots.

4. *Storm's Wake, 25–29 August*

Although both top commanders had decided to break off the main action, neither regarded the battle as finished. During the night of 24–25 August, five of Admiral Tanaka's destroyers pranced up and down off Lunga Point, bombarding the American perimeter while float planes from *Chokai, Kinugasa* and *Yura* dropped small but nasty "daisy-cutter" bombs. The disgusted Marines took advantage of a bright moon to retaliate. Eight dive-bombers led by Lieutenant Colonel Mangrum took off from Henderson Field and at 0300 August 25 relieved themselves over the intruding destroyers, made no hits and returned to Henderson to get ready for the first morning strike. That meant spending the butt of the night rearming and refueling by hand.

The Transport Group, unmolested throughout the 24th, was still pushing on toward Guadalcanal. Rear Admiral Tanaka, who commanded this group in light cruiser *Jintsu*, possessed more than his share of Japanese tenacity, a quality which he was to display on three important occasions during the next 90 days. While the Marines were undergoing their midwatch bombardment, Tanaka's soldiers enjoyed an untroubled sleep. But at 0935 Mangrum's Marine SBDs, full of bombs and fury, put in an appearance. They had been looking for the enemy carriers, missed them and encountered the transports by accident when returning. Second Lieutenant Lawrence Baldinus planted a direct hit on the famous flagship *Jintsu*, right between her two forward guns, which started fires, flooded the forward magazines, damaged the hull and left 61 men killed or wounded. Another hit on the 9300-ton *Kinryu Maru*, loaded with troops, gutted her with fire and brought her to a stop. Tanaka shifted his flag to destroyer *Kagero*, ordered *Jintsu* back to

Truk under escort of *Suzukaze*, and ordered *Mutsuki* to close the windward side of the transport to take off her passengers and crew. At 1015 eight Flying Fortresses from Espiritu Santo appeared over Tanaka's force. Commander Hatano, *Mutsuki's* skipper, glanced up at them and casually returned to his rescue work. Consequently, when the "Forts" let go a pattern of bombs, his destroyer was dead in the water. After three bombs had struck, she was dead under the water. Commander Hatano emerged, dripping, to remark quaintly, "Even the B–17s could make a hit once in a while!" [27] He claimed that his ship was the first to be hit by horizontal bombers during the war.

The same bombs which sank *Mutsuki* holed destroyer *Uzuki* with a near-miss. Even with these afflictions Tanaka would probably have continued to his destination had he not received orders from Rabaul to retire to Faisi Harbor, Shortlands. This change of plan was a significant tribute to *Enterprise* and *Saratoga;* they had so scaled down the enemy's air power that he no longer dared to try a daylight landing. But the troops were reloaded in fast destroyers for a "Tokyo Express" night landing three days later.

Nor did the enemy yield the air. At noon 25 August, 21 twin-engined bombers escorted by 13 fighters tried to bomb Henderson Field from 27,000 feet altitude, but killed only four men and caused slight damage. The concluding act of defiance by the Rising Sun came that night, when scout planes from cruisers *Chokai*, *Aoba*, *Kinugasa*, *Furutaka* and *Yura* bombed the Lunga area.

Off the eastern end of Guadalcanal, Admiral Noyes's *Wasp* group took station near the scene of the previous day's battle and conducted 200-mile air searches but found no enemy. Lucky for Kondo that he did withdraw, for *Wasp's* yet unblooded planes packed a nasty sting. Admiral Fletcher spent that day fueling and reorganizing his command at a point about 175 miles southeast of San Cristobal. *Grayson*, returning from her rescue mission, sighted

[27] Interrogation of Cdr. M. Okumiya, a friend of Cdr. Hatano, *Inter Jap. Off.* I 31. *Mutsuki* was the first Japanese destroyer sunk by high level bombers; other ships had suffered damage from this type of attack. *Myoko*, for instance, was heavily damaged at Davao, 4 Jan. 1942.

a Japanese periscope and, supported by depth charges from *Patterson* and *Monssen*, claimed destruction of the submarine. That same morning Ensign George C. Estes USNR plumped a bomb, as he believed, directly into the hull of another I-boat; and, although the postwar checkup indicates no submarines sunk at these times or places, it does show that *I–9* and *I–17* sustained damage from United States attacks at about this time. Damaged *Enterprise*, escorted by cruiser *Portland* and four destroyers, departed for Pearl Harbor via Tongatabu; *North Carolina*, *Atlanta* and two destroyers were taken over by the *Saratoga* group and most of the *Enterprise* planes and pilots were left in the Solomons to bolster the land-based organizations.

As the last *Wasp* search plane landed on 25 August, the Battle of the Eastern Solomons passed into history; and rather peculiar history at that. A major portion of the Imperial Fleet had gathered from far and near, ostensibly to safeguard the transportation of 1500 ground troops to Guadalcanal. This Fleet had exposed itself briefly and timidly for one day, had failed to protect the troop transports or to impose its will on the numerically inferior American sea forces, had failed even to inflict damage comparable to what it sustained. The memory of Midway was evidently fresh. American movements too were unaggressive, largely from want of intelligence about the enemy. Admiral Fletcher was certainly justified in hauling south for the night away from prowling surface raiders. But how badly did his destroyers need that drink of fuel oil for which he took *Saratoga* completely out of the battle scene on the 25th? As long as the issue was in doubt, every available carrier aircraft should have been used to protect our tenuous lease on Guadalcanal. That is what they were there for. Fletcher won the battle, to be sure; but only because the Japanese were more timid than he. His planes disposed of *Ryujo*, but the two big Japanese carriers were still afloat, and gave plenty of trouble later.

The Pacific Fleet profited much from the study of this engagement by tacticians and technicians. Immense carrier-pilot training programs and fleet-carrier building programs were already under way, and any practice or information was sure to count in the end. The American sailors who fought on 24 August shouted their opinions loud and long and, judging by subsequent events, their clamor was heard in Washington. Here are a few of the things they said: —

The aircraft identification system isn't good enough.

The increase in fighter plane complement since Midway (from 23 to 36 per carrier) is good dope, but we want fighters that can protect bombers and torpedo planes on long strikes.

Fighter-direction's got to be cleaned up; too many Nips get through without being jumped.

A carrier pilot doesn't get enough training while in the combat area to really keep his hand in.

What's the idea of separating carriers during battle? Just divides the anti-aircraft and fighter support. . . . No — you're wrong — we should separate the carriers further; suppose the Japs had sighted "Sara" and raped her too?

Carrier planes shouldn't be used for search. That's a job for the land-based outfits. Look at the Japs; they use 4-engined flying boats or cruiser float planes for their searches.

We could sure use some of that new 5-inch influence ammunition against those dive-bombers.[28]

The Battle of the Eastern Solomons, third of the great carrier engagements of the war and second of the naval actions centering around Guadalcanal, was not a decisive battle. But it did prevent the 1500 Japanese troops from landing and, as Admiral Nimitz wrote, "The Japanese had shot their bolt and with air forces seriously reduced were retiring." [29] And the diary of a Japanese officer at Guadalcanal remarked pertinently, "Our plan to capture Guadalcanal came unavoidably to a standstill, owing to the appearance of the enemy striking force." [30]

[28] All this can be found in Action Reports, but not in the wardroom vernacular which we have quoted.

[29] Cincpac *Solomons Islands Campaign — Action of 23-25 August.*

[30] This and other translations in this volume from captured Japanese diaries were seen at Nouméa early in 1943 through the kindness of Colonel Julian P. Brown USMC, Admiral Halsey's Intelligence Officer.

CHAPTER V

Attrition Tactics[1]

28 August–5 September 1942

1. Colhoun *Sunk*, "*Sara*" *Smacked*

THE SIX weeks following the Battle of the Eastern Solomons was the one period in the Guadalcanal campaign when gnawing at the other fellow's extremities was more fashionable than slashing at his vitals. Admiral Ghormley initiated a continuous movement of cargo ships from Nouméa to supply the Marines, and in order to protect these ships from air attack he established carrier patrols covering the main approaches. To augment and cover this defensive employment of naval vessels, he planned to harry the enemy at sea and in harbor with land-based aircraft from Guadalcanal, the New Hebrides, New Caledonia, New Guinea and Australia. At the same time several submarines were stationed where they could do the most harm. But Commander South Pacific wisely refused to commit his ships piecemeal, knowing they would still have to reckon with the Japanese Fleet. And the enemy, since the Henderson Field bombers were not numerous enough to stop him, accepted his losses at the Battle of the Eastern Solomons and kept reinforcing his Guadalcanal garrison by "Tokyo Express."

Although Lieutenant General Hyakutake in Rabaul still re-

[1] Comairsopac daily Intelligence Summaries, consulted at Admiral Fitch's headquarters at Espiritu Santo, and Cincpac files and papers are most useful for day-by-day events in the Guadalcanal campaign. On the Japanese side, details are supplied by the War Diary of Japanese Naval Operations ATIS 16268, and War Diary of Desron 2.

garded the Guadalcanal campaign as secondary to taking Port Moresby, he decided to commit some 3500 more troops, under Major General Kiyotake Kawaguchi. The first echelon, in four destroyers, entered Indispensable Strait on 28 August. Toward evening two Dauntless scouts spotted them, shouted for help and made an ineffectual bombing attack. At 1800 eleven of Mangrum's Marine Corps dive-bombers arrived over the enemy, then some 70 miles north of Guadalcanal, and did a very workmanlike job. Destroyer *Asagiri* blew up with a terrific explosion after being hit by a 500-pound bomb and sank almost immediately. Destroyer *Shirakumo* was stopped but left afloat; *Yugiri's* superstructure was well burned. The landing was called off and the one undamaged destroyer took *Shirakumo* in tow for a painful return trip to the Shortlands.[2] Only one American plane was lost in this highly successful raid.

It took more than that to discourage Hyakutake. Next day five destroyers sortied from the Shortlands and landed 450 soldiers on Taivu Point, east of the American perimeter, after dark. On 30 August, elements of General Kawaguchi's detachment were again embarked for a southward dash, in destroyer *Yudachi*, and a diversionary air attack not only protected her but exacted revenge for the loss of *Asagiri*.

The victim was fast transport *Colhoun*, converted from a four-stack destroyer. She and sister ship *Little* were covering a small auxiliary ship, *Kopara*, that was discharging stores at Guadalcanal. At 1415, in response to an air alert, the three vessels got under way for Tulagi. At 1512 a formation of twin-engined bombers appeared almost overhead, directly in the glare of the sun. *Colhoun's* men had but a short glimpse of 18 planes flying in two large Vees, when the enemy disappeared into the clouds. Lieutenant Commander Madden rang up full speed while his gunners prepared to shoot at any plane within range of *Colhoun's* pitifully inadequate anti-aircraft guns.

Those guns never had a chance. The enemy had already re-

[2] Desron 2 War Diary.

leased two sticks of bombs which, with phenomenal accuracy for horizontal bombing, hit all around and upon the little ship. On so thin-shelled a vessel the effect of several near-misses, exploding in the water only 50 feet away and evenly spaced from bridge to fantail, was devastating. The hull lurched violently to port, the foremast toppled, 4-inch guns were twisted from their mountings, main engines, boilers, pumps and piping were torn from their fastenings and the ship began to sink rapidly by the stern. Chief Quartermaster Saunders tried to work his way aft to the steering-engine room but was stopped when two more bombs struck, one on the after deckhouse, the other on the after engine room. Fuel oil burst into flames and prevented repair parties from approaching the damaged areas. Madden, realizing his command was a sinking shambles, ordered his executive officer to place the wounded in boats, but the boats were shattered. Within two minutes of the time the enemy planes were discovered, *Colhoun* went down with 51 men; the rest were picked up by tank lighters from Guadalcanal.

That night *Yudachi* landed her troops safely at Taivu.

The last day of August brought more grief to the United States Navy, this time in the warhead of a Japanese torpedo launched by a submarine some 260 miles southeast of Guadalcanal. It will be recalled that, after the Battle of the Eastern Solomons, *Saratoga* moved south to refuel and then took up a defensive patrol of the sea routes to Guadalcanal. *Wasp* and *Hornet* joined her in the same general area. Admiral Ghormley instructed the carriers to remain south of the 10th parallel unless pursuing an enemy. So Admiral Fletcher patrolled a rectangle about 150 miles long and 60 wide,[3] east and southeast of San Cristobal. On 27 August two *Wasp* planes drove down an I-boat only 50 miles from the carriers. At 0330 August 31, radar on *North Carolina* and *Saratoga* showed an indication that warranted an investigation by destroyer *Farragut*. She found nothing, and the "blip" disappeared from the

[3] Bounded by lats. 10°30′ S and 13° S, and longs. 163°30′ E and 164°30′ E.

radar screens. Possibly only a rainsquall, but it might have been a submarine. The task force continued on its northwesterly course.

At 0600 *Saratoga* sailors went to their battle stations for the dawn general quarters. As the darkness dissipated, they discerned the shapes of their screening ships: the battleship and three cruisers close aboard, seven destroyers dancing about their moving stations 3500 yards out, their sonar listening for submarine noises. At 0655 Admiral Fletcher reversed the base course from northwest to southeast, all ships zigzagging according to plan at 13 knots. His new track would bring him back to the general vicinity of the suspicious 0330 contact. At 0706, with sunlight flooding sea and sky, a cheery bugle blast released *Saratoga* men from battle stations and called all hands to breakfast. Since the Eastern Solomons affair, life had settled into a rather humdrum pattern at sea; this was just another morning watch — for half an hour.

As the chow lines formed, enemy eyes were watching *Saratoga's* movements through a periscope belonging to *I-26*. From a position on the carrier's bow but outside the screen, the submarine launched a spread of six torpedoes at the big target. At that moment destroyer *MacDonough* made a hot sound-contact dead ahead and close aboard, quickly followed by a sighting of the periscope barely 30 feet from her bow. She hoisted the submarine warning signal at 0746 and dropped two depth charges, unfortunately with no depth setting. Simultaneously a torpedo porpoised astern and harsh grating noises were heard against the ship's hull as *I-26* scraped it.

Captain Dewitt C. Ramsey of *Saratoga* saw *MacDonough's* warning, swung his rudder hard right and rang up full speed on all engines. As hundreds of alerted sailors in other ships watched and mentally strained, the big old ship began slowly and awkwardly to turn toward the torpedo wake. For two minutes only — and they seemed ten — the air was tense with expectation. Then a plume of water and oil erupted from the carrier's starboard side abreast the island. Men throughout the task force groaned, cursed and stamped their feet in futile rage. "Sara" had been nicked for the second time in 1942.[4]

At once the destroyers began a frantic hunt for the submarine. *Phelps* and *MacDonough* made sound contacts and dropped depth charges with no success. *Monssen*, ordered to keep the submarine down until dark and then rejoin, claimed to have sunk it with depth charges. But *I–26* escaped and, later in the year, sank cruiser *Juneau*.

On board *Saratoga* the situation was not too bad. Only twelve men, including Admiral Fletcher, had been wounded, most of them slightly. The torpedo had hit where it could do little structural damage, on the starboard side where tanks and voids were built out from the side of the ship. Only one fireroom was flooded; the slight list that developed was corrected by noon. *Saratoga*, however, was one of the few big ships in the Navy with electric propulsion units, and these caused her embarrassment. The torpedo explosion jarred a high-tension electrical switch which closed momentarily with an arc amounting to an explosion, filling the main control space with fumes, causing protective devices to function automatically and stopping two main generators. For several hours the engineer officer and his gang sought out and overcame many mechanical and electrical difficulties. It was late afternoon before the chief could give his captain 12 knots, and three days more passed before he could guarantee a steady 13.

Captain Ramsey, concerned with the danger of further attacks from aloft or below, was eager to fly off his valuable planes to a place of safety. A tow by cruiser *Minneapolis* and a brisk southeast wind helped the carrier's faltering engines to make sufficient windage for launching planes, and by midafternoon 21 bombers and

---

[4] See Vol. III of this History p. 260. Position of second hit lat. 10°34′ S, long. 164°18′ E. There was acrimonious debate about it. In his endorsement on Comdesdiv 22's report of this incident Admiral Ghormley remarked: "The point at which the *Saratoga* was torpedoed at 0748 was approximately 30 miles from the area where radar contacts [at 0330] indicated the possible presence of enemy submarines. . . . In the elapsed time of four hours and eighteen minutes from the radar contact until the *Saratoga* was torpedoed, the . . . movement of the disposition . . . was not sufficient to have taken it clear . . ."

nine fighters were on their way to Espiritu Santo, 347 miles distant. Thence they were dispatched to Henderson Field where the naval pilots — the "bell-bottom aviators" as the Marines called them — flew wing to wing with the flying leathernecks on many a combat mission. "Sara" made Tongatabu safely; but almost three months were required to put her in shape, and her absence from the South Pacific was sorely felt.

On 31 August, the same day that "Sara" was hit, the Japanese successfully ran the aërial blockade with seven or eight destroyers, which discharged 1200 more troops — including engineers, artillerymen, anti-tank units and General Kawaguchi himself — on the west flank of the Marines' perimeter. The attempts of General Geiger's airmen to hold up these "Tokyo Express" runs were as a rule unsuccessful. Their SBD–3s were only good for a 200-mile radius of action and for months there were not enough of them, or enough fuel, to launch an attack group every day. The Japanese were able to plan their reinforcement echelons, in the twelve-hour nights of that latitude, so as to start a fast run-in within an hour of darkness, debark troops and supplies in a few minutes, and be 175 miles or more up the Slot when day broke. Thus they were visible and vulnerable to air bombers only for a short time coming and going, and the SBDs had to figure on bucking a tropical thunderstorm at least one way. Efforts to hit vessels unloading were fruitless, except on the rare unclouded moonlit midnights, because the blacked-out Japanese ships soon learned not to give away their position by gunfire. And the primitive form of radar with which Catalinas tried to find them could not distinguish ships from an adjacent shore.

2. *Situation and Speculation, 1–6 September*

A curious tactical situation had developed at Guadalcanal; a virtual exchange of sea mastery every twelve hours. The Americans ruled the waves from sunup to sundown; big ships discharged cargoes, smaller ships dashed through the Sound, "Yippies"[5] and landing craft ran errands between Lunga Point and Tulagi. But as the tropical twilight performed its quick fadeout and the pall of night fell on Ironbottom Sound, Allied ships cleared out like frightened children running home from a graveyard; transport and combat types steamed through Sealark Channel while small craft holed up in Tulagi Harbor or behind Gavutu. Then the Japanese took over. The "Tokyo Express" of troop destroyers and light cruisers dashed in to discharge soldiers or freight, and, departing, tossed a few shells in the Marines' direction. But the Rising Sun flag never stayed to greet its namesake; by dawn the Japs were well away, and then the Stars and Stripes reappeared. Such was the pattern cut to fit the requirements of this strange campaign; any attempt to reshape it meant a bloody battle. The Japanese rarely, and then only disastrously, attempted daytime raids with ships; the Americans more frequently interfered with the night surface express, but any such attempt proved to be expensive.

Neither high command was satisfied, both wanted to break it up; and the concepts entertained by various commanders to alter the situation are revealing. On 1 September Admiral Turner voiced his opinion in a dispatch to Ghormley: —

While always in favor of the move to Tulagi[6] it may be remembered that I warned that such a move to be permanently successful would entail continuous support by strong naval and air forces. . . . Here in the Solomons we now have an unsinkable aircraft carrier which I believe may finally be multiplied into an invincible fleet adequate for a decisive move, but this will require patience, and the determined support by forces of a strength and character which you do not now have under your control. The enemy is now hampered by his adventures in the Aleutians and Eastern New Guinea. I believe that the immediate consolidation and extension of our Cactus position is now possible and

[5] YPs — district patrol vessels — small, slow craft varying in size from 50 to 175 tons' displacement; many were converted tuna fishermen from Hawaii. Wooden-hulled and slightly armed, they were not intended for combat. At Guadalcanal they were used as tugs, dispatch boats, rescue craft, troop and supply ferries, and as transports for minor amphibious assaults.

[6] He meant the entire Guadalcanal-Tulagi operation.

advisable, and is a golden military opportunity that ought not to be missed.[7]

General Vandegrift feared lest his Marines be hopelessly out-numbered, unless a stop were put to enemy troop landings. He wanted long-range search planes to be based on Henderson Field, nightly patrols by destroyers or motor torpedo boats, and another Marine regiment.[8] But General MacArthur, the neighboring area commander, naturally felt that his command should be given more consideration in the allotment of forces.

The whole question was threshed out at a conference on board Admiral Ghormley's flagship in Nouméa Harbor, 28 September, at which Admirals Nimitz, Ghormley and Turner, General "Hap" Arnold, head of the Army Air Force, General MacArthur's chief of staff General Sutherland, his air commander General George C. Kenney, and other high-ranking officers were present.[9]

The feeling between the Southwest and the South Pacific commands at this time was none too good; and the efforts of certain American politicians and journalists to play up General MacArthur as a forgotten hero were not calculated to improve matters. Neither appreciated the other's difficulties. MacArthur had 55,000 troops — two United States infantry regiments and two Australian divisions — in Port Moresby. Lacking transports, most of them had been flown up from Queensland in Army Air Force transport planes and B–17s — the biggest air lift so far in military history. The Japanese, thwarted by Fletcher's carriers in May from taking Port Moresby by sea, began trying to do it the hard way, by marching troops across the Owen Stanley Range, on 13 August. Two weeks before the Nouméa conference, the Japs were still coming, and were within 32 miles of Port Moresby, which was taking daily bombings from the Emperor's planes. MacArthur, warned by a

[7] CTF 62 to Comsopac, 1 Sept. 1942. "Cactus" was code name for Guadalcanal-Tulagi.
[8] To CTF 62, 1 Sept. 1942.
[9] Notes in Cincpac files, Pearl Harbor. General MacArthur was invited to be present but refused to leave Brisbane. Brig. Gen. Peck and Col. Pfeiffer represented the Marine Corps.

recent Japanese attempt to capture Milne Bay, feared they would try another Coral Sea operation and wanted the Pacific Fleet deployed to meet them; Nimitz felt confident the Japs would not try it. Turner asked why MacArthur did not try to occupy the north coast of New Guinea; Sutherland countered with the query, How could it be done without ships, adequate air coverage or trained amphibious troops? Nimitz admitted he could spare him none of these; Rear Admiral Barbey's famous VII 'Phib was still a dream, only authorized by the Joint Chiefs of Staff on the day of the Nouméa conference.[10] After the war it was ascertained that the Japanese had intended to send troops in barges around the tail end of New Guinea to take Port Moresby in conjunction with the forces marching overland; that their failure to capture the necessary staging point of Milne Bay, between 26 and 30 August, caused a change of plan — to concentrate again on the land route. On 31 August the Japanese high command finally decided to throw everything it had into Guadalcanal, and until that island was secured to leave their army in Papua on the defensive.[11] Knowledge of this decision would have been very depressing to Ghormley and Turner; but even without that knowledge the two Admirals gave warning at the Nouméa conference that unless they were reinforced the enemy could recover Guadalcanal whenever he really tried.

It is now evident that the entire Guadalcanal campaign was in the nature of what military writers call a "meeting engagement." Gettysburg is the classic example: Lee marching on a wide sweep toward Harrisburg and Philadelphia; Meade after him; clash of outposts near the town of Gettysburg, in which neither side had the slightest interest; major forces sucked into a great pitched battle. So with Guadalcanal, the island that nobody really wanted. The

[10] J.C.S. "Distribution and Composition of U.S. Amphibious Forces" 5 Sept. 1942.

[11] ATIS trans. of "Southeast Area Operation, Part I (Navy)" in Army Historical Division. The important but little known Milne Bay operation will be discussed in the next volume of this History, where the operations of MacArthur's forces will be taken up.

only Japanese interest in it was to protect the eastern flank of their advance on Port Moresby. The Allies reacted quickly to the "meeting," realizing that if they could not hold Guadalcanal they might never be able to climb the Solomons ladder to Rabaul. The Japanese strategists, notoriously inflexible, required almost a month to see the point. They continued to push the Port Moresby business, and reinforced their Guadalcanal garrison by driblets, hoping that a few hundred more troops and a few more air strikes and bombardment missions would wipe out the Marines. When they finally "threw the book" at Guadalcanal, it was too late; if they had done so in August or the first week of September, they could hardly have failed to clean up.

General Arnold concluded the Nouméa conference by remarking that the overall situation of the Allies looked much better, that Army–Navy coöperation was satisfactory, and that, since Rabaul was the common objective of both Southwest and South Pacific, they must pull together. And he reminded them that everything in the United States was turned toward Operation "Torch," the invasion of North Africa.

About three weeks before that (2 September) Mr. James Forrestal, Undersecretary of the Navy, was at Nouméa checking over the situation for himself. What he saw caused him to fly directly back to Washington and use all his efforts to send reinforcements to Ghormley and Vandegrift.

On 17 September MacArthur had stopped the overland advance of the Japanese only 32 miles from Port Moresby; but American possession of Guadalcanal was so seriously threatened that in Washington there was even talk of weakening Operation "Torch" to support Operation "Watchtower."

3. LITTLE *and* GREGORY *Lost, 5 September*

On 1 September a Flying Fortress on a scouting mission chanced upon seaplane carrier *Akitsushima* north of Choiseul and showered her with a salvo of bombs which failed to hit but did slight damage as near-misses. The Nipponese retaliated with vigorous air raids on Henderson Field by a score of bombers under fighter cover. Defending Marine fighter planes knocked down seven of the attackers, anti-aircraft gunners scored one kill, and no American planes were lost; but the enemy destroyed some precious aviation gasoline and ammunition.

During the night of 4–5 September an event occurred that recalled the tribulations of the Asiatic Fleet. Destroyer transports *Little* and *Gregory*, sister ships to sunken *Colhoun*, were still acting as water taxis for Marines and their supplies. Following an unconfirmed rumor that the enemy had occupied Savo Island, they ferried the 1st Raider Battalion from Tulagi to deal with the situation. But no Japs were on Savo. The raiders reëmbarked and were taken to Guadalcanal, where they landed at dusk. Under normal circumstances both ships would have returned to Tulagi Harbor, but the night was unusually dark and no landmarks were visible. Commander Hugh W. Hadley, division commander in *Little*, decided to patrol off Lunga Point during the night, steaming two to six miles off shore and parallel to the beach.

It so happened that the Japanese chose that night to land another group of Kawaguchi's detachment and, in addition to troop-carrying APDs, sent three destroyers, *Yudachi*, *Hatsuyuki* and *Murakumo*, to provide diversionary bombardment.

On entering Savo Sound in the opening hour of the midwatch, the Japanese bombardment force passed well to seaward of *Little* and *Gregory* so that neither force sighted the other. At 0100 September 5, just as *Little* was reversing course from 130° to 310°, occasional gun flashes were observed to the eastward; destroyer *Yudachi* and friends had opened fire on the beach. The deck watch in both American ships jumped to the reasonable conclusion that the gunfire came from a Japanese submarine conducting a nuisance bombardment. Both officers of the deck went to general quarters and called their skippers, in anticipation of an anti-submarine skirmish. Weary sailors, routed out of their bunks by

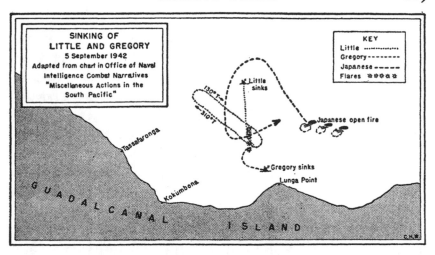

SINKING OF
LITTLE AND GREGORY
5 September 1942
Adapted from chart in Office of Naval
Intelligence Combat Narratives
"Miscellaneous Actions in the
South Pacific"

KEY
Little ·················
Gregory --------
Japanese — — — —
Flares ✿✿✿✿✿

Little
sinks

Japanese open fire

Gregory sinks
Lunga Point

Tassafaronga

Kokumbona

G U A D A L C A N A L   I S L A N D

the clamor of the general alarm, dressed hastily, sharing the feeling of one boatswain's mate that it was just routine gunfire "a good
piece off."

But *Little's* radar showed four distinct contacts almost dead
astern and only two miles distant. A tough choice lay before Commander Hadley. He could turn and run while still undetected,
a logical but distasteful decision for any skipper; or, relying on his
radar and on surprise, he could try a hit-and-run battle which
might scare the enemy off. As ill luck would have it, neither
choice could be followed.

The fatal agent in this case was a Navy Catalina flying over
Savo Sound and trying to be helpful. The pilot, probably unaware
of the presence of *Little* and *Gregory*, also believed that the gun
flashes came from a surfaced submarine, and decided to show it
up. Scarcely a minute after *Little's* radar had indicated the real
enemy, Helpful Harry released a string of five flares only half a
mile ahead of the two destroyer-transports. It was like one of those
bad dreams where you find yourself naked on Broadway. Japanese
gunners, at first startled by the illumination, soon spotted the
APDs and shifted their guns and a searchlight accordingly. *Little*
struck out at the enemy with every gun that could bear: one 4-inch,
some 20-mm, .50-caliber and .30-caliber machine guns — all woe-

fully ineffective against modern destroyers. The Japanese in the meantime were feeling for the range. Their first two salvos were over, the third short; but the fourth connected with the American's stern. One shot penetrated the steering-engine room, one entered the after fuel tanks, and another put the after 4-inch gun out of action. Fuel oil burst into brilliant flames. *Gregory* drew the attention of another searchlight and accurate 5-inch salvos followed. Explosions shredded her bridge, knocked down the after stack, pried open the galley deckhouse, burst a boiler and killed seamen with jagged hunks of metal. Flames pranced from stem to stern; *Gregory's* fighting days were over.

On board *Little*, Lieutenant Commander Lofberg decided to beach his ship. But the hit in the steering-engine room had jammed her rudder; other hits knocked out the few remaining weapons, ruptured the main steam line and ignited the Higgins boats. There was only one course open, to abandon ship. But before he could carry out his order, Lofberg and Commander Hadley were killed on the bridge.

Gregory, too, had to be abandoned, but a boatswain's mate and a coxswain [12] helped their badly wounded skipper, Lieutenant Commander Harry F. Bauer, over the side. They were pulling him clear of the suction and burning oil, when he heard through the darkness a sailor cry out that he was drowning; Bauer ordered his would-be rescuers to go to the man's assistance, and he was never seen again.

Both ships were already lifeless and burning hulks, but the Japanese, to make certain of their kill, steamed between them at high speed firing shells, some of which killed floating survivors; finally satisfied, they left the area at about 0135 September 5. The survivors spent a miserable night in shattered boats, overturned life rafts and shrapnel-torn life jackets. Planes sighted them at daybreak from Guadalcanal and directed landing boats to the rescue.

Admiral Turner in his report justly said: "The officers and men serving in these ships have shown great courage and have

[12] Clarence C. Justice and Chester M. Ellis.

performed outstanding service. They entered this dangerous area time after time, well knowing their ships stood little or no chance if they should be opposed by any surface or air force the enemy would send into those waters. On the occasion of their last trip in they remained six days, subjected to a daily air attack and anticipating nightly surface attack." [13]

During these early days of September the Japanese did not confine their troop ferrying to swift destroyers but also resorted to the use of landing boats and barges which could sneak along a coastline at night and tie up in jungle estuaries at daybreak. Army, Navy and Marine airmen attacked these barges at every opportunity, strafing and bombing them wherever found: at New Georgia, Santa Isabel, Cape Esperance and the eastern enemy outpost at Taivu. Such onslaughts occasionally caught the boats with troops in them, more frequently destroyed them when empty, and placed a heavy strain on Japanese supply lines.

Erosion of the Japanese air force also continued apace. Their lunch-hour raids on Guadalcanal almost always cost them dear. The average raid consisted of about two dozen bombers covered by a score of fighters; the usual loss ran anywhere from four to eight planes. Damage to the American airfield was negligible. American air strikes on enemy fields also accounted for many a Rising Sun aircraft. The Flying Fort was proving itself more than a match for any "Zeke" which dared come within range of its .50-caliber guns; one B–17 on a photo mission knocked down four enemy fighter planes. Mutual eagerness for air dueling was demonstrated on 5 September; Lieutenant Francis C. Riley USNR in a scouting PBY took on a Japanese counterpart, one of the umbrella-winged Kawanishi flying boats. The two cumbersome craft circled each other like a pair of flying elephants, spitting fire until the Kawanishi fell in flames.

Although the balance was in favor of the Americans, they too felt the pinch of air losses. In a month's operations, almost one

---

[13] Turner's Report "Loss of U.S.S. *Colhoun, Gregory* and *Little*," 13 Dec. 1942. *Little* lost 22 killed, 44 wounded; *Gregory*, 11 killed, 26 wounded.

quarter of the Catalinas in the area were lost. Army P–400s, low-altitude fighters ill adapted to the high-flying combat in the Solomons, went from a total of fourteen down to a meager three in four days. Operational losses were excessive; on 9 September nine planes crashed getting on and off a wet field at Guadalcanal. And, for every six Jap planes that crashed flaming, one Navy or Marine plane met a similar fate.[14]

[14] Details and PBY losses from Admiral Fitch's daily Intelligence Bulletin; P–400 losses from the contemporary A.A.F. publication *Counterblow*. Records were the least worry of the Marine and Navy airmen on Guadalcanal, so it is hard to put together an accurate tabulation.

CHAPTER VI

The September Crisis

1. *Raid on Tasimboko, 7–8 September*

E VENTS were building up to another crisis. Toward the middle of every month from August to November inclusive, the Japanese made a major effort to recapture Guadalcanal. Their pattern in every instance was the same; only the forces varied. First, for a week or ten days, the "Tokyo Express" made nightly runs landing reinforcements; owing to the excellent work by American airmen based on Henderson Field, the Japanese would not commit capital ships to Savo Sound in daylight. In the meantime Admiral Yamamoto mustered the Combined Fleet at Truk and drew up an operation plan which would be sparked off when the Emperor's ground forces captured the airfield; but he was also ready to accept a sea battle whenever challenged. For the September show, Yamamoto provided a carrier-battleship-heavy cruiser force, similar to the one engaged in the Battle of the Eastern Solomons, with orders to await developments north of Santa Isabel and Malaita.

General Kawaguchi, who, as we have seen, landed before the end of August with his first echelon at Taivu, east of the Marines' perimeter, had the mission of capturing Henderson Field. His plan involved three separate attacks against each flank and the rear of the Marine lines, to be followed by an amphibious assault on the beachhead.[1] D-day was to be 12 September, and Kawaguchi promised his superior officer, Hyakutake, that by 10 October the

---

[1] "Answers to Questionnaires on Guadalcanal Operations" ATIS 22729. Hyakutake had planned earlier to throw a whole new division into Guadalcanal but Kawaguchi, after taking Taivu, persuaded him that he had enough on hand to take Henderson Field.

Marines would be eliminated and he could shift his headquarters from Rabaul to Henderson Field. This strategy was a curious reversal of principles that had come down from the pre-air age. Instead of counting on a fleet to secure command of adjacent waters before pressing a land assault, the Japanese decided they must capture the air base before challenging their enemy's fleet. Billy Mitchell would have approved, but it didn't work.

Kawaguchi's engineers on 2 September began hacking a trail from Taivu through the jungle to a chosen point of attack southeast of Henderson Field. In the meantime, Allied native scouts and aërial reconnaissance caught occasional glimpses of Kawaguchi's main body of troops. The natives reported correctly that they were several thousand in number; but the Marines discounted Melanesian arithmetic and estimated enemy strength at about 500. Deciding that a full battalion of fresh troops would be sufficient to deal with them, Vandegrift ordered over from Tulagi the 1st Raider and 1st Parachute Battalions, amalgamated under the command of Colonel Edson. Tulagi could hardly be called a health resort, but it was a paradise compared with the sodden coastal plain of Guadalcanal, and Edson's men were both rested and eager. They were first brought to Kukum and there embarked at 1800 September 7 in destroyer transports *McKean* and *Manley*, *YP-346* and *YP-289*.

Edson's raiders landed east of Taivu Point at dawn 8 September. A lucky break gave them a pushover. Transports *Fuller* and *Bellatrix* happened to be steaming along the coast on other business, but Kawaguchi thought they were going to pull a major landing and withdrew his entire force inland. *McKean* and *Manley* made a second trip with reinforcements, and as the Marines moved westward, covered by strafing planes from Henderson Field, the enemy retreated, losing a battery of artillery. He made a desperate stand at Tasimboko village, then fled into the jungle. Tasimboko turned out to be a main supply depot stocked with artillery, ammunition, rice, medical supplies and equipment which the raiders gleefully destroyed. Late in the afternoon Colonel Edson reëmbarked his men, taking a fine haul of interesting enemy documents as well as General Kawaguchi's wardrobe of white full-dress uniforms with silk facings. "The bastard must have been planning to shine in Sydney society," was the comment of a Marine. Only two men were killed and six wounded out of nearly 600 in this successful foray.

The only flareback occurred because of the unconscious transport ruse. Admiral Kusaka ordered an air raid that gave *Fuller* and *Bellatrix* a few bad moments, and Admiral Mikawa dispatched cruiser *Sendai* and eight destroyers down the Slot after them. Failing to locate the transports that night, this force bombarded Tulagi Harbor and hit *YP-346*, wounding three men and driving the little craft aground.

2. *The Battle of the Bloody Ridge, 12–14 September*

General Kawaguchi, like so many of his compatriots, followed a pattern. His original plan with its devious complications was so pretty that he clung to it even after the Tasimboko tip-off. So on he went to his destruction.

In the Marine command post, General Vandegrift and staff studied the terrain map with misgivings. As there were not nearly enough troops properly to defend the entire perimeter, he decided to beef up the sectors most likely to receive the blow. The Ilu (Tenaru) River was one such, and to it went Lieutenant Colonel McKelvy's 3rd Battalion 1st Marine Regiment, which extended the eastern flank to a length of two miles inland. The western flank was deemed strong enough for anything that might come that way, but in the rear there was a weak two-mile stretch between the Lunga River and the western flank, open except for two strong points, one held by the 1st Pioneer, the other by the 1st Amphibian Tractor[2] Battalion. Since every Marine receives basic training as an infantryman, Vandegrift was confident that

[2] Prototypes of the LVT so extensively used in later amphibian operations.

these specialists could hold their own until reserves could be brought up. East of the Lunga River there was another two-mile hole in the perimeter, occupied only by knots of artillerymen, engineers and pioneers. Yet something could be done to thwart the enemy. Studying the map and the ground itself, Colonel Edson called Vandegrift's attention to a grass-covered ridge which ran south from the airfield. This is the feature that came to be known as "Edson's Ridge" or "Bloody Ridge." Higher than the surrounding jungle trees, it commanded the airstrip and would be a natural assault channel to Henderson Field, particularly as the jungle-covered flats on either side afforded excellent cover. Edson's combined Raider-Paratroop Battalion, returning from the Tasimboko affair, prepared positions on this ridge. Flank support on the right rear was furnished by the 1st Pioneer Battalion, and on the left rear by the 1st Engineer Battalion. And, right after the mêlée began, Brigadier General Pedro del Valle of the Marines' artillery regiment sited his 5th Battalion's 105-mm howitzers and his special weapons battalion's automatic weapons, in positions to render direct support.

September 12 was supposed to be Kawaguchi's day of victory. He had picked out the same ridge, just as Edson had anticipated, and committed the main body of his men to advance both alongside and on top of it. A small detachment took position still farther east. Daylight on the 12th saw numerous skirmishes between patrols; but, when evening fell, Kawaguchi began probing for weak spots in the Marine line. One group even broke through, cut off a company of Marine raiders and disrupted communications; but still Kawaguchi refrained from an all-out drive. Meanwhile, the Japanese air force based at Rabaul delivered a bombing attack which cost them 4 "Zekes" and 10 bombers, shot down by intercepting Wildcats and Marines' anti-aircraft fire, but placed a stick of bombs right down the center of the Ridge. Fortunately they inflicted little damage. One of Mikawa's cruisers and three destroyers chimed in with a haphazard night bombardment which failed to distinguish between friend and enemy.

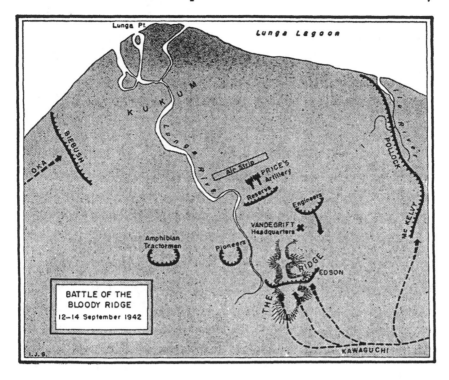

In this "rest area," as Colonel Edson jokingly described the Ridge when another officer asked where the Marines were going next, there was little sleep on the night of 12–13 September. When the Japs were not jabbering down on the jungle flats, they were charging the Ridge in bayonet attacks. By morning the Marines were worn out and General Vandegrift was worried, since he had few reserves. Edson's men dug in and prepared for another scrap. The 13th passed with a series of small raids; the Marines were too few to take the offensive, and the Japanese waited for night. A relief battalion under Colonel Whaling camped south of the airfield, ready to relieve the raiders.

Kawaguchi's soldiers were tired, too, after a long march through the jungle and successive charges; but they still felt confident when they saw their "Eagles" make raid after raid on Henderson Field. As night fell on the 13th, the last Nip plane left for Rabaul and Kawaguchi's soldiers whetted bayonets for the charge. They had no artillery preparation, because most of their big guns were on the bottom of Sealark Channel, where Edson's men had dumped them after their raid on Tasimboko.

A red rocket flared over the jungle, and the Japanese began to scream and drop heavy mortar fire into the Marine line. It held, but the enemy managed to find a hole in the jungle to the west of the Ridge, where he pushed back one raider company and outflanked another, while pressing heavily against the fronts of the rest. The outflanked company fought its way clear, then took up defensive position again. At 2100 General del Valle's 105-mm howitzers, commanded by Colonel Price, opened up and fired furiously all night long, slinging shells over the Ridge at the attackers. Communication was broken between the three batteries and their observers on the Ridge; the gunners then fired wherever the Japanese sent up rockets, their signal for each fresh attack.

At 2230 the Emperor's men delivered a howling charge on Edson's left flank. Hoping to demoralize the paratroops, enemy soldiers shouted in English: "Gas Attack! Marine, you die!" and laid down a covering smoke screen. The Marines were not fooled, but the ferocity of the assault pushed them out of position and exposed the flank. Edson now had his center company, 60 men under Captain John B. Sweeney, sticking out like the prow of a ship into a sea of maddened Japs. In the swirling darkness it was imperative to maintain contact, so the Colonel ordered his forward troops back to the last knoll of the Ridge, only 1500 yards short of Henderson Field. There they stayed while the Japs literally beat their brains out against a wall of steel from artillery, mortars, machine guns, rifles and grenades. General Vandegrift watched and listened from division headquarters only a quarter of a mile away, and a few intrepid men ventured near enough to be killed by his headquarters staff. Time and again a rocket flowered red, rallying the enemy to brave and bloody action. Time and again they were driven back. On each occasion some of the Japanese pressed resolutely through the dreadful barrage, halted briefly to illuminate the

Marines with calcium flares, then swept up the last few yards of the slope, screeching defiantly before crumpling under the impact of close-range automatic fire.[3] By 0230 September 14, Colonel Edson and his executive officer, Lieutenant Colonel Griffith, were certain their men's lines would hold. And at dawn the last charge flickered out.

Day broke silently except for bird calls and the shrilling of insects, but it uncovered a grisly scene. Those tumbled hillocks, soon to be named the Bloody Ridge, were littered with Japanese bodies sprawled in the pitiful and repulsive attitudes of death. Now every plane that could fly took the air, and with their strafing machine guns herded Kawaguchi's survivors back into the jungle.

Kawaguchi's two other attacks were more easily repulsed. His eastern prong also pushed in during the night of 13–14 September, choosing the inland flank of McKelvy's Ilu River defenses. Two companies attacked positions protected by barbed wire, skillfully placed machine guns and determined riflemen. They accomplished nothing. The western prong attacked a day late. Lieutenant Colonel Biebush's 3rd Battalion, well wired-in on a small grassy ridge south of Kukum and supported by 75-mm pack howitzers, fended it off easily.

Forty Marines died on Edson's Ridge and 103 were wounded, one fifth of all Americans engaged. But, of the 2000 or more Japs who participated, 600 fell on the Ridge and hundreds more died of wounds on their long, roundabout retreat to the coast. An estimated 200 more were lost in the fight with McKelvy. About 400 of those who straggled westward, cutting trails behind the perimeter, eventually staggered into Kokumbona. When Kawaguchi counted noses, almost half of his 3450 troops were no longer present or accounted for.[4] It would be another month before he could resume the offensive.

[3] The 105-mm howitzers alone poured out nearly 2000 rounds. "The Ridge could never have been held but for the outstanding support we had from Del Valle's artillery," wrote Col. Griffith.

[4] Figures from Miller *Guadalcanal: The First Offensive*. The Japanese official report was 633 killed, 505 wounded.

The Battle of the Ridge was one of the crucial ground actions of the Pacific War. It was won by Edson's inspired leadership, and the skill and courage of individual Marines. If this battle had been lost, Henderson Field would have been lost, and the Marines would have been hard put to hold the island.

3. WASP's *Sacrifice, 15 September*

On 14 September, when the Marines were engaged in burying enemy dead, a convoy of six transports carrying the 7th Marine Regiment sailed from Espiritu Santo, covered by cruisers and destroyers. It was well known that enemy battleships and carriers were lurking north of the Santa Cruz Islands, that other formidable forces were poised in the central and northern Solomons, that eager enemy bombers were nested on Rabaul and Bougainville fields, and that nearly a score of submarines were waiting for targets in Solomon Islands waters. But Guadalcanal had to be reinforced. To protect the transports against carrier or big-gunned opponents, Ghormley committed his two sound carriers, *Hornet* and *Wasp;* the latter had already run a plane-ferry mission to reinforce Henderson Field on the 12th. The task force built around them steamed in distant support, out of sight of the transports and their screen. In the hope of keeping knowledge of the troop convoy from the enemy until it was ready to land, Turner plotted a course well to the east of the normal approach. All day long on the 14th, the air was blue with reports of plane contacts on carriers and battleships to the north and "Tokyo Express" groups to the northwest. *Hornet* launched a search attack group but the enemy carriers retired before being found.

By the morning of 15 September Kelly Turner's mind was weighed down with responsibility and apprehension. The 7th Marine Regiment, the only one available in the South Pacific for reinforcement of Guadalcanal, could not be exposed to attack in the defenseless state before or during disembarkation. When, at noon, one of the lumbering Kawanishi bombers was detected snooping his formation, Turner felt certain of an ugly reception if he kept going. He made the hard decision to retire temporarily and await a more favorable opportunity, but held the convoy on its course until nightfall to deceive the enemy into thinking it was still closing Guadalcanal.

The carriers, meanwhile, were cruising from a position south of the 12th parallel of latitude and about a hundred miles from the Turner transports. Exploratory flights in quest of enemy forces developed nothing, and the two carrier groups ambled along at 16 knots on a westerly course, occasionally swinging to a southeasterly heading for flight operations. September 15 was a perfect South Pacific day, with a fresh 20-knot southeast tradewind, a white plume on every wave and hardly a cloud in the sky. Four cruisers and six destroyers surrounded *Wasp*, flagship of Rear Admiral Leigh Noyes, while five or six miles distant steamed *Hornet*, squired by battleship *North Carolina*, three cruisers and seven destroyers. Since early morn there had been but one brief flurry of excitement: a snooping "Mavis" detected by radar had been shot down by combat air patrol beyond visual range of the task force. On flight decks planes were gassed and fully armed, but there was no indication as yet of anything to attack.

Wasp, responsible that day for combat air and anti-submarine patrol, turned into the wind at 1420 and slowed down to launch and recover planes. In short order, 18 SBDs and eight Wildcats took the air from the flight deck; three of one and eight of the other landed on board. This operation was watched with keen interest by a submerged enemy submarine, *I-19*, one of those sent into the area to knock off the 7th Marine transports. None of the six destroyers around *Wasp* had yet picked up the boat on their sound gear when the carrier's commanding officer, Captain Forrest P. Sherman, sounded the routine whistle signal for a turn, bent on 16 knots, and brought rudder right standard for a return to her base course, W by N. While the ship was swinging in the turn, her lookouts shouted a warning of torpedoes on the starboard side.

I–19 had just fired a spread of four "fish" from a position to the southwest of *Wasp*. They were approaching from three points forward of the starboard beam, running "hot, straight and normal" and already very, very close. Captain Sherman ordered the rudder full right but it was too late. Two racing warheads struck deep, forward on the starboard side; a third broached, then dove under to hit the hull about fifty feet forward of the bridge; a fourth missed ahead and ran harmlessly under destroyer *Lansdowne*.

The ferocity of the explosions buffeted men and gear like a Kansas twister. Planes on flight and hangar decks took the air vertically only to fall back and smash their landing gears. Planes suspended from the hangar deck overhead ripped loose to fall on other planes and on men. An engine-room switchboard tumbled over; generators were pulled from their foundations. Fire broke out, spreading to ready-ammunition and to airplanes full of fuel and bombs. Oil and gasoline — the gasoline pumping system was in use — spread the scurrying tongues of fire. The writhing of the ship's hull broke all forward water mains, which boded ill for fire fighting. Decks canted crazily as the ship took a heavy starboard list.[5]

Captain Sherman discovered that he still had telephone communications with the engines, the damage control center and the after steering station. By telephone he ordered engines slowed to 10 knots and rudder full left to get the wind on the starboard bow; then he rang up "back" on all engines and ordered right full rudder until *Wasp* had the wind on her starboard quarter, blowing the fire away from her undamaged portion. The pilothouse was filled with smoke and flying fragments.

On watch in the engine room at the time of the hit was Chief Machinist Chester M. Stearns, who immediately took steps to correct the heavy list. At his direction Chief Watertender Coffee, the "oil king,"[6] shifted fuel from low to high side. Shortly thereafter, the engineer officer arrived and relieved Stearns. In a brief time the list was reduced to 4 degrees, the engines answered all

---

[5] Time 1445; location about halfway between San Cristobal and Espiritu Santo.
[6] A petty officer assigned the task of filling and measuring all fuel tanks.

bridge orders and repairmen busily worked on generators and switchboard. That was most important, for if electrical power failed steering would be impossible, the ship's head would fall off and smoke would suffocate the men throughout the ship. Machinist's Mate Holmes put an after generator in operation and furnished precious "juice" to the steering engine where Seaman Cornell followed the captain's telephoned instructions to the helm.

Wasp's troubles were bad enough for one afternoon but the Japanese were not yet through. Submarine *I–15*, keeping company with *I–19*, observed the success of her companion and attempted to duplicate the performance, selecting *Hornet* as the prospective victim. A spread of torpedoes slithered out of her tubes and headed for *Hornet's* position some five miles NNE of *Wasp*.

These torpedoes were not unheralded, for the sight of *Wasp* as a pyramid of flame had given rise to much conjecture. Had one of the carrier's planes caught fire, or was the trouble a result of enemy activity? *Lansdowne* squawked a warning by voice radio when the one torpedo which missed *Wasp* passed beneath her, but not every ship got the word and it remained for destroyer *Mustin* on *Hornet's* port bow to arouse the task force. She sighted a torpedo wake ahead and to port, turned hard left to avoid it, hoisted the torpedo warning signal and repeated the alarm by voice radio. She was lucky; the "fish" passed under her keel without touching. But it had only a 500-yard run from *Mustin* to *North Carolina* and, despite evasive measures instantly taken, the ponderous ship was unable to dodge. At 1452 the characteristic pillar of water and oil marked a score for *I–15*.[7]

North Carolina demonstrated that new battleships could take it as well as dish it out. The torpedo, striking forward on the port side and 20 feet below the waterline, killed five men, opened a wound 32 feet long by 18 high, caused flooding through four

[7] I assume that *I–15* did the job and not *I–19*. It is possible that *I–19* was responsible, but her torpedoes would have had a mighty long run. It is known that *I–15* was in the area, because she confirmed *Wasp's* sinking. *I–15* was sunk 2 Nov. 1942 by destroyer *McCalla* south of San Cristobal.

bulkheads from the skin of the ship and sent a flash into No. 1 turret handling room. The captain ordered the forward magazines flooded. But none of the damage kept "Carolina" from holding her station in formation, even at 25 knots. Damage control removed a 5.5-degree list in as many minutes.

That was only one of *I–15's* torpedoes. At 1454 *O'Brien*, a few hundred yards on *North Carolina's* quarter, sighted a torpedo to port and continued her swing to the right so that the warhead passed a man's length astern. Meanwhile the gunnery officer from his post above the bridge sighted another torpedo and shouted a warning. There was no time for the skipper to duck this one; with a resounding roar the explosion jerked open a section of the bow from keel to hawsepipe, leaving the destroyer looking like a huge fish with its mouth agape. The ship vibrated like a coachwhip, dislodging machinery and hull fittings and throwing men to their knees; happily there was no fire.

Wasp in the meantime was being eaten alive by fire. Faster and faster the swirling yellow flames moved, taller and taller they flared. Around 1500 a terrible explosion shook the entire ship, propelling gases into the bridge and island structure. Several men on the port side of the bridge were killed and Admiral Noyes had a close call when he was thrown onto the signal bridge deck, with singed face and burning clothes.

Captain Sherman and his assistants now evacuated the bridge to take control of the ship from Battle II, the after station. They were just in time, for another severe explosion on the hangar deck lifted the No. 2 flight-deck elevator into the air, crashing it down all askew.

Although nobody would then have believed it, there were still living men on *Wasp's* forecastle. Officers in the wardroom country and steward's mates taking their midafternoon siesta in their bunkrooms, both directly below the hits, were slaughtered. But many individuals, in forward staterooms, on gun stations and in bow compartments, were able to make their way forward. Asphyxiating gas billowed around these men and it soon became apparent that encroaching fires would drive everybody into the sea. But the water offered perils too, a film of burning oil and gasoline ringed the bow completely and it was not until several hardy souls had led the way by plunging in and swimming under the fires that the majority were convinced that salvation required the hazardous jump. On the hangar deck Lieutenant Raleigh C. Kirkpatrick could see nothing forward except an opaque wall of fire. He noted little knots of men vainly trying to use the various sprinkling systems, but no water came. A continuous din of popping machine-gun ammunition, bursting gas tanks and exploding bombs prevented orders from being given other than by gesture. A canvas curtain was pulled across the hangar deck and moistened in order to confine the fire; fire hoses were led from aft, but weak water-pressure made them of little use. The explosion which swept the Admiral off his feet tossed the hangar deck fire fighters aft, like chaff before the wind. The forward elevator pit was now an active volcano.

Captain Sherman held a conference with officers from the hangar deck and came to the reluctant conclusion that the fire was completely out of hand. He expressed this opinion to Admiral Noyes and with the latter's approval ordered Abandon Ship at 1520.

Strangely enough little of the ship's sore trouble was known in the engineering spaces. There were electrical difficulties, and escaping steam from a split condenser shell made conditions uncomfortable but not unbearable. The engineer officer, Lieutenant Commander Ascherfeld, and his assistants were somewhat startled when the word came to leave, and it was not until they reached the inferno of the hangar deck that they realized how far gone the carrier really was.

The conduct of the crew while leaving the ship was marked by courage and good will. The badly injured were tenderly lowered over the stern, to be given space on life rafts and floating mattresses. Chief Carpenter Machinsky, one of the last to leave, searched the hangar deck for lumber and mattresses to assist the men in the water. Finally, at about 1600, Captain Sherman left his ship.

Wasp survivors were picked up by escorting destroyers, but not before several depth-charge attacks on suspected submarines had given them some uncomfortable belly jolts. Rear Admiral Norman Scott in *San Francisco*, assuming from *Wasp's* inflamed appearance that Admiral Noyes was lost, took over command of the task force, and when Noyes was picked up by *Farenholt* he directed Scott to retain the command. It was obvious that *Wasp* could not be saved, so the sooner she went down the better. *Lansdowne*, selected to deliver the *coup de grâce*, fired five torpedoes. All hit and three exploded. At 2100 September 15 the carrier, which had survived all attempts by U-boats in the Atlantic and the Mediterranean and which had saved Malta,[8] succumbed at last.[9]

Of the 2247 souls on board, 193 were killed, 366 wounded. All but one of 25 airborne *Wasp* planes were safely recovered by *Hornet*. That evening radio operators of the task force had the humiliation of hearing from Radio Berlin "Enemy 22,000-ton carrier has been sunk." *I–19* had escaped and passed the word.

In *Hornet's* task group, *O'Brien* reported that she could make 15 knots and at 1600 she was detached with orders to proceed independently to Espiritu Santo, where she arrived the next day. At dusk *North Carolina* with two escorting destroyers was detached and directed to Tongatabu. She was repaired in Pearl Harbor, acquiring at the same time more and better anti-aircraft guns. *O'Brien*, temporarily patched in Espiritu Santo, made passage to Nouméa, where the crew of a tender made further repairs and a naval constructor passed her as fit to proceed to the West Coast. He made a bad mistake. The shock of the torpedo detonation had caused such a violent flexural vibration of the principal ship girder that her longitudinal strength was insufficient for a long voyage. She steamed 2800 miles before a temporary strengthening member let go. Then despite reduced speed the hull began to work, more

[8] See Vol. I of this History pp. 193–97.
[9] Position lat. 12°25′ S, long. 164°08′ E, about 250 miles NW of Espiritu Santo.

cracks opened up, leakage got out of control, and on 19 October, off Samoa, she broke in two and sank.

No one of the three ships torpedoed on the afternoon of 15 September could be easily spared. In the seven weeks since the first Americans had stepped ashore on Guadalcanal, Pacific Fleet carrier strength had dwindled from four to one; but the enemy, even after his carrier losses at Midway, could still muster two big ones and a number of light carriers. The damage to *North Carolina* left only one new battleship, *Washington*, operating in the Pacific. *O'Brien*, specially fitted with extra anti-aircraft fire power, carried guns which *Hornet* would miss in future battles.[10]

Admiral Turner and his six transports were still at sea awaiting a favorable chance to deliver the 7th Marine Regiment to Guadalcanal. He felt that their situation was hazardous but not hopeless, and on 16 September decided to push on so as to be off Lunga by dawn on the 18th. "Stout hearts make safe ships," the old adage in days of sail, was again tested by this bold amphibious commander; and he won through. Hazy weather concealed his convoy from lurking subs; MacArthur's fliers crashed through with some handsome bombing raids on Rabaul airfields; the Japanese task force that had been prowling about north of Guadalcanal withdrew. The convoy made Lunga Roads without further incident and, at 0550 September 18, the 7th Marines began flowing ashore in the

[10] Admiral Ghormley in forwarding Admiral Noyes's report stated: ". . . It is noted the *Wasp* remained in an area extending approximately 140 miles in a N-S direction and 170 miles in an E-W direction from 0500 on Sept. 12 until 1445 on Sept. 15. During this time she crossed her previous track approximately twelve times. Because the carrier groups remained in this comparatively small area for more than 3 days, enemy submarines were enabled to attain a position favorable for attack. It is obvious that carriers should not remain in the same general area for any length of time when enemy submarines are in the area, unless their mission requires such risk." Admiral Noyes replied in defense: "A reference to the track chart shows that the area referred to extends 300 miles in an E-W direction instead of the 170 miles stated. Also that the attack took place over 150 miles from the nearest point of crossing an old track, and in an area which had not been entered or approached previously." At Cincpac's orders Rear Admiral John F. Shafroth conducted an investigation into the sinking, on which our account is in part based. Nimitz's opinion after reading Shafroth's report was that "no persons should be blamed or censured for the loss of *Wasp*." Cominch concurred.

most orderly fashion of any American debarkation to date. Tanks, vehicles, weapons, bullets, food, fuel and assorted supplies along with nearly 4000 men were landed in twelve hours. Destroyers *Monssen* and *MacDonough* paraded up and down the enemy-held sections of the beach, throwing 5-inch shells ashore — to the vast delight of the Marines and distress of the enemy, as he himself reported.[11]

Admiral Turner's ships departed in the evening of 18 September for Espiritu Santo and Nouméa. No attack of any description occurred on the entire round trip. For that happy ending Turner could thank the American carriers, which had discouraged Yamamoto from taking positive offensive action.

Wasp was not vainly sacrificed.

4. *Chipping Away, 25 September–2 October*

The contest at Guadalcanal continued to be a struggle for advantage, not for decision. On 14 September the Flying Fortresses nicked heavy cruiser *Myoko*, causing slight damage; on the 25th they hit an after turret of light cruiser *Yura*. On 5 October two of the "Tokyo Express" destroyers, *Minegumo* and *Murasame*, were caught by Henderson Field fliers between Guadalcanal and the Shortlands, and received major damage from near misses.[12]

On 25 September the Japanese ferried to Rabaul 100 fighter planes and 80 bombers in order to conquer the air over the Solomons. But by this time the Wildcat pilots were skilled exterminators. On the 27th the enemy lost 9 out of 53 planes over Guadalcanal, the Americans none; on the following day the Japs returned with 62 planes and ran into an aërial buzz-saw; 23 of the Emperor's bombers and one of his fighters were shot down. General Vandegrift, with pardonable elation, radioed, "Our losses:

[11] "The effect on the morale of our ground forces was great" — "Southeast Area Operations Part I (Navy)" trans. by U.S. Army Historical Division.
[12] Japanese Naval War Diary.

no pilots, no planes, no damage. How's that for a record?" [13] Enemy air-combat losses since the Marines' landing now ran well over 200 planes as against 32 downed American aircraft.

These staggering plane losses prodded the Japanese into a change of tactics. Flights into the bullet-swept air over Henderson Field were now made by large numbers of fighters using a handful of bombers as bait. On 2 October these methods won them a score of 5 to 4, but the Americans soon caught on and brought the odds back in their favor. To pester the Marines, another new wrinkle in air activity was introduced in early October and continued throughout the campaign. Every night two aircraft, usually single-engined float planes based at Rekata Bay, arrived over Henderson Field and circled for an hour or more, releasing an occasional flare to brighten things up for bombarding naval forces, and dropping small bombs at irregular intervals to make sure that the Marines lost sleep. The exasperated Americans listening to the peculiar *chug-chug* of their engines named these nocturnal pests "Washing-Machine Charlie" and "Louie the Louse."

When, early in October, coastwatchers reported a great increase in Japanese shipping in the Shortlands, Admiral Ghormley guessed that another offensive was cooking. He wanted to break it up, but only the B-17s had the endurance to carry bombs that far, and they rarely seemed able to hit a ship. Ghormley decided to take a crack at this target — even though it meant risking the only big flight deck in the South Pacific, *Hornet's*. She departed Nouméa 2 October, screened by four cruisers and six destroyers, wearing the flag of Rear Admiral George D. Murray, and launched two strikes against the Shortlands on the 5th; but foul weather so muffled the planes that not one scored. The only thing accomplished by this strike was to scare the enemy into dispersing his shipping, which made it harder to get at next time.

The deadlock still held.

---

[13] Admiral Fitch's Intelligence Summaries.

CHAPTER VII

Fighting along the Matanikau[1]

23 September–9 October 1942

THE 18th of September, when Admiral Turner brought in Colonel Sims's 7th Marine Regiment, was a big day for Vandegrift's men. Although they had given the Japs a thorough whipping on the Bloody Ridge only four days before, they wanted reinforcements badly, and the arrival of the 7th Marines made it possible to draw up a plan which the General called "active defense." It was now known that the enemy's strength lay west of the Matanikau River, in a part of Guadalcanal made to order for defense: steep, jungle-clad hills, kunai grass ridges commanding every approach, and deep woody ravines running down to the sea. As a "cross corridor" advance would be very expensive and probably unsuccessful against an enemy in such terrain, Vandegrift's staff planned an enveloping movement from the interior; this they planned to start promptly in order to keep the Japanese off balance. Edson, now Colonel of the 5th Marine Regiment, was in overall command.

This operation made a bad start, on 23 September. Lieutenant Colonel Lewis Puller's 1st Battalion of the 7th Marines was given the inland route along the slopes of a series of hills (Grassy Ridge or Mount Austen) six miles southwest of Henderson Field. The land, furrowed like a crumpled wad of foolscap and matted with jungle growth like barbed wire, slowed the men to an exhausting crawl and the Japs rushed down on them from Mount Austen.

[1] Sources: the Zimmerman and Miller monographs (see chap. iii footnote above); conversations with these gentlemen and with Colonel Griffith.

Unable to cross the Matanikau in the time allotted, Puller turned north to parallel the stream and reached the mouth at night on the 26th. The 1st Raider Battalion, now commanded by Lieutenant Colonel Griffith was sent upstream from the mouth of the river that day, to make a crossing at the Nippon Bridge. Lieutenant Colonel McDougal's 2nd Battalion 5th Marines was poised at the river mouth, ready to assist either of the others. Before the raiders reached the bridge the enemy, from the other side of a clearing, let loose a vicious fire which killed Major Kenneth Bailey, one of the heroes of the Bloody Ridge. The only way to get at the enemy was to mount a steep, jungle-clad hill which commanded his position. It was a tough, four-hour climb up the hill, and after reaching the top Griffith was severely wounded and the raiders were recalled to the mouth of the Matanikau. It was now 27 September.

In order to solve the impasse at the river, three companies of Puller's 1st Battalion under Major Otho L. Rogers embarked in Higgins boats the same day, to land west of Point Cruz where, owing to a garbled transmission by portable radio, they supposed Griffith to be. They landed after a rough trip dodging air bombs, but had advanced only a quarter of a mile when Japanese troops got between them and the beach and killed Major Rogers. The Marines deployed in a circle on a kunai-grass knoll to fend off attack from all directions, laying their undershirts on the ground to spell the word HELP. A friendly plane spotted the improvised ground panel and reported by radio to division headquarters, but a bomb had just plumped into headquarters and knocked out communications. Colonel Puller, suspecting that his men were in difficulties, boarded the destroyer *Monssen* at Kukum and steamed right over to Point Cruz that afternoon. When the beleaguered Marines sighted her, Sergeant Raysbrook stood in full view of the enemy and arm-signaled their situation to the ship. Puller ordered them to move down to the coast while *Monssen* covered their withdrawal with a naval barrage. The two companies fought their way to the beach and established a tight defense ring. A Coast Guard petty officer, Douglas A. Munro, led in from *Monssen* five

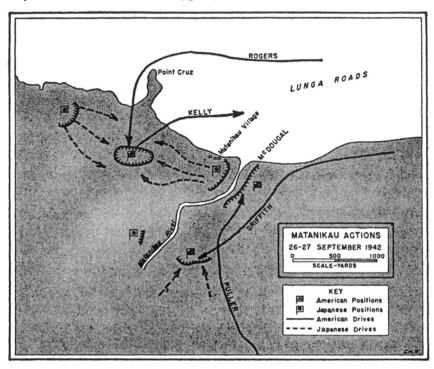

Higgins boats, occupying the Japs long enough with his two small
boat guns to get the Marines clear, and in so doing lost his own
life. Withering fire met the boats when they went in for a second
load, so Henderson Field sent an SBD to make a strafing run and
cover the retreat.

This four-day exchange of unpleasantries near the Matanikau
had cost the Marines 60 killed and 100 wounded, and gained nothing except experience. As one of the officers involved in it remarked to the writer, "high commanders of ground forces are apt
to lose their appreciation of time and distance; they forget how
long it takes a column to move over tortuous ground, to climb
rugged hills, and how long it takes for orders to be disseminated
to the echelons that do the fighting."

For the next ten days the Marines strung barbed wire, sowed
land mines and sited artillery in order to release men for a second

attempt to secure the Matanikau.[2] Six battalions were ordered to jump off on 8 October.

The Japanese chose the same day to start a similar drive, a warming-up for the monthly big show. General Hyakutake, in order to overwhelm the Marines, whose numbers he now estimated at 7500, reverted to his original plan of throwing in 25,000 men, including Lieutenant General Maruyama's 2nd Division. Part of another division was left at Rabaul in readiness to move into New Guinea as soon as Hyakutake should receive Vandegrift's surrender. His operation order even named the spot on the Matanikau where Vandegrift was to appear with a white flag on or about 15 October.[3]

"This is the decisive battle between Japan and the United States," read Maruyama's address to his troops on 1 October, "a battle in which the rise or fall of the Japanese Empire will be decided. If we do not succeed in the occupation of these islands, no one should expect to return to Japan alive." Apparently some of his men were becoming skeptical of this fanfaronade, judging from entries in captured Japanese diaries of a day or two later. For instance: "Where is the mighty power of the Imperial Navy? . . . The strength of the enemy is increasing . . . the morale of our forces is going down. . . . How long can we live on in this sort of a condition? When I think of it, the tears come out." [4]

The first step was to secure both banks of the Matanikau for the use of Maruyama's artillery. Colonel Nakaguma, commanding the 4th Infantry Regiment, brought his battalions into line on the west bank ready to thrust across the river in two prongs, one inland and the other along the beach. But the Marines took the initi-

[2] General Vandegrift's first intention was to drive the Japs beyond the Poha in order to protect Henderson Field from their artillery fire, but when advised of the impending enemy offensive, he revised his plans and decided to aim only at securing the east bank of the Matanikau. (Miller)

[3] Current rumor, to the effect that all surrendering Marines were to be taken to the Tenaru River and executed to wipe out the disgrace of that defeat, was intensely interesting to the Marines at the time; actually the Japanese issued no such order.

[4] Sopac Intelligence Center, translations of Japanese documents and a diary for 2 and 4 Oct.

ative. On 7 October two battalions of Colonel Edson's 5th Regiment swept forward along a front whose right flank rested on the shoreline. Before they reached the river they flushed an advance enemy force and backed it into the bend a few hundred yards upstream from the river mouth. The raiders were brought forward on the 8th to deal with this group. In the meantime Colonel Whaling's 3rd Battalion 2nd Marine Regiment marched upstream and bivouacked near the coconut-log Nippon Bridge.

During 8 October, a day of heavy rain, both sides were bogged down in jungle mud. At nightfall the Japs, cooped up on the east bank, came out of their foxholes screeching, shooting and hurling grenades, mauled the raiders severely in hand-to-hand fighting and broke through to a river sandspit where they were held up by a wire barricade and finally wiped out.

Vandegrift, seeing signs of the impending full-scale drive, decided to keep his reserves in the perimeter and ordered Edson to conclude his operation in a hurry. On 9 October, as the hot sun made the jungle steam and the Marines sweat, Whaling's battalion crossed Nippon Bridge and marched down the west bank unopposed. Lieutenant Colonel Hanneken's 2nd Battalion 7th Marines followed, pushed a little farther to the westward and then struck north to Matanikau Village on the coast. They too found no Nips. Where were they? Puller's battalion, which crossed third, probed along a trail about half a mile west of the river. As his men struggled over rugged ground they suddenly came upon two ravines filled with Nakaguma's troops, whose weapons enfiladed the coast road but afforded them no protection inland. Puller by radio asked Del Valle's artillery to lay down a barrage on a group directly in his path, and at the same time turned his own mortars on a group farther west. The resulting shower was more than Japanese flesh could bear. Panic-stricken soldiers scrambled wildly up the slopes, where Puller's machine-gunners sprayed them relentlessly, the survivors sliding back into the ravines to be chased up again by mortar and artillery fire. This grim routine continued until Puller had

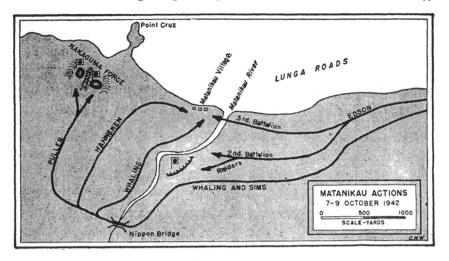

exhausted his ammunition and most of the human targets. A captured diary later revealed that 690 of Nakaguma's men had perished, most of them in the cul-de-sac.

Late in the afternoon of 9 October the attack force returned
to the American lines, having lost 65 killed and 125 wounded.
Vandegrift left his 5th Regiment guarding the east bank of the
lower Matanikau as the key to his western defenses, since the
shore road was the only possible approach for enemy tanks and
wheeled vehicles. His good judgment was later confirmed.

Across Ironbottom Sound, the 2nd Marine Regiment had been
enjoying a relatively quiet tour of duty on Tulagi. The only operation of consequence began on the same day as Puller's victory.
About 45 officers and men, under Lieutenant Colonel R. E.
("Bunker") Hill, were ferried to Aola Bay, Guadalcanal, 30 miles
east of Lunga Point where, in a two-day operation, they wiped out
a small Japanese base at the mouth of the Gurabusu River at small
cost to themselves. Vandegrift could now disregard any enemy
threat from the east.

Despite Nakaguma's reverses, Japanese preparations for the big
push continued. On 9 October General Hyakutake landed on

Guadalcanal to direct the campaign, and on the 11th ships came down the Slot carrying heavy artillery and protected by a covering group of heavy cruisers. But they encountered Task Force 64, commanded by Rear Admiral Norman Scott; and the ensuing Battle of Cape Esperance was one of the most interesting of the campaign.

CHAPTER VIII

The Battle of Cape Esperance[1]

11–12 October 1942

1. Looking for a Fight

THIS campaign of attrition was indecisive and unsatisfactory to both competitors in the bid for Guadalcanal supremacy. The American Navy in the South Pacific, still smarting from the sting of Savo Island and the loss of valuable carriers and destroyers, daily plagued by the submarine denizens of "Torpedo Junction,"[2] longed for active retaliation. The Marines, embittered by the nocturnal hammerings of the "Tokyo Express" and the apparent paucity of the supply and reinforcement effort, grew increasingly restive. On board Japanese ships and around their campfires there was an even stronger feeling of "On to Victory!" since they disliked war in less than blitz tempo. At the very depth of this winter of our discontent came the battle off Cape Esperance — which, if far short of glorious summer, gave the tired Americans a heartening victory and the proud Japanese a sound spanking.

Unwitting occasion of this naval battle was the 164th Infantry Regiment of the Americal Division, a former National Guard outfit from the Dakotas, now reinforced to about 2837 officers and

---

[1] At the time, called Second Battle of Savo Island, but after the number of "Savos" had got up to five each battle was officially assigned a distinctive name. The sources of this account are the Action Reports and War Diaries of American ships and commanders, and enemy reports procured by Lt. Cdr. Salomon in Tokyo.

[2] In the Pacific this term was used for that part of the Coral Sea between Espiritu Santo and the Solomons, which was patrolled by enemy submarines.

men. The 164th constituted the next echelon of reinforcement for the hard-pressed Marines. Admiral Ghormley, assuming that the Japanese would take a hostile view of the passage of this regiment from Nouméa to Lunga Point, marshaled naval forces to give them constant protection and cover.

The distant covering forces, three in number, consisted of Rear Admiral Murray's *Hornet* carrier group, Rear Admiral Lee's *Washington* group and Rear Admiral Norman Scott's cruiser group. It was this last on which fell the onus of blocking for Admiral Turner, who brought up the soldiers in *McCawley* and transport *Zeilin*, with eight destroyer-type escorts.

On 9 October this transport group sailed from Nouméa. Course was set to pass north of San Cristobal, head west through Lengo Channel and anchor in Lunga Roads on the morning of the 13th. Of the distant support forces, *Hornet* took station off Guadalcanal some 180 miles southwest of Henderson Field, *Washington* maneuvered about 50 miles east of Malaita, and Norman Scott's team (TF 64) was poised in the vicinity of Rennell Island. Admiral Scott,[3] flying his flag in *San Francisco*, considered himself lucky. He had orders from Admiral Ghormley to protect the convoy by offensive action, to "search for and destroy enemy ships and landing craft." It was the perfect assignment for an aggressive sailor. His staff was small and to his liking: four young and ambitious lieutenants.

Scott in three weeks had given his task force intensive training for night action, simulating battle conditions by keeping crews at stations from dusk to dawn; a Spartan procedure which taught them how to take it. He was ready to accept a night action, in which the enemy had hitherto shown superiority, and he intended

[3] Norman Scott of Indianapolis, born 1889, Naval Academy '11; outstanding service as "exec." of *Jacob Jones* when that ship was sunk by a U-boat in 1917; naval aide to the President; various C.O., gunnery and staff duties; instructor at Naval Academy and student at Naval War College; member of Naval mission to Brazil; C.O. of *Pensacola*; duty in office of C.N.O. 1941; where he "made things so miserable for everyone around him in Washington that he finally got what he wanted — sea duty" (Admiral Spruance); promoted Rear Admiral and commanded various task forces in the South Pacific, June 1942 to his death in action.

to be master of the situation. His scheme was to stay outside the enemy's air range until noon and then turn north to a position whence he could reach Savo Island before midnight. Scott, moreover, was one of the first task force commanders in the Pacific to enter combat with a carefully drawn battle plan. According to this plan his ships were to steam in column with destroyers both ahead and astern; destroyers were to illuminate with searchlight, fire torpedoes at large targets and guns at small targets; cruisers were to open fire whenever they saw a target without waiting for orders; cruiser planes would locate and illuminate the enemy with float lights; if the Japanese proved to be strong in destroyers, the force would be divided to reduce torpedo hazard.

On 9 and 10 October Admiral Scott made tentative advances toward Cape Esperance only to turn back when aërial reconnaissance reported no suitable targets.

Admiral Mikawa's scheme required that troops be landed off the northwestern cape of Guadalcanal every night, while the Marines were heckled with naval gunfire or aërial bombing. So far he had been successful: destroyers, carrying an average of 150 soldiers each, had on several occasions discharged as many as 900 men a night. But on the afternoon of 8 October, bombs from Henderson Field fliers derailed the "Express" so effectively that traffic down the Slot was snarled for twenty-four hours; but on the 9th, about midnight, *Tatsuta* and five destroyers landed General Hyakutake and troops at Tassafaronga, despite a bombing by American aircraft en route.[4]

These attacks by Henderson Field fliers sorely tried Admiral Mikawa's temper. He appealed to Vice Admiral Kusaka, Eleventh Air Fleet commander at Rabaul, to do something. Kusaka offered to neutralize Henderson Field on the 11th if Mikawa would run express that day, and he was as good as his word. On the afternoon of 11 October Henderson Field suffered a visitation of some 35 Japanese bombers protected by 30 fighters; but the former dumped their loads harmlessly in dense jungle and the latter shot down

---

[4] Japanese Naval War Diary and information from Capt. Omae in 1949.

only two American planes at a cost to themselves of 4 "Zekes" and 8 bombers. Yet they kept the American airmen so busy defending their base that Mikawa's southbound surface force was not molested.

Fortunately the long-legged patrol planes were not affected by this raid. It was a B–17 of Colonel L. G. Saunders's 11th Bombardment Group that first reported two cruisers and six destroyers tearing down the Slot. Two more air contacts were made that afternoon; at 1810, the enemy force was less than a hundred miles from Savo Island.

Admiral Scott received this intelligence eagerly. He signaled his approach order, and at 1600 throttlemen commenced building up speed to 29 knots. The enemy might reach Guadalcanal before midnight but Scott would be there first.

The search reports were correct as to enemy heading but short as to strength. Mikawa had sent a bombardment group consisting of heavy cruisers *Aoba, Kinugasa* and *Furutaka* (which we have already met off Savo Island) with two destroyers, and a reinforcement group, comprising seaplane carriers *Nisshin* and *Chitose* with six destroyers, to bring in troops and supplies.[5] The bombardment ships, like Scott's, had just completed several days' tactical and target practice in the Shortlands. Mikawa considered this a routine mission and let the cruiser division commander, Rear Admiral Goto, take the command.

Here is the Task Organization for each side: —

TASK FORCE 64, Rear Admiral Norman Scott

Heavy Cruisers

SAN FRANCISCO	Capt. Charles H. McMorris
SALT LAKE CITY	Capt. Ernest G. Small

Light Cruisers

BOISE	Capt. Edward J. Moran
HELENA	Capt. Gilbert C. Hoover

[5] Japanese Naval War Diary states midget submarines were in this group for supply purposes. Diary of a Jap officer in Annex J to Marine Report indicates that 150-mm howitzers were landed from the two tenders.

Destroyers, Capt. Robert G. Tobin (Comdesron 12)

FARENHOLT	Lt. Cdr. Eugene T. Seaward
BUCHANAN	Cdr. Ralph E. Wilson
LAFFEY	Lt. Cdr. William E. Hank
* DUNCAN	Lt. Cdr. Edmund B. Taylor
MCCALLA	Lt. Cdr. William G. Cooper

JAPANESE FORCES

Bombardment Group, * Rear Admiral Aritomo Goto (Comcrudiv 6)
Heavy Cruisers AOBA, KINUGASA, * FURUTAKA; Destroyers HATSUYUKI, * FUBUKI

Reinforcement Group, Rear Admiral Takaji Joshima (Comcardiv 11)
Seaplane Carriers CHITOSE, NISSHIN (carrying 728 Army personnel, 2 field guns, 4 howitzers, 4 tractors, 1 AA gun, ammunition, miscellaneous equipment, medical supplies, and six landing craft) [6]

Destroyers AKIZUKI, ASAGUMO, * NATSUGUMO, YAMAGUMO, * MURAKUMO, SHIRAYUKI

2. *Crossing the "T," 2100–2400*

On board Scott's speeding vessels sunset was marked by bugles and boatswain's pipes, followed by "All hands man your battle stations!" Sailors moved to their action posts on the double. Steel doors clanged shut. Over the complex telephone circuits reports streamed to the department heads, and from them to the quiet bridges: —

"Bridge! Bat Two, manned and ready for General Quarters."

"Bridge! Gunnery Department, manned and ready for General Quarters."

"Bridge! Damage Control, manned and ready for General Quarters, Condition Zed set throughout the ship."

"Bridge! Engineer Department, manned and ready for General Quarters, Condition Zed set. Boilers 1, 2, 3 (etc.) on the line."

As the tropical darkness shut down, Admiral Scott swept his eyes upward and around the horizon. Sky slightly overcast; the sliver of a new moon just setting; a smooth sea ruffled gently by

---

* Sunk or killed in this battle; *Natsugumo* and *Murakumo* by air attack 12 October.

[6] "Professional notebook of an Ensign in the Japanese Navy," JICPOA Item No. 4986, and "Japanese Carrier Achievements," WDC 161,709. Several of the landing craft were "Special Type," possibly a code name for midget submarines.

a 14-knot southeast breeze, a dark horizon brightened at intervals by flashes of distant lightning . . . Good weather for surprise. He knew his radar would be handicapped by the proximity of land, but the enemy had no radar. On the other side of the world, at New York and Norfolk, mighty forces were starting for North Africa. They had so much and he so little! Well, he'd show those fat boys of the Atlantic Fleet that Sopac could win victories "on a shoestring."

The Americans approached wide around the western coast of Guadalcanal. Shortly after 2100 course was changed from NNW to N. Half an hour later speed was reduced to 25 knots, then to 20. High on cruiser catapults pilots and crewmen groped in the darkness readying planes for launching. Scott, knowing what Mikawa had done at Savo Island, intended to employ his four Kingfishers to track the enemy. Two of the planes swooshed down the catapult tracks and flew off into the night, but *Salt Lake City* lost hers through the accidental ignition of aircraft flares in the fuselage, and *Helena* never got the word to launch and so dumped hers right overboard as an inflammable hazard. At 2228, Cape Esperance bearing SE by E distant 14 miles, Scott headed for sinister Savo, intending to skirt the coast and "contact the enemy, if possible, before he could effect a landing, but at any rate to contact him."

When the *Salt Lake* plane took its fiery plunge, Admiral Goto's bombardment group was more than 50 miles northwest of Scott's. His heavy cruisers were in column, with one destroyer on each beam of the leading flagship; the disposition was set up like a giant "T" rushing head-foremost down the Slot at 26 knots. His sailors were so preoccupied with navigating those black waters and with preparations for the bombardment that, when vigilant lookouts sighted the far-distant glare of the burning American plane, all brains on the flag bridge assumed it to be a signal from the beachhead or from the seaplane carriers. They answered with blinker, too dim for the Americans to see. Lack of reply made some of the officers suspicious, but Goto continued to flash his signal searchlights, hoping to lure away from the landing area any American forces that might be about. He did not really expect an attack. It was Savo Island again but in reverse; aircraft again gave the warning but this time it was the Japanese who brushed it off.

At 2228, as we have seen, Admiral Scott changed course to head directly for Savo Island. Seven minutes later he ordered his ships to execute the battle plan and form single column. Destroyers *Farenholt, Duncan* and *Laffey* were in the van; cruisers *San Francisco, Boise, Salt Lake City* and *Helena* in the center; destroyers *Buchanan* and *McCalla* in the rear.[7]

Entering a night sea battle is an awesome business. The enveloping darkness, hiding the enemy's agents of destruction, seems a living thing, malignant and oppressive; hardened "shellback" and timid "pollywog" alike hate to fight blind.[8] Swishing water at bow and stern mark an inexorable advance toward an unknown destiny. Men speak seldom and then only in short, clipped sentences. The gunners who perpetually fiddle with the complicated mechanism of their pieces, the navigators pricking off chart positions and the engineers manipulating valves are gratefully occupied, but hundreds just stand at battle stations and think long thoughts. Each sailor looks at his nearest shipmate, saying with his eyes, "What is going to happen? What will I be required to do? How well will I do it?"

In the American task force there was a slackening of taut nerves when *San Francisco's* spotting plane sent in a radio report at 2250: "One large, two small vessels, one six miles from Savo off northern beach, Guadalcanal. Will investigate closer." At last! Something for a man to put his teeth into. But Admiral Scott was not sure. Were all these ships together? Might they not be friendly craft? If unfriendly, where were the remaining Japanese ships reported that afternoon?

[7] Distance between cruisers 600 yards, between destroyers 500 yards, between types, 700 yards.
[8] Later in the war, radar repeating screens (P.P.I.) in various key positions in the ship gave them cats' eyes and whiskers and dissipated the instinctive fear of what darkness might conceal.

Actually, the ships sighted by the cruiser plane were of Joshima's reinforcement group, within Savo Sound. Goto's fighting ships were at this time thirty miles northwest of Cape Esperance.

Scott, fearing lest his course take him dangerously close to the shore, ordered column left to NE to pass six miles to the westward of Savo Island. His intention was to locate that large enemy force. Failing in that, he would go in after the small fry off Cape Esperance.

As the column-left was executed at 2308, there was still no definite contact with the enemy by Scott's ships. At 2325 the first radar waves bounced off a Japanese hull and back to *Helena*, who was equipped with the new SG search radar.[9] The target bore 315 degrees, distant 27,700 yards. An early plot of this "ship" separated into three, moving southeast at 20 knots.

Unfortunately, flagship *San Francisco*, equipped with radar of an earlier eccentric type, the SC, was unable to duplicate *Helena's* interesting finds; and *Helena* did not report her contacts for fifteen minutes. Furthermore, Admiral Scott knew that the Japanese had radar receivers capable of detecting his SC transmissions and so could track any ship making them; accordingly he had forbidden the use of SC radar in his force. And the flagship's gunnery radars, supposedly covering the 180-degree sector ahead, failed to pick up the enemy three points forward of the port beam. Nor did *Boise's* spotting plane help, since engine trouble forced it down near Savo Island at 2330. The only "hot" intelligence that reached Scott was an amplifying report from *San Francisco's* search plane at 2330, to the effect that the "one large and two small vessels" previously reported had now moved 16 miles eastward along Guadalcanal. These, again, were Joshima's, not Goto's ships that Scott was seeking.

Scott weighed the evidence and decided to continue covering the passage between Savo Island and Cape Esperance. In so doing,

---

[9] SG radar was just putting in its appearance in the Fleet. It became a scourge of the enemy, but *Helena* and *Boise* were the only ships in Scott's force so equipped, and few commanders as yet realized its potentialities.

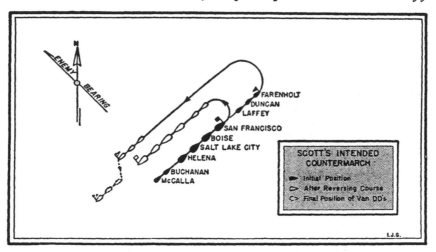

he should intercept either the force approaching or the other one retiring along Guadalcanal. To do either, he must now reverse course. His signal to countermarch, "Left to course 230 degrees!" went out over voice radio a few seconds after 2330. In this maneuver the cruisers, led by the flagship, reverse course by column movement, the rear destroyers follow in the same water as the cruisers, but the van destroyers make a separate column movement and then increase speed to resume their former positions in the van. There was nothing unusual in ordering this somewhat complicated procedure; but in close proximity to the enemy (of which Scott was ignorant) the execution of it very nearly cost him the ensuing battle.

At 2332 the signal was executed, *San Francisco* starting her wide turn to the left, followed by *Boise, Salt Lake City, Helena* and the two rear destroyers. Captain Robert G. Tobin, squadron commander in *Farenholt,* led his three van destroyers in a separate column movement, slowed down to make sure that it was proceeding according to book, then increased speed and came up on the starboard side of the cruiser column.

For ten minutes after the countermarch, *Helena's* SG radar tracked the suspected enemy; then Captain Hoover, certain of his analysis, informed the task force commander of a target six miles away "bearing 285 degrees." This was disturbing news to Scott. His flagship had no radar contacts. Captain Tobin's destroyers were somewhere out in the darkness, not yet back in column. *Boise,* who had detected the enemy group at 2338, contributed to Scott's bewilderment by reporting five "bogies" bearing 65 degrees relative, 295 degrees true. Now, "bogey" meant unidentified *aircraft;* but *Boise* meant to say unidentified *ships;* the Admiral guessed she did but was not certain. And several of his commanding officers missed a few words of the message, receiving the bearing merely as "65 degrees." Did that mean a true compass bearing or relative to the course of the cruiser — a difference of some 130 degrees? With the bearing understood as true, the message made no sense compared with *Helena's;* both cruisers' radars might be merely recording Tobin's destroyers. *Boise's* contacts might be either surface or air, either on the port quarter or the starboard bow.[10]

The first step in clarification must be to locate Tobin. Scott voiced a query to the squadron commander, "Are you taking station ahead?" Captain Tobin, aware that his three destroyers were in a dangerous and awkward position, attempted to dispel doubt by replying: "Affirmative. Coming up on your starboard side."[11] *Farenholt* by that time was abreast the center of the cruiser column. But, unknown to Tobin, *Duncan* was no longer astern of him. She alone of the destroyers had recorded suspicious indications to the westward with her fire control radar, just before the countermarch, and when the course change was more than half completed these contacts strengthened and closed to four miles' range. *Duncan's* skipper saw *Farenholt* apparently steady on a westerly course and assumed that Tobin had seen what he saw and was closing to attack. He bent on 30 knots and pointed *Duncan's* bow in the direction of the radar contacts. The third destroyer, *Laffey,* observed *Duncan's* aberration but steadied her

---

[10] At a later date the word "skunk" was used to mean "unidentified surface radar contact" and true bearings became compulsory in radio reports.
[11] *Salt Lake City* Action Report.

helm and followed *Farenholt*.[12] Admiral Scott's concern for his destroyers was amply warranted.

By fifteen minutes before midnight his four cruisers with destroyers *Buchanan* and *McCalla* were in column on the new southwesterly course (230°) at 20 knots; *Farenholt* was on a parallel course about 800 yards to starboard with *Laffey* closing from astern; *Duncan* was charging in to attack the enemy singlehanded. *San Francisco* had just made her first radar contact bearing 300 degrees distant 5000 yards — was it the enemy or one of Tobin's destroyers?

There was no doubt in the minds of *Helena's* gunners. Their new SG radar persistently tracked the original contacts. With the range down to 5000 yards, word reached the bridge: "Ships Visible to the Naked Eye." Now the old communications jinx bedeviled Scott's task force. On the voice radio, Captain Hoover broadcast a two-word signal, "Interrogatory Roger," which meant "Request Permission to Open Fire." [13] It so happened that the code word "Roger" was employed also to acknowledge receipt of a voice transmission, and on the flag bridge of *San Francisco* Hoover's question was interpreted as a mere request for acknowledgment of a previous message. So Scott answered, "Roger," intending to indicate "Message Received." But an unqualified "Roger" also meant "Commence Firing!" To be certain, Captain Hoover repeated his inquiry and received the same one-word response. It was a sardonic paradox of the signal book that both Scott and Hoover were correct, yet victims of a word owning several meanings. Captain Hoover, however, extracted from "Roger" the meaning he wanted and at 2346 *Helena* opened fire with her 6-inch main battery and her 5-inch guns also.

While Scott was trying to resolve these various perplexities, his

[12] *Laffey* and her records were lost in the Battle of Guadalcanal, 13 Nov. 1942. Her actions have been reconstructed with the assistance of Cdr. W. T. Doyle, her former executive officer, and Lt. Cdr. A. H. Damon, officer of the deck during the battle.

[13] Scott intended that his captains open fire without orders, but his pre-battle memorandum was not clear on this point. Also, with friendly destroyers in the line of fire, it was prudent for any captain to request permission before shooting.

Japanese counterpart remained oblivious to everything except the execution of his bombardment mission. The Americans need not have fretted about radar-controlled torpedo attacks or interception of radar transmissions. Admiral Goto had no radar and never suspected the proximity of enemy forces. He was almost precisely in the situation of the American cruisers on the other side of Savo Island two months earlier: telltale warnings discounted, all guns secured fore and aft, ignorant there was a battle on until hit. And *Helena's* first salvo, or perhaps her second, hit and hit hard.

The other ships were quick to follow suit. *Salt Lake City*, her 8-inch sights laid on an enemy cruiser broad on her starboard bow and only 4000 yards distant, was only seconds behind *Helena* with gunfire and star shell, and one Japanese ship was only seconds behind her, getting a hit on *Salt Lake* that killed several men. *Boise*, next ahead, laid her 6-inch guns on the cruiser column while her anti-aircraft batteries barked at destroyer *Hatsuyuki* on the left flank. *San Francisco* picked on a cruiser which her lookouts reported 4800 yards distant. The destroyers, too, were quick to fire. *Farenholt*, with friendly cruiser shells screaming overhead, concentrated on the enemy column. *Laffey*, caught in the line of cruiser fire, went emergency full speed astern and turned hard left, intending to fall in astern of *Helena*. Three of her 5-inch guns raked *Aoba* while a fourth lighted the Japs with star shell. *Duncan* on her lone assault found herself less than a mile from the Japanese, enemy ships closing her rapidly and on both sides. Her skipper, Lieutenant Commander Taylor, maneuvered desperately to avoid friendly gunfire and unmask his torpedo batteries. Swinging right, he recognized *Furutaka* by her slender No. 2 stack. The cruiser, too, turned right and in so doing opened range, which was not to Taylor's taste; he ordered hard left rudder to pursue, pumped several gun salvos into *Furutaka* and then shifted fire to an enemy destroyer, probably *Hatsuyuki*. *Duncan* was now in a precarious position in the line of fire between the two forces, as a shell-hit in No. 1 fireroom indicated.

It still lacked 13 minutes of midnight. Admiral Scott now made

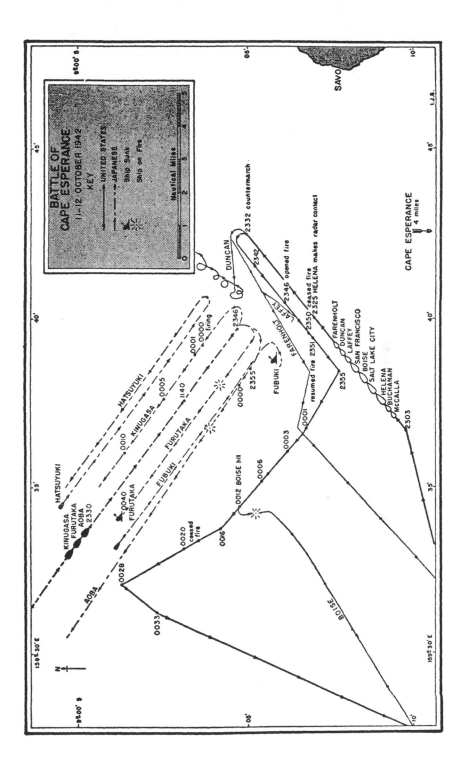

BATTLE OF
CAPE ESPERANCE
11-12 OCTOBER 1942
KEY
⟶ UNITED STATES
---- JAPANESE
Ship Sunk
Ship on Fire
Nautical Miles
0 1 2 3 4 5

SAVO

CAPE ESPERANCE
4 miles

DUNCAN

2332 countermarch
2342
2346 opened fire
2350 ceased fire
2325 HELENA makes radar contact
FARENHOLT
DUNCAN
LAFFEY
SAN FRANCISCO
BOISE
SALT LAKE CITY
HELENA
BUCHANAN
MCCALLA
2303
2355
2351 resumed fire
0001
0003
0006
0012 BOISE hit
0016
0020 ceased fire
0028
0033
BOISE

LAFFEY
FARENHOLT
FUBUKI
2355
0000
0001
2346
FUBUKI
FURUTAKA
0000
1140
KINUGASA 0005
0010
0000 firing
0001
HATSUYUKI
0040 FURUTAKA
FURUTAKA
FUBUKI
AOBA
HATSUYUKI
KINUGASA
FURUTAKA
AOBA
2330
N

a serious mistake, from the best of motives. Convinced, by the position of his destroyers, by the deceptive similarity of silhouettes and (on the negative side) by lack of radar intelligence, that his cruisers were firing on American destroyers, he ordered Cease Firing at 2347, only one minute after *Helena* had fired her first salvo. But the gods were laughing at both sides that night. Fantastic as it may seem, the startled and confused Japanese Admiral fumbled to a similar conclusion — that he was being shot at by the Japanese Supply Force! He ordered a column movement to the right. Seconds later he was mortally wounded by one of an avalanche of shells exploding around *Aoba's* bridge.

Little could Goto have done to extricate his ships. Scott had inadvertently achieved the classic crossing of the "T" — enabling his guns to enfilade an enemy unable in that position to fight back. Goto's column movement unmasked his own gun batteries but permitted the Americans to concentrate on each ship in succession as it approached the knuckle of white water at the turning point. Nor did Scott's order to stop shooting save the enemy. *Aoba* and *Furutaka* were now burning from numerous hits and the enthusiastic American gunners were slow to comply with their Admiral's command; some never did. Scott repeated the unpopular order several times and personally visited the bridge of *San Francisco* to insure compliance by his own flagship. Then by voice radio he asked Tobin the vital question, "How are you?" Tobin replied that he was all right and was taking his ships up ahead on the starboard side. Scott, still not satisfied, wanted to know if his cruisers had been shooting at Tobin's destroyers. The squadron commander replied, "I don't know who you were firing at." Still uncertain, Scott ordered Tobin's three ships to flash their battle recognition lights. Lights green over green over white in a vertical position flickered momentarily to starboard. Satisfied at last — and four minutes had elapsed — Scott at 2351 ordered Resume Firing.

During this four-minute partial lull in American shooting, the surprised and uncertain Japanese returned a desultory and ineffective fire. *Aoba* with difficulty negotiated a 180-degree right turn.

Furutaka, caught with several salvos at the turning point, staggered drunkenly in *Aoba's* wake, turrets and torpedo tubes immobilized by American shellfire. Captain Masao Sawa of *Kinugasa* unwittingly turned left in the wrong direction, thereby saving his ship. So did destroyer *Hatsuyuki*.

When Admiral Goto was mortally wounded the command devolved upon his senior staff officer, Captain Kikunori Kijima. The effects of surprise were now wearing off. It would be only a few moments before the astonished Japanese would bare their fangs and strike.

A hit in *Duncan's* fireroom was probably the first serious one received by any United States ship, and she collected plenty more; a second hit knocked out the gun director, but *Duncan* continued to shoot on local control and launched one torpedo at *Furutaka*. The torpedo officer, Lieutenant (jg) Robert L. Fowler USNR, was mortally wounded, but Chief Torpedoman Boyd quickly aimed and fired another torpedo at the cruiser. *Duncan* sailors reported seeing *Furutaka* "crumble in the middle, then roll over and disappear." [14] Unfortunately, this was an illusion and the same salvo that felled Lieutenant Fowler knocked over the forward stack and started a fire in the No. 2 ammunition handling room. The skipper, acutely conscious of his situation, turned on battle recognition lights. It was too late. Another salvo, probably American, put lights and ship out of action. [15]

Farenholt was hit about the same time as *Duncan*, two shots exploding in the rigging to pepper the superstructure with a hail of jagged fragments. Shortly thereafter her hull was hit. A gaping hole just above the waterline flooded gun plot, destroying communications and gunfire control wiring. Another shot pierced the

[14] *Duncan* Action Report; timing of events based on memory of survivors. The observations of her men were typical of the distorted impressions received by individuals in all ships. What these sailors saw may have been destroyer *Fubuki*, may have been an illusion concocted of darkness, smoke, fire and supersensitive imagination. *Furutaka*, although hit in the forward engine room at 2354, did not go down until 0228, long after the battle's end.

[15] A post-battle inspection of *Duncan* revealed hits on both port and starboard sides, the majority entering from port. *Kinugasa* claimed sinking a destroyer at 2354, which may have been *Duncan*.

forward fireroom, releasing a cloud of scalding steam which drove the crew topside. Since these hits were on the port side, away from the enemy, and were recorded as "apparently 6-inch" it seems regrettably certain that *Farenholt* too was the victim of American gunfire.[16]

When Captain "Soc" McMorris of *San Francisco* received Admiral Scott's orders to resume fire, the attention of his lookouts and gunners was attracted by an unidentified warship steaming a parallel course only three quarters of a mile to the westward. This strange craft flashed a combination of red and white lights, signaled indistinguishable characters for a minute or two and then turned right. The cruiser snapped open searchlight shutters and disclosed the typical latticework foremast and white-banded second stack of destroyer *Fubuki*. All Scott's ships assaulted *Fubuki* so fiercely that she stopped dead, exploded and sank at about 2353.

Admiral Scott, now rid of uncertainty and furiously eager to let no enemy escape, at 2355 swung his column to the northwest to parallel the Japanese. During this course change two or three shells nicked *Boise* but did little damage. She, *Salt Lake City* and *Helena* were tracking targets, and shooting, but it is now impossible to tell which enemy vessels were favored by their attentions. *Buchanan* and *McCalla*, the rear destroyers, pulled into range of the same highly attractive targets. Commander Wilson of the former "shot the works," a steady stream of 5-inch bullets and five torpedoes; Lieutenant Commander Cooper of *McCalla* sighted *Aoba* and *Furutaka* burning, their guns still trained amidships, and slugged away at them with his main battery. At 2354 a torpedo from either *Buchanan* or *Duncan* struck *Furutaka's* forward engine room but failed to sink or even to stop her. *Laffey* fired no torpedoes during the battle but was one of those that ganged up on *Fubuki* and, after she sank, chased destroyer *Hatsuyuki* out of sight with gunfire.

[16] *Farenholt* Action Report. Comdesron 12 Action Report. The reports conflict as to times.

3. *Flareback, 0000–0245*

Precisely at midnight Admiral Scott ordered all ships to cease firing. It appeared to him that "some shaking down was necessary in order to continue our attack successfully." Again, a number of gunnery officers and gunners turned deaf ears to this order. All ships were directed to flash recognition lights and form column. All complied excepting crippled *Farenholt* and *Duncan*, and the stern chase commenced.

Sunday the 11th ended unhappily for the Imperial Navy. Cruiser *Furutaka* crawled toward her grave 22 miles northwest of Savo Island. A swirl of bubbling water and a few floating survivors were all that remained of destroyer *Fubuki*. Cruiser *Aoba* was on fire. Cruiser *Kinugasa* and destroyer *Hatsuyuki*, the only whole survivors, were in flight. Admiral Goto was dying. And seven undamaged American ships, led by a purposeful admiral, were intent on making 12 October memorable for something besides Columbus Day. But the Japanese were still full of fight. At the same instant that Scott ordered his formation to cease firing, *Kinugasa* opened up on the American cruisers 8000 yards to the southward. Sailors in the American flagship had an unwanted thrill when a typical Japanese tight salvo pattern straddled their wake. *Boise* had another when torpedoes launched by the enemy cruiser at 0001 were spotted on a collision course. Sailors below decks, informed of the torpedoes' approach, sweated the seconds out while Captain "Mike" Moran ordered hard right rudder and successfully combed the wakes.

After this skillful maneuver *Boise* returned to column. Shortly thereafter her radar gave notice of a target just abaft the starboard beam. *Boise* directed a searchlight at it and quickly opened gunfire, but the light gave her position away and the enemy ship, probably *Aoba*, returned fire with good effect, puncturing *Boise's* hull in four places. At the same time, *Kinugasa* found the American searchlight a superb point of aim, and for three minutes *Boise* was given a demonstration of accurate Japanese gunnery. Near-misses closely bracketed her and two 8-inch hits inflicted cruel damage; the enemy had her in a groove. She was only saved by *Salt Lake City*, the next ship astern, turning right deliberately and interposing herself between the burning *Boise* and the enemy. A courageous move, this, on the part of Captain Small; foolhardy, some would call it — but he silenced one of the ships that was pounding *Boise* and gave Moran a chance to turn hard left at 0012 and pull free.

San Francisco, like *Boise*, first fired at a target some 7000 yards away until her gunners, through the smoke, briefly sighted and attacked *Kinugasa* with radar-controlled gunfire. *Aoba*, too, was roughly handled by the American cruisers, collecting some 40 hits; but *Furutaka* was still under way, although listing heavily to port; *Hatsuyuki* was scarcely touched. After *Boise* left the formation, *Salt Lake* continued her duel with *Kinugasa* until 0016 with no great damage to either. That Japanese cruiser received only four hits during the battle; *Salt Lake* was hit twice but fortunately the enemy ammunition was not up to snuff; armor turned one 8-inch shell away and the other exploded with a low order of detonation in a fireroom, killing one man and starting an oil fire that did extensive damage to electrical equipment.

In this furious night clash there were few men who could qualify as spectators only. None of our ships were air-conditioned and ventilation was nil with Condition Zed set; temperature below rose to over 150° F. and sailors working in closed compartments heard little and saw less. Men on darkened bridges were too engrossed in keeping station on the black loom of ships ahead — no easy task this, to apprehend a sudden speed and course change through the blinding flash and smoke of forward guns. Gun control crews, like men with tunnel vision, saw only the target under fire, viewing it down a long lane of tracers. The gunners themselves kept their eyes on dial, valve or powder case; each team member had a single special function. But as the battle reached its climax two men in *San Francisco's* scout plane saw the whole thing as a panorama. The pilot, Lieutenant John A. Thomas, flew over the antagonists where his flares and float lights could be used if requested. He reported his presence, inquired in which direction the Americans were firing and circled to await orders. Against an ocean glistening with a delicate sheen from star shell, he saw red ribbons of tracer fire, the white thin cones of searchlight beams, the sullen red glow of hits, the multicolored fountains raised by shell splashes, more beautiful than any *grandes eaux* of a princely park. Then *Boise's* punishment began. A massive orange blossom of flame arose from her, unfolding as it flew skyward. Good-by *Boise*, thought Lieutenant Thomas.

Boise was indeed in dire peril. One 8-inch shell had penetrated No. 1 turret, exploding within and setting fire to the gun chamber. Another had entered the hull nine feet below the waterline to detonate in a forward 6-inch magazine. Blast, penetrating all the forward magazines, propelled flames and gas up through the handling rooms and two forward turrets. Magazine and handling-room crews were wiped out, to a man. The flames, gaining access to the forecastle through the turret openings, scorched more men to death and enclosed the entire forward part of the ship. Captain Moran gave the order to flood forward magazines, but the men at the flood control panel were dead. It seemed even to him that his ship was lost; at any moment the tons of explosives in magazines would destroy her like Britain's ill-fated battle cruiser *Hood*.[17] But the "luck of the Irish" prevailed. Enemy shell had so ripped *Boise's* hull that sea water did what dead men could not do; it flooded her magazines and quenched the flames. Even so, she was definitely out of the fight.

By 0020 fire had ceased. During the last of it, other ships had strayed from the column to avoid torpedo wakes. Admiral Scott, fearing lest those in the rear mistake *San Francisco* for the enemy, terminated the pursuit at 0028 by changing course from NW to SSW, and set about collecting his flock. Most ships answered and indicated their positions by flashing recognition lights, but re-

[17] See Vol. I of this History p. 64.

peated calls by voice radio got no reply from *Boise, Farenholt* or *Duncan.* Destroyer *McCalla* was ordered to assist them.

Shortly after his last change of course the Admiral warned "Stand by for further action. The show may not be over." But over it was.

By 0100 *Helena, Laffey* and *Buchanan* were back in formation with the flagship. *Boise,* although trailing streamers of flame from her devastated bow, lost little speed. Her retirement was made good at 20 knots while damage control parties wrestled with the double problem of mastering both fire and flooding. By 0240 all fires were out, shaky bulkheads were shored, underwater holes stuffed with bedding, submersible pumps chuffing effectively. Captain Moran eased his ship into column astern of *San Francisco,* justly proud of his crew's magnificent damage-control effort. But she had lost 107 officers and men, and 35 more were wounded.

Farenholt, damaged in the first minutes of the action, was handicapped by flooding through shell holes on the waterline. By pumping oil and water and shifting topside weights, the crew listed the ship nine degrees to starboard, which brought the holes clear of water. Inclined to this jaunty angle, *Farenholt* scampered out of the battle zone at 20 knots, escorted by the newly arrived destroyer *Aaron Ward.*

With day at hand Admiral Scott called for and received air coverage from Rear Admiral Fitch's land-based aircraft, a wise but unneeded precaution. As no Japanese planes appeared, he set about recovering cruiser planes from Tulagi, and escorting cripples.

4. *Loss of* DUNCAN

Duncan had but a few hours left of life's fitful fever. The details of her death struggle had no influence on the battle but we shall tell them as an example of what destroyer sailors did and suffered that night, and on many other nights.

She had been out of action since the beginning of the engagement. One shellburst killed everyone in the charthouse. Fragments from another slew men on both the bridge and the gun-director platform. The main radio, coding, radar plotting, gunnery plotting and interior communications rooms were demolished. Forward fireroom, damaged by a previous hit, was the goal of another shell. This additional havoc, added to fires already raging on the forecastle, turned the forward third of the ship into a white-hot caldron. The starboard wing of the bridge was isolated by fires forward and aft and to port and below, and the fires were closing in on it. Lieutenant Commander Taylor, after trying in vain to communicate with the after part of his ship, ordered bridge abandoned by the only possible route, over the side and into the water. *Duncan* still had way on, steaming in aimless circles at about 15 knots, when the wounded were lowered into the water and the able-bodied followed. From a life raft Taylor watched his ship steam away, uncontrolled and deadly.

There were still plenty of men on board. Gunners had continued to shoot the after guns until targets disappeared out of sight and range. Ensign Frank A. Andrews had then left his gun for the after conning station and established communication with the engineer officer, Lieutenant Herbert R. Kabat, now senior officer on board. Andrews and Chief Torpedoman Boyd attempted to beach the ship on Savo Island, then gave up the idea when diminishing fires suggested that the ship might be saved.

The crew made a game fight and might have succeeded but for the spread of the conflagration below decks. Men were gradually driven from the forward engine room. The after fireroom was unable to obtain needed boiler feed-water. Steam pressure dropped rapidly. Without steam, no power; without power, no pumps. Lieutenant (jg) Wade H. Coley USNR and Chief Watertender A. H. Holt attempted to run a boiler on sea water pumped in by a gasoline hand-billy. It was no use. Cold water boiled into steam and backed up into the pump. The medical officer made his way through heavy smoke toward sick bay to get a few needed drugs, and disappeared. One group of men in the flaming midships section dropped over the side, watched the ship slow to a stop, then swam back to assist in the fire fighting.

Heroic efforts were not enough and at 0200, with flames swarming over the topsides and ammunition exploding, *Duncan* was abandoned. Life jackets, floats, empty powder cans, any and every buoyant material were pressed into service to keep the survivors floating. During the remaining hours of darkness the swimmers unhappily watched the explosions of their beloved ship.

At the time of abandonment, *McCalla* was in the vicinity searching for *Boise*. Lieutenant Commander Cooper made a wary approach on a burning wreck so shrouded with fire and smoke that she was hard to identify. At 0300 a boat was lowered with a party, under the executive officer, which boarded the ship and made a cursory examination. The "exec" thought she could be saved and for two hours his men tried. *McCalla* in the meantime was looking for *Boise* and did not return until daybreak. She then fished the waters to the west of Savo Island, competing with sharks for human lives.[18] The sharks, lured by the bright aluminum powder cans serving as lifebuoys, were slashing viciously at the helpless human bait. *McCalla* sailors drove off several of the brutes with rifle fire. The result of their rescue effort was most gratifying: 195 officers and men from *Duncan* recovered, as against 48 lost.[19]

Salvage efforts by *McCalla's* men were not successful. Shortly before noon progressive flooding got *Duncan* down to main-deck level, the salvage party abandoned her and she sank, six miles north of Savo Island.

5. Scott's Score

Destroyer *Hatsuyuki* stood by *Furutaka* until she went down, and cruisers *Aoba* and *Kinugasa* retired up New Georgia Sound,

---

[18] The waters around Savo Island were infested with sharks because the natives for generations had been in the habit of setting their dead adrift.

[19] *McCalla* Report of Rescue of *Duncan* Survivors. The casualties of *Duncan* are only rough guesses by her skipper.

the 40 hits on *Aoba* no deterrent to high speed. Captain Kijima told the expiring Admiral Goto that he could die happy because two United States heavy cruisers had been sunk. The Orientals were miserably apprehensive of an American air attack at daybreak, and at 0700 it came; but the planes from Henderson Field failed to make a hit. By mid-morning the three surviving ships were anchored off Shortland Island. *Kinugasa* returned to action within twenty-four hours; *Aoba* went home for major repairs; *Hatsuyuki* had suffered only minor damage.

While Admiral Goto fought, Admiral Joshima landed men, stores and 150-mm guns from his Reinforcement Group, near Kokumbona. At 0230 the drifting float plane that belonged to *Boise* sighted these ships steaming swiftly out of the Sound. Destroyers *Shirayuki* and *Murakumo* returned to recover survivors from Goto's group, rescued 400 Japanese from the water, but broke off when an American destroyer hove into sight. They tried to entice the American into a chase within range of Japanese aircraft, but got a reverse twist on that. *Murakumo*, while jammed with survivors, became a victim of Henderson Field dive-bombers and fighters and had to be scuttled. Relief destroyer *Natsugumo* later in the day suffered a similar fate from the weapons of these same aviators. The only countermove of the Japanese on the 12th was an unsuccessful effort of submarine *I–2* to attack *McCalla*, still scouring the waters north of Savo for signs of life. At 1430 this destroyer sighted a large cluster of close-shaven Japanese heads. Lines were thrown to the enemy sailors but they preferred sharks to survival. *McCalla* men forcibly captured three struggling samples; minesweepers *Hovey* and *Trever*, out from Tulagi, snared 108 more unwilling Nips on the 13th.

Captain Kijima, O.T.C. of the Japanese Bombardment Group after the death of Goto, wished he had shared the Admiral's fate. Despite his claim of having sunk two heavy cruisers and one destroyer, he was promptly relieved by order of Admiral Mikawa. He and his fellow officers had reason to lose face. Proceeding as they were on an offensive mission, they should have been reason-

ably alert. They would have been annihilated, except for the confusion caused by Scott's countermarch and *Kinugasa's* wrong but
lucky turn to the north.

Admiral Scott, on the contrary, became the hero of the South
Pacific during the short month that remained of his valiant life.
The Navy in general, misled by overoptimistic reports of commanding officers in accepting a score of four cruisers and four
destroyers sunk, regarded Cape Esperance as adequate revenge for
Savo Island. As West Coast yards were crowded, Captain Moran
was ordered to bring *Boise* to Philadelphia for repairs. There she
was accorded an enthusiastic welcome — unfortunately marred by
a journalist's nickname of this gallant cruiser as the "one-ship task
force," grossly unfair to other participants whose names were
withheld for security reasons. *Salt Lake City* was repaired at Pearl
Harbor before going on to greater glory in the Aleutians.

Norman Scott fought the Battle of Cape Esperance with a cool,
determined courage. Despite the trouble caused by an intricate
countermarch, he never let the situation deteriorate into a mêlée.
His ignorance of the varying capabilities of different types of radar
was almost universal in the United States Navy in 1942. Later
commanders learned that proper use of radar could eliminate the
searchlights and recognition lights which attracted enemy gunfire
as a candle attracts moths.[20]

Unfortunately, because it is human to conclude that the result
justifies the means, some fallacious conclusions were drawn from
this battle. Thus, Scott was convinced that his long single-column
formation was all right and that American gunfire could master any
night battle situation. Actually his disposition was dangerously un-
wieldy and prevented the destroyers from exploiting their proper
weapon, the torpedo. And because the surprised enemy did not get
off his usual torpedo attack, that was assumed to be no longer a
serious threat. So, because we won the Battle of Cape Esperance,
serious tactical defects were carried over into subsequent engage-

---

[20] An electronic identification system was introduced on board ships so that
the radar signals of friendly vessels could be recognized.

ments with unfortunate results. One learns more from adversity than from success.

Savo Island was a victory for the Japanese, but the American transports were not touched; Cape Esperance was an American victory but the Japanese accomplished their main object. Not only did fresh troops get ashore at Tassafaronga while Goto and Scott were fighting, but seaplane carriers *Nisshin* and *Chitose* unloaded heavy artillery, which meant trouble for the Marines. Nor did Scott's victory prevent the Japanese from inflicting a heavy air raid on Henderson Field on 12 October (fortunately with very bad aim) or the heaviest bombardment yet two nights later (unfortunately with very good aim).

Cape Esperance helped American morale, spared the Marines one night of bombardment, and punctured Japanese confidence in their superiority at night fighting. "Providence abandoned us and our losses mounted," says one of their official reports.[21] But the decisive naval battle of the Solomons was yet to be fought.

[21] "Southeast Area Operations Part I (Navy)."

CHAPTER IX

Mid-October Misery

13–17 October 1942

1. *"The Bombardment,"* 14 October

SUNRISE 13 October revealed the gray hulls of Admiral Turner's transports bringing up the 164th Infantry Regiment of the Americal Division; a heartening sight for Marines, particularly for the 1st Raider Battalion which was scheduled to provide these transports with return passengers. Out on the fringes of the perimeter things were looking much better; patrols pushed to the west of the Matanikau River without hindrance. On Henderson Field also there was cause for optimism. Ninety operational aircraft, about equally divided between dive-bombers and fighters, were scattered in the dispersal areas; and though the gasoline supply was low replacement prospects were good.

Events shortly proved that American optimism was premature. At noon about 24 Japanese bombers, flying nearly six miles high, made an unexpected and accurate bombing run over Henderson Field. Two hours later, while American fighter planes were fueling, 15 more bombers came in and left the field looking like a slice of Swiss cheese. No sooner had the Seabees filled the holes than a new and disgusting Japanese character made his bow with a shrill whine followed by an explosive thud, smack in the middle of the airstrip. This was "Pistol Pete," — the heavy field artillery unloaded on the 11th, and now laid on Henderson from well-concealed positions beyond the Matanikau. When he opened up again on the evening of 13 October, destroyers *Sterett, Gwin* and *Nicho-*

las, covering the unloading, took him under fire and silenced him, though not for long.[1]

While this was going on Japanese naval officers were talking on the darkened flag bridge of battleship *Kongo,* headed for Guadalcanal. Vice Admiral Takeo Kurita, Combatdiv 3, discusses with his staff gunnery officer, Commander Yanagi, the details of an interesting operation planned for that night. Over nine hundred 14-inch bombardment shells are ready in battleships *Kongo* and *Haruna,* but less than three hundred of them are the thin-skinned HE (high explosive) kind especially designed to tear Marines and their planes apart. The rest, all AP (armor-piercing) may not even explode against soft ground and yielding coconut palms, and at best will only blow a big hole in the ground. The two officers review their plan carefully. Four destroyers, already sweeping ahead of the battleships, will give warning of any ships in the area, then torpedo them. The battleships, screened by light cruiser *Isuzu* and four or five destroyers, will pass between Santa Isabel and Florida Islands, leaving Savo Island on the port hand, and catapult float planes for gunfire spot. Then watch the fireworks!

Shortly before midnight the drone of a low-powered observation plane is heard over Henderson Field, and at a few minutes after 0100 October 14, sixteen 14-inch guns break the silence with monstrous thunder which echoes from the mountains of Guadalcanal. A bright, unwinking flare descends from the observation plane, affording the aviator and Japanese observers in the hills a sharply defined picture of the airfield. The first shells plant orange-red seeds of flame to mark the target. Kurita's fire control parties calculate range data and apply corrections radioed in from plane pilots and land observers. The Admiral and his gunnery officer note with growing elation how each salvo starts new blazes until the entire airfield is a field of fire.[2]

[1] A few days later several hundred enemy dead were found in this area; *Sterett* and *Nicholas* claimed they were their victims.

[2] "Japanese Bombardment Report" ATIS 16567-B. Capt. Watanabe, formerly of Yamamoto's staff, informed us in 1949 that the HE shells used in this bombardment had been ordered as early as Jan. 1942, in order to give profitable employ-

Marines crouch in their foxholes and speculate. There is something disturbingly different about this bombardment. The ground shakes as the shell pattern walks back and forth, shattering planes and storehouses, setting off fuel dumps, knocking down trees, killing men or tearing their bodies with jagged fragments. One 14-inch shell bursts in General del Valle's command post. Newly arrived soldiers of the 164th Infantry wonder if this is what life on Guadalcanal is always like.

On the beach at Lunga Point, searchlights waver to and fro seeking the source of this misery; star shell daubs the darkness with flickering yellow splotches. Five-inch naval guns ashore bark savagely but ineffectively; the battleships are outside their range. Over on Tulagi, Lieutenant Alan R. Montgomery is awakened by the thud of distant explosions. He can do something. Only the day before he had brought four motor torpedo boats to Tulagi for just such an emergency. Montgomery calls his four young skippers — all junior grade reserve lieutenants: Henry S. Taylor of *PT–46*, Robert C. Wark of *PT–48* and the Searles brothers, John M. of *PT–60* and Robert L. of *PT–38*. Go get 'em!

All four pile in eagerly. A spirited but baffling action is joined with the Japanese destroyer screen, the PTs firing torpedoes, shooting machine guns and receiving plenty of near-misses from 5-inch shells. The PT men are certain they are making hits but what they probably see is the flash of enemy gunfire. The brawl has its effect, however, in helping Admiral Kurita decide to break off. American searchlights have picked up his battleships; he knows not what may develop behind the PTs; he has already been shooting for 80 minutes and his initial ammunition allowance is expended. So at 0230 he orders Cease Fire and retires according to plan. *Kongo, Haruna* and escorts, untouched by a single hit, slip around Savo Island and head northward for the fleet rendezvous. Kurita knows that his colleague Kusaka will have bombing planes over

---

ment to battleships subsequent to the demonstration of their vulnerability to land-based air attack. This was the first use of the new shells, some of which were incendiaries, others fragmentation.

the field next day, so he has little fear of retaliation from the air.

Kurita is right. In the morning the Marines crawl out of fox-holes to find yawning chasms spotting the airfield and dispersal areas. Only 42 planes (35 fighters and 7 dive-bombers) remain operational out of 90. The aviation gas supply, critically low before, is nearly all gone. Forty-one men are dead, others wounded. And every 15 minutes "Pistol Pete" spits up geysers of dirt around the field. Then at noon, without warning, an air raid hits the field hard, followed by another an hour later. Henderson Field is through for the time being. Whoever flies must use the new grass-covered fighter strip. A Marine colonel from division headquarters appears at the field and delivers a short pronouncement to the Army aviators: —

We don't know whether we'll be able to hold the field or not. There's a Japanese task force of destroyers, cruisers and troop transports headed our way. We have enough gasoline left for one mission against them. Load your planes with bombs and go out with the dive-bombers and hit them. After the gas is gone we'll have to let the ground troops take over. Then your officers and men will attach yourselves to some infantry outfit. Good luck and good-by.[3]

On board *Kongo*, now well to the northward, an orderly hands the Admiral a copy of an intercepted Marine dispatch: "Last night we received a terrific bombardment from surface ships." [4] Kurita grunts with satisfaction and thinks of the tremendous victory to follow.

2. Rebound, 14–15 October

Admiral Kurita's punitive visit bore down heavily on Marine morale; the more so because, following hard on the Battles of the Matanikau and of Cape Esperance, it seemed to prove that the enemy's resources were unlimited. The men knew that they could

[3] Quoted from "67th Fighter Squadron History Mar.–Oct. 1942" pp. 26–27.
[4] Desron 2 War Diary.

not stand many more such drubbings. For the rest of the war Guadalcanal veterans would talk of Kurita's shelling as "The Bombardment," as if there had never been any other.

On 14 October the last echelon of General Hyakutake's troops was on its way down the Slot in six transports, escorted by destroyers on the surface and overhead by "Zekes." Four Dauntless dive-bombers (all that would fly at the moment) and seven Army fighter planes armed with bombs took the air in a pathetic effort to stop this reinforcement. They did their best, but the only ship to suffer, and that lightly, was destroyer *Samidare*. When darkness set in, she was still heading south.

The night of 14–15 October was another bad stretch for the Marines. Admiral Mikawa personally entered "Sleepless Lagoon" (as the Marines were beginning to call it) in cruiser *Chokai*, followed by lucky *Kinugasa*, to churn up the Henderson Field community with 752 eight-inch shells. Four PT crews looked on but could do nothing; one boat had been damaged by grounding the night before, one was out of torpedoes and the other two were compelled to remain with a small-craft convoy moving between Tulagi and Guadalcanal. Dawn of the 15th revealed a spectacle highly humiliating to the Marines who saw it, and to the Navy that did not. In full view were enemy transports lying-to off Tassafaronga, unloading troops and supplies with as much ease as if they had been in Tokyo Bay. Hovering around and over them were destroyers and planes.

General Geiger, Marine air commander, was told there was no gas at Henderson Field. "Then, by God, find some!" he ordered. Men scoured the dispersal areas, collected some 400 drums of aviation gas from swamps and thickets where they had been cached and trundled them to the field. Even the two disabled B–17s had their tanks siphoned dry. By these pint-pot methods enough fuel was procured to enable the planes to make the ten-mile hop to the targets and back. And by mid-morning, Marine and Army transport planes began to fly in gasoline from Espiritu Santo.

Off Tassafaronga, Army, Navy and Marine pilots bombed and

strafed the transports all day long 15 October, fighting off "Zekes" and dodging the darting tongues of anti-aircraft tracers. Flying Forts flew up from Espiritu Santo and lent a hand. A visiting PBY, General Geiger's personal "hack" piloted by Lieutenant Colonel Jack Cram, contributed a pair of torpedoes, and returned to Henderson Field full of holes, with swarms of enemy fighters on its tail, but safe. High over the revitalized airfield, Wildcat bullets and anti-aircraft shells brought down twelve Nip bombers and five fighters. Everybody who flew claimed damage that day, and for once they were right. Three large transports not yet completely unloaded (*Azumasan Maru*, *Kyushu Maru* and *Sasako Maru*) had to be beached and became a total loss. By 1550 things had become so hot that the Japanese task force commander decided to withdraw with the other three transports.[5] Not one transport escaped damage, not one troop unit landed without casualties and loss of equipment. This field day cost the Americans three dive-bombers and four fighter planes.

That night, breathing was a bit easier for all hands. Even a downpour of 1500 eight-inch shells from cruisers *Myoko* and *Maya* failed to quench the spark of hope kindled by the feeling that the enemy had done his worst. But, alas, he had not.

Carrier *Hornet*, keystone of Task Force 17 under Rear Admiral George D. Murray, also lent a hand. On 16 October she launched an air raid on Rekata Bay, Santa Isabel, which chewed up twelve enemy seaplanes. On the same day her planes flew over Guadalcanal, socking beached Japanese transports and troop and supply concentrations.

United States submarines in these waters were not very successful in October, but *Sculpin* and *Gudgeon* between them sank three freighters amounting to 13,500 tons; and *Sturgeon* sank a large aircraft ferry, *Katsuragi Maru*.[6]

---

[5] "Southeast Area Operation Part I (Navy)" Special Staff U.S. Army Historical Division pp. 31–2.
[6] Details will be found in Vol. IV of this History.

3. *Supply-train Sufferings*

"It now appears that we are unable to control the sea in the Guadalcanal area. Thus our supply of the positions will only be done at great expense to us. The situation is not hopeless, but it is certainly critical."

On 15 October Admiral Nimitz expressed his estimate of the situation in these three sober sentences. Past events had justified this gloomy assessment; future events would substantiate it. Naval spokesmen in Washington acted as though preparing the public for the worst. Even Secretary Knox, optimist by nature, when asked on the 16th whether he thought we could hold Guadalcanal, said he "would not make any prediction, but every man will give a good account of himself. . . . Everybody hopes that we can hold on." [7]

The Nimitz-Ghormley-Vandegrift team were determined to hold on; but they staggered under a multitude of afflictions, number one being the Japanese Navy; Nimitz had no doubt whatever that it was making an all-out effort. He and his service force had to provide the South Pacific with the tools of war at a time when the North African operation acted as an absorbent sponge for ships, planes and fuel, beans and bullets. Fortunately Admiral King in Washington never for a moment forgot Guadalcanal. Ghormley was harassed by the need for doing too much with too few ships. Vandegrift was plagued with the problem of hanging onto valuable acres of jungle-surrounded airfield in the face of air bombs, naval and heavy artillery shells, supply deficiencies, fanatically fighting Japs and enervating diseases. It could hardly be expected that such a doubtful issue could be quickly resolved. The battles of October were not decisive but they defeated the second serious attempt of the Japanese to retake Guadalcanal and afforded the Americans a much-needed opportunity to catch their breath and strike back.

[7] *N.Y. Times* 17 Oct. 1942.

The extremity of the American situation in mid-October is illustrated by gallant if pitiful efforts to keep the lifeline intact. The Japanese had ironically relieved the fuel shortage by destroying most of the American planes, but there still remained enough to burn gas at an alarming rate. The twin-engined Douglas Skytrooper became a flying work-horse, bringing in enough aviation gas from Base "Button" (Espiritu Santo) each trip to keep twelve Wildcats aloft for an hour. Submarine *Amberjack*, fitted to carry 9000 gallons of gasoline together with ten tons of bombs, did her part. To swell the trickle, a barge-towing expedition was made up, to arrive at Lunga Roads on the 16th. It comprised cargo ships *Alchiba* and *Bellatrix*, motor torpedo boat tender *Jamestown*, ex-minesweeper (now fleet tug) *Vireo* and destroyers *Meredith* and *Nicholas*, each towing a barge carrying 2000 barrels of gasoline and 500 quarter-ton bombs.

On 15 October, 75 miles from Guadalcanal, these lucrative targets were sighted and reported by a Japanese search plane. The American ships, with the exception of *Vireo* and *Meredith*, hastily retired. At 1050 these two beat off a two-plane attack. At the same time word was received that two enemy ships were close at hand. Course was reversed and at noon *Meredith* ordered the slow and vulnerable *Vireo* to be abandoned and sunk, after taking off her crew. At 1215, just as *Meredith* was about to torpedo *Vireo*, a 27-plane raid, from the big Japanese carrier *Zuikaku*,[8] plastered the destroyer with bombs, torpedoes and machine-gun fire, and sank her almost instantaneously.

Vireo, abandoned but still undamaged, was drifting so rapidly to leeward that only one life raft from *Meredith* succeeded in boarding her, and those men were saved. The other life rafts became floating horrors. Horribly burned sailors lay on the sea-washed gratings while able-bodied survivors clung to the rafts' lifelines, fighting off sharks until the death of a wounded man released a place for them inside. Lieutenant Commander Harry E. Hubbard, *Meredith's* skipper, was one of many who so died. One shark

---

[8] "Japanese Carrier Achievements" (WDC 161,709).

even boarded a life raft and gouged a chunk from a dying man's thigh before his exhausted raft mates could heave the beast over by the tail.

After three days and three nights of suffering, 88 men were rescued by destroyers *Grayson* and *Gwin*, but *Meredith* lost 185 and *Vireo* 51 officers and men.[9] The tugboat and both gasoline barges were salvaged.

This lamentable affair had one compensation: *Meredith* collected most of the enemy bombs and torpedoes which might have been used against the freighters and tender. *Bellatrix* was attacked by two dive-bombers whose near-misses only started minor flooding. She, with *Alchiba*, *Jamestown* and *Nicholas*, headed back to Espiritu Santo and arrived safely. But it was not there that they were needed.

Destroyer seaplane tender *McFarland* and destroyer minesweepers *Southard* and *Hovey* also were drafted for the "B., T. & B." (Button, Tulagi and Back). *McFarland's* adventures were reminiscent of the dark days at Cavite. Literally a floating ammunition and fuel dump, she stood into Lengo Channel on the morning of 16 October carrying twelve torpedoes, a quantity of 37-mm ammunition, crates of aircraft flares and 40,000 gallons of gasoline in tanks below and drums topside. That kind of cargo robbed her skipper (Lieutenant Commander John C. Alderman) and his crew of all peace of mind. At 1320 they anchored off the beach at Lunga and began discharging cargo with great alacrity. Passengers were taken on board — 160 ambulatory hospital patients and "war neurotics," an emotionally inflammable cargo. At 1700 the sighting of a submarine periscope convinced Alderman that he was too good a target at anchor, so he got under way with the gasoline barge alongside still taking fuel from *McFarland's* tanks. Then,

[9] Comairsopac Intelligence Bulletin; Comdesdiv 22 Report, 27 Oct. 1942; account by Lt. (jg) Charles J. Bates usnr in Navy "History of *Meredith*." Cdr. Frederick J. Bell (of *Grayson*) *Condition Red* (1943) pp. 121–52 gives the story of the rescue and that of the medical officer of *Meredith*. This book is the best existing account of life on board a destroyer during the Guadalcanal campaign, and for conditions at Espiritu Santo.

at 1750, out of the sky plunged nine enemy dive-bombers. The ensuing action lasted only a couple of minutes during which *McFarland's* bridge rang up full speed, her gunners shot down one "Val" and damaged another, and the gasoline barge was cast off, exploding furiously. The last "Val" scored a hit on the depth-charge racks which made a shambles of the fantail and threw the poor neurotics into uncontrolled panic. While *McFarland's* blue-jackets calmly carried out damage control and defense measures, these unfortunate passengers stampeded the passageways, tried to take weapons and life jackets from the crew, and otherwise added tension to an already taut situation. But the ship's company were determined to save *McFarland*. Rudderless, leaking aft, engines damaged and passengers demoralized, the ship was a problem. Yet the black gang in the engine room soon found that they could give her five knots on a generally straight course by running the damaged port engine astern and the intact starboard engine ahead. It was nearly midnight before this tough little ship anchored in Tulagi, towed the last few miles by *YP–239*. She had lost 27 men with 28 wounded.

That was only the beginning of *McFarland's* improvisation. Next day (17 October) her crew moved her up the narrow Maliali River mouth on Florida Island, covered her with a camouflage of jungle greenery and began repairs. This involved raiding the for-mer Japanese seaplane base for steel and fashioning a jury rudder out of telephone poles. During a three-week period Alderman and his hearties not only repaired the damage but established the new U.S. Naval Base, Tulagi. Thanksgiving Day found *McFarland* once more on her own, steering for Espiritu Santo. Her experi-ence was an inspiration, but she could deliver no more liquid gold to hungry planes at Guadalcanal. Admiral Nimitz was right; supply was very expensive.[10]

[10] O.N.I. Combat Narrative *Miscellaneous Actions in the South Pacific* p. 40. A far more serious supply-train casualty, although it cost but two lives, was the total loss of the big army transport *President Coolidge* at Segond Channel, Espiritu Santo, on 25 Oct. She was carrying the 172nd Infantry 43rd Division. Her merchant skipper, although repeatedly warned by patrol craft and shore blinker, blundered

Another effort of small but significant nature was a naval bombardment on 17 October by *Aaron Ward* and *Lardner*, a two-destroyer force commanded by Captain Robert G. Tobin. Two thousand rounds of 5-inch ammunition plowed into enemy positions west of Kokumbona, touching off a couple of ammunition dumps and arousing a chorus of radio squawks from indignant Japanese. Air observers did a fine job spotting targets for the destroyers' gunners, the material damage was considerable, the moral effect on ground forces excellent, and the precedent valuable. The Japanese admitted the loss of "large quantities of ammunition and rations" which were irreplaceable, and, in Captain Omae's words after the war, "was the most fatal reason for further failures." [11]

4. *Enter Halsey*

Admiral Nimitz was confronted with many problems of which the question of leadership in the South Pacific was the most pressing. Admiral Ghormley, a meticulous and conscientious man with a long record of achievement, apparently lacked the personal qualities needed to inspire American fighting men in a tough spot. As area commander, he received blame for many things beyond his control, for employing too many ships around "Torpedo Junction," [12] for landing too few American troops and supplies on Guadalcanal and letting too many Japanese soldiers get there, for supply bottlenecks at Nouméa and Espiritu Santo. [13] Yet, could any

---

into a protective mine field and she sank. All the troops' equipment and their heavy weapons were destroyed and their reinforcement of the Guadalcanal garrison was delayed for weeks. Earlier, on 4 Aug., destroyer *Tucker* had run into the same mine field with the same result.

[11] "Southeast Area Operations (Navy) Part I," p. 34, U.S. Army Historical Division. Conversations of Lt. Pineau with Capt. Omae in 1949.

[12] Ironically enough, the next "Torpedo Junction" casualty came two days after Ghormley had been relieved, on 20 Oct. Heavy cruiser *Chester,* operating in a task group under Rear Admiral W. A. Lee in *Washington,* when about halfway between Espiritu Santo and San Cristobal was hit at night in No. 1 engine room by a torpedo from submarine *I-176.* She had to go around to Norfolk for repairs and rejoined the Pacific Fleet only in time for the Gilberts operation.

[13] The writer believes that Admiral Ghormley did as well as anyone could have

new leader do as well; would not a change at this time create even more confusion? Admiral Nimitz weighed the matter scrupulously. On the evening of 15 October, after a conference with his staff, he decided that "the critical situation requires a more aggressive commander," and that he wanted Vice Admiral William F. Halsey. Next day Admiral King granted authority for the change, and Nimitz acted at once.

Since May Admiral Halsey had been on the binnacle list with aggravated dermatitis, but mid-October found him in the South Pacific on an inspection tour preparatory to taking over command of a carrier task force. In health and spirits he was "back to battery," but he had no inkling of the load about to be dumped into his lap. On 18 October he landed at Nouméa to be confronted with a terse order: "You will take command of the South Pacific Area and South Pacific Forces immediately." That same day with feelings of "astonishment, apprehension and regret," he relieved his old friend Ghormley.[14] "Bill" Halsey had won golden opinions in the Fleet for his aggressiveness and his character. The announcement was received on board ships of the South Pacific Fleet with cheers and rejoicing.

Besides replacing the top commander, Admiral Nimitz considered and took other positive measures. A task group powered by new battleship *Indiana* was ordered through the Panama Canal to the South Pacific. The 25th Infantry Division U.S. Army at Oahu was given word to pack its gear for a voyage to the southern seas. A flock of 50 Army fighter planes was told to migrate

---

done; that he was the victim of circumstances. His health was excellent. He believed that he was relieved on account of the question of reinforcement; frequently he demanded troops from the West Coast but was always told that there were none ready, and that he must "roll up" the garrisons of his rear areas, Fiji and Samoa. That he refused to do, because he feared denuding these islands of defense forces would tempt the enemy to attack them. An unfortunate concomitant of his relief was the fact that Halsey, unlike Nimitz, brought his own staff, to the detriment of his old flagship *Enterprise* and replaced many of Ghormley's experienced staff, four of whom were killed at the Battle of Guadalcanal.

[14] *Admiral Halsey's Story* p. 10; for the Admiral's previous career see Vol. III of this History p. 211. His nickname "Bill" was corrupted by news reports to "Bull." Nobody who knew Halsey personally ever called him that.

from the Central to the South Pacific. A plan was devised to infest enemy-held waters in the Solomons with an additional 24 large submarines. A similar number of Army B–17s droned across the Equator to join Admiral Fitch's brood.[15] Most important, carrier *Enterprise,* recovered from her 24 August wounds, rushed pell-mell to the Solomons.

Insistent demands of the South Pacific were met as far as possible, but Nimitz could not allow himself or his forces to become too absorbed with one locale. The Aleutian situation required attention, for repeated air bombing missions had failed to dislodge the Japanese from Kiska and Attu. Another whack at Midway or Hawaii was an enemy capability that kept the old-style battleships milling around Oahu as insurance.[16] There was anxiety about holding Funafuti, which about a thousand Marines and Seabees of the Samoa garrison had occupied on 3 October, because the Japanese were strongly reinforcing their positions in the Gilbert Islands, the next group north. Heckling missions against enemy patrol craft in that area became routine for warships steaming to and from the South Pacific. Nimitz was interested also in sniping at the expanded Hirohito empire from another direction. On 20 October he wrote to Admiral King, "Now is a golden opportunity for the British Eastern Fleet to take action on the Japanese west flank." Such action would more than compensate for the loss of New Zealand cruisers *Achilles* and *Leander,* withdrawn for overhaul; but the British Far Eastern Fleet remained in the Indian Ocean.

In Washington Admiral King had his hands full. Our predicament in the Solomons was more than matched by that caused by the German submarines, which, during the month of October, sank 88 ships and 585,510 tons in the Atlantic.[17] The North African venture was already at sea; British forces in Egypt still had

[15] Rear Admiral Aubrey W. Fitch relieved Vice Admiral J. S. McCain as Comairsopac 20 Sept. 1942, retaining the same headquarters at Segond Channel, Espiritu Santo.
[16] A single enemy submarine sighted 500 miles southwest of Oahu on 23 Oct. was thought to be possibly the harbinger of another Pearl Harbor attack.
[17] See Vol. I of this History p. 315.

to be supplied by the Cape of Good Hope and Suez route. Guadalcanal had to be fitted by the Joint Chiefs of Staff into a worldwide strategic panorama, but Guadalcanal could be reinforced only by drawing on forces originally committed to the build-up in the United Kingdom (Operation "Bolero") for a cross-channel operation in 1943. General Arnold wished to concentrate air forces in Europe for the strategic bombing of Germany; Admiral King and General MacArthur argued against risking disaster in the Solomons and New Guinea in order to provide for the eventuality of a future operation in Europe. President Roosevelt broke the deadlock on 24 October by sending a strong message to each member of the Joint Chiefs of Staff, insisting that Guadalcanal must be reinforced, and quickly.[18]

5. *Cras Ingens Iterabimus Aequor* [19]

The nerve center of this campaign was not, however, at Washington or Pearl Harbor but at Nouméa, where Admiral Halsey and his chief of staff Captain Miles Browning, with about 15 seasoned staff officers and 50 bluejackets, ran the entire South Pacific Force of Navy, Army, Marine Corps; ships, boats, freighters, net tenders; search radars, anti-aircraft batteries and barrage balloons; N.A.S. and N.O.B.; service of supply and repair stations; Flying Forts, Cats, SCAT, Cubs, Acorns, Seabees; camps, hospitals, officers' and enlisted men's clubs; a hundred other groups, units and forces; not to mention the thousands of men who were just passing through, and the unwanted and troublesome "do-gooders" who were occasionally flown across from the States. No Waves

[18] The message, partly written by Harry Hopkins, is reproduced in Robert E. Sherwood *Roosevelt and Hopkins* (1948) p. 624; it is undated, but the J.C.S. records show that it was presented 24 Oct.

[19] Horace *Odes* I vii, the last stanza of which may be translated: —

> All right, tough guys, we've had it worse before;
> Hey, barkeep! drinks for the whole gang on me —
> Tomorrow once again we sail the Ocean Sea.

or Wacs, however; since Congress, jealous of the virtue of American womanhood, refused to allow them to cater to these rude
fighting men of the South Pacific. But New Zealand filled their
places acceptably with a contingent of their auxiliaries, a fine
upstanding group of girls, efficient in work and merry at play.
The French governor kept sulkily (but not silently) aloof in his
"palace" on the hilltop, conceding to Admiral Halsey a gimcrack
villa vacated by the Japanese consul. Its yard was cluttered up
with Quonset huts for the senior officers and the juniors over-
flowed into "Havoc Hall" down the hill. Naval headquarters were
in an old warehouse-like building with adjoining stable, near the
waterfront. For recreation there were year-old movies at several different outdoor screens under the cool night sky. Sundays
one had a choice between mass in the noble Catholic cathedral,
with a sermon in Bossuet's French by a priest as remote from this
war as Bossuet himself; or a chaplain-conducted service with familiar hymns at the Protestant *temple* after the French service (at-
tended by one old gentleman and five old ladies in black) was over.
The local French colonials were divided into pro- and anti-
Vichy compartments, but even the stoutest DeGaullists appeared
to be consumed by a frustrated pride that led them to raise innu-
merable difficulties and make vociferous demands. The Annamite
laborers simply did not care. Nouméa itself is an unpainted, ram-
shackle town but the climate and the surrounding scenery are
superb: a picturesquely indented coast, dazzling coral sand, vales
wooded with the fragrant niaouli tree, well cultivated fields, the
right amount of rainfall, thermometer never above 86°, cool nights
with the tradewind always blowing fresh, and no malaria-carrying
mosquitoes. New Caledonia is the one island in the South Pacific
that Americans wished they could keep; but President Roosevelt
had promised France to restore her empire intact, so that could
not be.

In other times Nouméa might have been a place to relax, but
not so now. Lights burned late on the docks where soldiers and
sailors tried to relieve supply-line congestion, and in naval head-

quarters where staff officers worked over reports, orders and dispatches. The native population went their placid ways, but there was hardly a calm American in the place except Admiral Halsey, and he was not always calm. Almost daily, damaged ships brought wounded men and neurotics evacuated from Guadalcanal to swell the haggard crowd at the fleet landing. Then, what an uproar in the courtyard and around the bar at the Grand Hôtel du Pacifique! Scraps of overheard conversation, such as: My God, *you* still alive! Yeah, there wasn't enough left of Bill to bury at sea — Bravest little bastard I ever saw, stood off a whole *Banzai* charge with his tommy gun — Harry ran out of gas; but you know Harry, probably raising a family now up in the Stewart Islands.

Nobody since Q. Horatius Flaccus has so well expressed that feeling of immediacy at Nouméa on the last night ashore. Tomorrow our task group sorties to meet a new Japanese threat; tomorrow we fly up to reinforce Henderson Field, where everyone is expended sooner or later; tomorrow our transport leaves for the 'Canal — can the Navy even get us there? Why doesn't Washington *see* that this is *it*, why take the war into Africa when we are locked in deathly embrace with the most relentless foe America has ever known? Don't they know that if we lose the 'Canal we lose the war? Well, thank God for Halsey, exuding strength and confidence; for his slogan, which "Scrappy" Kessing painted up over the fleet landing at Tulagi in letters two feet tall: —

KILL JAPS, KILL JAPS, KILL MORE JAPS!

This may shock you, reader; but it is exactly how we felt. We were fighting no civilized, knightly war. We cheered when the Japs were dying. We were back to primitive days of Indian fighting on the American frontier; no holds barred and no quarter. The Japs wanted it that way, thought they could thus terrify an "effete democracy"; and that is what they got, with all the additional horrors of war that modern science can produce.

CHAPTER X

The Battle for Henderson Field

19–26 October 1942

1. *The Japanese Plan and the Matanikau Drive*

WHILE the Americans were counting their several woes and infrequent blessings, the Japanese high command concluded that the time had come to unsheath a myriad Samurai swords and chase the enemy out of the Solomons. Preliminary to this great joint operation were General Maruyama's attacks on Henderson Field, the Combined Fleet's sailing from Truk 11 October, the successive night bombardments, the landing of 4500 troops on the 15th, and the accelerated tempo of air raids. The new fighter strip at Buin in southern Bougainville was being pushed to completion, and as early as 20 October thirty of the one hundred "Zekes" at Rabaul were advanced to the new field, to escort Rabaul-based bombers to Guadalcanal.

The Japanese plan stemmed from an Army-Navy agreement for operations in mid-September, revised as the situation altered. In this agreement Guadalcanal was given top billing by the Emperor's chiefs of staff, and the Papua operation dropped to second place. The substance of the Tokyo order was contained in its opening paragraph: —

[1] So called by the Marines and soldiers at the time, but both the name and the events have dropped out of general accounts. For general sources see chap. iii footnote 1, above. The writer made a personal examination of this battlefield in company with Col. Puller and Col. Timboe. We have the enemy version with an excellent map in "Answers to Questionnaires on Guadalcanal Operations" ATIS 22729.

After reinforcement of Army forces has been completed, Army and Navy forces will combine and in one action attack and retake Guadalcanal Island airfield. During this operation the Navy will take all necessary action to halt the efforts of the enemy to augment his forces in the Solomons Area.[2]

This plan was a sincere compliment to Henderson Field and its fliers. The Emperor's high military advisers would not risk another battle until the field was captured. But, as it turned out, they would better have stuck to Mahan, because unexpected delays by the Japanese ground forces gave Admiral Kinkaid time to bring up carrier *Enterprise* to take a decisive part in the sea action. We are accustomed to sea battles deciding a land campaign; in this instance, Japan lost a naval engagement because her army bogged down.

By 15 October the Japanese reinforcement phase was completed. The third week of October was to be devoted to softening up the Marines in preparation for "Y-Day," the 22nd, when the Rising Sun was to be planted on Henderson Field by General Maruyama. The Combined Fleet, impatiently circling north of the Solomons, would then "apprehend and annihilate any powerful forces in the Solomons area, as well as any reinforcements." [3]

The Marines and their fellow soldiers of the 164th Infantry Regiment United States Army declined to soften. Despite breakages in the supply train, food was now sufficient for almost everyone to have three meals a day. Japanese thrusts had been tossed back wherever made. Henderson Field fliers were daily demonstrating their combat superiority. On the other hand, the nocturnal ship bombardments and diurnal air attacks continued. There was also the certain knowledge that the enemy was shoving in troops at the rate of 900 a night, not to mention the 4500 who had come ashore from the transports on 15 October. These troops could, in theory, be deployed all over Guadalcanal while the Ma-

---

[2] Imperial Headquarters Navy Staff Section Directive No. 135 (WDC No. 216,769).

[3] Japanese Report "Battle of Santa Cruz" (WDC No. 15,687).

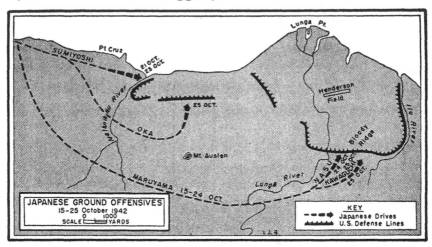

rines were pinned down to their perimeter around Henderson Field. But the hated 'Canal jungle now turned American ally, thwarting neat Japanese plans for envelopment.

General Hyakutake made the assignments, as before; fortunately he still underestimated both the strength and quality of his antagonists and had very inaccurate information on the nature of the terrain his troops were to traverse. To Major General Tadashi Sumiyoshi, commanding Seventeenth Army artillery, was given the honor of making a frontal attack on Marine positions along the Matanikau. This was to be coördinated with a two-pronged assault on Henderson Field from the south, the eastern prong to be directed by Major General Kawaguchi, the western one by Major General Yumio Nasu, both under Lieutenant General Masai Maruyama, Commanding General 2nd Division. Air strikes and surface bombardment were to be provided as softening agents.

Sumiyoshi jumped off against the Marines' defensive sectors along the Matanikau on 20 October. Colonel McKelvy's battalion, stationed near the river mouth, became the recipient of heavy mortar and artillery fire. On the 21st, nine light tanks tried to force a crossing by the coast road but were easily repulsed by Marine Corps artillery. Next day destroyer *Nicholas*, which had just escorted a small supply echelon to Guadalcanal, saw her charges safely anchored (as she thought) at Lunga Roads, and pranced over to make four bombardment runs on enemy shore positions, firing over a thousand rounds of 5-inch shell by 0830. A Japanese shore battery retaliated by opening up on one of *Nicholas's* charges, the small freighter *Kopara*, but *Nicholas* scurried back to pump an additional 181 rounds into the offending battery, which silenced it. After severe artillery preparation on 23 October, Sumiyoshi just before midnight 23 October sent in his tanks with infantry support for another try. The 11th Marines' 105-mm howitzers took care of the tanks, destroying twelve, and McKelvy's battalion disposed of several hundred soldiers at small cost to themselves. Thus, the western attack was a complete failure, and the occupation of Henderson was already two days overdue.[4]

Next morning, 24 October, the enemy unexpectedly appeared upstream on the Matanikau. Marines of Colonel Farrell's 3rd Battalion 7th Regiment sighted a strong Japanese force on a ridge to their left and rear. They shouted for artillery fire and air support, and got both, together with Hanneken's 2nd Battalion of their regiment, which during the previous night had shoved off from its defensive position south of the airfield.

2. *Coffin Corner, 24–25 October*

This withdrawal of the 2nd Battalion forced Colonel Puller's 1st Battalion of the same regiment to "single-up its lines"[5] along the U-shaped perimeter south of Henderson Field. An action, which for bloody devilment came close to the earlier Battle of the Ridge, was fought here on the edge of the woods, only half a mile south of the Ridge.

Puller's lines lay in the jungle, partly along the south edge of a

[4] Del Valle in *Marine Corps Gazette* Feb. 1944; *Nicholas* War Diary.
[5] An expressive nautical phrase; a ship singles-up her doubled mooring lines before getting under way. The Marines used it to describe the attenuation of defensive lines when half the defenders are withdrawn and the other half have to spread out.

large field of kunai grass that sloped up to a grassy knoll 2000 yards away. On his left, the lines bent back along the course of the river which the troops called the Tenaru, and this sector was guarded by Lieutenant Colonel Timboe's battalion of the 164th Infantry. A second battalion of the same regiment was posted to the rear, as reserve. The lines were prepared for assault with barbed wire on which shell fragments and other metal oddments were hung to jingle a warning if a Jap tried to cross them at night. Fields of fire were cut with bayonets through the seven-foot-tall kunai grass and pickets were connected with their outfits by strings — two jerks to mean "Japs coming." A detachment of 48 Marines was posted on the summit of the grassy knoll, 3000 yards from the lines.

All day on the 24th signs of an approaching Japanese force were observed. This was General Nasu's prong; Kawaguchi had been delayed in the jungle. After nightfall at 2130 the Marine outpost on the grassy knoll was overrun, and half an hour after midnight Nasu's men poured down through the kunai into the Marines' lines. It was raining buckets. Colonel Hall's reserve battalion of the 164th Infantry was ordered up from the rear in support, and made it in spite of rain and darkness.

Along "Coffin Corner," as the soldiers named this point where their lines came out of the woods, the Japs tried all their tricks and fought savagely all night; but the Marines and GI Joes had their weapons properly sited and slaughtered them as fast as they came. By daylight General Nasu (or his second in command, for he was killed at some time during the action) withdrew to reform. The Marines and the 164th spent daylight of the 25th readjusting their lines, as soldiers of the two outfits were completely commingled by morning; and many found time to walk across the field and bathe in the river.

At nightfall the attack was renewed with the aid of part of Kawaguchi's brigade which had found its way there. "Coffin Corner" still held, and the only result was more piles of bodies added to those heaped up in the grass, and along the edge of the woods.

Puller's and Timboe's outfits together buried 941 of the enemy in that small sector.

A pathetic personal notebook of a Japanese colonel who committed suicide after this battle was captured. He presents a watch to Captain Suzuki and a pair of spectacles to Sergeant Yamakawa. Apologizes for embarrassing his division commander. Begs pardon of his regiment for spoiling their reputation through ignorance. Admires American soldiers for not talking. Will tear up his regimental colors.[6]

In the meantime Hanneken's 2nd Battalion 7th Marines, whose departure for the Matanikau had caused the 1st to "single-up its lines," had taken an east-west position along an irregular line of grassy ridge parallel to the coast, facing a steep-sided and heavily-wooded valley. There they were attacked by Colonel Oka's unit with heavy artillery support, subjected to sniping fire from tall trees on the other side of the valley, and infiltrated at night. One company of Marines was almost wiped out, and when the survivors withdrew the enemy emplaced two machine guns on the ridge and enfiladed the rest. Dawn 26 October revealed this unpleasant fact to the battalion command post, only a few yards distant. Major Odell M. Conoley, the battalion "exec.," formed his communication personnel, company runners, cooks and messboys, to the total number of 17, into an assault force which knocked out the two machine guns with hand grenades and cleared the crest.

---

[6] Sopac Intelligence Center translation. What he meant by "not talking" is that the captured Americans refused to give information under torture. There was plenty of yelling and back talk during the action. Two dialogues were especially remembered. Japanese: "Blood for the Emperor!" Marine: "Blood for Elea-nor!" GI: "Tojo eat s——!" (much gabbling among Japanese in search of a suitable return insult, followed by) "Babe Ruth eat s——!"

3. *Skirmishes in the Sound and the Strait, 25 October* [7]

On the 25th, while Marines and soldiers were preparing for the next night assault, a small Japanese bombardment force was tangling with four little American ships out in Ironbottom Sound. An "assault unit," consisting of three destroyers of the Eighth Fleet, *Akatsuki, Ikazuchi* and *Shiratsuyu,* had come down that morning to try a daylight surface raid. They were supported by an "attack unit" of five destroyers led by light cruiser *Yura.* What the mission of the "assault unit" was we do not know; possibly to bombard, probably to land troops; but whatever it was, the "attack unit" was supposed to pile in immediately after and help Maruyama's overdue assault on Henderson Field with a bombardment.

That same morning destroyer-minesweepers *Trever* and *Zane* entered the Sound laden with good things for the PT boys at Tulagi. Piled high on the decks of these erstwhile four-stackers were torpedoes, ammunition and gasoline; astern of each were towed two new motor torpedo boats. They discharged their cargoes quickly and stood by, expecting an order to bombard enemy-held beaches across the Sound. Then, at 1000, the Japanese destroyers appeared. Lieutenant Commander Agnew of *Trever,* the senior skipper, decided to escape via Sealark Channel. At 1018, with the range under ten miles, the hostile group commenced a high-speed approach on Agnew's old-timers. At a range under five miles the Japs opened up. *Trever* and *Zane* fired back, although their 3-inch shells could not carry more than four miles. The Japanese salvos began slapping the water "feet, not yards" from *Zane.*

On the bridge *Trever's* helmsman steered an erratic zigzag course; in the firerooms boiler casings burned clear through as the engineers sweated out an incredible 29 knots. The enemy, how-

[7] O.N.I. Combat Narrative *Miscellaneous Actions in the South Pacific;* Action Reports of American ships concerned; and conversation with Cdr. Amos T. Hathaway, former navigator of *Zane;* translations of Japanese "Combat Report No. 13, Comdesron 4" USSBS files; "Merit Report of Various Naval Units" (WDC No. 161,011).

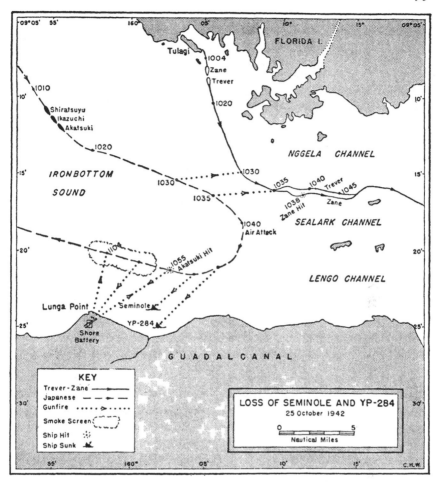

ever, was making at least 35. Lieutenant Commander Agnew made up his mind that there was no escape by way of Sealark Channel; but his chart showed another way, through shoal-studded waters south of Nggela Channel. He signaled his intent to *Zane's* captain (Lieutenant Commander Wirtz) and both ships heeled under the force of hard left turns. At about 1038 [8] the Japanese drew first blood, a hit on *Zane* that killed three men and knocked out a gun.

[8] Times recorded by *Trever* have been used. *Zane* report is at variance.

At this critical juncture help came from the heavens in the shape of an American air attack on the Japanese. The enemy commander, perhaps remembering orders to bombard the airfield, turned abruptly away and headed toward Guadalcanal, fighting off the bombing planes as he went. This change of plan was greeted with incredulous sighs of relief in *Trever* and *Zane*, but their good luck turned sour for the only other American shipping then in the Sound, tug *Seminole* and "yard bird" *YP–284*.

These two craft of the "Cactus Navy" had made a routine ferry run from Tulagi to Lunga loaded with troops, ammunition, gasoline and weapons and were in the process of discharging cargo when *Akatsuki*, *Ikazuchi* and *Shiratsuyu* were sighted. Lieutenant Carl Rasmussen, skipper of the "Yippie," hopefully asked radio Tulagi if the vessels were friendly. The reply was a dismal negative, so both craft rang up full speed — which wasn't much — and headed for home. They had not gone far when the Japanese began paying them a few compliments. At 1050 *YP–284* was hit; the cargo caught fire, and a few minutes later the engine room was holed. Dead and defenseless, the patrol craft quickly sank, with the loss of three Marine passengers. And at 1120 *Seminole*, with gasoline cargo blazing, followed *YP–284* to the bottom. As most enemy shells had passed through her thin hull without exploding, only one life was lost.

The enemy destroyers next let go at the Lunga Point shore batteries but accurate return fire scored a hit on *Akatsuki* at 1055 and persuaded the trio to retire behind a smoke screen. United States submarine *Amberjack*, bringing in her cargo of gasoline, had a fish-eye view of the action but was too far distant to join.

This little affair had more effect than met the eye. The heavy rain during the night of 24–25 October, while battle raged at Coffin Corner, had made the new fighter strip, and a good part of Henderson Field too, inoperable by dawn. If the *Yura* "attack unit" had commenced bombardment at daybreak, instead of waiting while the "assault unit" picked on the little fellows, they might have kept the field out of action for the rest of the day. As it was,

Illustrations

Point Cruz, Guadalcanal, January 1943

Mouth of Lunga River and lagoon

Savo Island from the north shore

Guadalcanal Scenery

Rear Admiral Gunichi Mikawa

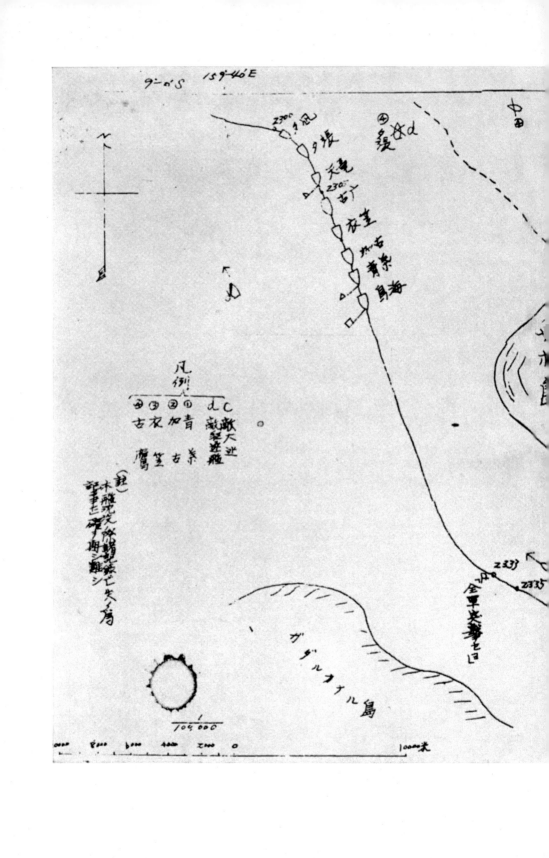

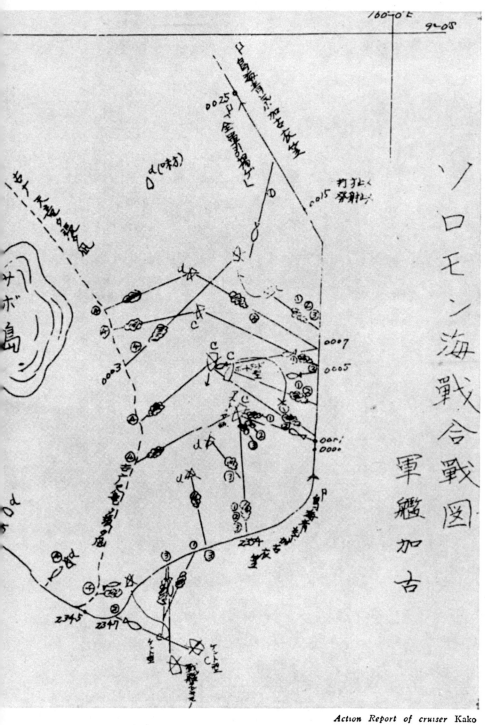

Japanese Track Chart of the Battle of Savo Island

KAKO. FURUTAKA. AOBA. KINUGASA.
巡洋艦 加古.古鷹.青葉.衣笠.

排水量噸 七、一〇〇
速力(節) 三三・〇
航続 (浬)
馬力数 一〇二〇〇 (六)
発射管 (四)
八糎高角砲 (二二)
進水年度 一、九二五
青葉.衣笠 一、九二七

Japanese Navy photo

Kako class heavy cruisers

Photo taken from a Japanese cruiser

U S S *Quincy* during the battle

Ships in the Battle of Savo Island

The coconut grove

The river mouth

After the Battle of the Tenaru River

Henderson Field, Guadalcanal, Shortly after the American Occupation

Vice Admiral Nobutake Kondo

Japanese Naval Commanders

Admiral Isoroku Yamamoto

Bomb hitting flight deck

Under attack

U S S Enterprise, *Battle of Eastern Solomons*

Front row, left to right Col G R Rowan, Col Pedro del Valle, Col W C
James, Maj Gen A A Vandegrift, Col G C Thomas, Col C B Cates
Second row Col W J Whaling, Col Frank B Goettge, Col LeRoy P Hunt,
Lt Col F C Biebush, Lt Col E A Pollock

A Group of Marine Officers, 11 August 1942

Marine Corps photos

The Bloody Ridge after the Battle

Wasp *Burning*, O'Brien *Hit*

Wasp, *Just before Abandonment*

Rear Admiral Norman Scott USN

U S S *Duncan*

U S S *San Francisco*

Ships in the Battle of Cape Esperance

Marine camp near Henderson Field

USS *Meredith*

At Guadalcanal

The large ship is seaplane tender *Akitsushima*, the plane a new "Hamp" fighter
Taken 13 October 1942

Tonolei Harbor, Shortlands, under Air Raid

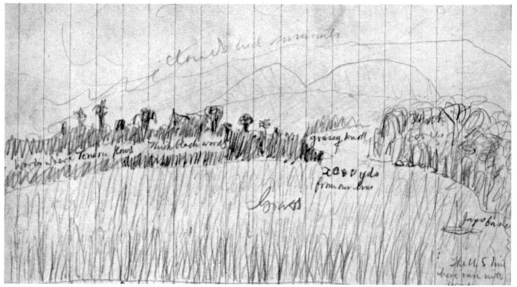

Coffin Corner

Mouth of the Matanıkau Rıver

The Battle for Henderson Field

U S S South Dakota *and* Enterprise *during the*
Battle of the Santa Cruz Islands

Torpedo-bomber approaching USS *South Dakota*

USS *San Juan* repelling air attack

The Battle of the Santa Cruz Islands

Japanese Bomber Diving on U S S Hornet

Rear Admiral Daniel J Callaghan USN
(Photo taken when CO of *San Francisco*)

USS *President Jackson* and *San Francisco*

USS *Atlanta*

Air Attack 12 November 1942

Rear Admiral Willis Augustus Lee USN

Japanese transports burning on beach

USS *Washington*

15 November 1942

Rear Admiral Raizo Tanaka

USS *Minneapolis*, in Tulagi Harbor

The Battle of Tassafaronga

"Black Cats" on prowl

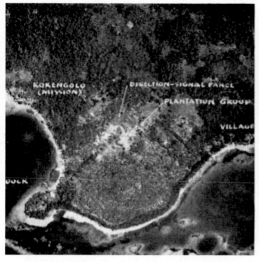

First installations (24 November)

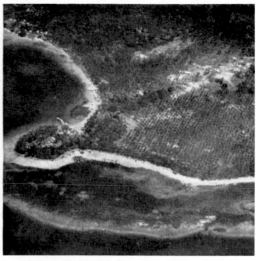

Buildings erected, airstrip
visible under palms (5 December)

Airstrip completed,
marks of bombardment
(12 December)

Airstrip and dispersal area
after more bombardment
(22 December)

The Building of Munda Airfield, 1942

Scene of General Patch's January advance looking south Note "Sea Horse" and "Galloping Horse" at upper left

U S S *Chicago* going down

Guadalcanal and Rennell Island

the time so dearly purchased by four American ships allowed the bright tropical sunlight to soak up enough moisture so that fighters and dive-bombers could take off before noon. Some of these planes caught the *Yura* group at 1255 when they were proceeding south through Indispensable Strait to execute their bombardment mission. *Yura* and destroyer *Akizuki* both were hit. Bomb explosions flooded the after engine room of the cruiser, causing her to slow down. She turned north to escape, but Henderson Field fliers pursued her with bombs. At 1620 the captain received permission to beach her on Fara Island, close to the north coast of Santa Isabel. At 1700, when *Yura* was crawling along south of Ramos Island and west of Cape Astrolabe, she was attacked by six B–17s and six SBDs, one of which scored a direct and final hit. Burning throughout her length, she was abandoned and torpedoed by destroyers *Harusame* and *Yudachi*.

While his SBDs were ganging up on the light cruiser, General Geiger sent aloft the 20 miscellaneous fighter planes still operational to intercept air raids on the field; they shot down 17 "Zekes" and five bombers.

This was the best and final day's work in a remarkable ten-day effort by the handful of American planes at Guadalcanal. From 16 to 25 October inclusive, they had accounted for 103 enemy planes (not including 10 shot down by anti-aircraft guns) at a cost of only 14 American aircraft.[9] And they had disposed of an enemy cruiser.

There was no "Tokyo Express" on the night of 25–26 October. Word reached Rabaul that Admiral Lee in battleship *Washington*, with three cruisers and a number of destroyers, was on the prowl west of Savo; and the nightly run was canceled.

Thus, the Battle for Henderson Field ended shortly after daylight 26 October with the sinking of a bombardment force flagship by Henderson Field fliers and the repulse of Japanese land attacks at all three points — Matanikau, Hanneken's Ridge and

[9] Marine Air Group 23 War Diary, through courtesy of Mr. Robert Sherrod who is writing the history of Marine Corps Aviation.

Coffin Corner. Japanese ground force casualties were numbered by the thousands, and on our side they were heavy. The 7th Marine Regiment lost 130 killed; the 164th Infantry Regiment, 78 killed and wounded. Marine–Army–Air Force coöperation had been well-nigh perfect under Generals Vandegrift and Geiger;[10] GIs had proved they could fight Japs as well as could the Leathernecks.

As the sounds of battle faded out on land, the two Navies were hurling planes against each other's ships in the great Battle of the Santa Cruz Islands.

[10] Relieved 7 Nov. as Commander Aircraft Guadalcanal by his First Wing chief of staff, Brig. Gen. Louis E. Woods USMC. Geiger returned to Espiritu Santo, where First Wing had set up headquarters on 14 Sept.

CHAPTER XI

The Battle of the Santa Cruz Islands[1]

26–27 October 1942

1. Preliminary Maneuvers, 23–25 October

Y AMAMOTO'S orders to his subordinate naval commanders, all poised for action awaiting word of the capture of Henderson Field, were "to apprehend and annihilate any powerful forces in the Solomons area, as well as any reinforcements." Yamamoto had every confidence that the word "annihilate" would mean just that, for he could deploy against Halsey no fewer than 4 carriers, 5 battleships, 14 cruisers and 44 destroyers. These were divided as usual into several groups, spotted over that part of the ocean between the Marianas and the Solomons in a manner difficult to follow. The giant battleship *Yamato* lay at Truk, flying the flag of Admiral Yamamoto. Under him Admiral Kondo commanded all surface forces that it was the Commander in Chief's intention to commit: Kondo's own Advance Force of battleships *Kongo* and *Haruna* (which had just had search radar installed) and four heavy cruisers, including also two carriers under Kakuji

---

[1] Originally called "Third Battle of Savo Island," although fought nowhere near it. Sources similar to those for Cape Esperance – plus Cincpac's Report "Solomon Islands Campaign, Battle of Santa Cruz"; individual ships' Action Reports; Japanese report "Battle of Santa Cruz" ATIS 15687; Desron 10 Combat Report No. 2 (WDC No. 160,985). The writer was given a play-by-play account of this battle by the damage control officer of *South Dakota* a year later, and some interesting facts came out in *Bureau of Naval Personnel Info. Bulletin* for Feb. 1943. Sidney Shalett *Old Nameless* (1943) is fantastically inaccurate.

Kakuta of Aleutians fame; Nagumo's Striking Force containing his own carrier group, ahead of which operated Hiroaki Abe's vanguard of battleships and heavy cruisers. About 220 land-based planes were at Rabaul, where also lay Mikawa's work-horse Eighth Fleet of two heavy cruisers and 16 destroyers. A submarine screen completed the setup. There were no transports because Yamamoto, taking heed from the Eastern Solomons battle, had sent them down in advance — unsuccessfully, as we have seen.

The first brush occurred on 23 October about 650 miles north of Espiritu Santo. One of Admiral Fitch's PBYs spotted an enemy carrier and radioed the alarm. That night several torpedo-toting Catalinas went after the flattop. Lieutenant (jg) George A. Enloe USNR was the only pilot lucky enough to locate an enemy ship, a large cruiser which his torpedo missed.

October 24 passed quietly at sea, as far as enemy contacts were concerned. The best news was the arrival of the "Big E" accompanied by the new, fast battleship *South Dakota*. The latter, on her way out in early September, had had her bottom sliced open by a coral pinnacle near Tongatabu. But this accident proved a blessing in disguise because the Pearl Harbor Navy Yard, not content with patching her bottom, installed dozens of new 40-mm anti-aircraft guns that stood her in good stead in the forthcoming battle. No ship more eager to fight ever entered the Pacific, for Captain Gatch, by constant target practice, neglecting the spit-and-polish things that vex bluejackets, and by exercising a natural gift for leadership, had welded his green crew into a splendid fighting team.[2]

[2] These remarks about Capt. Gatch are based on conversations with several officers who served under him. They were all somewhat puzzled by Gatch's extraordinary power over his men. Some said it was due to his religion; he revived the old Navy practice of reading the lesson at divine service, and always urged his men to make their peace with God before going into action. Others said it was because, as a close student of the Civil War, Gatch had reached the conclusion that taut, spic-and-span units never fought well; so he let the men wear anything or nothing — "they looked like a lot of wild men." He let the ship get abominably dirty and directed all his men's energies to perfecting their shooting. Whatever the reason, Capt. Gatch was adored by his men and received a splendid ovation when he returned to duty after his wound. There is a good article on him by Capt. J. V. Claypool, the ship's chaplain, in *Chicago Tribune* 13 May 1944.

Admiral Halsey now had two carriers, two battleships, nine cruisers and 24 destroyers organized into three teams: Kinkaid's *Enterprise* group (TF 16), Murray's *Hornet* group (TF 17) and Lee's battleship-cruiser group (TF 64). The rendezvous of the two carrier groups was set at a point 273 miles NE by E of Espiritu Santo, and Halsey gave them explicit and daring routing instructions. They were to make a sweep north of the Santa Cruz Islands and then change course to the southwest in order to be in a position to intercept enemy forces approaching Guadalcanal.

The Santa Cruz archipelago, lying to the north of the New Hebrides and to the east of the southern Solomons, includes four volcanic islands of which the better known are Ndeni and Vanikoro. They are so infested with malaria of the malignant cerebral type that few white men have succeeded in surviving, and their inhabitants are more primitive than those of the Solomons. The original plan for Operation "Watchtower" provided for the occupation of these islands in order to guard the supply route and provide another airfield; but the terrain proved to be too rugged for airfield construction, and many of the Army Engineers sent in to survey died of malaria. In late October the islands were a no man's land.

Admiral Yamamoto, out of patience by the 24th after Kondo's ships had been milling about these waters for nearly two weeks, advised his Army friends that if they did not mop up Henderson Field in a hurry his ships would be obliged to retire as fuel was running short. With this blunt prodding, the Army announced that Henderson Field would be in the Emperor's hands that very evening.

That is what the plan said; but what happened that night did not follow the book, and the Japanese Admiral was bewildered. At 0126 October 25, his naval liaison officer on Guadalcanal jubilantly radioed: "*Banzai!* Occupied airfield at 2300." [3] At 0200 this officer

[3] Diary kept by yeoman of a Japanese DD, recovered from a survivor, trans. in Cincpac "Orange Naval Task Force Operations 10–30 Oct. 1942" 17 Jan. 1943. Capt. Omae in 1949 told us that this phony report started because a Japanese scout pilot thought he saw green-white-green flares, the prearranged signal for "Hender-

amplified his report to indicate that fighting still continued in the vicinity. Finally, at 0623, he was forced to retract the *Banzai* statement and admit that the field was still in Marine custody. In the meantime his premature pæan had set naval forces in action. Kondo's force, including four carriers,[4] steamed to and fro in a fog of indecision 300 miles north of Guadalcanal. During the morning Yamamoto directed carrier *Junyo* to conduct air raids on enemy shipping in Lunga Roads, but the planned surface force rampage south of San Cristobal was postponed. The riddle of the airfield was partially solved by early afternoon on the 25th, when the liaison officer at Guadalcanal reported that "because of difficulty in handling the force in the complicated terrain" the previous night's attack had failed. But there still remained another baffling question: where were the American carriers? A Japanese patrol plane out of the Gilbert Islands had sighted *Enterprise* some days previously, but the search planes which should have found the other carriers were coming back with empty dispatch blanks, owing to the wide sweep to the eastward taken by Kinkaid. Admiral Lee's battleship group, the only American force of any consequence whose position was known to Nagumo, was then between Rennell and San Cristobal Islands, out of range of his carrier planes. All that Nagumo could do was wait and wonder.

While the Japanese fretted, *Hornet, Enterprise* and their screens were well embarked on their run around Santa Cruz. Furthermore, they had information on enemy movements, since one of Admiral Fitch's efficient PBYs sighted two enemy carriers at noon of the 25th, on course SE by S, speed 25 knots. The American force was then west of the Santa Cruz Islands and 360 miles from the reported Japanese position, which lay northwest of the islands.[5] Owing to thick overcast and rain squalls the PBY was unable to hang on

---

son Field captured." Omae added that this was the reason why the *Yura* attack unit, whose movements on 25 Oct. are described in Section 3 of the last chapter, was called off from its original mission of bombarding the field; and that the attack on them by land-based aircraft made the destroyers "very suspicious" that the field was still in American hands!

[4] Carrier *Hiyo* developed engine trouble on 22 Oct. and returned to Truk with two destroyers; her planes flew to Rabaul.

[5] U.S. force at 10°04′ S, 170°18′ E. Japanese at 08°51′ S, 164°30′ E.

to the contact. Admiral Kinkaid was now faced with three choices:
—to await further developments, conduct a search or launch a
strike. He chose a combined search and strike, the former leaving
Enterprise at 1330, the latter at 1420. Unfortunately the presence
of the American PBY had alarmed the Japanese into reversing
course to the northward, so Kinkaid's 12 search planes and 29
attack planes saw nothing. Returning after dark, the first plane
crashed the flattop and six others were lost by landing in the water,
a tough break at a critical time.

Admiral Fitch's Catalinas and Flying Forts were hustling all day
on the 25th. Besides making and developing contacts on the Kondo
fleet, they went after Abe's battleships. Bombs fell close to *Kirishima* but no hits were made. The "Cats" did not try to scratch
until after dark, when five of them lumbered into the air, armed
with torpedoes and bombs. During the small hours of 26 October
two of them very nearly hit carrier *Zuikaku* and destroyer *Isokaze*.

The Japanese naval commanders realized that a sea battle was
inevitable despite the failure of the army ashore to take Henderson
Field. They were bothered by the failure of their planes to locate
the American carriers. Nevertheless, in the early evening they
scorched the air with radio directives indicating how the enemy
would be found and destroyed. Shortly before midnight 25 October Yamamoto came out with a revised overall concept: Army will
storm the airfield at 2100; "accordingly there is great likelihood
that the enemy fleet will appear in the area northeast of the Solomons, and the Combined Fleet will seek to destroy it on the 26th."
Aircraft will continue searching and tracking "regardless of weather
and enemy planes, in an attempt to discover size and nature of
enemy forces." [6]

At 0105 on the 26th Guadalcanal reported to Yamamoto that the
Army was still fighting for the airfield, but "the condition of the
first line is not clear." The PBY attack on *Zuikaku*, at 0250, also
alarmed the Japanese admiral. Was this a trap? Indecision reigned
again. Admiral Nagumo ordered his Striking Force to reverse

[6] Dispatches of 2118 and 2240. Desron 10 Combat Report No. 2 (WDC No.
160,985).

course to the north to await the outcome of the Henderson Field attack and the results of the aërial scouting.

Admiral Kinkaid spent the night of 25–26 October zigzagging steadily on an aggressive northwesterly course at 20 knots. He intended to make trouble for the Nips and expected to be repaid in kind. *Hornet* kept a deckload of aircraft readied for a moonlight strike; ships' companies were alerted to expect attack. At 0011, one of the faithful PBYs reported the enemy fleet about 300 miles to the northwest. Three hours later a second PBY contact went on the air; one large carrier and six other vessels about 200 miles away on the same bearing. This was the hottest dope yet received, and would have been of inestimable value to the task force commander if only delivered promptly; but it did not reach him until 0512, a two-hour delay. Fitch's headquarters at Espiritu Santo received the PBY broadcast and retransmitted that information.

In the gray hours before dawn Admiral Halsey in Nouméa riffled through the dispatches, glanced at his operations chart and sent out these words: "Attack ✦ Repeat — Attack!"[7] The single message had an electrifying effect on every ship in the Solomons. That was the stuff!

2. *Composition of Forces*

a. United States

SOUTH PACIFIC FORCE
Vice Admiral William F. Halsey, at Nouméa

TASK FORCE 16, Rear Admiral Thomas C. Kinkaid

ENTERPRISE   Capt. Osborne B. Hardison

Air Group 10: 1 TBF–1 (Avenger), Cdr. Richard K. Gaines

VF–10:	34 F4F–4 (Wildcat)	Lt. Cdr. James H. Flatley Jr.
VB–10:	18 SBD–3 (Dauntless)	Lt. Cdr. James A. Thomas
VS–10:	18 SBD–3	Lt. Cdr. James R. Lee
VT–10:	12 TBF–1	* Lt. Cdr. John A. Collett

SOUTH DAKOTA   Capt. Thomas L. Gatch

* Lost in this action.
[7] *Admiral Halsey's Story* p. 121.

Rear Admiral Mahlon S. Tisdale (Comcrudiv 4)

PORTLAND	Capt. Laurence T. DuBose
SAN JUAN	Capt. James E. Maher

Destroyer Screen, Capt. Charles P. Cecil (Comdesron 5)

* PORTER	Lt. Cdr. David G. Roberts
MAHAN	Lt. Cdr. Rodger W. Simpson

Desdiv 10, Cdr. Thomas M. Stokes

CUSHING	Lt. Cdr. Christopher Noble
PRESTON	Lt. Cdr. Max C. Stormes
SMITH	Lt. Cdr. Hunter Wood Jr.
MAURY	Lt. Cdr. Gelzer L. Sims
CONYNGHAM	Lt. Cdr. Henry C. Daniel
SHAW	Lt. Cdr. Wilbur G. Jones

TASK FORCE 17, Rear Admiral George D. Murray

* HORNET	Capt. Charles P. Mason

Air Group 8: 1 TBF–1, Cdr. Walter F. Rodee

VF–72:	36 F4F–4	Lt. Cdr. Henry G. Sanchez
VB–8:	18 SBD–3	Lt. James E. Vose
VS–8:	18 SBD–3	Lt. Cdr. William J. Widhelm
VT–6:	15 TBF–1	Lt. Edwin B. Parker Jr.

Rear Admiral Howard H. Good (Comcrudiv 5)

NORTHAMPTON	Capt. Willard A. Kitts III
PENSACOLA	Capt. Frank L. Lowe
SAN DIEGO	Capt. Benjamin F. Perry
JUNEAU	Capt. Lyman K. Swenson

Destroyer Screen, Cdr. Arnold E. True (Comdesron 2)

MORRIS	Lt. Cdr. Randolph B. Boyer
ANDERSON	Lt. Cdr. Richard A. Guthrie
HUGHES	Lt. Cdr. Donald J. Ramsey
MUSTIN	Cdr. Wallis F. Petersen
RUSSELL	Lt. Cdr. Glenn R. Hartwig
BARTON	Lt. Cdr. Douglas H. Fox

TASK FORCE 64,[8] Rear Admiral Willis A. Lee

WASHINGTON, SAN FRANCISCO, HELENA, ATLANTA, AARON WARD, BENHAM, FLETCHER, LANSDOWNE, LARDNER, MCCALLA

TASK FORCE 63

Land-based Air Forces, Rear Admiral Aubrey W. Fitch

At Henderson Field: 26 F4F–4, 6 P–400, 6 P–39, 20 SBD, 2 TBF
At Espiritu Santo: 23 F4F–4, 39 B–17, 12 Hudson of R.N.Z.A.F., 32 PBY, 5 OS2U (Kingfisher); tenders CURTISS and MACKINAC

* Sunk or lost in this battle. Lt. Albert P. Coffin succeeded Lt. Cdr. Collett as VT-10 commander.

[8] Operating separately. Did not engage.

At New Caledonia: 46 P–39 (12 en route Guadalcanal), 15 P–38, 16 B–26, 13 Hudson of R.N.Z.A.F.

Action of 25 October in Ironbottom Sound

TREVER	Lt. Cdr. Dwight M. Agnew
ZANE	Lt. Cdr. Peyton L. Wirtz
* SEMINOLE	Lt. Cdr. William G. Fewel
* YP–284	Lt. Carl W. Rasmussen

b. Japanese

COMBINED FLEET

Admiral Isoroku Yamamoto in *Yamato* at Truk

GUADALCANAL SUPPORTING FORCES

Vice Admiral Nobutake Kondo (C. in C. Second Fleet)

ADVANCE FORCE, Vice Admiral Kondo

Crudiv 4: ATAGO, TAKAO
Crudiv 5 (Rear Admiral Sentaro Omori): MYOKO, MAYA
    Screen, Rear Admiral Raizo Tanaka (Comdesron 2) in CL *Isuzu*
DDs NAGANAMI, MAKINAMI, TAKANAMI, UMIKAZE, KAWAKAZE, SUZUKAZE

Air Group, Rear Admiral Kakuji Kakuta (Comcardiv 2) [9]
JUNYO (24 VF, 21 VB, 10 VT); *Screen:* Destroyers KUROSHIO, HAYASHIO

Support Group, Vice Admiral Takeo Kurita (Combatdiv 3)

BBs KONGO, HARUNA; DDs OYASHIO, KAGERO, MURASAME, SAMIDARE, YUDACHI, HARUSAME

STRIKING FORCE, Vice Admiral Chuichi Nagumo (C. in C. Third Fleet)

Carrier Group, Vice Admiral Nagumo (Comcardiv 1)
    SHOKAKU (18 VF, 20 VB, 23 VT)
    ZUIKAKU (27 VF, 27 VB, 18 VT)
    ZUIHO (18 VF, 6 VT)
Screen, Heavy cruiser KUMANO; Destroyers AMATSUKAZE, HATSUKAZE, TOKITSUKAZE, YUKIKAZE, ARASHI, MAIKAZE, TERUZUKI, HAMAKAZE

Vanguard Group, Rear Admiral Hiroaki Abe (Combatdiv 11)

Battleships HIEI, KIRISHIMA
Crudiv 8 (Rear Admiral Tadaichi Hara): TONE, CHIKUMA
Crudiv 7 (Rear Admiral Shoji Nishimura): SUZUYA
    Screen, Rear Admiral Susumu Kimura (Comdesron 10) in CL *Nagara*
DDs KAZAGUMO, MAKIGUMO, YUGUMO, AKIGUMO, TANIKAZE, URAKAZE, ISOKAZE

* Sunk in this action.
[9] Flagship *Hiyo* developed engine trouble on 22 October and returned to Truk with DDs *Inazuma* and *Isonami;* planes sent to Rabaul and flag transferred to *Junyo.*

Supply Group

Oilers KOKUYO MARU, TOHO MARU, TOEI MARU, KYOKUTO MARU, Destroyer NOWAKI

LAND–BASED AIR FORCE

Vice Admiral Jinichi Kusaka (C. in C. 11th Air Fleet) at Rabaul
About 220 operational planes

ADVANCE EXPEDITIONARY FORCE

Vice Admiral Teruhisa Komatsu (C. in C. Sixth Fleet) in CL *Katori* at Truk

Force "A": Submarines I-4, I-5, I-7, I-8, I-22, I-176
Force "B": Submarines I-9, I-15, I-21, I-24, I-174, I-175

OUTER SOUTH SEAS FORCE

Vice Admiral G. Mikawa in CA *Chokai* at Shortland

These ships were in Actions of 25 October in Ironbottom Sound and Indispensable Strait. *Assault Unit:* Destroyers AKATSUKI, IKAZUCHI, SHIRATSUYU; *Attack (Bombardment) Unit*, Rear Admiral Tamotsu Takama (Comdesron 4), CL * YURA with DDs AKIZUKI, HARUSAME, YUDACHI, MURASAME, SAMIDARE

* Sunk in this action.

3. *The Carrier Plane Battle, 26 October*

The sun rose at 0523 on a fair South Sea day, low broken cumulus clouds apportioned haphazardly to about half the sky, the soft belly of the ocean rising and falling in a gentle swell, a languid 8-knot breeze from the southeast scarcely raising ripples on the sea's smooth skin. It was weather to the taste of dive-bomber pilots who could lurk in the clouds, but to the distaste of anti-aircraft gunners — no cloud has a silver lining for them.

At 0500, still lacking the patrol planes' reports, Admiral Kinkaid directed Captain Hardison of *Enterprise* to launch a 200-mile search of the sector between SW by W and due north. Sixteen Dauntless planes took off, each armed with a 500-pound bomb "just in case." For anyone with a penchant for danger and excitement, this flight was a bonanza.

The 16 SBDs paired up. The couple piloted by Lieutenant

Vivian W. Welch and Lieutenant (jg) Bruce A. McGraw USNR were the first to smell game — a "Kate" flying an opposite course about 85 miles from *Enterprise*. Neither plane paid heed to the other, since both were after something bigger. Next, at 0617, Welch and McGraw sighted Admiral Abe's Vanguard Group, reconnoitered it carefully, transmitted a report at 0630, and then proceeded to search farther for the carriers but failed to find them. On the way back to their carrier the two lieutenants gave Abe another inspection which drew anti-aircraft fire. Returning to *Enterprise* they passed "Kate" again. She had been snooping Kinkaid and telling her pals about it.

Lieutenant Commander James R. Lee and Ensign William E. Johnson USNR at 0650 were the first to pick up Nagumo's carriers and the first to let Admiral Kinkaid know their position — less than 200 miles northwest of him. As Nagumo laid smoke and altered course, the Lee-Johnson team commenced a two-plane bombing attack. Eight "Zekes" buzzed into action against them. Johnson got two and Lee one; then both Americans sought cloud cover.

Meanwhile, Lieutenant Stockton B. Strong and Ensign Charles B. Irvine USNR, searching on another leg, had seen nothing and decided that the Lee-Johnson report was an invitation to battle. At 0740, by a combination of skill and luck, they were able to sneak in undetected, push over in unopposed dives and make two hits which started fires on *Zuiho's* stern. These hits opened a 50-foot hole in the flight deck, knocked out the after anti-aircraft batteries, and canceled further flight operations on the flattop; but her strikes had already flown off. Combat air patrol chased the Americans as they pulled out and two "Zekes" fell victim to the rear-seat gunners of the SBDs.

The other planes of the search, finding nothing in their assigned sectors, went after reported targets to the westward and unsuccessfully bombed cruiser *Tone*. No enemy fighters bothered them, but on the way home they teamed up to destroy an enemy "Kate." All *Enterprise* search planes returned safely; a remarkable record, when it is considered that they found what they were looking for, disposed of seven "Zekes" and made two bomb hits on a carrier.

Japanese flag officers received simultaneous intimations of Kinkaid's proximity and position about 0630 when their own float searchers sighted *Hornet* [10] and one of the American search couples was recognized as carrier-based. A 65-plane strike was already spotted on *Shokaku, Zuikaku* and *Zuiho* decks. At 0658 the initial report came in from a *Shokaku* plane "Large enemy unit sighted, one carrier, five other vessels." Twelve minutes later "Zekes," "Kates" and "Vals" were aloft burning up the miles toward the American force 200 miles to the southeastward. The two big carriers readied a second strike of 44 planes. *Junyo*, not included in the first, readied a 29-plane group; but *Zuiho*, thanks to the Strong-Irvine attack, could not participate.

The Americans were a good 20 minutes behind the enemy in launching the first strike. At 0730 Lieutenant Commander William J. Widhelm led off 15 dive-bombing SBDs, 6 Avenger torpedo planes and 8 Wildcats from *Hornet*. Half an hour later, *Enterprise* sent off 3, 8 and 8 under her air group commander, Lieutenant Commander Gaines. At 0815 Commander Rodee led 9, 9 and 7 from *Hornet*, bringing the total number of striking American planes to 73. Time and fuel were so vital in an estimated 200-mile run to the enemy that all three strike groups took departure without waiting to form a single large cluster. They were strung along over a distance of several miles. When the leaders were about 60 miles out, the Japanese and American air groups passed close aboard, each eying the other and wondering who was going to have a flight deck to come back to. The *Hornet* group passed the enemy unmolested but the smaller *Enterprise* outfit fared badly. A dozen "Zekes" peeled off to make a vicious attack from upsun, shot down three Wildcats and damaged a fourth, then turned to the torpedo planes and made the same score on them, but this time lost two of their own. The four remaining Wildcats piled in and drove off the enemy after shooting down one more. *Enterprise* had lost nearly half her attack group over a hundred miles short of their target.

[10] Information from Capt. Layton, former Intelligence Officer Cincpac staff.

The only benefit derived from this inopportune meeting was a timely alert to *Hornet* and *Enterprise*.

Now came the most tense moment for the opposing commanders, Kinkaid and Kondo. Each had found the other, each was lashing out at the other. Vital decisions had been made; there was naught to do but hope and pray that Fate, winging closer to each force, would favor one's own side.

Admiral Kinkaid had every confidence that his offensive would press in with determination and courage. As for the defense, he could rely on savage resistance by the ships and planes of his heavily defended task force. Flagship *Enterprise* was the hub of a tight little circle rimmed by battleship *South Dakota*, heavy cruiser *Portland*, anti-aircraft cruiser *San Juan* and eight destroyers. Ten miles to the southeast cruised Murray's flagship *Hornet*, similarly surrounded by floating gun platforms: two heavy cruisers, two anti-aircraft cruisers and seven destroyers. Stacked in layers overhead were 38 fighters of the combat air patrol, all under *Enterprise* fighter-direction. This number was well under the 54 which had defended *Enterprise* at the Battle of the Eastern Solomons, but should be sufficient to rough up the enemy if properly placed. Unfortunately the *Enterprise* fighter-director officer was new to the job. Admiral Halsey had taken the veteran of Midway for service on his staff.

Admiral Kondo had the same faith in the fighting quality of his fliers as did Admiral Kinkaid. He was further heartened by a report that the enemy force had but one carrier.[11] For the defensive, he too had a few tricks. The old gambit might work again; battleships and cruisers some threescore miles out front might absorb air attacks intended for the carriers. If the Americans did break through, a goodly number of "Zekes" would be waiting to drive them off. Kondo did not think too well of his anti-aircraft weapons, but radical maneuvering by his tender-helmed ships had always

---

[11] Reported to him as the *Saratoga*. Old "Sara" appears to have been the only American carrier known by name to the enemy; she was repeatedly "sunk" in their propaganda broadcasts but always reappeared.

been an effective defense. The situation at 0900 was akin to the start of a basketball game, the ball centered but not yet in either team's possession.

The Japanese strike, first to depart, was also the first to arrive. A report of approaching Japanese aircraft was received at 0840 but the radar operators had great difficulty in separating friendly and enemy contacts on the same bearing, so that verification was not achieved until 0857 when the enemy was but 45 miles distant. Two minutes later combat air patrol sighted the "Val" dive-bombers at 17,000 feet, coming in fast.

When carriers are battling carriers, there is only one foolproof means of defense — to bomb the other fellow's flight decks before he can launch a strike. Failing that, the next best method is to knock down his planes with fighters before they reach their attack position. But if his strike gets through, the chance of escaping damage is slim. Radar screens are cluttered, the enemy is split into small groups on several bearings at various altitudes, easily concealed by clouds; one's own fighter planes are restricted by the dense anti-aircraft fire of the task force. On this occasion American combat air patrol was stationed too near and too late — 22,000 feet altitude and ten miles out at 0906. So the third and least desirable defense, a battle over the carriers, was forced on Kinkaid.

Lieutenant Albert D. Pollock, leading four Wildcats of the combat air patrol, first saw *Hornet* planes dogfighting with "Zekes"; next he saw anti-aircraft fire from the task force; and finally he picked up three "Vals" just entering their dives. He and his teammates, chasing the enemy craft down through the flak, managed to destroy all three, but by that time had lost their altitude advantage. Another fighter division leader, Lieutenant S. W. Vejtasa, saw no enemy planes until they were at the diving point. *Hornet* fighters had little better success, with insufficient altitude for timely interception of enemy planes. The fighter-director officers were up against a tough situation; we must not forget that this was still 1942, and the materials, gadgets and techniques worked out two years later were not available.

Captain Mason of *Hornet* had little time to watch the progress of his fighters. His ship and men were primed for battle: decks clear of inflammable planes, gasoline system filled with inert CO_2 gas, watertight compartments buttoned up, bow slicing the water at 28 knots, guns pointed and eyes turned skyward, damage control parties checking tools on station. The galley gang even had thousands of mince pies and doughnuts cooked and ready to serve in a lull in the battle; but as one of the bakers observed, "There just wasn't any lull!"

At about 0900 *Enterprise* entered a local rain squall which concealed her from the approaching Japanese. *Hornet*, however, was in the clear and the enemy concentrated on her, commencing at 0910. "Vals" dove down, loosing a series of explosive bombs. *Hornet* and her protectors blackened the sky with shell bursts which knocked down many but failed to prevent damage to the carrier. One bomb hit the starboard side of the flight deck aft; two near-misses hammered the hull. Next, the Japanese squadron commander, crippled by a shellburst, made a spectacular suicide crash. His plane hit the stack, glanced off and burst through the flight deck, where two of its bombs detonated. Even more deadly were the torpedo-carrying "Kates" boring in low from astern, slugging nastily at *Hornet's* tender groin. Two torpedoes exploded in the engineering spaces. The carrier, in a thick cloud of smoke and steam, lurched to starboard, slowed to a stop, lost all power and communications. She was now immobile, deaf, dumb and impotent. Three more quarter-ton bombs hit the flight deck; one detonated on impact, one penetrated to the fourth deck before exploding, one plowed through four decks before its delayed-action fuze touched it off in a forward messing compartment. *Hornet* was still writhing from the onslaught when a flaming "Kate" with a doomed pilot made a suicide run from dead ahead, piled into the port forward gun gallery and blew up near the forward elevator shaft. Captain Mason estimated that 27 planes had jumped his carrier; the enemy admitted the loss of 25.[12]

[12] This does not jibe with the Japanese account of 65 planes in the first wave. A large number were fighters, which may account for the discrepancy.

Within ten minutes of the first bomb hit, the sky was clear of enemy planes, and salvage work began. Fires were raging from bow to stern and from signal bridge to fourth deck. Torpedo hits had let in the sea and given the carrier an 8-degree list. Damage control under Commander Henry G. Moran and engineers under Commander Edward P. Creehan turned to with a will.

At 0925, when *Hornet* looked like a poor risk, 52 planes of her air group led by Lieutenant Commander "Gus" Widhelm were approaching the Japanese force. The 15 dive-bombers and 4 fighters of the leading wave had first sighted enemy cruisers and destroyers at 0915 and minutes later passed to the eastward of Kondo's Advance Force. Nine planes of combat air patrol tried to interfere with Widhelm's plans, but were engaged by his fighter escort and kept clear of the bombers, at a cost of two Wildcats. The SBDs continued without escort. At 0930 they encountered *Shokaku* and *Zuiho*, the latter still smoking from her early morning bomb dose. A cloud of "Zekes" closed in on the undefended bombers. Widhelm's plane was soon hit, but he continued doggedly toward the carriers until his plane could no longer fly, made a water landing, promptly inflated his rubber raft and sat back with his gunner to watch the show. Another bomber was shot down and two were forced to turn back because of damage, but the remaining eleven under another determined individual, Lieutenant James E. Vose, fought their way through to the pushover point, drew a bead on *Shokaku* and roared down through flak with "Zekes" still on their tails. It was worth the risk. Three to six 1000-pound bombs ripped the Japanese carrier's flight deck to shreds, destroyed the hangars and most of the guns and ignited severe fires.[13] *Shokaku* was out of the war for nine months.

Hornet's first wave of torpedo planes had early become separated from her dive-bombers; and that was too bad, because a couple of torpedoes might have finished *Shokaku*. The six Avengers

[13] Japanese reports vary from 3 to 6 hits; Widhelm from his life raft saw 6, Vose claimed 4. Widhelm and his gunner happily watched *Shokaku* burn and saw a Japanese destroyer passing so close it nearly swamped their raft. A searching PBY rescued them on the 28th.

failed to hear Widhelm's broadcast of Nagumo's position and never found the carriers, so launched their "fish" ineffectually at *Suzuya*, one of Abe's cruisers, around 0930. *Hornet's* second wave also missed the carriers. After another futile search, Lieutenant John J. Lynch at 0920 led his SBDs in a dive on cruiser *Chikuma*. Two bombs whooshed onto the bridge, wounded Captain Komura and killed most of the personnel; a burst below slowed her down, two near-misses sprinkled the superstructure. *Chikuma* was out of the fight but could get home. Two Avengers of this second wave, armed with bombs, attacked cruiser *Tone* unsuccessfully. *Hornet* had shot her bolt.

The one small *Enterprise* wave, disorganized by the disastrous attack by "Zekes" en route, separated into two groups. Three dive-bombers made an ineffective run on battleship *Kirishima;* four TBFs, discovering that their fighter escort was very short of gas, launched torpedoes at a heavy cruiser but missed.

As the last American plane pulled out from its attack run, the outcome of the battle was very doubtful. *Hornet* was out of action and dead in the water, but *Enterprise* was untouched; and despite losses there were enough planes for another strike. On the other side, *Shokaku* and *Zuiho* could no longer indulge in flight operations but *Zuikaku* and *Junyo* were intact and mounting further assaults. And, by intercepting voice radio transmissions, at 0927 the enemy learned that a second American carrier was in the area. One lucky bomb planted on that carrier's flight deck, and the battle would be over — as at Midway when *Hiryu* was done in. The Japs determined to place that bomb.

On board *Hornet* the fire menace was serious but not deadly. Bucket brigades were hastily organized, carbon-dioxide fire extinguishers, hand-carried, were liberally used and chemical "foamite" was scattered on the flames manually. These measures were moderately effective but the major fire-fighting medium was water from hoses of destroyers *Morris* and *Russell* alongside. By 1000 all fires appeared to be under control. But it was a herculean task to regain propulsion. Commander Creehan's black gang made a hurried inspection and decided that three boilers might possibly make steam which, by ingenious use of unruptured pipes, could be delivered to the after engine room. It was worth a try. Men stumbled through coal-black passageways cluttered with debris, crawled into stifling firerooms, prayed, cursed and performed engineering miracles. The other vessels of the task group steamed in slow circles around the stricken giant. Cruiser *Northampton*, assigned the ticklish job of taking *Hornet* in tow, left her position in the screen at 1005. Just four minutes later there came out of the sky a single "Val," hell-bent for *Hornet*. Its bomb missed close aboard one of the fire-fighting destroyers, but the effect of this surprise package was to delay towing operations as ships milled about apprehensive of further raids. Their concern was unnecessary, for the lone raider's pals, some two dozen all told, were at that moment whistling down on *Enterprise*, twenty miles to the eastward.

While Admiral Murray's sailors were struggling to save *Hornet*, Kinkaid's group began to have trouble. At 1002 came a torpedo salvo, probably from Japanese submarine *I–21*.[14] One "fish" bored into both firerooms of destroyer *Porter*, which was then engaged in picking up a downed air crew. Destroyer *Shaw* took off all *Porter's* crew except 15 killed in the firerooms and sank her with gunfire [15] — sad but necessary with the enemy so near.

Even without these two destroyers *Enterprise* was better off than *Hornet* in the matter of anti-aircraft batteries. While in Pearl Harbor both *Enterprise* and *South Dakota* had acquired the new 40-mm anti-aircraft weapons, an American version of the Swedish Bofors, that proved vastly superior to the 1.1-inch. These guns, mounted in quads, were capable of terrific execution at intermediate ranges, a fact about to be demonstrated.

The "Val" which attacked *Hornet* at 1000 was the only one of a 44-plane strike that had left *Zuikaku* and *Shokaku* at 0822 that

[14] Japanese records do not show which boat fired the torpedo but credit *I–21* with a "battleship" next day.
[15] Position lat. 8°32′ S, long. 167°17′ E.

did not concentrate on *Enterprise*. A coördinated dive-bombing and torpedo attack similar to the one on *Hornet* was planned, but the dive-bombers, nearly half an hour ahead of the "Kates," dropped down without waiting. *South Dakota's* radar had picked up this group 55 miles away; yet neither fighter planes nor anti-aircraft opposed the enemy until his diving started. This sort of fighting was old stuff for *Enterprise* gunners, who methodically set about making the enemy's ride down plenty bumpy. Their professional efforts were accompanied by a large amount of enthusiastic gunfire support from the screen, particularly from *San Juan* and *South Dakota;* the latter here demonstrated conclusively how useful a fast battleship could be to a carrier during an air attack. She maneuvered about 1000 yards from "Big E" — a neat bit of ship-handling by Lieutenant (jg) William D. Moody usnr, the assistant navigator and junior officer of the watch. *Enterprise* observed 7 planes crash in the immediate vicinity; *South Dakota* claimed 32 and was officially credited with 26. Out of 23 bombs dropped, the enemy made two hits and one near-miss.

The first bomb to sear *Enterprise* smashed through the flight deck close to the bow and traveled some 50 feet through the forecastle deck and the ship's side before exploding. The blast blew a parked airplane over the side and with it a stout fellow of the "ground crew," S. D. Presley, who from the rear cockpit of the plane was firing a machine gun. The second bomb landed just abaft the forward elevator and broke in two at the hangar deck where one half exploded and the other drilled down to the third deck before going off. This bomb killed and wounded many men and caused scattered fires. The third detonated close to the hull on the starboard side aft, started numerous plates and damaged a main turbine bearing.

As at the Battle of the Eastern Solomons, the repairmen were on hand dousing fires, patching holes, adjusting machinery and stemming leaks before the firing ceased. Right with them were the first-aid parties caring for the 75 wounded; but 44 sailors were beyond aid. The enemy torpedo planes had not yet been heard from, but Lieutenant Vejtasa, whose Wildcat division had shot down three planes during an attack on *Hornet,* was ready and waiting as eleven dark-green "Kates" came in from the south. He led his wing man into the thick of them, expertly destroyed six and then ran out of ammunition. Other fighter sections destroyed three or four more "Kates" but all were handicapped by ammunition shortages. About 14 of the torpedo planes succeeded in reaching Kinkaid's ships where, naturally, *Enterprise* was number one attraction. Anti-aircraft took out 5 more, but the 9 remaining dropped four torpedoes to port and five to starboard. Captain Hardison, seeing three torpedo tracks forward of the starboard beam, brought *Enterprise* hard right and combed the wakes. Another quick turn dodged a fourth torpedo which zipped by 100 feet away. The torpedo planes on the port side were given a long, hot approach run when *Enterprise* made her hard right turn; they were splashed by anti-aircraft guns but only after cruiser *Portland* had been jarred by some three dud warheads.

While guns were still spitting, one torpedo plane charged in for a suicide try, curiously picking on destroyer *Smith.* Carrying his torpedo under his belly this 1942-style Kamikaze hurtled into the destroyer's forecastle. The entire forward part of the ship erupted in flames. Lieutenant Commander Hunter Wood ran to the after control station, and Chief Quartermaster F. Riduka to the steering-engine room. Following telephoned directions from the skipper, Riduka steered *Smith* smartly through the formation, nuzzling the ship's burning bow close under *South Dakota's* quarter where the battleship's foaming wake helped to quench fires. Yet, even before the fires were out, *Smith* with her after guns helped defend *Enterprise* during her next air attack. She lost 28 dead and 23 wounded.

Enterprise had a forty-minute spell of hard breathing after the torpedo plane attack. Overhead now were dense, low, beetle-browed clouds offering shelter for any aërial ambuscade. Near by, planes from both carriers were demanding to come on board for gas and bullets. On the carrier flight deck there was trouble clearing up the mess from the bomb hits. To make matters more difficult, a submarine periscope appeared.

Meanwhile a 29-plane strike, the first from carrier *Junyo*, was closing. *South Dakota's* radar picked up a suspicious indication to the west at 1101. At 1110 she mistakenly opened gunfire at six SBDs trying to get on board *Enterprise*. The SBDs beat a hasty retreat and *Enterprise* reported "no unidentified aircraft" at 1120. One minute later the *Junyo* "bastards" [16] tumbled out of the low overcast with their bomb and torpedo loads. Although the clouds afforded excellent cover for the enemy, they gave him no opportunity to pick a choice carrier and forced him to make shallow dives which offered good targets for anti-aircraft gunners. In two minutes, some 20 enemy planes pushed through the cloud drapery; eight were shot down and only one paid off, a near-miss on *Enterprise* causing minor damage. Fair enough, so far. But at 1127 stragglers from *Junyo's* strike broke into the open with sudden attacks on *South Dakota* and *San Juan*. These pilots did better. A quarter-ton bomb from a bow-on attack hit the battleship's No. 1 turret on its after starboard corner and exploded. The turret crew, with the exception of one officer at the periscope, were not even aware that their tough armored roof had been hit, but a shell fragment wounded Captain Gatch in the neck as he stood erect on the walkway outside the armored conning tower. In the ensuing confusion, steering control was shifted to "Bat 2," the executive officer's station aft, and there the telephone went dead; so that for one minute *South Dakota* ran amok, heading straight for the "Big E," who quickly got out of her way. Fifty men were wounded but only one died.

Anti-aircraft cruiser *San Juan* was struck by an armor-piercing bomb which bored through the ship's bottom before detonating. She lost steering control with rudder jammed hard right, and Captain Maher experienced several anxious moments as his ship spiraled through the formation, guns shooting, whistle blowing,

---

[16] In radar slang unidentified aircraft were termed "bandits." *South Dakota's* chronological log of battle whimsically substituted "bastards."

breakdown flag flying. No collisions resulted and the damage, open circuit breakers, was rectified in a matter of minutes. Cruiser *Portland* also had a steering casualty in the course of the morning and was conned from the after control station during much of the action. Steering casualties are much dreaded by sailors, for in the short time required to shift control a high-speed ship can get herself into really hot water.

About ten planes were shot down in this, the last go. *Enterprise* then turned into the wind to recover aircraft whose gas tanks were almost dry. As the inoperative forward elevator caused delay in striking planes below, several were forced to splash, but destroyers picked up their crews. In order to reduce congestion on the flight deck, 13 SBDs were flown off to Espiritu Santo. *Enterprise* launched a new combat air patrol and at 1400 retired from the battle zone. *Hornet* had been out of sight since early morning.

4. HORNET *Abandoned; All Hands Retire*

The prospect of saving *Hornet* looked a little brighter when at 1123 October 26 Captain Kitts of *Northampton* kicked his engines slowly ahead, towing the carrier on the end of an inch-and-three-quarters wire. Then the line parted. A two-inch towing cable, stowed deep in *Hornet's* after elevator pit, was roused out and secured at 1330. A towing speed of three knots was gradually built up. At noon Admiral Murray transferred his flag to *Pensacola*, the better to command his task group. The wounded were gathered on the fantail where dressings were applied, splints fastened and medication administered. In the early afternoon Captain Mason ordered all wounded and nonessential men removed from the ship to destroyers *Russell* and *Hughes*. Breeches buoys, stretchers and cargo nets were used for a mass exodus of some 875 sailors, completed at 1440.

Admiral Kondo had some reorganizing to do before he could send off more strikes. As Nagumo's carriers had been heading away from Kinkaid since daybreak, he ordered undamaged *Zuikaku* and most of the screen destroyers to reverse course toward the enemy. Crippled *Zuiho* and *Shokaku* continued on a northerly course and withdrew from the battle. Command of the carriers now passed to Admiral Kakuta in *Junyo*.[17] The loss of nearly 100 planes during the morning left him neither quantity nor uniformity in air strength. At 1315 *Junyo* sent a mixed strike of five of her own planes and ten that belonged to *Shokaku* to hit the Americans, who had plenty of warning of this latest effort. But no planes were over the task force to stop it. At 1515 half a dozen torpedo planes started in, weaving from side to side. *Northampton* hastily cut loose her tow and turned hard left, avoiding the torpedoes intended for her. Unfortunately anti-aircraft cruiser *Juneau*, having misunderstood a signal, had pulled out of formation and joined Kinkaid's group, thus depriving wounded *Hornet* of the protection of her 16-gun 5-inch battery. The carrier was an easy target, almost dead in the water, and it seems strange that only one torpedo hit her.

What happens below when a torpedo explodes in a carrier is well told by *Hornet's* engineer officer, Commander Creehan, who was on the third deck port side, over the aviation storeroom, when the torpedo hit the starboard side of that storeroom: —

A sickly green flash momentarily lighted the scullery compartment and seemed to run both forward toward Repair Station 5 and aft into the scullery compartment for a distance of about 50 feet. This was preceded by a thud so deceptive as to almost make one believe that the torpedo had struck the port side. Immediately following the flash a hissing sound as of escaping air was heard followed by a dull rumbling noise. The deck on the port side seemed to crack open and a geyser of fuel oil which quickly reached a depth of two feet swept all personnel at Repair 5 off their feet and flung them headlong down the sloping decks of the compartment to the starboard side. Floundering around in the fuel oil, all somehow regained their feet and a hand chain was formed to the two-way ladder and escape scuttle leading from the third

[17] Nagumo transferred his flag at 1930 to destroyer *Arashi*, which steamed southeast to place him on board *Zuikaku*, which she did on 27 October at 1530.

deck to the second deck. . . . All managed to escape in some fashion through this scuttle . . . and presented a sorry appearance upon reaching the hangar deck.[18]

With her after engine room flooding rapidly, *Hornet* was in a hopeless predicament. The starboard list increased to 14 degrees. Captain Mason told his crew to stand by to abandon ship while his gunners searched the sky for the dive-bombers, which were expected to follow the torpedo planes. At 1540 the "Vals" arrived and doled out their bombs. No score; all bombs missed and anti-aircraft fire missed the bombers.

At 1550 Captain Mason left his bridge and five minutes later six "Kates" in a perfect Vee formation made a neat horizontal bombing run on the helpless ship. A radioman about to abandon ship saw them and manned a machine gun, shouting to another radioman as he opened fire, "Come on over pal, three shots for a quarter!" But *Hornet* took another hit, on the starboard after corner of the flight deck.

Abandoning ship is a sad business. A man-o'-war is home, club, office, pride, joy and worry of her crew. *Hornet*'s men had a bellyful of carrier warfare that bloody Monday, yet they hated to leave the old stinger. As sailors slid down lines into the water one asked another, "Are you going to reënlist?" The reply was, "Goddamit, yes — on the new *Hornet!*"

At 1702 October 26 Nagumo's fliers made their last stab at the dying flattop; 6 fighters and 4 dive-bombers from *Junyo* exploded a bomb on the carrier's empty hangar deck and started a brief fire. The destroyers soon resumed rescue work so that by dark all living men of *Hornet*'s crew were safe. She lost 111 killed; 108 wounded survived.

It now appeared that there was no alternative to destroying the carrier and retreating from the scene. Destroyer *Mustin*, a mile away on the carrier's beam, carefully fired eight torpedoes at her in slow succession. Results were not complimentary to American

[18] Capt. Mason's "Report of Action 26 Oct. 1942 and Subsequent Loss of *Hornet*," 30 Oct. 1942.

torpedo performance: two erratic runs, three indeterminate runs and only three hits. *Hornet* refused to sink. At 1920 *Anderson* fired her eight torpedoes. One angled to the right, one blew up prematurely, six hit. But the carrier continued to ignore mistreatment at the hands of old friends.

Meanwhile Kondo, having early decided to follow up his success, had dispatched Abe's Vanguard Group and his own Advance Force on night search and attack missions, *Zuikaku* and *Junyo* following to exploit any victory resulting from gunfire battle. Scouting float planes relayed a steady stream of information on the sad plight of the American carrier, and Abe's group was closing fast. *Mustin* and *Anderson* were uneasily aware of aërial snoopers but they were beholden to bury *Hornet. Anderson* resorted to shellfire, pouring 130 rounds into the carrier's logy hull. Then both ships gave her nearly 300 more rounds. By 2040 *Hornet* was incandescent with flame throughout her length and the destroyers took to their heels, Japanese planes encouraging them with a display of flares and float lights. Forty minutes later, Abe's force was treated to the sight of the carrier blazing and exploding. Unable to take her in tow, Abe detached a destroyer division in a vain effort to catch *Mustin* and *Anderson* and sent destroyers *Makigumo* and *Akigumo* to close *Hornet* and sink her with torpedoes. Four big Japanese 24-inch "fish" finished what aërial torpedoes, bombs and American "fish" had started. At 0135 October 27 Japanese sailors had the satisfaction of watching *Hornet* — seventh ship of that name in the United States Navy, and the first of any navy to bring bombers to Tokyo — as she plunged into a 2700-fathom deep off the Santa Cruz Islands.[19]

Kondo now set a retiring northerly course for all his force and laid plans for the morrow — a search for enemy forces and more carrier-air attacks. During the night, however, he was offered some convincing reasons for not prolonging his stay south of the fifth parallel. Two hours after midnight, a "Black Cat" from

---

[19] The position was lat. 8°35′ S, long. 166°45′ E, 145 miles NNE of Ndeni. The eighth ship and second carrier named *Hornet* was commissioned 29 Nov. 1943.

Espiritu delivered a close-in torpedo attack on *Zuikaku* which the carrier barely avoided. Another Cat, piloted by Lieutenant Melvin K. Atwell, crippled destroyer *Teruzuki* but not fatally. The Japanese continued to steam slowly around 300 miles to the northward of Ndeni until early afternoon, when order was given for a general retirement to Truk.

Kinkaid's force moved southward during the night of 26–27 October and by daybreak was well on its way to Nouméa. En route, *South Dakota* and *Mahan* collided while avoiding a submarine contact; the battleship's damage almost forced a Stateside return for overhaul. To the westward Admiral Lee's flagship *Washington*, which as yet had seen no action, had a brief bit of excitement in the early hours of the 27th when Japanese submarine *I–15* let fly at her with torpedoes. Later in the same morning a high-speed "tin fish" chased Lee's force for some distance, its wake visible to lookouts, who considerately passed the word to all hands in compartments under the waterline. Fortunately the warhead exploded while still 400 yards short of *Washington*. This incident convinced Halsey that he must no longer operate capital ships continuously at sea in submarine-infested waters — a decision which brought hearty Amens from the long-suffering denizens of Torpedo Junction. Lee's task force was split, part heading for Nouméa, part for the New Hebrides.

The Santa Cruz set-to was the fourth carrier battle in six months. Something of a pattern had been established and little new occurred. There was much criticism of the poor fighter-direction. The standard doctrine of carrier tactics, operating each flattop as the center of a special group, came up again for discussion; and the older practice was abandoned during sorties of the carrier task forces in early 1943.

American pilots and gunners remarked that the Japanese flier was losing his touch. Possibly so, owing to five months' heavy losses; but the main reason why the enemy seemed less efficient in the air was an improvement in American fighting technique, both in the air and on deck. The new 40-mm anti-aircraft gun featured by *Enterprise* and *South Dakota* showed the Jap up by knocking him down. In two techniques only were the Americans inferior: torpedo attack and long-range search. Torpedo hits were infrequent and detonations still more rare.[20] Search planes were doing wonders but the information was not getting to the people who needed it.

What effect did the battle have on the situation? Was it still "not hopeless but certainly critical," as Nimitz had said? Measured in combat tonnage sunk, the Japanese had won a tactical victory; but other losses forced them back to the Truk hideout. The land assault against the Marines had ended in a fizzle; the sea effort had dangerously reduced Japanese air strength. Tokyo claimed "three carriers, one battleship, three cruisers and one destroyer," but the Imperial Rescript that followed suggested that the Emperor was not too sure he had won: —

The Combined Fleet is at present striking heavy blows at the enemy Fleet in the South Pacific Ocean. We are deeply gratified. I charge each of you to exert yourselves to the utmost in all things toward this critical turning point in the war.[21]

American claims for the battle were moderate and accurate. The loss of an aircraft carrier was promptly made known to the public. Several days after the battle Admiral Nimitz observed, "The general situation at Guadalcanal is not unfavorable" — a much more hopeful view than his mid-October statement. But he well knew that the Japanese were more determined than ever to retrieve Guadalcanal. All right, let 'em try; the Battle of Santa Cruz Islands had gained priceless time for the Americans — days in which to reinforce and prepare.

[20] For reasons, see Vol. IV of this History chap. x.
[21] Desron 2 War Diary, Enclosure B to Cincpac "Orange Naval Task Force Operations, 10–30 Oct. 1942" 17 Jan. 1943.

CHAPTER XII

The Naval Battle of Guadalcanal[1]

12–15 November 1942

1. *Great Expectations*

AT the end of October a feeling of frustration respecting
Guadalcanal pervaded both Japanese and American high
commands. Allied ships afloat and aircraft aloft had failed in their
efforts to seal off Guadalcanal from enemy access, or even to en-
sure the safe arrival of American reinforcements. Admiral Halsey, after two weeks as Commander South Pacific Force, felt
exasperated. On shore an alleged irresistible force, the Imperial
Japanese Army, had met a demonstrably immovable object, the
United States Marine Corps. Something had to give soon. The
break came in the great three-day Naval Battle of Guadalcanal.

Each side decided to attack the other during November, each
believing that his strength was sufficient to hammer the issue into
a favorable and final shape. In Nouméa, Admiral Halsey and staff
prepared to accelerate the movement of supplies and reinforcements and, at the same time, disrupt the enemy's efforts. In Truk,
Admiral Yamamoto completed an operation plan designed to se-

---

[1] Earlier called "Battle of the Solomons" or "Third and Fourth Battles of Savo
Island." The sources, other than the Action Reports of vessels and commands concerned and the personal experiences of Cdr. James C. Shaw in *Atlanta*, are Cincpac Report "Solomon Islands Campaign – Battle of the Solomons, 11–15 November
1942" 18 Feb. 1943; Allied Translator and Interpreter Section of General Headquarters (General MacArthur's Command) "Naval Battle of Guadalcanal" ATIS
15931, prepared in Japan under the direction of Lt. Cdr. Henry Salomon USNR;
Commander Amphibious Forces South Pacific "Report of Operations of TF 67
and TG 62.4, Nov. 8–15 1942 and Summary of Third Battle of Savo," 3 Dec. 1942.

cure supremacy in the Solomons. Characteristically, the American plan was simple and direct — to bring in troops and supplies over airways and sea lanes — while the Japanese drew up an involved schedule of interdependent troop and ship movements.

On 30 October anti-aircraft cruiser *Atlanta* and destroyers *Aaron Ward, Benham, Fletcher* and *Lardner* escorted to Guadalcanal the transports bringing General del Valle's 155-mm artillery — a welcome present for the Marines, who now had something with which to outshoot the Japanese "Pistol Petes." Shortly after sunrise on the 30th, while the big guns were being unloaded, the escort gave rousing bombardment support to a westward push of the Marines which carried them to Point Cruz by 3 November. For an hour on the morning of the 2nd, *Shaw* and *Conyngham* shelled Japanese shore positions between Point Cruz and the mouth of the Umasani River with 803 rounds of 5-inch ammunition. But that night the enemy pulled his old trick of sneaking through the Sound to land 1500 troops and some artillery near Koli Point, east of the American lines. This exploit appears to have produced a greater impression in America than in the South Pacific. The *New York Times* in announcing it included a warning against optimism by Secretary Knox: "It is a bitter, tough fight and the whole Japanese Fleet is involved." Yet, a few hours before this bad news reached the public, cruisers *San Francisco* and *Helena* and destroyer *Sterett* had drenched the new enemy positions with a destructive bombardment. The Marines followed up relentlessly and by 9 November had practically exterminated the Koli Point force.

Nevertheless, between 2 and 10 November the enemy brought in 65 destroyer loads and 2 cruiser loads of troops to western Guadalcanal. Seabees worked overtime to repair and enlarge Henderson Field, and planes based there inflicted major damage on destroyers *Takanami* and *Naganami* on the 7th. On the same day destroyer *Lansdowne* brought up 90 tons of ammunition for the Marines. Her unloading was interrupted at 0929 when *Majaba*, an 1800-ton Navy cargo ship anchored near by, was hit by a torpedo from a Japanese submarine. United States destroyers in the vicinity were ordered to go get the offender, thought at the time to be a midget.[2] *Lansdowne* joined in the search, which proved unsuccessful; then finished discharging her cargo and spent the afternoon bombarding Japanese shore positions east of the Metapona River. Next day, 8 November, the Tulagi motor torpedo boat flotilla thrust a damaging but not fatal torpedo into destroyer *Mochizuki*, at the cost of two PT boats hurt. And on the 10th, sweeper *Southard* sank submarine *I-172* off Cape Recherché, San Cristobal. Times were not exactly dull, but neither were they momentous.

Execution of American plans was still in the hands of Rear Admiral Richmond K. Turner, Commander Amphibious Forces South Pacific. Incorporated under his command were two task groups of transports loaded with troops, food, ammunition and aviation material; and a support group of cruisers and destroyers. Three attack cargo ships (AKAs), escorted by Rear Admiral Norman Scott in *Atlanta* with four destroyers, left Espiritu Santo 9 November and arrived Lunga Point on Armistice Day. The second transport contingent, commanded by Rear Admiral Turner in *McCawley*, sailed 8 November from Nouméa and made Lunga on the 12th. Escorting Turner's four transports were two cruisers and three destroyers from the support group commanded by Rear Admiral Daniel J. Callaghan. The rest of this group, three cruisers and five destroyers, rendezvoused with the transports off San Cristobal on 11 November.

Intelligence reports indicated such a press of enemy shipping at Truk, Rabaul and the Shortlands that American commanders were not sanguine of discharging their own transports safely and at the same time preventing the enemy from landing heavy reinforcements. So Admiral Halsey sent a formidable team of troubleshooters to the area, with Rear Admiral Kinkaid in command.

[2] Japanese submarine *I-20*, no midget, claimed "sinking" a transport off Lunga Point this date; but she was overoptimistic, because *Majaba* was successfully beached and later salvaged.

This was Task Force 16, comprising carrier *Enterprise*, battle-ships, cruisers and destroyers. If the "Big E," still under repair at Nouméa from her bout off Santa Cruz, could not get there in time, the battleships and four destroyers would be detached for independent action, under the command of Rear Admiral Willis A. Lee in *Washington*.

That is exactly what happened — and mighty fortunate that it did.

Indirect support for Turner, Callaghan and Kinkaid was pro-vided by the 24 submarines deployed in the Solomons, and by Rear Admiral Fitch's South Pacific planes in Espiritu Santo.[3] General Geiger's First Marine Air Wing at Henderson Field gave direct support.

Poised in the enemy base at Truk, under Admiral Kondo, were two light carriers, four battleships, eleven cruisers and over three dozen destroyers to cover eleven high-speed *Marus* for a major movement of supplies and men into Guadalcanal on 14 Novem-ber. Henderson Field would be heavily bombarded on the two previous nights. The operation plan indicated that Kondo antici-pated stout opposition, and he was not disappointed.

Intelligence on both sides of the enemy's intentions and compo-sition of forces was fairly accurate. There was no question of sur-prise here. Admiral Turner's letter of instructions to Admiral Cal-laghan, dated 10 November, covered about everything that the Japanese could and did do. They, on the other hand, made a very close estimate of the forces that Halsey would employ.

As the American transports steamed northward, D-day dawned on the other side of the world in North Africa. An auspicious event for Allied fighting men everywhere, it was particularly wel-come to those of the South Pacific, so long inured to delay and disappointment. Copies of the morning press were passed eagerly from hand to hand; details of the African adventure became cur-rency of conversation. If the Atlantic Fleet could handle the

---

[3] See Task Organization List in next section for details; Appendix for air squadrons.

Krauts and their Vichy friends, surely Turner's outfit could take a round turn on the Nips!

Admiral Scott's convoy hoped to elude long-range enemy air detection by passing north of San Cristobal, but the wily Japanese had sent to the lower Solomons an I-class submarine carrying a seaplane, which sighted the force on 10 November and maneuvered maddeningly for two hours beyond anti-aircraft range.[4] That meant trouble off Lunga. Accordingly, at daybreak on the 11th when anchor chains roared down the hawsepipes of transports *Zeilin*, *Libra* and *Betelgeuse*, the Marine passengers lost no time landing; and their shore movement was expedited by a dive-bombing attack delivered by about a dozen enemy planes from carrier *Hiyo*, then northwest of Guadalcanal.[5] Ample warning from a coastwatcher and from radar resulted in a vigorous anti-aircraft reception for the bat-winged "Vals," few of which escaped. No ship was hit, but *Zeilin's* hull was ruptured and flooded by near-misses. She continued unloading until midafternoon when, having discharged all passengers and half her cargo, she departed for Espiritu Santo escorted by *Lardner*. Another attack later in the day by some 27 "Bettys" from Rabaul, flying too high for anti-aircraft fire to reach, dropped bombs around Henderson Field.

Meanwhile, Turner's four transports had been pushing northward, closely covered by Callaghan's Support Group. Turner, too, was snooped by a Japanese plane and so ordered the troops ashore immediately upon their arrival at 0540 November 12, carrying only one unit of fire and two days' rations per man. During the previous midwatch Callaghan's group had searched Ironbottom Sound and found it empty of enemy shipping. For protection of transports during the unloading, cruisers *San Francisco*, *Portland* and *Helena* steamed in a close semicircle while *Atlanta*, *Juneau*, eleven destroyers and two large minesweepers afforded anti-submarine protection about three miles out.

[4] Japanese Army Report to MacArthur Command "Southeast Area Operations, Part I (Navy)" (Special Staff U.S. Army Historical Division No. 851-100) p. 42.
[5] Lt. Roger Pineau's translation of Board of Merit Report (WDC No. 161,709).

The first diversion that day was a submarine contact at 0600, only six miles from Lunga Point. Vessels of the screen depth-bombed vigorously but hit nothing. "Pistol Pete" then started whacking away at the transport area — much to the discomfiture of landing craft — but, again, hit nothing. Destroyer and cruiser fire and Marine shore batteries silenced the big guns temporarily and then turned their attention to enemy beach positions to the westward. The unloading proceeded at accelerated pace, anticipating an air attack. And at 1317 November 12 a coastwatcher in Buin sent word that enemy bombers and fighters were coming.

Admiral Turner immediately broke off unloading, got his ships under way and formed anti-aircraft disposition. The transports were placed in two parallel columns of three ships each, while anti-aircraft guns on the support vessels bristled up like the hackles on so many Kerry Blues. Course and axis were set in the general direction of Savo Island. At 1405 enemy planes were sighted circling low around the Asses' Ears, the eastern point of Florida Island; these were twin-engined "Bettys" getting into position for a coördinated torpedo attack. Presently they split into two groups so that a bracketing approach could be made. But Admiral Turner was a master at eluding torpedo plane attack. He turned his ships right so as to present their broadsides temptingly to the northern group of "Bettys," who accepted the bait and charged in, skimming the surface. While the ships were pouring out anti-aircraft fire, Turner again changed course, this time to the left so that sterns were rudely presented to the onrushing ladies, and their torpedoes ran harmlessly parallel to the course. In the meantime the other Japanese plane group, to the southward, was being pursued by Wildcats from Henderson Field, which forced them to attack prematurely and disadvantageously. Again Turner's captains combed the dangerous torpedo tracks. During the eight-minute period of action, anti-aircraft batteries averaged one kill per minute, while the fighters accounted for all but one of the remaining "Bettys." Other fighter planes disposed of a flight of dive-bombers as well as nine high-level bombers who had been making holes in the landscape around the flying field.

On the debit side there were two serious incidents. Destroyer *Buchanan* received so much topside damage from friendly anti-aircraft fire that she was ordered out of the area at nightfall. A wounded enemy plane deliberately crashed cruiser *San Francisco* on the after control station, knocking out a fire control radar, disabling an anti-aircraft gun director, and inflicting casualties on some 50 men including the executive officer, Commander Mark H. Crouter. The wounded were transferred to *President Jackson*, but Commander Crouter, eager to return to duty at the earliest moment, insisted on remaining on board, a decision that shortly cost him his life.

2. *Composition of Forces*

a. United States

SOUTH PACIFIC FORCE
Vice Admiral William F. Halsey, at Nouméa

TASK FORCE 67
Rear Admiral Richmond K. Turner

TG 67.1 TRANSPORT GROUP, Captain Ingolf N. Kiland

MCCAWLEY	Capt. Charlie P. McFeaters
CRESCENT CITY	Capt. John R. Sullivan
PRESIDENT ADAMS	Cdr. Frank H. Dean
PRESIDENT JACKSON	Cdr. Charles W. Weitzel

Embarking 182nd Infantry (less 3rd Battalion), 4th Marine Replacement Battalion and Naval Local Defense Force personnel. This Group was escorted Nouméa–Guadalcanal by ships marked (T) in TG 67.4.

TG 67.4 SUPPORT GROUP, Rear Admiral Daniel J. Callaghan *

SAN FRANCISCO		* Capt. Cassin Young

Rear Admiral Mahlon S. Tisdale (Comcrudiv 4)

PENSACOLA	(E)	Capt. Frank L. Lowe
PORTLAND	(T)	Capt. Laurance T. DuBose
HELENA		Capt. Gilbert C. Hoover
* JUNEAU		* Capt. Lyman K. Swenson

* Lost or killed in this battle.

Destroyer Screen

| * BARTON | (T) | * Lt. Cdr. Douglas H. Fox |
| * MONSSEN | (T) | Lt. Cdr. Charles E. McCombs |

Cdr. Thomas M. Stokes (Comdesdiv 10)

* CUSHING		Lt. Cdr. Edward N. Parker
* LAFFEY		* Lt. Cdr. William E. Hank
STERETT		Cdr. Jesse G. Coward
O'BANNON	(T)	Cdr. Edwin R. Wilkinson
SHAW	(E)	Cdr. Wilbur G. Jones
GWIN	(E)	Lt. Cdr. John B. Fellows Jr.
* PRESTON	(E)	* Cdr. Max C. Stormes
BUCHANAN		Cdr. Ralph E. Wilson

Ships marked (E) were detached on arrival Solomons to *Enterprise* (TF 16)

TG 62.4,⁶ Rear Admiral Norman Scott *

| * ATLANTA | Capt. Samuel P. Jenkins |

Destroyer Screen, Captain Robert G. Tobin (Comdesron 12)

AARON WARD	Cdr. Orville F. Gregor
FLETCHER	Cdr. William M. Cole
LARDNER	Cdr. Willard M. Sweetser
MCCALLA	Lt. Cdr. William G. Cooper

AKAs (Attack Cargo Ships)

BETELGEUSE	Cdr. Harry D. Power
LIBRA	Cdr. William B. Fletcher Jr.
ZEILIN	Capt. Pat Buchanan

Embarking 1st Marine Aviation Engineer Battalion; Marine replacements; Marine Air Wing 1 ground personnel; provisions, ammunition and materiel.

In the Night Action of 12–13 November, the composition of TG 67.4 (Rear Admiral Callaghan *) was: SAN FRANCISCO, PORTLAND, HELENA, * ATLANTA, * JUNEAU, * CUSHING, * LAFFEY, STERETT, O'BANNON, * BARTON, * MONSSEN, AARON WARD, FLETCHER.

TASK FORCE 63

Land-based Aircraft, Rear Admiral Aubrey W. Fitch

At Henderson Field: 27 F4F-4, 18 P-38, 37 SBD, 9 TBF; one each of F4F-7, P-400, P-39.

At Espiritu Santo: 8 F4F-4, 13 F4F-3P, 16 TBF, 37 B-17, 5 B-26, 2 PB4Y, 5 Hudson of R.N.Z.A.F., 24 PBY, 1 PBY-5A.

TASK FORCE 16

Rear Admiral Thomas C. Kinkaid

As in air action of 14 November. Also ships marked (E) in TG 67.4.

* Lost or killed in this battle.

⁶ Combat ships in this task group merged with TG 67.4 at Guadalcanal 12 Nov.

ENTERPRISE   Capt. Osborne B. Hardison

Air Group 10: 1 TBF-1 (Avenger), Cdr. Richard K. Gaines

VF-10:	38 F4F-4 (Wildcat)	Lt. Cdr. James H. Flatley Jr.
VB-10:	15 SBD-3 (Dauntless)	Lt. Cdr. James A. Thomas
VS-10:	16 SBD-3	Lt. Cdr. James R. Lee
VT-10:	9 TBF-1	Lt. Albert P. Coffin

Rear Admiral Howard H. Good (Comcrudiv 5)

NORTHAMPTON   Capt. Willard A. Kitts III
SAN DIEGO   Capt. Benjamin F. Perry

Destroyer Screen, Captain Harold R. Holcomb (Comdesron 2)

CLARK   Lt. Cdr. Lawrence H. Martin
ANDERSON   Lt. Cdr. Richard A. Guthrie
HUGHES   Cdr. Donald J. Ramsey

Desdiv 4, Commander Arnold E. True

MORRIS   Lt. Cdr. Randolph B. Boyer
MUSTIN   Cdr. Wallis F. Petersen
RUSSELL   Cdr. Glenn R. Hartwig

TASK FORCE 64
Rear Admiral Willis Augustus Lee

(As in night action of 15 November)

WASHINGTON   Capt. Glenn B. Davis
SOUTH DAKOTA   Capt. Thomas L. Gatch

Destroyer Screen

* WALKE   * Cdr. Thomas E. Fraser
* BENHAM   Lt. Cdr. John B. Taylor
GWIN and * PRESTON (also in TG 67.4)

b. Japanese

COMBINED FLEET
Admiral Yamamoto in *Yamato* at Truk

ADVANCED FORCE
Vice Admiral Nobutake Kondo in *Atago*

RAIDING GROUP, Vice Admiral Hiroaki Abe (Combatdiv 11)

Battleships * HIEI, * KIRISHIMA
Desron 10: Rear Admiral Susumu Kimura in light cruiser NAGARA with destroyers
AMATSUKAZE, YUKIKAZE, * AKATSUKI, IKAZUCHI, INAZUMA, TERUZUKI

* Lost or killed in this action.

Sweeping Unit: Rear Admiral Tamotsu Takama (Comdesron 4), destroyers
ASAGUMO, MURASAME, SAMIDARE, * YUDACHI, HARUSAME
Patrol Unit: Capt. Yasuhide Setoyama (Comdesdiv 27), SHIGURE, SHIRATSUYU,
YUGURE

MAIN BODY (ATTACK GROUP),[7] Vice Admiral Kondo

Bombardment Unit: heavy cruisers ATAGO, TAKAO; battleship * KIRISHIMA
Screening Unit: Rear Admiral Kimura in NAGARA with destroyers TERUZUKI,
INAZUMA, SHIRAYUKI, HATSUYUKI, ASAGUMO (Rear Admiral Takama), SAMIDARE
Sweeping Unit: Rear Admiral Shintaro Hashimoto (Comdesron 3) in light cruiser
SENDAI with destroyers URANAMI, SHIKINAMI, *AYANAMI

Late Reinforcement Unit: destroyers OYASHIO, KAGERO

CARRIER SUPPORT GROUP, Vice Admiral Takeo Kurita (Combatdiv 3)

Supporting Unit: battleships KONGO, HARUNA; heavy cruiser TONE
Air Striking Unit, Rear Admiral Kakuji Kakuta (Comcardiv 2): JUNYO (27 VF,
12 VB, 9 VT), HIYO (15 VF, 23 VB, 9 VT); four to eight destroyers[8]

OUTER SOUTH SEAS FORCE

Vice Admiral Gunichi Mikawa (C. in C. Eighth Fleet)

SUPPORT GROUP, Admiral Mikawa

Main Unit: heavy cruisers CHOKAI, * KINUGASA; light cruiser ISUZU; destroyers
ASASHIO, ARASHIO
Bombardment Unit (Rear Admiral Shoji Nishimura): heavy cruisers SUZUYA,
MAYA; light cruiser TENRYU; destroyers MAKIGUMO, YUGUMO, KAZAGUMO,
MICHISHIO

REINFORCEMENT GROUP, Rear Admiral Raizo Tanaka (Comdesron 2)

Escort Unit: destroyers HAYASHIO, OYASHIO, KAGERO, UMIKAZE, KAWAKAZE, SUZUKAZE,
TAKANAMI, MAKINAMI, NAGANAMI, AMAGIRI, MOCHIZUKI
Transport Unit: * ARIZONA MARU, * KUMAGAWA M., * SADO M., * NAGARA M., * NAKO M.,
* CANBERRA M., * BRISBANE M., * KINUGAWA M., * HIROKAWA M., * YAMAURA M.,
* YAMATSUKI M.

LAND–BASED AIR FORCE

Vice Admiral Jinichi Kusaka (C. in C. Eleventh Air Fleet) at Rabaul

25th and 26th Air Flotillas: about 215 operational planes

* Sunk in this battle.

[7] This is the "emergency organization" in effect from evening of 13 Nov., incorporating
certain ships from the Raiding Group, and 4 destroyers originally with the Carrier
Support Group and 2 destroyers from the Escort Unit, Reinforcement Group, Outer
South Seas Force, which joined during the night battle of 14–15 Nov.

[8] *Hatsuyuki, Shirayuki, Uranami, Shikinami;* until 13 Nov., when they joined the
Main Body (Attack Group) and were replaced by 8 survivors of the Raiding Group
several of which were also ordered to "engage in the rescue of personnel from distressed
vessels." "Report on the Naval Battle of Guadalcanal" ATIS 15931.

ADVANCE EXPEDITIONARY FORCE (Submarines)

Vice Admiral Teruhisa Komatsu (C. in C. Sixth Fleet), in CL *Katori* at Truk

Patrol Groups "A," "B" and "D": I–16, I–20, I–24, I–15, I–17, I–26, I–122, *I–172, I–175, RO–34

Scouting Units: I–7 (off Santa Cruz): I–9, I–21 and I–31, with seaplane, reconnoitering San Cristobal, Nouméa and Suva.

* Sunk in this battle; *I–172* on 10 Nov. by *Southard* between San Cristobal and Guadalcanal.

3. Prologue, 12 November

A tense calm followed the afternoon's elimination shoot. As Turner's ships steamed back to the unloading area through floating remains of downed planes, they realized that the enemy had just begun to show his hand. Five cruisers of varying capabilities and eleven destroyers of assorted origin were available to chop it off.

An abundance of aircraft intelligence, routed to all flag bridges during the day, indicated the convergence of heavy surface forces north of Guadalcanal that night. Morning observation revealed two battleships or heavy cruisers, one cruiser and six destroyers 335 miles to the northward. Another group of five destroyers lay less than 200 miles to the NNW. In mid-afternoon two carriers and two destroyers were reported 265 miles to the westward.[9] That was bad enough, and Admiral Turner suspected that it was not all. Since no troop ships had been sighted, he guessed that the enemy was intent on attacking the American transports or else bombarding Henderson Field and adjacent troop positions. Since 90 per cent of their lading was already on the beach, these vulnerable targets could be sent away; but a bombardment could be countered only by a night battle.

In his appraisal, Turner listed enemy strength as two battleships, two to four heavy cruisers, two light cruisers and ten to twelve

[9] Admiral Turner did not believe enemy flattops were in that area, and he was right. Actually, carriers *Junyo* and *Hiyo* were to the northward and had not been sighted. Board of Merit Report (WDC No. 161,709).

destroyers — obviously too large a bite for Callaghan's two heavy and three light cruisers and eight destroyers. Yet, with Kinkaid's carrier-battleship force too far away to help, there was nothing else to be done but for Callaghan to block, and block hard.[10]

Admiral Turner's decision was embodied in a dispatch to Admiral Callaghan, which confirmed his earlier written orders. Transports would retire and Callaghan's Support Group, after shepherding them safely to sea, would return to Guadalcanal that night and strike enemy ships present.[11] Turner left Callaghan to work out the tactics of this desperate effort.

Dusk of 12 November found the four transports (with Admiral Turner embarked in *McCawley*) and the two cargo vessels of Scott's group (*Zeilin* had already departed) — escorted by the damaged *Buchanan*, destroyers *Shaw* and *McCalla* (selected because they were short of fuel) and minesweepers *Southard* and *Hovey* — hauling out for Espiritu Santo, where they safely anchored on 15 November.

Rear Admiral Callaghan[12] was now on his own, faced with an urgent situation. His two-starred flag now flew in the ship he had commanded six months earlier before serving on Ghormley's staff. Austere, modest, deeply religious; a hard-working and conscientious officer who possessed the high personal regard of his fellows and the love of his men, who called him "Uncle Dan," Callaghan had reached the acme of his career. There was something a little detached about this man, since his thoughts were often not of this world; something, too, that recalled the chivalrous warriors of other days. One could see him in the rôle of Don Alonso de Aguilar, or of dark-haired Duth-maruno, Fingal's

[10] *Enterprise* was not in the area because of unrepaired bomb damage. The two battleships remained with her.

[11] CTF 67 to CTG 67.4, 12 Nov.; Cominch Inf. Bull. No. 4, *Battle Experiences Solomon Islands Actions* pp. 28–63.

[12] Daniel Judson Callaghan, b. San Francisco 1890, Naval Academy '11. During World War I in *New Orleans* on convoy duty; asst. fire control officer of *Idaho* 1920–3; 1st Lt. *Colorado* 1925–6; engineer officer *Mississippi* 1926–7; U. of Calif. 1933–5; exec. *Portland* and staff Cdr. Cruisers Scouting Force 1936–8; Naval Aide to President 1938–41; C.O. *San Francisco* May 1941–May 1942; chief of staff to Admiral Ghormley June–Oct. 1942.

second in command: "Near us are the foes, Duth-maruno. They come forward like waves in mist, when their foaming tops are seen at times above the low-sailing vapor." [13]

Included in Callaghan's force were anti-aircraft cruiser *Atlanta* flying the flag of Rear Admiral Norman Scott, and two of his destroyers. Scott, the victor of the Battle of Cape Esperance, was junior to Callaghan, who thus became O.T.C.

Callaghan ordered his group to assume battle disposition B–1, a snakelike column, the van consisting of destroyers *Cushing, Laffey, Sterett* and *O'Bannon;* the center, of cruisers *Atlanta, San Francisco, Portland, Helena* and *Juneau;* and the rear, of destroyers *Aaron Ward, Barton, Monssen* and *Fletcher.*[14] This disposition, resembling the old line-of-battle of sailing ship days, was chosen because it appeared to have worked well under Scott at the Battle of Cape Esperance. A long column helped one to navigate restricted waters and facilitated communication between ships. Unfortunately, the three cruisers and two destroyers that mounted the latest search radar were not placed in lead positions; anti-aircraft cruiser *Atlanta* with inferior radar steamed ahead of flagship *San Francisco* and the rear destroyers were in no position to join the van in a torpedo attack.

At 2200, after seeing the transports safely away, Callaghan reversed course and passed back through Lengo Channel into Ironbottom Sound. A 9-knot easterly breeze scarcely rippled the surface. The stars shone brightly and jagged flashes of lightning over the islands fitfully illuminated low-lying clouds. The new moon had vanished below the dark horizon. Sailors peered from darkened bridges, waited in crowded plotting rooms and sweated in stifling engine rooms, wondering what the score would be. Few of these ships had operated together before that afternoon; yet no intelligence of enemy movements was distributed to commanding officers and no battle plan was issued.

[13] *Poems of Ossian,* "Cath-loda," part 2.
[14] Distance between types 800 yards; between cruisers 700 yards; between destroyers, 500 yards.

Enemy forces were heading southward, planning to leave Santa Isabel Island on their starboard hand, pass south of Savo and round up on an easterly bombardment course parallel to the Guadalcanal shore. The battleships and destroyers which had departed Truk 9 November, and the additional destroyers which left Shortlands on the 11th, were the elements reported by American air patrols on the morning of the 12th. At 1530 that day they rendezvoused 70 miles north of Indispensable Strait and became Vice Admiral Hiroaki Abe's Raiding Group, consisting of two battleships, light cruiser *Nagara* and 14 destroyers. Their mission was to knock out Henderson Field completely. Shell hoists were crammed with thin-shelled, quick-fused bombardment projectiles. Special flashless powder was on hand to assure concealment during action.[15] If challenged on the surface, the destroyers could brush off the intruder with torpedoes.

The core of Abe's formation was a bombardment unit of two battleships, *Hiei* leading *Kirishima*, with six destroyers and *Nagara* screening. On both advanced flanks rode destroyers (two on one side, three on the other) prepared to deal with motor torpedo boats.[16] Both the disposition chosen and his lack of armor-piercing projectiles indicate that Abe was not looking for a major surface encounter. This miscalculation cannot have been caused by lack of Intelligence, because the Admiral had been informed that nine United States cruisers and seven destroyers were near Guadalcanal; it must rather have been based on the assumption that the Americans as usual would be gone with the sun, leaving Dai Nippon to prowl the Sound at will.

The first deviation from plan occurred at midnight. Abe's Raiding Group entered a squall northwest of Savo Island and the Admiral reversed course, apparently fearing lest the weather prove too thick in Ironbottom Sound for a shore bombardment. Upon

[15] "Report on the Naval Battle of Guadalcanal" ATIS 15931. The Americans did not then have flashless powder for major-caliber guns. The advantage it gave the Japs was the subject of much comment in action reports.

[16] As an additional precaution Desdiv 27 (*Shigure*, *Shiratsuyu* and *Yugure*) was sent to patrol the passage between Guadalcanal and Russell Islands.

obtaining a favorable weather report from Japanese headquarters on Guadalcanal, he put about again for Lunga; but he had lost 40 minutes and set forward to 0130 the time for the bombardment to commence. In maneuvering, the right-flank destroyers *Asagumo*, *Murasame* and *Samidare* fell out of position and were now far back on the starboard quarter instead of on the port bow of the battle-ships.

4. *The Night Action of Friday the Thirteenth*

a. Mutual Surprise

It was now Friday the Thirteenth, last day of life for eight ships and many hundred sailors, including two American admirals.

Early in the midwatch a *Helena* radar operator detected a suspicious "blip" on his scope. Then appeared two traces that were neither friendly ships nor neutral land masses. The report went out at 0124: "Contacts bearing 312 and 310, distant 27,000 and 32,000 yards." Obviously one was a group of ships screening another 5000 yards behind it.

Three minutes after this first contact, Admiral Callaghan ordered his 13-ship column to change course two points to starboard, to course 310°. Apparently he desired a head-on clash rather than the more subtle run-around accompanied by torpedo launchings from the flanks. At 0130 *Helena* informed all ships that the enemy disposition was on their port bow distant 14,500 yards, steaming at speed 23 knots on course 105°. Opposing forces were closing at a rate of over 40 knots, and as the range decreased the initial American advantage of radar vanished. Fire control men, intent on the complicated controls of rangekeepers, watched the relentless spinning of the range dials, heard the drone of the range talker's voice, "Range one three O double O — range one two O double O," wondering why no word came to let fly "fish" or commence gunfire. For ten long minutes their questions remained unanswered. Course was changed to due north, speed upped to

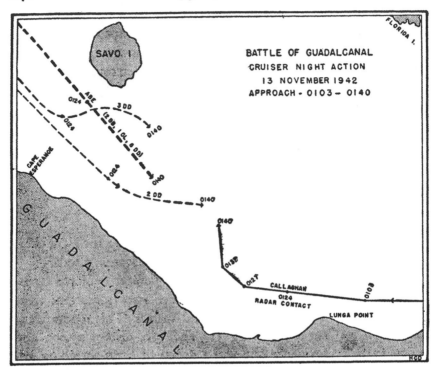

20 knots. On board *San Francisco* Admiral Callaghan, blind for want of adequate radar, was continually and urgently calling on his seeing-eye dogs, *Helena* and *O'Bannon*, for vital ranges, bearings, courses and composition. Yet this same voice radio (TBS) channel was the tactical control circuit; imperative directions for course, speed and gunfire had to be sandwiched between information requests. The outlets of the "squawk box" (voice radio) on the ships' bridges delivered a confused medley that baffled listeners and fast typists alike.

The fast-approaching Japanese did not listen in on this circuit; they were unaware of an enemy in the Sound. But they were not to be caught with defenses down. In anticipation of the scheduled shore bombardment, stocky gunners waited in their turrets while torpedomen, secondary battery gun crews, and searchlight operators stood alert at battle stations. Without radar, Admiral

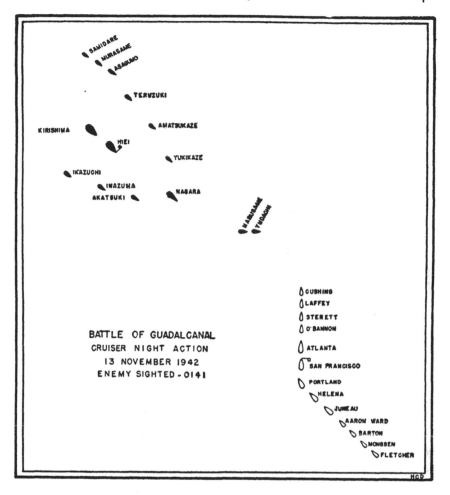

BATTLE OF GUADALCANAL
CRUISER NIGHT ACTION
13 NOVEMBER 1942
ENEMY SIGHTED - 0141

Abe realized that any surface action would be quick, close and decisive.

Inexorably the range closed. Commander Stokes of Desdiv 10, embarked in van destroyer *Cushing*, suddenly sighted Japanese destroyers crossing ahead, port to starboard, at the uncomfortably close range of 3000 yards. A flash radio report was passed down the line as *Cushing's* skipper, Lieutenant Commander Parker, turned left from a northerly heading at 0141 in order to unmask his torpedo batteries. His quick turn avoided collision with the enemy but resulted in a pile-up of the van, in which every ship struggled to keep station while swinging to the new course 315°. *Atlanta,* heavier than the destroyers, had to swing hard left. "What are you doing?" asked Callaghan over voice radio. "Avoiding our own destroyers," answered Captain Jenkins.

The ships seen by Stokes were destroyers *Yudachi* and *Harusame,* whose skippers may have been startled but were certainly not asleep. By 0142, a minute after first sighting, the entire Japanese force knew of the contact, surprise was lost, and the American delay in opening fire gave Admiral Abe's ships eight good minutes to prepare for action.

The United States ships were doubly confused by the sudden left turn and the resulting press of voice radio transmissions. Nobody could be certain whether reported target bearings were true or relative to the reporting ships. Nobody knew which target to take under fire, or when. Commander Stokes could stand it no longer. "Shall I let them have a couple of fish?" he asked. Permission was granted, but by this time the enemy destroyers had scudded into the darkness. Finally, at 0145, Admiral Callaghan gave the word, "Stand By to Open Fire!"

The prologue was now over and the principals in place; Americans confused, Nipponese surprised. Through the darkness Japanese night glasses picked up the loom of ships almost within their own formation, *Atlanta's* high superstructure standing above the low destroyer silhouettes. At 0150 Japanese searchlight shutters clicked open; beams shot out, feeling right and left; one probably from *Akatsuki* quickly came to rest on the port wing of *Atlanta's* bridge, bathing the whole superstructure with the kind of light that sailors rightly fear. The cruiser's gunnery officer shouted two orders, "Commence Firing! Counter-illuminate!" The range was a scant 1600 yards, with solution already set on the rangekeeper; the cruiser's 5-inch guns spewed forth a stream of shells which extinguished the offending light, but not quickly enough. While *Atlanta* sent salvo after salvo crashing into the Nips on both bows, they and their sister ships concentrated on her. Enemy shells

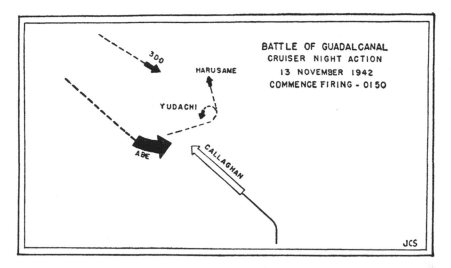

BATTLE OF GUADALCANAL
CRUISER NIGHT ACTION
13 NOVEMBER 1942
COMMENCE FIRING - 0150

crunched into the misnamed "Lucky A." One of them killed Admiral Scott, all but one of his staff, and others on the bridge. Simultaneously, from *San Francisco* came the long-awaited order: "Odd ships commence fire to starboard, even ships to port."[17]

Atlanta's participation in the battle was brief. Japanese destroyers, ever ready to exploit torpedo opportunities, dispatched several salvos at the confused American column. One, perhaps two, hit *Atlanta*. Their explosion lifted her bodily from the water, then set her down shuddering and crippled. In the plotting room, fire control men watched the needle on the pitometer log (the ship's speed indicator) slide down the scale until it rested against zero. *Atlanta* was dead in the water, and the battle scarce begun. The ship's mascot terrier, misnamed "Lucky," whimpered pitifully in a corner of the damage control station, while the officer in charge telephoned vainly for reports from damaged areas.[18]

[17] This order added to the confusion, in ships which could not see or bear on targets on their designated sides but did see targets on the opposite side, and it took no account of variations in gun caliber between ships.
[18] "Engagement with Japanese Surface Forces off Guadalcanal Night of 12–13 Nov. 1942, and Loss of U.S.S. *Atlanta*" 20 Nov. 1942; personal recollections.

b. General Mêlée

From now on, Japanese and American ships mingled like min-
nows in a bucket. It is impossible to reconstruct their tracks; we
can only relate what happened to each. Van destroyer *Cushing*
sent several salvos screaming after a destroyer to starboard, but
within two minutes received shell hits amidships which severed
all power lines and slowed her down. Her bow was pointing almost due north when her skipper sighted *Hiei* on his port beam,
on a collision course. Using hand steering control and what little
way remained, he swung *Cushing* right and, by local control,
fired six "fish" at the enemy battlewagon less than half a mile distant. None hit *Hiei,* which was also the target of destroyer and
cruiser gunfire; but she didn't like it and turned slowly away to
the westward. *Cushing* had only a few moments to exult like David.
A probing searchlight beam picked her out and enemy gunfire
reduced her to a sinking wreck in short order.[19]

Laffey, directly astern of *Cushing,* also entered a disastrous ar-
gument with *Hiei,* passing so close that collision was barely averted.
Her torpedoes, launched at too short a range, failed to arm and
bounced harmlessly off the battleship's sides. Topside machine-
gunners sprayed the pagoda-like bridge with 20-mm and 1.1 bullets as *Hiei* passed, shooting. Then two large-caliber gun salvos and
a torpedo in the fantail put *Laffey* out of action for all time. She
was promptly abandoned, the third to go. Many swimming survivors were killed when the burning hull exploded.

Destroyers *Sterett* and *O'Bannon,* respectively third and fourth
in column, had better luck. The former, as an odd-numbered ship,
ordered Action Starboard and took an enemy vessel under rapid
fire at 4000 yards' range. Although the *Hiei* fracas on her port
had rendered visual fire control difficult, radar and early fire-ignit-
ing hits on the target solved the problem. Three minutes after

[19] "Report of Engagement off Savo Island on Nov. 13, 1942 and Destruction of
the U.S.S. *Cushing*" 20 Nov. 1942.

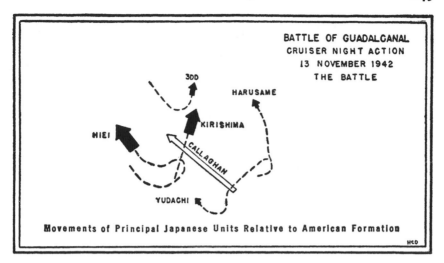

BATTLE OF GUADALCANAL
CRUISER NIGHT ACTION
13 NOVEMBER 1942
THE BATTLE

3DD

HARUSAME

KIRISHIMA

HIEI

CALLAGHAN

YUDACHI

Movements of Principal Japanese Units Relative to American Formation

HCO

Sterett had opened fire, an enemy salvo found its mark in her port side aft, disabling her steering gear. This was followed by a hit on her foremast which destroyed the radar. But *Sterett* and her wiry little skipper, Commander Jesse G. Coward, were still full of fight. Maneuvering her with the engines, Coward turned his attention to *Hiei* and pumped out four torpedoes at 2000 yards' range. Simultaneously *O'Bannon* was getting in a few licks; she had opened fire when the first searchlight burst out and so continued throughout the battle. The illuminating Jap took a pummeling from her guns before *O'Bannon* turned on *Hiei*, then some 1200 yards on her port bow. Commander Wilkinson, in the midst of a maneuver to avoid collision with *Sterett*, ordered fire on the big battleship.

At that moment came a puzzling order from Admiral Callaghan: "Cease firing own ships!" *O'Bannon's* skipper checked fire momentarily and then launched two carefully aimed torpedoes at *Hiei*. He thought they had scored, but actually they either failed to hit or did not explode. The range was so short that the battleship was unable to depress her guns sufficiently to hit back. As her 14-inch salvos shrieked harmlessly over their heads, *O'Bannon's* sailors had the pleasure of seeing this enemy ship of the line completely enveloped in sheets of incandescent flame. A moment later, *O'Bannon* sheered left to avoid the sinking *Laffey's* bow, and tossed life jackets to survivors as she passed. Torpedo wakes crossed her bow. Suddenly an enormous underwater explosion jolted the ship, disrupting light and power and rattling the teeth of all on board. This quake may have been *Laffey's* explosive death rattle or it may have been an enemy torpedo exploding at the end of its run.[20]

Admiral Abe had already disposed of a light cruiser and two destroyers; but his position on the flag bridge of *Hiei*, cynosure of American gunfire, blinded him to the actual progress of the battle and he ordered a change of course in order to get clear. The American column had actually penetrated the center of his formation between his van destroyers, and between his two battleships. This was not according to book, and the Admiral did not like it. While *Hiei* was bearing the brunt of American fury, her sister battleship *Kirishima*, about 800 yards on the flagship's quarter, was dishing out 14-inch punishment but receiving only near-misses in return. She was nicked but once during the entire engagement, by an 8-inch shell. Both battleships turned left in compliance with the retirement order; *Hiei* so slowly that she was rapidly left behind, but she had not yet been torpedoed and was in not too bad a shape.

Flagship *San Francisco*, sixth in the American column and astern of *Atlanta*, had entered the fray promptly, taking under fire an enemy vessel on her starboard beam less than two miles distant. For illumination she used 5-inch star shell, fired to burst above and beyond the target. The unblinking beam of a searchlight, originating on her starboard quarter, wavered and then settled on her; and the illumination of American ships astern served to silhouette her to the enemy. After delivering seven hefty salvos, *San Francisco* shifted to a target described as a "small cruiser or a large destroyer." Two full main-battery salvos were pumped into the vessel, "setting her on fire throughout her length." [21] It will be recalled

---

[20] *O'Bannon* and *Sterett* Action Reports 20 Nov. 1942.
[21] *San Francisco* Action Report 16 Nov. 1942 with chronological log of battle.

that *Atlanta* was now dead in the water and ahead of *San Fran-cisco;* the crew of *Atlanta* believe that she was the victim.[22] How else can one explain Admiral Callaghan's order to cease fire? Before he gave that order, however, the flagship's main-battery control officer had sighted *Hiei* and contributed some well-placed salvos toward the devastation of that ship. When the Cease Firing order took effect, *San Francisco* was the first to suffer. *Kirishima* on her starboard hand dealt out heavy blows; another enemy ship on her starboard quarter employed searchlight illumination and gunfire to good effect; a destroyer darting down her port side raked the superstructure. Steering and engine control were temporarily lost, and as she slowed down, an avalanche of shellfire from three different ships snuffed out the lives of Admiral Callaghan and his staff, of Captain Cassin Young and of nearly every man on the bridge.

At this juncture, cruisers astern of *San Francisco* rallied to her support. *Portland,* seventh in line, had closed firing keys when the enemy illuminated. Her shells located a starboard-hand target whose return fire registered but one hit, which wounded the executive officer. Five minutes after the battle's start, Captain Laurance DuBose received the Cease Firing order but disregarded it except for an incredulous inquiry addressed to the flagship: "What's the dope, did you want to cease fire?" Callaghan had time to answer "Affirmative," and to order a course change to the northward. *Portland* checked fire briefly while turning, then picked up a target three miles to starboard and commenced gnawing away at it with her turret guns. A Japanese torpedo tore through the water toward her. A terrific wallop rocked the cruiser as the explosion ripped a huge chunk from her stern, bending the structure so that projecting hull plates acted as an unwanted auxiliary rudder and she made an involuntary complete circle. As she came

[22] This conjecture was strengthened by the presence of scattered projectile fragments with *San Francisco* green dye color later found on *Atlanta* decks. Lt. Cdr. Bruce McCandless of *San Francisco* stated to the writer, 2 Nov. 1945, that his ship was not firing at *Atlanta* but at a Japanese ship beyond *Atlanta*, and that the short-range flat trajectory resulted in shells passing through *Atlanta.*

out of it *Hiei* loomed up in her sights, range 4000 yards, and *Portland* let her have it from both forward turrets. This concluded the evening's main-battery performance for the "Sweet Pea," as her crew called this happy ship.

Helena, next astern, was favored by fortune. Opening fire at the same instant as the ships ahead of her, she directed her tracers at the inquisitive searchlight on her port beam some two miles away. Enemy shell splashes reared up in ugly gouts astern but *Helena* received only minor superstructure damage. During the next few minutes Captain Hoover made strenuous efforts to avoid the damaged ships ahead while his guns shifted from target to target. Almost simultaneously his 6-inch main battery lashed out at a ship that was pummeling *San Francisco,* his 5-inchers went after a destroyer on the starboard quarter, and his heavy machine guns worked over a ship of unfriendly contour only 3000 yards distant, probably *Nagara.* When the enemy's retirement opened the range, bullets from "Helen" hastened him on his way.

Juneau, last cruiser in column, fired along with the rest of the task force during the hectic quarter-hour between 0148 and 0203. In common with other ships, she had difficulty in identifying targets; Callaghan's Cease Firing order belayed a brief spraying of *Helena.* An enemy torpedo sundered *Juneau's* forward fireroom with a shock which put the ship completely out of action, dead in the water and probably with a broken keel. From that moment her main concern was to clear out and keep afloat.[22]

Bringing up the rear, and thus late for the initial slugfest, were destroyers *Aaron Ward, Barton, Monssen* and *Fletcher.* Captain Robert G. Tobin, the squadron commander who flew his pennant in the first-named, was handicapped by lack of orders and an ineffective radar. His opening ranges were considerably greater than the side-scraping distances at which the van destroyers fought, and the jumbled state of the column rendered target selection and sta-

[23] Buships *Summary of War Damage to U.S. Battleships, Carriers, Cruisers and Destroyers, 17 Oct. 1941 to 7 Dec. 1942,* 15 Sept. 1943; recordings in Office of Naval Records and Library by Lt. (jg) Charles Wang usnr; Lt. R. W. O'Neill and L. E. Zook sm1, in Jan. 1943.

tion-keeping almost impossible. *Aaron Ward* opened up on a target 7000 yards on her starboard bow, discharged 10 salvos and then checked fire because friendly cruisers fouled her range. Commander Gregor was forced to stop and back engines to avoid collision with a ship ahead — probably *Helena*. Ten minutes elapsed before he could feel certain that an enemy target was in the optics, and then *San Francisco* charged into his line of sight. A target showing unfamiliar recognition lights sharp on the starboard bow was next taken under fire at a mile-and-a-half range, and firing continued until the ship appeared to explode and sink. *Aaron Ward* then used enemy searchlights as points of aim. She received one hit in the director which occasioned a shift to local control of gun batteries.

Destroyer *Barton*, commissioned as recently as 29 May, had a total combat life of exactly seven minutes. She opened fire, launched four torpedoes to port, stopped to avoid collision and, when almost dead in the water, received a torpedo in the forward fireroom which was followed almost instantly by another in the forward engine room. She broke in two and sank in a matter of seconds, taking with her all but a handful of the crew.

Monssen, her conning party eagerly listening to the jabber of the voice radio, trailed *Barton*. She had lost the use of her fire control radar during the afternoon air fight and was forced to rely on radio information and optics. Her knowledge of the situation was slight but her interest was great, particularly after a torpedo passed directly under her keel. *Monssen* fired a 5-torpedo salvo at a battleship on her starboard bow, then turned her attention to another vessel two miles on the starboard beam, launching a spread of five more torpedoes. The 5-inch guns meanwhile went after targets on the port side while the 20-mm guns raised havoc on the topside of a destroyer a quarter of a mile to starboard. Star shell began to burst over and around *Monssen*, lighting up the ship like a night-club floor show. Lieutenant Commander McCombs, believing the star shell to be friendly, switched on his fighting lights; and the click of that light switch was the death knell of his ship. Two blinding tentacles of light grasped her, a deluge of explosives followed, torpedoes hissed by. Some 37 shell hits reduced *Monssen* to a burning hulk.

Destroyer *Fletcher*, despite her station in the very rear of the column, had excellent information from a superior search radar. When the enemy first illuminated *Atlanta*, Commander Cole triggered his firing keys at the offending ship, then some 5500 yards on his port bow. Next, observing that many other ships had chosen the same target, *Fletcher* shifted to a more distant target and had the satisfaction of starting some bright blazes. The order Cease Firing caused her to check momentarily and then resume firing at a third target still farther back in the enemy formation. Eight minutes after the first shot, *Fletcher* sailors witnessed the sudden disintegration of *Barton* and the riddling of *Monssen*. Now that the column was in complete disorder, Commander Cole decided to leave this cluttered area, make another evaluation and return to launch his yet unused torpedoes. Aided by a constant flow of information from the radar room, he threaded his way through the maelstrom of friends and foes, turned south, bent on 35 knots and rounded up to a firing position ahead of the enemy. Torpedo wakes swirled under and around her, gun salvos bracketed her, but *Fletcher* had a charmed life; she emerged without even her paintwork scratched.

Four bells of this sinister midwatch had struck during these fifteen minutes of raw hell. A literally infernal scene presented itself to the participants. The struggle had deteriorated into a wild and desperate mêlée. The greenish light of suspended star shell dimmed the stars overhead. Elongated red and white trails of shell tracers arched and crisscrossed, magazines exploded in blinding bouquets of white flame, oil-fed conflagrations sent up twisted yellow columns. Dotting the horizon were the dull red glows of smoldering hulls, now obscured by dense masses of smoke, now blazing up when uncontrolled fires reached new combustibles. The sea itself, fouled with oil and flotsam, tortured by underwater upheavals, rose in geysers from shell explosions.

By 0200 November 13, the main issue had been decided by Admiral Abe's order to *Hiei* and *Kirishima* to turn left and steam north. Henderson Field and its precious planes were safe for that night at least, but nobody on the American side knew it.

c. Exeunt Fighting

Fighting continued with little respite after the battlewagons retired, *Hiei* to the south of Savo, *Kirishima* to the north. A short lull gave *Cushing* opportunity to fight fires on board, but just as they were brought under control several enemy salvos came her way. The flames then took charge and finally, at 0315, with magazines in volcanic action, the skipper ordered Abandon Ship. *Laffey* was already on the iron bottom. *Sterett*, with steering gear disabled, encountered destroyer *Yudachi* some 600 yards on her starboard bow at 0220 and launched two torpedoes followed by gunfire which took her apart; but, shortly after, *Sterett* was hit by 14-inch shells and forced to retire southeastward, slowing down periodically to reduce the windage on the flames.

Commander Wilkinson in *O'Bannon* decided, since the scene was utterly confused, to haul off to the southeastward in an effort to locate friend or foe. At 0215 he sighted a smoking vessel on the port bow but wisely withheld torpedo fire on what later proved to be *San Francisco*. Thinking that enemy transports might have entered the Sound, *O'Bannon* turned south and investigated the shoreline. Saint Christopher, Saint Barbara and the luck of the Irish must have been with plucky *O'Bannon* on this fearful night.[24]

Atlanta's fighting men by 0200 were mere spectators, a status which they had neither time nor inclination to enjoy. Their ship was ravaged by more than 50 large-caliber shell hits, holed by torpedoes and consumed by fire. Survivors found devastation behind every bulkhead and in almost every compartment. Below decks men groped in complete darkness through acrid smoke and sloshed

[24] *O'Bannon* Action Report. Luck, ably assisted by a spirited and capable crew, enabled her to come through the entire war unscathed by enemy action.

heavily in oily waters on flooded decks. Cursing and coughing, they labored to seal hull ruptures, succor the many wounded and bring fires under control. The main deck was a charnel house. Burned and eviscerated corpses, severed limbs and chunks of flesh mixed with steel debris, littered it from stem to stern. Blood, oil and sea water made a nasty, slippery slush through which one could move only on hands and knees. The "spud locker" amidships had burst open, strewing the decks with potatoes; no joke to groaning men who slipped on the treacherous tubers. Muzzles of useless guns drooped silent over the motionless dead. Seven out of the eight 5-inch turrets had been hit, all but four of the machine guns were smashed. Flames ate greedily into the superstructure, belching out as burning ammunition detonated. Shadowy figures, the only living part of this macabre setting, moved perilously back and forth as bucket brigades or to jettison the cumbersome weights which threatened to capsize the ship, or to carry the wounded to improvised dressing stations. Admiral Scott was dead but Captain Jenkins and his executive officer, Commander Campbell D. Emory, were spared serious injury. They were able gradually to establish communications with the little knots of survivors around the ship and to direct a coördinated effort to save *Atlanta*. Gasoline handy-billys were rigged to fight fire, a damage control party worked to get one fireroom back into operation, the remaining guns were manned, the injured were taken to comparative safety aft.[25]

As the battle drew to a close, *San Francisco's* topsides were in almost as bad shape as *Atlanta's*, but three circumstances saved the flagship from annihilation. The close range had prevented the enemy from depressing his guns sufficiently to score hits below the waterline; thin-skinned bombardment shells, fatal to human lives and damaging to superstructure, had been deflected by armor; she had suffered no torpedo hits. On the navigation bridge Lieutenant Commander Bruce McCandless, communications officer, found himself the only able-bodied survivor. In central station, Lieutenant Commander H. E. Schonland, acting first lieutenant,

[25] *Atlanta* Action Report; personal recollections.

learned that he had succeeded to command. Realizing that his knowledge of damage control was vital to the ship's survival, he elected to lead the fight against the twenty-five fires then raging, and ordered McCandless to conn the ship out of harm's way. That he did very well, skirting the coast of Guadalcanal.

Portland, with her warped stern, continued to steam in tight circles for the remainder of the night. Captain DuBose at one time counted nine burning vessels in the Sound. *Helena* ceased firing at 0216 and, except for brief searchlight scrutiny, received no more attention from the enemy. Captain Hoover, unable to contact either Scott or Callaghan and believing his to be the senior undamaged command, called all ships (only two answered) and at 0226 ordered them to follow him and retire via Sealark Channel. *Juneau* got way on by the end of the midwatch and moved toward Indispensable Strait.

Meantime, Captain Tobin's three remaining destroyers of the rear were acting individually. *Aaron Ward* with guns in local control lashed out at enemy searchlights that were guiding salvos her way. She cleared out after being pierced by nine medium-caliber shells. The damage was cumulative and progressive, so that by 0235 she lay dead in the water with a flooded engine room, and spent the rest of the night in efforts to get way on. *Monssen* burned and exploded with such fury that she was hastily abandoned. The crew, clinging to life rafts, watched their ship flame and erupt throughout the remaining hours of darkness.

Fletcher, the apparently untouchable Shadrach of the American task force, was now in an excellent position to reënter the contest with torpedoes. A large target was selected and radar commenced tracking as the ship stalked her prey. The enemy vessel, on an easterly course, was shooting to the northward, probably at her friends, when *Fletcher* dispatched ten "fish" on a three-and-a-half-mile run at 36 knots. Having shot her bolt, *Fletcher* retired in the general direction of Sealark Channel.

On the enemy side, it is probable that most torpedo tubes were emptied during the first ten minutes. At any rate, after 0200 the

Martian display diminished rapidly. *Hiei* steered an erratic north-westerly course, limping from damage to steering and communication systems and loss of fire power. She had taken over 50 topside hits. Destroyer *Akatsuki*, one of the forward screening vessels, had gone down. *Yudachi* of the advanced flank, emerging from a penetration run through the American forces, underwent a severe explosion at 0220 which stopped her dead some five miles south of Savo Island. Three destroyers had been hit but not stopped: *Ikazuchi*, forecastle gun damaged; *Murasame*, forward boiler room out; *Amatsukaze*, minor scars. These three retired to the north in company with undamaged ships, *Samidare* took off *Yudachi* survivors and followed them later, and the Patrol Unit of three destroyers stood by the stricken battleship.

d. Daylight Disasters

> Thus pass'd the night so foul, till morning fair
> Came forth with pilgrim steps in amice gray,
> Who with her radiant finger still'd the roar
> Of thunder, chas'd the clouds, and laid the winds
> And grisly spectres, which the Fiend had rais'd . . .[26]

A glassy, metallic sea, stippled by the floating litter of death and destruction, reflected the sun's first rays. The mountains of Guadalcanal turned from black to purple and then to lush green. Sailors on crippled warships of both nations stood by their damaged guns, grimly aware that between ship and ship no quarter would be given. Early birdmen could see eight crippled ships scattered without order between Savo Island and Guadalcanal. Five were American: unsteerable *Portland*, shattered *Atlanta*, immobile *Aaron Ward*, burning and abandoned *Cushing* and *Monssen*. The Rising Sun was still flying on rudderless *Hiei* and her loyal protectors and on flaming and abandoned *Yudachi*. It was inevitable that more compliments would be exchanged.

Portland, still churning in circles, embraced *Yudachi* 12,500 yards distant, with six salvos. Enough of these 36 projectiles hit

[26] *Paradise Regained* iv 426–30.

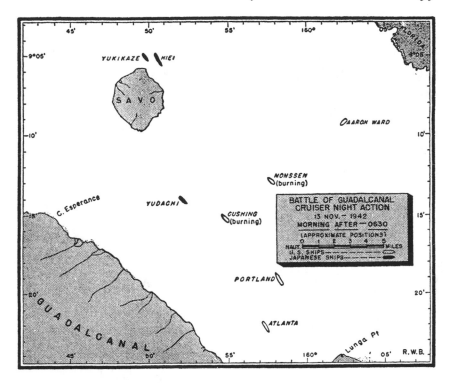

to produce a magazine explosion which completely erased the destroyer, a cheering sight to many a swimming American. *Hiei* sent four 2-gun salvos careering down the 13-mile range to *Aaron Ward;* the third straddled but did not hit. Fortunately, the Marine Corps aircraft which promptly appeared on the scene proved so interesting to *Hiei* that she laid off the destroyer until tugs could tow her out of range, eventually to an anchorage in Tulagi Harbor.

On board *Atlanta* all efforts were concentrated on saving the ship. Captain Jenkins, wounded painfully in the foot, urged his bedraggled seamen to superhuman efforts. First, it was necessary to get the pumps going to counteract the continual seepage of water. Apprehensive of beaching off the enemy-held shore of Guadalcanal, the Captain ordered the port anchor walked out and issued small arms to all hands. Wounded and nonessential ratings were sent ashore in Higgins boats hastily provided by the Lunga base. Even after 0939, when tug *Bobolink* had taken her in tow, *Atlanta* shot at a Japanese "Betty" which ventured too close; the seamen of *Bobolink*, rendered bloodthirsty by previous experiences, machine-gunned every dark head they saw afloat until Captain Jenkins begged them to desist lest mistakes be made. By 1400 the cruiser was anchored off Kukum, but she could not be kept afloat. No salvage facilities were available, she was listing heavily to port and the enemy was expected again that night. So the crew was ordered to scuttle the old girl with a demolition charge. *Atlanta* went down three miles off Lunga Point shortly after dark on Friday evening, the Bloody Thirteenth.

Cushing and *Monssen* continued to burn but did not sink until late in the afternoon. The water around them was blanketed with debris. At daylight three gallant sailors boarded burning *Monssen* to rescue eight helpless wounded and place them in a life raft.[27] Rescue craft from Guadalcanal plowed through wreckage and oil, picked up friends and were evaded by foes who had been indoctrinated not to accept rescue.

All day *Portland* continued her efforts to recover steering control. A score of Higgins boats nosed her bow, huffing and puffing in a vain struggle to offset the torque of the bent stern. Every conceivable maneuver and gadget were tried. Sea-anchors improvised of canvas and garbage cans were streamed. Finally *Bobolink*, after leaving *Atlanta*, pushed *Portland's* starboard bow so vigorously that she was able to crawl along on a steady course. "Sweet Pea" finally anchored in Tulagi Harbor at 0100 November 14.

The American vessels which had retired from the hot spot around Savo found themselves at dawn in a formation proceeding southeasterly down Indispensable Strait. Captain Hoover of *Helena*, now senior officer present, took charge of *San Francisco*, *Juneau*, *O'Bannon*, *Sterett* and *Fletcher* — three of them lame ducks. Zigzagging through a smooth sea at 18 knots, they set course for the New Hebrides. In order to provide anti-submarine protection, *Fletcher* and *Sterett* were placed 4000 yards ahead of the heavy ships. As *O'Bannon's* sound gear had been damaged by the previ-

[27] G. C. Storey, L. F. Spurgeon and J. G. Hughes; *Monssen* Action Report.

ous night's underwater explosion, she was sent ahead to transmit a radio message to Admiral Halsey. At 0950 *Sterett* made a sound contact and delivered an urgent depth-charge attack with indeterminate results.

An hour later, this task force touched the nadir of its fortune. *Helena* was steaming 1000 yards ahead of *San Francisco; Juneau* was 1000 yards on the latter's starboard beam. Submarine *I-26*, cruising at periscope depth, drew a bead and fired a spread of torpedoes.[28] Two of them shot past *San Francisco* but she, with no means of rapid communication left, could not broadcast the alarm. Straight and true, one enemy torpedo traveled toward *Juneau*, and at 1101 detonated against her port side under the bridge. Horrified sailors in *San Francisco* saw the light cruiser disintegrate instantaneously and completely, sinking with apparently no trace except a tall pillar of smoke and a little debris. Nobody waited to look for survivors. A Flying Fortress, attracted thither by the force of the explosion, was informed of the disaster and asked to relay a rescue request to Admiral Halsey's headquarters.[29]

Unfortunately this message never got through. Of more than a hundred men who miraculously survived the eruption and who clung pitifully to the flotsam that marked their ship's end,[30] all but ten perished. Three paddled their raft to a small island where friendly natives and a European trader brought them back to life, and a Catalina carried them home. Another PBY rescued six; *Ballard* picking up the sole survivor of one raft on 20 November. Almost 700 men, including the five Sullivan brothers, went down with *Juneau* or died in life rafts.[31]

*   *   *

[28] *I-26* skipper aimed at and thought he had hit *San Francisco*. War Diary of Sixth Fleet, Advance Force Battle Report No. 12 (WDC No. 160,268 Group 20 Item 20A).

[29] *Helena* Action Report. Text of message: "*Juneau* torpedoed and disappeared lat. 10°32′ S, long. 161°2′ E at 1109. Survivors in water. Report Comsopac."

[30] Signalman 1st class L. E. Zook. His account of the dying wounded, the rapacious shark attacks and the madness consequent to privation is one of the grimmest survivor stories of the war.

[31] Report on sinking of *Juneau* 22 Nov. 1942; reports of other ships present, and Office of Naval Records recordings already mentioned. Admiral Halsey deprived

So ended the wildest, most desperate sea fight since Jutland, one that recalls the Anglo–Dutch battles of the seventeenth century. Ship losses were fairly well balanced; two light cruisers and four destroyers as against two destroyers and a battleship so badly damaged that airmen could sink her next day. Casualties on the American side were many times those of the enemy.[32] But the Japanese bombardment mission was completely frustrated — Yamamoto admitted as much by relieving Abe and depriving him of any further sea command.[33] Callaghan, on the other hand, completed his mission; he saved Henderson Field from a bombardment which might well have been more serious than "the" bombardment of mid-October, and certainly would have stopped the American air operations, which next day disposed of eleven troop-laden transports.

Thus, in the end, all mistakes were canceled out by valor. While the shells that were to strike him down were being loaded into enemy gun breeches, Admiral Callaghan called out over voice radio, "We want the big ones!" — meaning Japanese battleships.[34] His men stopped one; on the following night Admiral Lee consigned another to the iron bottom. Let none deny praise, glory and honor to those who fell on Friday the Bloody Thirteenth with two great seamen and gallant gentlemen, Daniel J. Callaghan and Norman Scott.

Capt. Hoover of his command for abandoning *Juneau.* Later he admitted that Hoover, with an inadequate screen and expecting the B-17 to send his message, had acted for the best. But it would seem that he might have left boats or life rafts in the water before steaming on.

[32] Bureau of Medicine and Surgery casualty figures for this battle are so obviously wrong (e.g. 377 killed on *Juneau* when she had 700 on board, 5 for *Atlanta* when Bupers listed 18 officers and 151 men lost) that I have thought it inadvisable to repeat them.

[33] Vice Admiral Hiroaki Abe was ordered to the Naval General Staff 21 Dec. 1942, a face-saving job, and retired the following March although only 53 years old. He is not to be confused with Vice Admiral Koso Abe who had a command at Coral Sea and caused the Marines taken prisoner at Makin to be executed. There were at least 4 flag officers named Abe in the Japanese Navy during World War II.

[34] *Helena* TBS log, enclosed with *Helena* Action Report.

5. *Kinkaid Moves Up, Nishimura Bombards, 13 November*

Abe's failure in no way softened Admiral Kondo's determination to land troops and supplies on Guadalcanal. His cruisers and destroyers, idling off the coral reefs of Ontong Java some 250 miles to the northward, were summoned to save *Hiei* at 0630 November 13. At the same time, Vice Admiral Mikawa in *Chokai* sallied forth from the Shortlands with four heavy cruisers, two light cruisers and six destroyers to bombard Henderson Field. That left Rear Admiral Tanaka with eleven destroyers to escort eleven troop-laden transports to Guadalcanal. This Reinforcement Group had departed Shortlands at nightfall 12 November, prudently retired to its Faisi base early on the 13th, and that day made preparations to dash into Guadalcanal and discharge troops after sunset on the 14th. In preparation, Kondo's Main Body would assimilate undamaged remnants of Abe's Raiding Group — *Kirishima, Nagara* and four destroyers — to make way for the Emperor's transports. Air cover would be provided by two carriers, supported by two *Kongo* class battleships and cruiser *Tone*.[35]

After a foul night, American prospects looked fair on the morning of the 13th. Henderson Field still supported an aggressive brood of aircraft. Admiral Kinkaid's Task Force 16 with carrier *Enterprise* and two new battleships, which had departed Nouméa on the 11th, was boiling up from the south. "Big E" rang day and night with hammer blows and the sputter of welders' arcs as she steamed north, but still the forward elevator refused to operate.[36] Cruiser *Pensacola* and destroyers *Gwin* and *Preston*, detached from Callaghan's command before the night action, were on their way down from the Solomons to beef up Kinkaid's screen.

Admiral Turner, as we have seen, had discounted the contact

---

[35] "Report on the Naval Battle of Guadalcanal."
[36] Tender *Vestal* supplied repair crews who rode *Enterprise* throughout the ensuing action.

report of two enemy carriers 150 miles west of Lunga at 1450 November 12. Admiral Kinkaid could not afford to ignore it — he knew to his cost what carrier planes could do to carriers. So, at dawn 13 November, when Task Force 16 was still 340 miles SSE of Guadalcanal, *Enterprise* launched ten planes to search 200 miles out over a 120-degree northerly sector. An attack group was readied on "Big E's" flight deck, but the questing planes found nothing; *Junyo* and *Hiyo* were well beyond their range. Kinkaid then decided to contribute some *Enterprise* planes to Henderson Field, for his carrier was still incapable of her usual fast flight operations. Accordingly, nine Avengers and six Wildcats took off with orders to report to General Vandegrift, after searching for enemy ships en route and attacking any that might be sighted.

The first target encountered by these planes was the long-suffering *Hiei*. Lieutenant John F. Sutherland, leading the TBFs, sighted this wounded battlewagon with her attendant destroyers about ten miles north of Savo Island, approached through a protective cloud blanket, made runs on both bows simultaneously and, at 1020, emerged unscathed by anti-aircraft fire. The Avengers made two hits, one of which disabled the rudder so that *Hiei* steamed in circles; but the "unsinkable old so-and-so," as the aviators were beginning to call her, needed more punishment than that. Sutherland had his planes reserviced at Henderson Field and took the air again at 1330 in company with eight Marine Corps SBDs and two additional Wildcats. This time the Avengers launched torpedoes at 90-degree angles to the almost stationary battleship. Two bounced harmlessly off the armored sides and a third ran wild, but two exploded; and these, although they did not sink *Hiei*, left her dead in the water at 1430 so that other planes could work her over. The next to do so flew up from Espiritu Santo.[37] Fourteen Flying Fortresses dropped 56 bombs, only one of which possibly hit. By 1800 *Hiei*'s crew had been taken off by

[37] CTF 16 "Operations of TF 16 in the Action for the Defense of Guadalcanal, 12–15 Nov. 1942," 23 Nov. 1942; *Enterprise* Action Report 19 Nov. 1942.

three destroyers, who left her going down stern-first, about five miles NNW of Savo Island.[38]

Other land-based aircraft of Admiral Fitch's from Espiritu Santo were active on 13 November. Scout planes ran into more than their share of excitement. Flying Forts, snooping Admiral Kondo's ships near Ontong Java, on two occasions were attacked by "Zekes." Another B–17, cruising up the Slot, reported four cruisers, six destroyers and twelve transports. These were Tanaka's group, whose schedule had been delayed as a result of Callaghan's night action. Navy Catalinas, too, had several brushes and sighted enemy ships. But *Enterprise* had only one brief flurry of excitement. About noon a 4-engined Kawanishi reported her location and was shot down by her combat air patrol. Apparently the Japanese were too busy to make any use of the plane's contact report.

Admiral Halsey from Nouméa had ordered Admiral Kinkaid to cover the retirement of American ships damaged in the night action by remaining south of lat. 11°40′ S; but information of enemy movements that flowed in during the day indicated more important work to be done. In midafternoon Halsey ordered Lee's heavy gunfire component of Task Force 16 (*Washington, South Dakota* and four destroyers) to be readied for a quick run to Guadalcanal, when he gave the word. Halsey had determined to keep *Enterprise* south of Guadalcanal, whatever happened.[39] So it was up to the battlewagons.

At about 1700 November 13, Kinkaid turned his entire task force due north, to close Guadalcanal at 23 knots. About an hour and a half later, during the second dogwatch, word came from Halsey to send Lee's group ahead to prevent a bombardment of Henderson Field. Unfortunately, Kinkaid's northward advance had been slowed by emergency turns to avoid submarine contacts, and by flight operations which had required fast steaming into a gentle southeast breeze; and by the time Halsey's order reached the

---

[38] ATIS 15931, Sec. 9.
[39] Admiral Halsey remarked after the Battle of Santa Cruz that he would never again permit Yamamoto to "suck" his carriers into waters north of San Cristobal.

task force it was still 350 miles from Savo Island. No battleship could get there that night. Kinkaid sent destroyer *Mustin* 50 miles to the eastward to let Halsey know by radio that it would be impossible for Lee to reach Savo before 0800 November 14. So, as a result of poor staff work at Nouméa, there was nothing to put between Henderson Field and the Japanese bombardment ships except the Tulagi motor torpedo boat contingent.[40]

Admiral Mikawa's cruisers and destroyers, after taking the long way north of Choiseul and Santa Isabel to escape detection, arrived off Savo Island shortly after midnight. Mikawa then detached Nishimura's bombardment group to enter the Sound, while he patrolled to the westward as a precaution against interference. Star performers for the scheduled fireworks were Nishimura's flagship *Suzuya* and another heavy cruiser, *Maya*, each carrying some 500 rounds of high-capacity 8-inch shells destined for Henderson Field. Covered by light cruiser *Tenryu* and four destroyers, the two heavies steamed south of Savo, turned to parallel the Guadalcanal coast, and let fly off Lunga.

On the receiving end of this lethal deluge was Henderson Field, whose aviators and ground crews were playing host to several hundred survivors from *Atlanta* and the sunken destroyers. Sleepy and indignant, these weary Americans groped their way to the familiar muddy foxholes to sit out the show. All hands had hoped that Callaghan's last fight had put a stop to such doings; yet here was another "Tokyo Express" right in the old groove. For thirty-seven minutes the Japanese shells whistled, screamed and caromed through the coconut palms while soldiers and sailors, furious at their inability to strike back, ran the gamut of profanity and

---

[40] Admiral Halsey states in his *Story* that, "confident of the wind's loyalty," he counted on Kinkaid's speed of advance being sufficient to put the battleships within striking distance of Ironbottom Sound that night. He seems to have asked too much of the gods; for a northerly wind, which would have allowed *Enterprise* to conduct flight operation toward instead of away from Guadalcanal, is a rarity in the Coral Sea at that season. It is now obvious that Halsey should have ordered Lee detached much earlier; but we must remember that *Enterprise* was then the only operational American carrier in the Pacific and that she wanted the protection of Lee's force during daylight hours.

prayers. "Washing-Machine Charlie," the Japanese aërial spotter, added insult with bright flares as he sent corrections to the cruisers' fire control teams. When losses were counted in the morning, they were much less than had been anticipated: one dive-bomber and 17 fighter planes destroyed and 32 more fighters damaged, but the field was still operational.[41] Nishimura's bombardment was a poor show compared with what Abe's big boys might have staged the previous night, if let alone.

During the bombardment two motor torpedo boats bravely sortied from Tulagi, made three runs at the heavy cruisers and launched six torpedoes. They made no hits but possibly influenced the enemy to hurry up and get out. At 0205 November 14, when Nishimura had expended his allowance of bombardment ammunition, he led his ships around the north end of Savo, and rendezvoused with Mikawa's patrol group; both retired toward the Shortlands.

Back in Washington it was still the morning of Friday the Thirteenth. Everyone hoped that Callaghan's sacrifice had stopped the enemy; it was a shock to hear that heavy surface forces had broken through and were shelling Henderson Field. And when, a few hours later, word came that Japanese transports were heading down the Slot unopposed by surface forces, even President Roosevelt began to think that Guadalcanal might have to be evacuated. "The tension that I felt at that time," recalled Secretary Forrestal, "was matched only by the tension that pervaded Washington the night before the landing in Normandy."[42]

6. *Smacking the Transports, 14 November*

As the sun rose over Sealark Channel, airmen and ground crews at Henderson Field rolled out of their foxholes. Reinforcements

---

[41] Cincpac Action Report; "Pacific Counterblow," published by Hdqrs Army Air Force as "Wings of War Series No. 3." Army planes damaged were of the 67th Fighter Squadron.

[42] Letter to the writer 22 Oct. 1948.

from *Enterprise*, missing their good Navy chow, shared an exiguous breakfast with Army aviators, Marines and Navy survivors, and Henderson warmed up to one of the busiest days in its hectic history.

Search planes from Henderson and Espiritu Santo were out scouring suspected waters by daybreak, and shortly after 0700 their reports started to roll in: two large groups of combatant ships and transports up the Slot 150 miles northwest of Henderson Field and headed southeast; [43] Mikawa's retiring Support Group bearing W by N, distant about 140 miles. Six Avengers, 7 Dauntless and 7 fighter planes took to the air, hot after the nearer contingent; found it at 0800 and attacked. Torpedo planes, visitors from *Enterprise*, and others of the Marine Corps, holed heavy cruiser *Kinugasa*, while dive-bombers zipped through anti-aircraft fire to plant bombs on light cruiser *Isuzu*. The jubilant pilots left the leading cruiser burning vigorously, and the other emitting clouds of smoke. The entire American flight returned safely to base by 1015; a good early morning's work. [44]

Enterprise, now some 200 miles SSW of Guadalcanal, was eager to get in on the fight. Bad weather delayed her dawn search until 0608 when two planes were launched to cover a northwesterly sector for 200 miles out and eight planes to cover a northerly sector for 250 miles out. Ten fighters and 17 dive-bombers armed with 1000-pound bombs were ready on the flight deck. At 0708 one of the search planes reported ten unidentified planes 140 miles to the northward, flying toward *Enterprise*. What these planes were never was ascertained, but the report caused Captain Hardison to head into the wind and launch his attack group with instructions to head north, look and listen. Their early departure served them well when an exciting contact report came through: "Two battleships, two heavy cruisers, one possible converted carrier, four destroyers, position 8°45′ S, 157°10′ E, course 290°." [45]

[43] Lat. 8° S, long. 157°55′ E.
[44] *Enterprise* Action Report p. 75.
[45] Radio report of Lt. (jg) Robert D. Gibson USNR of VB–10 at 0915; *Enterprise* Action Report.

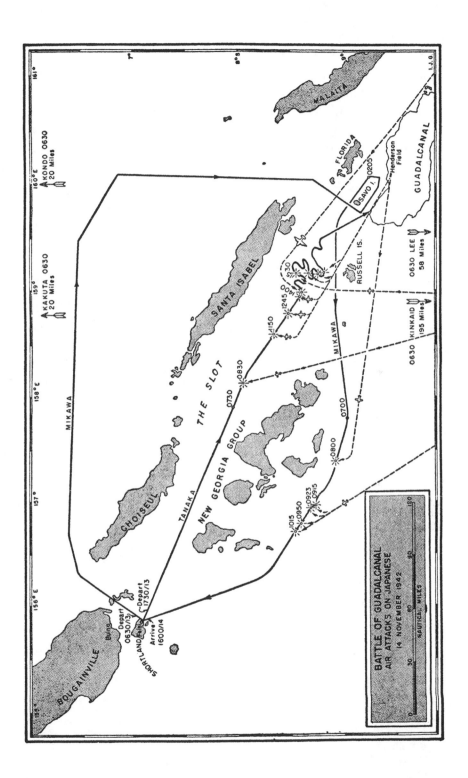

BATTLE OF GUADALCANAL
AIR ATTACKS ON JAPANESE
14 NOVEMBER 1942

NAUTICAL MILES
0   30   60   90   120

That group again was retiring Mikawa's, to the southward of New Georgia; it included no battleships, however. While the two search planes which had made the contact report trailed Mikawa, and at 0915 took a crack at *Kinugasa* which started flooding and gave the heavy cruiser a 10-degree list,[46] Lieutenant Commander James R. Lee in command of the *Enterprise* attack group was making a beeline for the enemy.

At 0950 Mikawa's disorganized command hove into sight. After searching the area carefully for carriers, the bomber leader selected cruiser targets. Planes went into their dives and were rewarded with two apparent hits. A near-miss ruptured *Kinugasa's* gasoline tanks and started another fire and, a few minutes later, the pilots had the satisfaction of seeing this heavy cruiser take the plunge.

Admiral Mikawa, whether he intended it or not, was serving his country somewhat expensively as a decoy, leading American air power away from the crowded troopships. In a series of attacks over a period of two hours he lost *Kinugasa* and suffered damage to heavy cruisers *Chokai* and *Maya*, light cruiser *Isuzu* and destroyer *Michishio*. But the cripples and undamaged ships reached Shortland safely.

Admiral Tanaka's heavily escorted Reinforcement Group, following the direct route down the Slot, had been sighted at 0700 and identified at 0730 by Henderson scout planes when north of New Georgia; but it was not until an hour later that two *Enterprise* SBD pilots[47] found these ships in the Slot midway between New Georgia and Santa Isabel. The planes selected a fat transport and scored one near-miss and one probable hit. As they pulled out, strafing, they encountered a buzz-saw of seven furious "Zekes" which had flown down from carrier *Hiyo*, then operating to the northward. One SBD was shot down but the other managed to escape, returning to *Enterprise* with tanks almost dry after nearly five and a half hours airborne.[48]

[46] Nav. Tech. Jap. Trans. 054 (S-06-3) Jan. 1946.
[47] Lieutenants (jg) Martin D. Carmody USNR and William E. Johnson USNR.
[48] *Enterprise* Action Report; but, according to the Japanese report, the transports suffered their first attack at 0755. Another *Enterprise* SBD piloted by Ensign

Guadalcanal-based airmen now turned their entire attention to the transports approaching Savo Island. A mixed group of Marine Corps and Navy planes — 7 torpedo and 18 dive-bombers escorted by 12 fighters — rose from runways still scarred from the night bombardment. They picked up Tanaka's convoy at 1150, attacked, and opened gaping holes in several transport hulls.

The next relay — 17 dive-bombers with a fighter escort of mixed antecedents — drew a bead on the transports at 1245, zoomed down from 12,000 feet to drop bombs, pulled out strafing and had the satisfaction of seeing at least one enemy ship break in two. Fifteen Flying Fortresses started out from Espiritu Santo at 1018. Their turn arrived at 1430 when, from an altitude of three miles, they loosed 15 tons of bombs over the transports, scoring one hit and several near-misses. "Zekes" were present in equal number to the Forts, and a lively aërial skirmish ensued, six of the enemy falling victim to the American gunners.[49]

Henderson Field was hot in every sense of the word that afternoon. Scattered high cumulus clouds and shell-torn coconut palms gave little shade. Ground crewmen burned up the minutes and themselves too, grunting and sweating to get planes back into action. Pilots scorched landing-gear rubber as they fishtailed, skidded and braked onto the runway, shouting to the ground crew to bear a hand. A fever of excitement pervaded the dusty strip. This was the long-awaited chance to sock the soft bellies of Tojo's transports. Wounded sailors from Callaghan's sunken ships, and other casualties awaiting the arrival of flying ambulances to take them to hospital in Espiritu, watched each aircraft take off and

---

Jeff Carroum was brought down by flak from a transport that afternoon, about 25 miles north of the Russells. The rubber boat was dragged down by the plane, but the pilot and gunner started to swim to the island. Carroum alone made it, after 73 hours in the water. Natives cared for him and he was flown home by a PBY. Source of the "Zekes" is Japanese Board of Merit Report (WDC No. 161,-709), which does not make it clear what carrier *Junyo* was then doing. Both carriers reported shooting down several Wildcats and one or two B-17s, but I have found no American records of those contacts.

[49] CTF 63 Action Report; "Pacific Counterblow" p. 53; *Enterprise* Action Report. At 1500 CTF 63 also sent out 10 Army B-26s, loaded with torpedoes and bombs, and 4 PBYs with torpedoes. None of these made attacks.

prayed for its safety and success; many a whispered "Go get 'em!" escaped burned lips and pain-racked bodies.

Get 'em they did. At 1245 another score of Navy and Marine dive-bombers whipped over Lunga Point palms. An hour later, disregarding combat air patrol and diving in through anti-aircraft fire, these airmen added to the chaos in the broken transport ranks below. And close behind them was another wave of ten bombers.

In Task Force 16 Admiral Kinkaid made the sound decision to shoot the works. *Enterprise's* 8 bombers accompanied by 12 fighters and led by skipper Flatley of "Fighter Ten," skimmed skyward at 1310, "pouring on the soup" in an effort to reach the targets before they were all gone. Flatley had his first glimpse of Tanaka's disordered ranks about 60 miles northwest of Savo Island at 1530. The Japanese admiral was attempting to reform his ships. Some seven or eight transports and five or six destroyers were turning southeast again, leaving three or four others dead in the water and on fire. The attendant "Zekes," much diminished in number, actually flinched from attacking Flatley's Wildcats. Each SBD selected a target and peeled off from 15,000 feet while the Wildcats guarded its tail and then came in strafing. Some bombs hit their marks; fighter-plane bullets whipped troop-crowded decks. Every one of the *Enterprise* planes was safely grounded at Henderson Field by 1600.

Tanaka was in a dilemma. If he retired, his mission would be a failure and he would lose face; if he continued he might possibly deliver some troops to Guadalcanal but would certainly lose his ships. He chose the bolder alternative. Bringing his eleven destroyers close aboard the burning and sinking transports, he succeeded in transferring between 600 and 1000 men to each, and at the same time organized such transports as were still navigable to continue doggedly on their advance.

It was too much to expect that American planes could continue the slaughter all day without cost. Lieutenant Commander Thomas, commanding *Enterprise* "Bomber Ten," departed Henderson Field at 1530 leading a seven-plane flight without fighter escort. That gave the "Zekes" guarding Tanaka their chance. They shot down three of the unprotected SBDs, seriously damaged and turned back two others, and gave a hot reception to the two which penetrated the fighter curtain. One of these played hide-and-seek with a Nip, up through the clouds and down through the Russell Island jungles, finally shaking him off to return to base with 68 holes in his Dauntless and a firm belief in the merits of fighter protection. And two more Marine flights were dispatched from Henderson before nightfall.

Thus, in one day Tanaka lost seven transports, with all their supplies and many of their troops, to air attack alone.[50] Four transports and eleven destroyers remained afloat, still boldly steaming toward Guadalcanal.

To the south of the island *Enterprise*, with only 18 fighter planes remaining on board, passed into a weather front at 1400. An enemy snooper's error in reporting her position resulted in a large flight of would-be attackers passing far to the westward while Kinkaid snuggled into the squall. Next day, Halsey ordered the carrier and her screen back to Espiritu Santo and Nouméa.

The 14th of November offered a striking illustration of what happens to lightly protected ships that venture under enemy-controlled skies. At a cost of only five planes the Americans had sunk a heavy cruiser and seven transports and inflicted serious damage on several others. Both sides learned much that day. The Japanese observed that a destroyer screen with fighter cover was not enough to protect feebly armed ships; they must have close support from heavily gunned men-of-war. And they also learned the need of an additional airfield to help protect the "Tokyo Express." The Americans noted how greatly the effectiveness of carrier planes was increased when they were provided with an optional land base.

[50] Transports sunk on 14 Nov. were *Arizona, Shinanogawa, Sado, Canberra, Nako, Nagara* and *Brisbane* — all *Marus.*

7. *Joust of Giants, 14–15 November* [51]

a. The Encounter South of Savo

These pulverizing air blows against Mikawa and Tanaka obscured the activities of Lee's heavy gunfire group and Kondo's Emergency Bombardment Group, both of which had missions of great import.

Task Force 64 was the first flag command of Rear Admiral Willis Augustus Lee. Behind his lined and weather-beaten face was one of the best brains in the Navy. As director of fleet training just before the war he had been responsible for many improvements in the equipment of combat ships and "he knew more about radar than the radar operators." In addition he had the quality of imperturbability, the capacity to keep in mind the details of a complicated and rapidly changing situation, and the gift of quick and accurate decision that characterized Spruance at Midway. The Navy would need everything he had in the rough night action ahead. [52]

It will be recalled that Lee's group peeled off from Kinkaid's carrier task force on the evening of 13 November, the two battleships and four destroyers hightailing northward. Unable to reach Savo in time to thwart Nishimura's cruiser bombardment, Lee

[51] In addition to using sources previously listed, the writer went to sea in *Washington* about five months after the battle when Admiral Lee had the same staff and the ship the same captain (Glenn B. Davis) and heads of departments. For several days he discussed the action with the Admiral, the Captain, Cdr. Harvey T. Walsh ("exec."), Cdr. Edwin S. Schanze (navigator), Cdr. John A. Strother (engineer), Lt. Cdr. Edwin B. Hooper ("Guns"), Cdr. William F. Jennings (chief of staff) and Lt. Cdr. Richard D. Zern (flag secretary). And in Aug. 1948 both Schanze and Zern read and criticized the first draft of this section.
[52] Willis Augustus Lee of Natlee, Ky., b. 1888; Naval Academy '08; at Vera Cruz 1914; World War I Atlantic destroyer duty; U.S. Olympic rifle team prizewinner; C.O. of destroyers *Fairfax, W. B. Preston* and *Lardner;* student at Naval War College; "exec." *Pennsylvania;* C.O. *Concord;* staff of Cdr. Cruisers Battle Force; director of fleet training; asst. chief of staff to Cominch. In Aug. 1942 became Combatdiv 6. He served in various task forces during the remainder of the war, dying just at its close when engaged in research to counteract the kamikaze menace.

stood off during the 14th, about 100 miles S by W of Guadalcanal, hoping to avoid detection. The enemy did snoop him, but Lee on his side was picking up everything that went on elsewhere. Reports of what was being done to Mikawa and Tanaka, though encouraging, were not nearly so interesting to him as other contacts which crackled in from the north: enemy battleships in Ontong Java waters, big combatant force southbound some 150 miles north of Guadalcanal at 1600. That was Kondo's. It confirmed Lee's suspicion of a forthcoming "Tokyo Express" run that night. His sailors checked their big guns and armor-piercing shells with the certainty that both would find employment.

Admiral Kondo's Emergency Bombardment Group — battleship *Kirishima*, heavy cruisers *Atago* and *Takao*, two light cruisers and an entire destroyer squadron,[53] started south from its stand-by position near Ontong Java at about 1000 November 14, to enter the Slot east of Santa Isabel. During the afternoon this group was attacked by U.S. submarine *Trout*, three of whose torpedoes passed underneath a destroyer and almost nicked the flagship. *Trout* sent an urgent plain-language report of the episode, which Kondo overheard and from which he concluded that a warm reception would await him off Lunga Point. His intention was to brush off American air and surface interference and carry out the devastating airfield bombardment originally assigned to Abe but frustrated by Callaghan.

Early in the evening of 14 November, Lee began prowling around the western end of Guadalcanal, within nine miles of the shoreline. Leading his six-ship column were destroyers *Walke*, *Benham*, *Preston* and *Gwin*, followed by battleships *Washington* and *South Dakota*.[54] He was suffering from the same lack of practice in teamwork that had plagued Callaghan. The four destroyers, from four different divisions and with no division commander on board, had been assigned to him because at the moment they had

[53] Identical with Main Body or Attack Group in above Task Organization.
[54] *Washington* Action Report. At 2100 the flag navigator fixed the position at lat. 9°20' S, long. 159°27' E, course 20°, speed 23 knots.

more fuel than any others under Kinkaid. The battleships had not operated together before leaving Nouméa. Admiral Lee had no opportunity to prepare a formal operation order, but signaled his intentions by visual dispatch. Many at Comsopac headquarters doubted the wisdom of committing two new 16-inch battleships to waters so restricted as those around Savo Island, but Admiral Halsey felt he must throw in everything at this crisis. And he granted Lee complete freedom of action upon reaching Guadalcanal.

Lee's task force, sweeping to the west of Savo, made no contact but saw the distant flares from Tanaka's burning transports on the western horizon. Shortly after 2100 November 14 the Admiral signaled a course change to 90° to take the ships into Ironbottom Sound. He intended to intercept the enemy bombardment group first and early, then deal with the covering group. With Savo on the starboard beam at 2148, course again changed to 150°, SE by S. Now they were steaming over the hulls of ships lost in the battles of 9 August and 13 November, as one could ascertain by watching the needle deflect on the magnetic compass. Ironbottom Sound was flat and calm. A light 7-knot breeze sharp on the port bow hardly ruffled the surface. The first-quarter moon, due to set at 0100, was now and then obscured by low clouds which cast dark shadows on the water. Lookouts could pick up looming heights of land on every side; shore outlines appeared on the radar screen; but neither eyes nor radar discerned any trace of Nips. A rich, sweet odor like honeysuckle floated out from the land over the calm waters, a pleasant change from the normally fecal smells exuded by the Guadalcanal jungle. It seemed a good omen to sailors topside.

Lee badly wanted exact intelligence of the enemy. As he had been assigned no radio call sign in the hurry of departure, he tried to contact radio Guadalcanal ("Cactus"), asking for any late information and signing with his last name. To this he received the snub, "We do not recognize you!" As a last resort he signaled again, "Cactus, this is Lee. Tell your big boss Ching Lee is here and wants the latest information" — for he was a personal friend of General Vandegrift, who knew him by his old Naval Academy nickname. Before "big boss" could be reached, flagship *Washington* picked up voice radio chatter between three motor torpedo boats that were patrolling northeast of Savo. Someone was saying "There go two big ones, but I don't know whose they are!" Admiral Lee, believing it highly desirable to resolve their doubts, at 2230 called Guadalcanal headquarters: "Refer your big boss about Ching Lee; Chinese, catchee? Call off your boys!" The PTs immediately chimed in that they knew Lee and were not after him. Shortly after, "Cactus" called and said, "The boss has no additional information." [55] So all that Lee knew before the battle opened was that the Japanese were coming down in force.

Admiral Kondo's express was now running in three sections: a distant screen consisting of light cruiser *Sendai* (Rear Admiral Hashimoto) and three destroyers; a close screen composed of light cruiser *Nagara* (Rear Admiral Kimura) and six destroyers; and the big bombardment group, Kondo's flagship *Atago*, her sister ship *Takao* and battleship *Kirishima*.[56] Hashimoto's ships were two or three miles ahead as pickets. Kimura's were steaming close to the bombardment ships. Admiral Kondo had scheduled his bombardment to commence simultaneously with the landing of reinforcement troops from Tanaka's tough remnant, the four transports and accompanying destroyers which also were approaching Savo.

Sendai, leading Hashimoto's pack, first sniffed trouble at 2210

[55] The flag radio log merely states that Lee established his identity with Base "Cactus" at 2240. What Lee said became legendary in a very short time. An officer in *Washington* told me that the Admiral replied in rhyme: "This is Chung Ching Lee — you mustn't fire 'fish' at me!" and I have since heard five or six different versions. Lt. R. W. Thompson, Lee's flag lieutenant who was on the bridge with him, says (1948) that what really happened was this: Lee overheard the PTs reporting his position, course, etc. in a code he did not have. He told Lt. Cdr. Zern to tell them over voice radio, "This is Lee," which Zern did. PT retorted "Who's Lee?" Admiral replied "Tell your boss this is Ching Lee." My version is a combination of the radio log in *South Dakota's* Action Report with what Admiral Lee told me on 15 Apr. 1943.

[56] Of these ships, *Kirishima*, *Nagara*, *Samidare*, *Teruzuki*, *Inazuma* and *Asagumo* participated also in the action of 13 Nov.

when she sighted "two enemy cruisers and four destroyers" north of Savo, heading into the Sound. Destroyers *Ayanami* and *Uranami* were detached to reconnoiter south of Savo, passing to the westward of the island, while *Sendai* and *Shikinami*, unknown to Lee, took off in eager pursuit of him. *Sendai's* report caused instant action on the flag bridge of *Atago*. Kondo issued his attack order. He divided Kimura's group into two elements: cruiser *Nagara* and four destroyers as an advance guard, destroyers *Asagumo* and *Teruzuki* remaining with the firing unit to lead it west and north of Savo. The *Nagara* group was to enter the Sound at full speed south of Savo Island behind *Ayanami* and *Uranami*. Kondo's plan could be considered the ultimate in the Japanese tactical pattern of dispersion. Fourteen ships were split four ways in a ten-mile-square area which had to be shared with the antagonist.

At 2252 as the moon set behind the mountains of Cape Esperance, Admiral Lee, at the limit of the southeasterly leg, executed a column movement to the right to course west. *Washington* had barely settled on this course when her radar picked up a target distant nine miles, a point and a half west of north. This, cruiser *Sendai*, was tracked until 2312 when the main battery director actually saw her through his telescopes. *South Dakota* also saw her but none of the destroyers did. At 2316 Lee ordered his captains to open fire when ready. A minute later 16-inch projectiles were burning up the air toward Admiral Hashimoto's flagship. *Sendai*, alarmed by this dubious welcome, laid down a blanket of smoke, and at high speed doubled back to the northward in company with destroyer *Shikinami*, pursued by battleship salvos out of radar range.

b. Destroyers' Slaughter

Fortunately this indecisive bout had not distracted the leading American destroyers sufficiently to cause them to relax vigilance in other quarters. Enemy destroyers *Ayanami* and *Uranami*, sneaking along the south shore of Savo, were by this time within visual, gunfire and torpedo range. *Walke*, at the head of the American column, sounded the alarm with a 5-inch salvo at 2322. *Benham* and *Preston* followed with rapid gunfire. *Gwin*, which had been firing star shell in the direction of the battleship targets, attracted by the rumpus on the starboard bow, swung optics and trained guns at 2326, just in time to pick up Admiral Kimura's advance guard cruiser *Nagara* and four destroyers. A private gun duel started between *Gwin* and the Kimura contingent. The enemy, concealed by the overhanging mountains of Savo, replied heartily with gunfire, and was not slow in employing his customary equalizer, the torpedo. *Ayanami* and *Uranami* laid their tubes carefully, the ugly shark-shaped engines swooshed overboard at 2330; others from Kimura's force five minutes later. At about this time *Walke* was struck by enemy shells and began to fall off to port, shooting furiously and endeavoring to get onto the target with her torpedoes. *Benham*, 300 yards astern of her, continued to fire whenever a target could be seen but refrained from shooting torpedoes at what were thought to be destroyers. *Preston* shot at a ship, probably *Nagara*, but like *Walke* received more than she gave, one salvo putting both firerooms out and toppling the after stack. Shortly thereafter, shells coming in from the quarter practically demolished her topsides from amidships aft; *Preston* was out of action with torpedoes still on board. *Gwin*, tailing her, also was a mark for Japanese destroyer guns; one shell detonated in an engine room, another struck the fantail, and the shock disrupted her torpedo safety links so that the "fish" slid harmlessly out of the tubes. By the time enemy torpedoes began to boil around the destroyers, only *Benham* had escaped serious damage by gunfire. And at 2338 enemy warheads began to find their marks. *Walke* had her forecastle blown off as far aft as the bridge; *Benham* had a large chunk of her bow destroyed in one massive eruption.

While the destroyers were bearing the brunt of enemy attention, the battleships were striving to lend a hand, their secondary batteries hammering away at vessels in the shadow of Savo. But *Washington* had trouble sorting out the numerous targets on her radar screen and, at 2333, *South Dakota* had a stroke of bad luck: electrical circuit breakers jumped out and caused loss of electrical power throughout the ship. Faith in radar had become so great that the loss of both SG and SC equipment had a most depressing effect on officers and men; it gave all hands the feeling of being blindfolded.

If Kondo's intention was to confuse by splitting his forces, the ruse was certainly succeeding. Milling about in the narrow channel between Savo and Guadalcanal at 2335 were three separate groups. Kimura's advance guard was retiring close to Savo after firing torpedoes; *Ayanami* was damaged and with *Uranami* was striving to extricate herself from a hot spot less than two miles from the Americans; and, finally, Hashimoto's pugnacious cruiser *Sendai* and destroyer *Shikinami* were resuming action with a stealthy attack from astern. Small wonder that American radar screens made no sense to the puzzled operators and that American commanders were confused by reports of motor torpedo boats, flares, lightning, phantom contacts and completely contradictory "dope" as to enemy movements. Even after the battle many gunners were convinced that their targets were shore batteries on Savo. But the Japanese, aware that their enemy was in one concentrated formation, were able to follow Lee's movements and disregard the comings and goings of their own various groups. By 2335 all four American destroyers were out of action without having launched a single torpedo; one battleship was blinded by power failure and the other handicapped by floundering cripples ahead and confused by radar echoes against Savo Island. *Ayanami* alone of ships flying the Rising Sun was injured, and *Uranami* stood ready to rescue her crew or protect her against further attack.

In the individual American destroyers conditions were sickeningly similar to the horrors of Friday the Thirteenth. *Walke*, dismembered and blazing, was down by the head and sinking fast. Commander Fraser ordered Abandon Ship in the nick of time; the after two-thirds of the ship sank at 2342 and depth charges previously reported as "safe" exploded directly under the survivors. *Benham,* her bow partially destroyed, limped painfully clear of friendly ships, then turned to a westerly course, passing through swimming and shouting survivors. *Preston,* gutted by an internal fire, was ordered abandoned at 2336. Seconds later she rolled heavily on her side, hung ten minutes with bow in air and then sank. *Gwin,* least damaged of the destroyer quartet, passed through the swirling water marking *Preston's* grave, shaken by exploding depth charges. She continued to fire at the enemy as long as anything remained within range. *Washington's* sailors found time to toss life rafts overboard as the flagship tore past the stricken destroyers.

Round One ended at 2335 when Admiral Lee changed course left from 300° to 282° in order to pass to the southward of burning destroyers. *South Dakota* started to follow in her wake but had to turn to starboard to avoid *Benham* and so got herself silhouetted by the burning *Preston* and *Walke.* At 2336 all hands in the battleship heaved a sigh of relief as steady power flowed back once more to operate gyros, radars, guns and motors. Gunners took advantage of their rejuvenation to pour out a few main battery salvos at *Sendai* astern. At 2342 *South Dakota* was again in trouble of her own making; a turret gun blast set fire to planes on the fantail catapults. Fortunately, a succeeding salvo blew the planes overboard and the fires out.[57]

c. Battlewagon Duel

At 2348 Admiral Lee, recognizing that his destroyers were no longer capable of offensive action, ordered them to retire while he altered his own course slightly to the northward. The time was now at hand for *South Dakota* to pay dearly for her electric power failure earlier in the game. When she turned to starboard instead of

[57] Cincpac "Solomons Islands Campaign — Battle of the Solomons, 11–15 Nov. 1942," 18 Feb. 1943. Cincpac criticized the presence of planes on board, remarking that they should have been flown off. Admiral Lee had considered sending the planes to Tulagi to stand by for possible night use, but he doubted that Tulagi had facilities for them.

to port to clear the burning destroyers, she inadvertently closed the range on Kimura's retiring advance guard and completely lost track of her own flagship.[58] Kimura sighted *South Dakota*, shouted an alarm to Kondo and at 2355 launched a swarm of 34 torpedoes. Fortunately, all missed.

Kondo's bombardment unit had been tacking back and forth on the sheltered northwest side of Savo throughout the entire first phase of the battle. At 2348 his ships were in column on a westerly course eight miles due north of Cape Esperance; order of ships: destroyers *Asagumo* and *Teruzuki*, heavy cruisers *Atago* and *Takao*, battleship *Kirishima*. Upon hearing Kimura's warning, Kondo swung this column completely around to a southeasterly course in order to join the fight.

South Dakota, with the radar picture incomplete as a consequence of that untimely power loss, continued to close both Kimura and Kondo. The former, making a complete loop after delivering his torpedo attack, fell back and somehow lost sight of both American battlewagons. At the same time Kondo's leading destroyers picked them up. At a scant 5000 yards searchlight shutters were snapped open to expose *South Dakota* to the combined fury of the entire bombardment force. Again the torpedoes missed, but large-caliber shells plowed into the battleship's superstructure. She replied with everything she had, directed against the offending beams of light. She was in a tough spot, the primary target of three heavy ships.

Lee was of no mind to let this situation deteriorate further. With radar humming accurately, *Washington* had tracked a big target for several minutes but had refrained from shooting for fear it might be her sister ship; *South Dakota* actually was in the "blind spot" of *Washington*'s radar on her starboard quarter. All doubts were resolved when the Japanese illuminated, and at midnight Lee's flagship opened fire. Selecting *Kirishima*, the fattest

---

[58] *South Dakota's* chronology differs by 10 minutes from *Washington's*. In view of the power loss and subsequent damage, I believe *Washington* times to be the more reliable.

target, bearing almost due north, the 16-inch main battery cut loose at a range of 8400 yards. The 5-inch mounts divided their attention between her and the ship that was illuminating *South Dakota*, while one 5-inch gun sent up star shell which showed Lee what the big fellow was. One of the few actions of World War II between line-of-battle ships was joined.[59]

In Kondo's ranks there was a general rush to get at the brightly illuminated *South Dakota*. *Asagumo* fruitlessly launched torpedoes. Other ships spat out rapid-fire salvos of large- and medium-caliber shells. So intent were they on this obvious target that they failed even to locate the American flagship. The results were fatal to *Kirishima*; 9 out of 75 sixteen-inch shells from *Washington* scored, as did about 40 fast-shooting 5-inchers. Within seven minutes *Kirishima* was out of the fight, steering gear hopelessly wrecked, topsides aflame. Meanwhile *South Dakota* and *Washington* had registered a few hits on cruisers *Atago* and *Takao*, revealed by their own searchlights.[60]

South Dakota took numerous hits topside, from 14-inch down to 5-inch. She had lost track of *Washington*; her radio communication had failed; only one radar in the entire ship was unhurt; radar plot was demolished; one main battery turret was damaged in train; gunnery control stations were depleted by casualties; many small but dangerous fires were creeping throughout the superstructure. The redoubtable Captain Gatch, finding his ship no longer under fire and without means to reënter the engagement, moved to retire; course was set at 235° and the battered ship drew clear at full speed.

d. *Washington* Wins

Admiral Lee tried without success to raise *South Dakota* by radio; he could only hope that she was retiring, not sinking. In an

[59] The others were Battle of Calabria, 27 June 1940, Battle of Surigao Strait, 25 Oct. 1944, the hunting and sinking of *Bismarck*, and *Renown* vs. *Scharnhorst* 8 Apr. 1940. *Massachusetts* against immobile *Jean Bart* was not a sea action.
[60] Lt. Cdr. Horishi Tokuno in *Inter. Jap. Off.* I 141.

effort to draw enemy fire away from her and to encounter any Japanese ships that might be coming down from the north, he turned his flagship to a northwesterly course. *Kirishima* and the rest of the bombardment group were left behind on her starboard quarter as *Washington* pushed on alone. At 0020 November 15 the Admiral changed course to 340°, a move which (judging from the radar screen) set the entire enemy force in motion to the northward. The Japanese were hastening to protect their transports. Their bombardment unit (minus *Kirishima*) roughly paralleled Lee, with Kimura in hot pursuit; Tanaka, justifiably concerned about his remaining transports, detached destroyers *Oyashio* and *Kagero* to make a torpedo attack on any American that approached them.

At 0025 Admiral Kondo thought better of his decision to pursue and ordered all ships not actively engaged to withdraw. Led by *Atago*, the bombardment unit turned sharp right to course NNE, laid down a smoke screen and retired. Admiral Lee observed this move with satisfaction. Convinced that the enemy troopships would now be delayed until daylight, when Henderson Field airmen could take care of them, and that *South Dakota* was out of harm's way, he ordered an abrupt right turn at 0033 and commenced retirement. With Chinese cunning he charted a course far to the westward, at one point only 4000 yards from one of the Russell Islands, in order to draw trailing enemy destroyers away from the tracks of damaged American ships. This decision was good joss, for at 0039 *Kagero* and *Oyashio* of Tanaka's screen and Kimura's advance guard destroyers launched torpedoes at *Washington*, some of which exploded on entering her troubled wake. Through moonless darkness keen lookouts sighted the torpedo tracks and Captain Davis's clever maneuvering dodged their embarrassing caresses as nimbly as a young girl eluding a sailor on a park bench. At 0040 she changed course again to 210° and speeded up to 26 knots in order to shake off these persistent destroyers.

While *Washington* was acting as a lone-ship task force, *Benham* was struggling to survive with her bow shattered and keel damaged. *Gwin,* although making sluggish recoveries from dangerous rolls, was in no immediate danger. *South Dakota* was out of the battle zone, heading at high speed for a prearranged rendezvous. Admiral Lee, apprised of *Benham's* woes, directed *Gwin* to escort the noseless destroyer to Espiritu Santo, and further authorized *Benham's* skipper to abandon ship if necessary. Necessity arrived next afternoon and abandoned she was by 1724 without loss of life. *Gwin* sank *Benham* by gunfire and made Espiritu Santo without further incident.[61]

South Dakota fell in with *Washington* at 0900 November 15, and the two ships proceeded in company toward Nouméa. *Washington* had come off unscathed; but *South Dakota,* with superstructure badly damaged by 42 large-caliber hits, 38 men killed or missing and 60 wounded, returned to the States for refitting.[62]

The battle was over. Admiral Kondo abandoned his bombardment plan and faced the problem of succoring the burning and exploding *Kirishima. Sendai* and *Shikinami* had previously been ordered to stand by the wounded queen, and three destroyers were added to her ladies in waiting. In addition to her steering gear, the engines had been slightly damaged. But her skipper wanted no repetition of *Hiei's* daytime ordeal and so lost little time in ordering the abandonment and scuttling of his ship. Destroyers closed to take off her crew, sea valves were opened, and the ship settled slowly, sinking northwest of Savo Island at 0320 November 15.

One more Rising Sun had set. Destroyer *Ayanami,* in hopeless shape after running close aboard the American ships, was given

---

[61] *Benham* went down at lat. 10°11′ S, long. 160°7′ E. An ironic feature of the sinking was the failure of *Gwin's* torpedoes to hit. One exploded prematurely, one missed ahead, one had an erratic run, and one missed astern.

[62] *Washington,* despite an enviable war record, received less publicity than any other capital ship in the U.S. Navy. The reasons for this are: undamaged by the enemy, she furnished no "drama," and *South Dakota* by going home grabbed all the publicity for this action, as *Boise* had for Cape Espérance. I cannot here refrain from calling attention to the presumptuous mendacity of Mr. William B. Huie who, in the *Reader's Digest* for Dec. 1948, says of the 15 U.S. battleships that operated in World War II, "They were manned by thousands of scarce men. The Navy spent millions on propaganda for them. *Yet no super-battleship ever sank an enemy ship; not one of them ever fired a justifying shot.*"

the deep six by her skipper after the crew had been transferred to *Uranami*.

For sheer tenacity of purpose, every sailor owes a salute to Rear Admiral Raizo Tanaka. When the sea was finally cleared of dueling warships, Tanaka resumed his "Cape Esperance or Bust" mission with four remaining transports escorted by eleven troop-laden destroyers. By 0400 the transports had been grounded on the beach off Tassafaronga, and the soldiers were joining their unfortunate fellows in the Guadalcanal jungle. It is doubtful whether the destroyers disembarked their passengers because, according to the Japanese, only 2000 troops in all got ashore. At any rate, the destroyers scampered back to the Shortlands, arriving at midnight on the 15th.[63]

The battleship action of November 14–15 was vastly better fought by the United States Navy than the unorganized brawl of two nights earlier. Admiral Lee had a positive doctrine that he maintained, despite the absence of his entire destroyer screen. An able and original scientist as well as a flag officer, he appreciated the value of radar, used it to keep himself informed of enemy movements and tactics, and made quick, accurate analyses from the information on the screens. Yet some mistakes of earlier night battles were repeated. Lee's task force was a scratch team, destroyer and battleship captains alike being unfamiliar with each other and with their commander. Apparently the recurring urgencies in the South Pacific imposed a haphazard composition for every task force thrown together to meet the enemy. Again, and not for the last time, the Japanese taught the Americans a lesson in the use of torpedoes. *South Dakota* was lucky to escape alive. *Washington*, conned by Captain Glenn Davis and directed by Admiral Lee with a skill and imperturbability worthy of her eponym, saved the day for the United States.

[63] Cdr. Tadashi Yamamoto, Tanaka's communications officer, in *Inter. Jap. Off.* II 468.

e. Survivors' Holiday

Sunrise November 15 found the sultry air hushed over the quiet waters of Sleepless Lagoon with many thousand more tons of iron resting on the bottom and several hundred bluejackets clinging to flotsam or floating in their life jackets. Before long, survivors from *Walke* and *Preston*, who had remained cheerful and hopeful all night, became moist ringside spectators of interesting events. First ship to meet their eyes was a Japanese transport beaching herself on Guadalcanal. This was *Yamatsuki Maru*, last of Admiral Tanaka's brood. As the floating destroyer sailors followed her movements, they noticed that three other transports were already grounded. These were *Kinugawa Maru*, *Hirokawa Maru* and *Yamaura Maru*. Trouble arrived for all four in the form of strafing Army fighters followed shortly by Navy and Marine bombers. *Enterprise* Air Group 10 came early on the scene and stayed late; between 0645 and 1530 about 17 "Big E" bombers worked over the helpless transports, dropped "Molotov breadbaskets" (incendiary clusters) on adjacent beaches with excellent results, and touched off an ammunition dump ashore which exploded and burned most of the day and night. They were aided and abetted by Marine and Army fliers who entered into the game with great gusto but whose sporting instincts were so sorely tried by this necessary butchery, and by bloodstained waters covered with dissevered human members, that they retched and puked.[64]

Not so with the floating destroyer survivors who had been on the receiving end of Nipponese fury; the higher the score, the more they enjoyed the game. And the Marine and Army shore batteries, concentrating on the wretched transports, never had enough to suit them. But the star performance was staged by a United States destroyer that darted out of Tulagi Harbor at 0915. At a range of 12,500 yards she opened up on a large Japanese ship in Doma Cove north of Tassafaronga, closed to 8000 yards and continued

[64] Army information contained in A.A.F. pamphlet "Pacific Counterblow"; *Enterprise* Action Report with letters of *Walke* and *Preston* survivors.

shooting, with the aid of a spotting plane. At 1021, feeling she had finished off one transport, she trained on a second beached at Tassafaronga Point, then shifted to a third at Doma Cove, then peppered the Japanese-held beaches with her 40-mm machine guns (among the first to appear in these waters) and bombarded them with her main battery. Finally she gave the transport in Doma Cove a concentrated dose of rapid fire which in five minutes' time caused it to split longitudinally.[65]

From their fish-eye view, *Preston* and *Walke* bluejackets witnessed this unknown warrior's performance with wonder and delight, mingled with hope that she might take up survivor rescue as a side line. Sure enough, the destroyer pranced over to the bobbing heads and commenced picking up their owners. With the help of landing and patrol craft, a motor torpedo boat and airplane spotters, 135 men of *Walke* and 131 of *Preston* were pulled out of the water by midafternoon. Survivors then learned that their benefactor was the *Meade*, skippered by Lieutenant Commander Raymond S. Lamb, new to Guadalcanal and, for the time being, cock-of-the-walk where mighty battlewagons had slugged it out a few hours earlier.[66]

Some *Walke* survivors drifted away and were never recovered, but at least two of them swam ashore after spending two days and nights in the water, and their adventures on Guadalcanal testify to the toughness and unbreakable spirit of American bluejackets. These were Seaman Dale E. Land and Machinist's Mate Harold Taylor. They got ashore within enemy lines and made their way eastward very slowly, because Land had no shoes and they were forced to travel through jungle to avoid military patrols of the beach. They lived on coconuts and a few enemy supplies that they filched, and on one occasion were near enough to a Japanese

[65] The destruction of the four grounded ships brought the Japanese transport losses for 14–15 Nov. to 77,608 gross tons.

[66] *Meade* had been escorting auxiliary *Kopara* and tug *YT–130* to Tulagi. Because of the tactical situation, Admiral Turner had directed them to retire, but changed his mind and they arrived Tulagi on the afternoon of the 14th. *Meade* had never before been in action. *Walke* and *Preston* "Additions" to Action Reports 6 Dec. 1942.

bivouac to see men run and hear them scream when Army P–39s strafed the group. After two weeks of painful progress they picked up a Japanese rifle and a bandolier full of cartridges and, thereafter, fired on nearly every enemy sighted, killing a good dozen all told. But they did a little too much of that. On 5 December Taylor, who had the rifle and was about 50 yards ahead of Land, fired into a group of Japs sitting around a fire and killed three or four, but the rest got him. Land escaped, crawled to within shouting distance of the 182nd Regiment front lines, and was well received by the soldiers. He had a temperature of 106 degrees but made a rapid recovery.[67]

8. *Fork in the Road*

When *Meade* entered Tulagi with her cargo of survivors on the afternoon of 15 November, curtain fell on the Naval Battle of Guadalcanal. Both fleets retired from the field of battle; both countries claimed a tremendous victory. In view of what each was trying to do, and in the light of future events, who really won?

Both objectives were similar: to reinforce one's own garrison on Guadalcanal but deny it to the enemy by air and sea. With that yardstick the conclusion is unmistakable: Turner got every one of his troops and almost all his materiel ashore, while Tanaka the Tenacious managed to land only about 2000 shaken survivors, 260 cases of ammunition and 1500 bags of rice.[68] The Americans dominated the air from start to finish and kept possession of Henderson Field. On the surface, Callaghan chased one force out of Ironbottom Sound, losing his life and several ships in the process, and Lee disposed of Kondo's second attempt to follow Mahan doctrine. Air losses were far greater on the Japanese side. Of combat ships the United States Navy sustained the greater loss, but the elimination of two battleships and 11 transports from the Japanese Fleet

[67] Comairsopac Intelligence, 18 Dec. 1942.
[68] "Southeast Area Operations, Part I (Navy)" Special Staff U.S. Army Historical Div. No. 851-100 p. 45.

was far more serious. The enemy could accept a heavy loss of troops because he had plenty of replacements, but he could not replace battleships or transports, and he depended on air and surface fleets to stop any American offensive against Greater East Asia.

The Battle of Guadalcanal was decisive, not only in the struggle for that island, but in the Pacific War at large. Only a day later, 16 November, important elements of MacArthur's Army were ferried around the tail end of New Guinea to land seven miles south of Buna and clear the enemy out of the Buna–Gona hinterland, an operation that received scant notice in the United States but bothered the Japanese high command almost as much as did Guadalcanal. The Imperial Army did not give up Guadalcanal for another ten weeks, but the Navy performed its ferryboat duties with increasing reluctance and made no further bid to rule the adjacent waves.

In torpedo tactics and night action, this series of engagements showed that tactically the Japanese were still a couple of semesters ahead of the United States Navy, but their class standing took a decided drop in the subject of war-plan execution. Why was Admiral Mikawa permitted to abandon the area and the transports on the morning of the 14th? Without his muscle-men, the big-bellied transports waddled into a veritable slaughterhouse. Again, with Henderson Field still a going concern and an American carrier snorting back and forth southward of Guadalcanal, why did carriers *Hiyo* and *Junyo* hang far back to the northwestward, instead of steaming down to help square an unfavorable balance of air power? Lastly, why were the transports not recalled to Shortland to reorganize (as at Wake in December 1941) when it became apparent that the operation was not proceeding according to book?

The conclusion of this great battle was marked by a definite shift of the Americans from the defensive to the offensive, and of the Japanese in the opposite direction. The United States Navy felt that it could never again be defeated; the Marines and soldiers, confident at last of real naval support, fought with greater vigor and lighter hearts; the airmen had won a definite ascendancy over and around Ironbottom Sound. And during the first two weeks of November, fortune for the first time smiled on the Allies everywhere: North Africa, Stalingrad, Papua, Guadalcanal. President Roosevelt, while mourning the loss of his friend Dan Callaghan, announced, "It would seem that the turning point in this war has at last been reached." [69] Churchill chose this moment to proclaim "the end of the beginning." And a captured Japanese document admitted: "It must be said that the success or failure in recapturing Guadalcanal Island, and the vital naval battle related to it, is the fork in the road which leads to victory for them or for us." [70]

From 15 November 1942 until 15 August 1945 the war followed the right fork. It was rough, tough and uncharted, but it led to Tokyo.

[69] Robert E. Sherwood *Roosevelt and Hopkins* p. 656.
[70] Cincpac Action Report on the Solomons.

CHAPTER XIII

The Battle of Tassafaronga[1]

30 November 1942

1. *Point Cruz and* ALCHIBA, *15–29 November*

THE Americans were quick to profit by mid-November victories, but there was plenty to do before Guadalcanal could be converted from a precarious foothold into a solid platform for the long overdue advance up the Slot. First, the island must be tidied up; the enemy must be destroyed or pushed into a corner where he would be impotent.

A fair start for this clean-up would be the relief of the long-suffering 1st Marine Division. For 15 long weeks — seven-day weeks and twenty-four-hour days — these stout fighters had taken all that the enemy offered, and the jungle as well. They were enervated with malaria and combat fatigue after double the tour of duty that medical officers considered possible under such conditions. For the last month they had had the help of the 164th Infantry Regiment and, since 4 November, of the 8th Marine Regiment (Colonel Jeschke's). Plans were completed for bringing the 6th Marine Regiment up from New Zealand and the 182nd Infantry, Americal Division, from New Caledonia. As an orderly and

[1] Also called "4th," "5th" and "6th Battle of Savo I." and "Battle of Lunga Point." Principal sources: Cincpac "Solomon Islands Campaign, 5th Battle of Savo — 30 Nov. 1942"; Action Reports of U.S. ships and commands involved; 1st Marine Division "Final Report on Guadalcanal Operation"; Capt. Toyama in *Inter. Jap. Off.* I, 254; Allied Japanese Report "Battle of Tassafaronga" ATIS 16086; Henry Salomon Jr. notes taken in Japan. The writer spent some time on board *New Orleans* and *Pensacola* after their temporary repairs were made, and had two tours of duty on board *Honolulu* which enabled him to gather many incidents of this action not elsewhere recorded.

uneventful troop movement to and from Guadalcanal began, Thanksgiving Day was not forgotten; a shipload of turkeys was sent up to the troops.

Much could be done and was done to better the condition of troops who stayed and of those coming. Improvements were effected in sanitation and care by sending up the 101st Medical Regiment United States Army, which landed at Guadalcanal 13 November just in time to help the victims of the great three-day battle. They collected 1156 casualties in two nights and a day. But of these the battle casualties were very much less than those from fatigue and disease.[2]

General Vandegrift wished to follow up the naval victory of Guadalcanal by pushing forward to new lines westward. The ensuing action was called the Battle of Point Cruz, a small cape between the Matanikau River and Kokumbona where Mendaña had landed in 1568. At this point the shores of Guadalcanal rise steeply from the sea, leaving only enough flat land for the dirt road; numerous defiles and ravines gave the defense ample opportunity to enfilade any advancing force. The hills and ridges, in fantastic shapes, are covered with kunai grass.

This operation proved that the Japanese on Guadalcanal, though disappointed of their expected reinforcements, still had plenty of fight and savvy. Vandegrift pushed his forces ahead in three prongs. The 1st Battalion 182nd Infantry Regiment took the coast road, and by 19 November cut off the Japanese on Point Cruz from their fellows in the interior, and pushed about 300 yards beyond. On their left marched a company of Marines; some 1000 yards to the Marines' left, the 2nd Battalion 182nd Regiment, which took position on a grassy knoll. Between this battalion and the Marines, the Japanese strongly held another grassy knoll and were not

[2] Conversations with Capt. A. E. Roberts USA MC, statistical officer of 101st Regiment, 1 May 1943; Sanitary Survey by Col. Dale G. Friend USAMC in Report to Surgeon General 1 Mar. 1943. Average sick rate Americal Division on Guadalcanal 15 Nov. 1942–15 Mar. 1943 was 7 per 1000; battle casualties only 0.3 per 1000. Incidence of malaria 15 Nov. averaged 8.7 per 1000 per day, and in some units that rejected atabrine (owing to a rumor that it impaired virility), rose as high as 20. But by 15 March, it had fallen to 1.7.

completely dislodged until the 1st Battalion 164th Regiment was called up to help on the 21st. The entire enemy front was very strongly held; the 182nd and the Marines found Nips on three sides of them and suffered a very harassing mortar fire. They had little artillery and no naval support, as every ship left whole after the battle had retired. On the 22nd the American troops had to fall back to a position a little in advance of Point Cruz, which they proceeded to clean out. And the lines which they then occupied were substantially unchanged for the next fifty-four days.[3]

In the meantime, Lieutenant Colonel Carlson's 2nd Raider Battalion went on a manhunt in early November which afforded them a good dozen fights in which over 400 of the enemy were killed at the cost of only 17 Marines. The route chosen by these colorful raiders carried them through some of the most forbidding country on Guadalcanal: the upper valleys of the Tenaru and Lunga Rivers and a long detour around Mambulo (Mt. Austen), a hilly mass on the central part of the coast. It was December before they returned to the perimeter, lean from a diet of rice, bacon and tea.[4]

Air strength on Henderson Field increased during the last fortnight of November from 85 single-engined planes to 124 aircraft, including 5 New Zealand Hudsons and 8 Flying Fortresses. At the same time, Seabees were grading and laying steel mat on the mile-long bomber strip and the two fighter strips. Logistics could barely keep pace; on 30 November only four days' supply of aviation gasoline was on hand.

Afloat there were changes, too; the motor torpedo boat flotilla by 30 November mustered 15 PTs and tender *Jamestown*. Antisubmarine patrol boats and aircraft put in their first appearance at Tulagi. Eight destroyers were assigned to escort duty between the Solomons and South Pacific bases. Base "Ringbolt" (Tulagi) was becoming solidly embedded.

The attrition of naval power incident to five big naval battles

[3] This action was personally investigated by the writer on the spot 5 months later, and he is satisfied that the story of a "rout" of one of these units is untrue.
[4] Maj. John L. Zimmerman USMCR *The Guadalcanal Campaign*. Carlson's Raiders arrived on the island 4 Nov. 1942.

forced Admiral Halsey to reorganize his South Pacific Force. *Saratoga* was on her way back to the South Pacific, to become the pivot of a carrier group under Rear Admiral DeWitt C. Ramsey. Around *Enterprise*, in spite of her recalcitrant forward elevator, Rear Admiral Frederick C. Sherman formed a second carrier group. *North Carolina's* torpedo damage of September had been repaired; she and sister battlewagon *Washington* became nuclei of a big-gun task force, presently augmented by *Indiana*. Down in the Fijis battleships *Maryland* and *Colorado*, commanded by Rear Admiral Harry W. Hill, were awaiting employment; escort carriers *Altamaha* and *Nassau* ferried planes to New Caledonia and Espiritu Santo. To replace Callaghan's shattered command, Rear Admiral Kinkaid was assigned a task force powered by heavy cruisers *Pensacola, New Orleans* and *Northampton* and light cruisers *Honolulu* and *Helena*. Nouméa and Espiritu Santo were the bases for these revamped forces. No more would task forces mill around "Torpedo Junction"; henceforth ships entered the Coral Sea only with a destination to reach or a combat mission to perform.

There were also administrative changes in the South Pacific Force. Halsey was promoted to Admiral on 26 November in recognition of his success and the growing importance of his command. And, since the majority of ground troops on Guadalcanal were henceforth to be of the Army, it was decided to relieve Major General Vandegrift usmc by Major General Alexander M. Patch usa of the Americal Division.

American commanders still had to consider the possibility of another Japanese attempt to win back Guadalcanal. Yet, confidence that any such effort could be thwarted allowed bolder planning than heretofore. Assurance was justified. The enemy carriers were refitting in Japan, and the rest of the Combined Fleet was held in readiness to serve Yamamoto's ambition for one big decisive battle with the entire Pacific Fleet, a battle that was not to occur until after Yamamoto's death. As for Guadalcanal, the very name was anathema to the Nipponese; an evil place like quicksand, where ships and men sank out of sight without ever finding *terra firma* for victory. Tojo's planners began to shift interest to the middle Solomons. Perhaps New Georgia, a potpourri of irregular islands, could be blended into a stew unpalatable to the Americans. In the meantime, Tanaka the Tenacious must employ destroyers to supply the unhappy troops on Guadalcanal. No more nightly naval bombardments, however.

While so much else changed for the better, the American supply train continued to suffer. U.S.S. *Alchiba*, rated an AK or naval freighter, departed Nouméa 21 November in company with transport *Barnett* and a destroyer escort for Guadalcanal. She carried a touchy cargo of aviation gasoline, bombs and ammunition, and towed a barge full of Marston mats. On the morning of the 28th, when she was starting to unload at Lunga Point, Japanese midget submarine No. 10 (launched by *I–16*) boldly and precisely fired a single torpedo past the screen of five destroyers into *Alchiba's* No. 2 hold.[5] In a flash the forward part of the ship was ablaze and she took a 17-degree list. Her skipper, Commander James S. Freeman, apprehensive lest his ship blow up or sink, made straight for the beach two miles west of Lunga unloading point and drove her bow hard into the sand so that over 150 feet of her keel rested on the solid bottom. Meanwhile the executive officer, Lieutenant Commander Howard R. Shaw, organized damage control to fight the fires, flood magazines and pour CO_2 into the blazing hold. Ammunition was unloaded, fire hoses were passed over from minesweeper *Bobolink* (now doubling as fleet tugboat), and every effort was made to control the conflagration. All day the work went on in a cloud of smoke and a shower of exploding machine-gun ammunition. Men would go down into a hold, come out exhausted, then plunge back into the smoke-filled compartment. That night

[5] Sixth Fleet War Diary (WDC No. 160,268). *I–16*, which had taken part in the midget attack on Pearl Harbor, was now based at Visale Bay near Cape Esperance. See document salvaged from a midget sunk at Visale and raised by U.S.S. *Ortolan* 7 May 1943, in *Pearl Harbor Attack* Part 13 p. 532. For full story of *Alchiba*, see O.N.I. Combat Narrative *Miscellaneous Actions in the South Pacific*.

the flames grew more intense and all hands except fire-fighters were evacuated. Japanese aircraft, attracted to a well-lighted target, splashed a salvo of bombs close aboard at 0330. Throughout 29 November, unloading and fire-fighting continued, simultaneously. *Alchiba* was destined to burn for four days, to be in peril for nearly a month and even to be announced a total loss by the Navy Department; but never was the old Navy maxim "Don't give up the ship!" more faithfully and skillfully honored. *Alchiba* survived.

2. *The Scratch Team*

Commencing 24 November there was a suspicious increase of enemy shipping in the Buin–Shortlands area, and in the Central Solomons. On the 25th, destroyer *McCalla* shot up 40 landing barges off Tassafaronga. Three days later, Guadalcanal aircraft inflicted bomb damage on two transports moving out of Munda, New Georgia; one of them, *Chihaya Maru*, was rendered unnavigable. Natives reported activity in Rekata Bay, Santa Isabel. It seemed that the enemy might be using New Georgia as a staging base for troops to be landed on Guadalcanal.

Rear Admiral Thomas C. Kinkaid had arrived at Espiritu Santo on 24 November to take command of the cruiser force assembled there. Receiving an order from Halsey to counter any night landing attempt by the enemy, Kinkaid completed an operation plan by the 27th; but he never had a chance to use it as he was detached next day by Cominch,[6] and in his stead Rear Admiral Carleton H. Wright, newly arrived in cruiser *Minneapolis*, was given command of the cruiser-destroyer team.[7] The change was unfortunate.

[6] Kinkaid's orders took him to Pearl Harbor and the West Coast. Thence he went to the North Pacific Force, assuming command 3 Jan. 1943.

[7] Carleton Herbert Wright, b. Iowa 1892, Naval Academy '12. During World War I, served in *Jarvis* based at Queenstown, later had duty assembling mines for North Sea barrage; ordnance postgraduate course 1918–20; various ships and staff assignments afloat and ordnance posts ashore 1920–35; Comdesdiv 18, 1935–6; Staff Comscofor 1936–8; Naval Mine Depot, Yorktown 1938–41; C.O. *Augusta* 1941; cruiser task force commander in Pacific July–Nov. 1942.

"Tommy" Kinkaid was a veteran of the South Pacific and there were no pressing duties for him elsewhere as yet; "Bosco" Wright, a competent and respected flag officer, had had some experience in these waters, but a combat mission fell into his lap on the second day of his command.

On 29 November Rear Admiral Wright held a conference with Rear Admiral Mahlon S. Tisdale and with the commanding officers of his task force, heavy cruisers *Minneapolis*, *New Orleans*, *Northampton* and *Pensacola*; light cruiser *Honolulu*; destroyers *Drayton*, *Fletcher*, *Maury* and *Perkins*. Admiral Kinkaid's plan was both clear and detailed. Taking heed of errors in previous battles, it divided the force into one destroyer group and two cruiser groups, each including at least one ship fitted with SG surface-search radar. There were to be no more misunderstandings about "Roger" and other signals as at Cape Esperance. The cruisers' float planes would scout over suspected waters and provide night illumination, when and if requested by the officer in tactical command. In night action the destroyers stationed on the engaged bow of the cruiser column would use their radar advantage to deliver a surprise torpedo attack, then clear out to prevent fouling their own cruisers, which would try not to close within 12,000 yards of the enemy and would withhold gunfire until the destroyers' torpedoes were at or near their targets. Use of searchlights was forbidden and recognition lights were to be used only to check fire by friendly ships. The plan was sound, and Admiral Wright wisely adopted it.

Early in the evening of the same day he received a dispatch from Halsey calling for prompt action by Task Force 67. An enemy force of eight destroyers and six transports was expected off Guadalcanal on the night of 30 November. Wright must intercept it. There was a short, unexplained, yet unfortunate delay of a few hours, ending around 2300 when Halsey ordered the task force to depart immediately. It negotiated the tortuous, mine-rimmed Segond Channel in the dark shortly after midnight, and commenced

[8] Light cruiser *Helena* and four additional destroyers, nominally a part of Wright's organization, were absent on detached duty.

the 580-mile run to thorny "Cactus" at 28 knots. Along with orders came supplementary but indefinite information that the enemy *might* substitute combatant ships for transports, *might* send destroyers only, and *could* arrive before 2300 November 30.

In order to make Ironbottom Sound in time to meet this enemy, Admiral Wright selected the shortest course — to the eastward of San Cristobal, via Indispensable Strait and Lengo Channel. His float planes were useful for dropping flares but a liability on board ships in action, so each cruiser sent two planes back to Segond Channel and dispatched the rest at about 1700 to Tulagi, to be on hand when needed for illuminating the enemy.

Admiral Tanaka's scheme of reinforcement was modest in comparison with the one that had met disaster at the Battle of Guadalcanal. On 30 November, and every four days thereafter until 12 December, high-speed destroyers under cover of darkness would jettison floating drums of provisions off Tassafaronga, where they could be recovered by small craft operating from the beach, and promptly retire. At almost the very moment when Wright departed Espiritu Santo, Rear Admiral Tanaka weighed anchor at Buin at the south end of Bougainville for his first try. His stout old flagship *Jintsu* was still under repair, so he shifted his flag to a destroyer, one of eight that were laden with 1100 drums and a few troops. This time, Tanaka was not looking for a fight. His ticklish mission would best be accomplished without firing a shot. In order to escape snooping Allied planes, he set a course north through Bougainville Strait, then east toward Roncador Reef, and finally made a sharp break south for Indispensable Strait.

Tanaka was much chagrined by the appearance of an American search plane over his force at 1000 on the 30th. Strangely enough, that plane never reported his ships; may never have seen them. But an Australian coastwatcher counted masts at Buin on Monday morning 30 November, noticed the absence of nearly a dozen destroyers and radioed the information to Guadalcanal. This was the only positive intelligence of Tanaka's movements available to Admiral Wright, or at Henderson Field; and it was not much.

Failure of the search plane to report was the first of many bad breaks for Wright; Guadalcanal bombers would have liked nothing better than to try the nerves and persistence of Tenacious Tanaka.

It would take much more than the intelligence he received that afternoon to deter Tanaka, although most flag officers would have been worried. Japanese headquarters at Guadalcanal informed him that a dozen American destroyers were off Lunga Point. That was the anti-submarine patrol for the unloading transports. A second radiogram from Rabaul warned him that American cruisers were approaching the Sound. Tanaka merely told his ships to prepare for a fight, and continued his course.

In the early evening of 30 November, when Admiral Wright's force was about to enter Lengo Channel, it narrowly avoided collision with a friendly eastbound group consisting of three transports and five destroyers. Two destroyers of the transport group, *Lamson* and *Lardner*, on orders from Halsey, immediately joined Wright. Although Commander Abercrombie in *Lamson* now became senior destroyer officer present, Admiral Wright found it impossible to send him either his operation plan or special instructions, and, in any case, these destroyers had only SC radar. So Wright ordered the somewhat bewildered Abercrombie to tag along astern of the cruiser column.

Task Organizations, Battle of Tassafaronga

TASK FORCE 67
Rear Admiral Carleton H. Wright

TG 67.2, Rear Admiral Wright

MINNEAPOLIS	Capt. Charles E. Rosendahl
NEW ORLEANS	Capt. Clifford H. Roper
PENSACOLA	Capt. Frank L. Lowe

Rear Admiral Mahlon S. Tisdale

| * NORTHAMPTON | Capt. Willard A. Kitts |
| HONOLULU | Capt. Robert W. Hayler |

* Sunk in this action.

TG 67.4 (Destroyers), Commander William M. Cole
FLETCHER	Commander Cole
DRAYTON	Lt. Cdr. James E. Cooper
MAURY	Lt. Cdr. Gelzer L. Sims
PERKINS	Lt. Cdr. Walter C. Reed

Desdiv 9, Commander Laurence A. Abercrombie
LAMSON	Lt. Cdr. Philip H. Fitz-Gerald
LARDNER	Lt. Cdr. William M. Sweetser

DESTROYER SQUADRON 2, Imperial Japanese Navy

Rear Admiral Raizo Tanaka

DESTROYER PATROL UNIT: NAGANAMI, * TAKANAMI

TRANSPORT UNIT NO. 1, Capt. Torajiro Sato: MAKINAMI, KUROSHIO, OYASHIO, KAGERO

TRANSPORT UNIT NO. 2, Capt. Giichiro Nakahara: KAWAKAZE, SUZUKAZE

* Sunk in this action.

3. *Wright Attacks, 2225–2325*

The American ships transited Lengo Channel in the following order: destroyers *Fletcher, Perkins, Maury* and *Drayton;* cruisers *Minneapolis, New Orleans, Pensacola, Honolulu* and *Northampton;* destroyers *Lamson* and *Lardner.* This sequence was maintained until the battle opened. Unfortunately no destroyer pickets were stationed ten miles ahead to obtain early information, as provided in the operation plan.

It was 2225 when the task force shook off the spray of Lengo Channel and set course 320° at speed 20 knots, the cruisers 1000 yards apart with two miles separating the last of the van destroyers from flagship *Minneapolis.* At 2238 a simultaneous ships' turn brought the course left to 280° with ships in line of bearing. Pitchy darkness surrounded the formation and there was no prospect of better visibility before a last-quarter moonrise at midnight. Radar operators became the most important individuals in the force as, with hands on dials and eyes glued to the scope, they endeavored to sort out ghostlike blobs indicating the shoreline from "pips" that might be ships. A trying business, this screen-gazing; the appearance of the tiny luminous glow of a foreign body on the radar screen brings relief rather than apprehension. At 2306 the flagship radar operator picked up the first "stranger," bearing almost dead ahead (284°), distant 23,000 yards. Admiral Wright at once informed his ships and signaled a 40-degree turn right, which put them in column again. On the screen this contact first appeared as a small wart detaching itself from Cape Esperance; then the wart broke up into several distinct pips indicating ships in formation on a southeasterly course. Eight minutes after initial contact, Wright brought his column 20 degrees left, to course 300°.

On that calm night the surface of Ironbottom Sound was like a black mirror. Destroyer *Fletcher*, leading the van, had traversed these same waters on the night of Friday the Thirteenth when her position in the extreme rear had precluded effective use of her radar. Commander Cole was now in the best position to make a radar contact count. *Perkins*, next astern of him, and *Drayton*, last destroyer of the van, also felt the enemy coming and readied their torpedoes.

Admiral Tanaka and his chief of staff, Captain Yasumi Toyama, with no radar and no means of monitoring the American radio circuits,[9] were both literally and figuratively in the dark. At 2245, when Wright's force passed north of Henderson Field, Tanaka's destroyer squadron was on a southerly course west of Savo Island. The squadron steamed in column in this order: *Naganami*, *Makinami*, *Oyashio*, *Kuroshio*, *Kagero*, *Kawakaze* and *Suzukaze*, with *Takanami* on the port bow of the flagship, as a sentinel to warn of hostile forces. She and *Naganami* carried no supplies and were prepared to fight on instant warning. Upon entering the Sound and preparatory to releasing the floating drums and transferring the few troops to boats, Tanaka ordered speed reduced to 12 knots, on a course parallel to the shoreline and less than two miles distant.

Fate now gave Admiral Wright the second of his many tough

[9] Admiral Nimitz in his report hazarded a guess that Japanese were listening on our frequencies, but they do not appear to have done so.

breaks. With the enemy almost at hand, no flare planes had yet reported over his force. The reason was infuriatingly simple; for an hour and a quarter the pilots had been taxi-ing over the glassy-calm Tulagi Harbor, unable to lift their little seaplanes from the surface. When they finally got the aircraft aloft, it was too late.

At 2316 Commander Cole in *Fletcher*, whose radar showed the enemy to be broad on the port bow 7000 yards distant, asked Admiral Wright for permission to fire torpedoes. Wright should immediately have turned the destroyers loose to make an independent torpedo attack. He not only did not do that, he hesitated to authorize them to fire torpedoes, believing that the range was excessive. By TBS he interrogated Cole, who replied that the range was satisfactory. So at 2320 Wright told the destroyer commander to "go ahead and fire torpedoes," an order immediately relayed by Cole to his van destroyers. But four precious minutes had been lost since Cole had requested permission to launch; and in the meantime the yet unsuspecting enemy force had been whizzing by — now broad on the bow, now abeam, now abaft the beam. That delay was fatal.[10]

Within a minute of Wright's order, nimble *Fletcher* launched ten torpedoes in two salvos. The range was 7300 yards to the closest enemy destroyer (*Takanami*) but 9600 yards to the leading enemy destroyer, a long but not impossible range *if* torpedoes and target are approaching each other. In this case the targets were already abaft the beam, steaming along on a course opposite to that of the American ships, which gave the American torpedoes a long, overtaking run. *Perkins*, astern of *Fletcher*, got much the same solution, and launched eight of her torpedoes to port. *Maury*, third ship, with only SC radar, had to pick her range and bearing out of the air, so held her torpedoes and awaited developments. *Drayton*, last of the van, had radar worries too, and the skipper decided

[10] According to Kinkaid's Op Plan, the destroyer squadron commander had the right to fire torpedoes without permission only if the target was distant less than 6000 yards. Otherwise he must await an order "Turn and Attack" from the O.T.C., and that Wright had not given. Wright must have assumed that the enemy was closing, not opening, range.

to shoot only two "fish" at a target bearing 250° distant four miles.

As at the Battle of Cape Esperance, the Americans had beaten the Japanese to the draw by using radar; and, better yet, had a score of torpedoes darting through the water. But for bad errors, they should have cleaned up on the still unsuspecting enemy.

Admiral Wright in *Minneapolis* learned that the destroyers were launching torpedoes and that the enemy's range had now dropped to five miles from his cruisers. Eager to cash in on radar superiority, he gave the order to commence firing, over the voice radio: "Roger! and I do mean Roger!" He wanted none of that signal-book confusion which had bedeviled Admiral Scott six weeks before.

Fletcher's last torpedo had barely smacked the water when the cruiser firing line opened up with 8-inch, 6-inch, and 5-inch guns. As the order to close firing keys reached the director pointers of *Minneapolis*, her target was 9200 yards away, 10 degrees forward of the port beam. *New Orleans's* target, probably picket destroyer *Takanami*, was taken under fire at a range of 8700 yards. *Pensacola* felt the lack of the new SG radar and did not succeed in finding a target until two minutes after the start of the gun action. Then one of her fire control radar screens outlined an enemy and guns began to roar. *Honolulu* had some difficulty in locating a proper target but, once started, her fire became so rapid and voluminous that all hands topside were blinded by the muzzle flashes. *Northampton* used her fire control radars to coach guns onto the enemy. Several of the cruisers tossed out 5-inch star shell for illumination. Now all four van destroyers joined in with their guns, using both star shell and high explosive. As *Lamson* and *Lardner*, the two tail-end destroyers, saw no targets on their old-fashioned radars, the former furnished illumination and the latter fired whenever her director crews could sight a ship. Eleven vessels staining the velvet darkness with gun flashes, projectile tracers and star shell candles produced a fearsome sight even for old Guadalcanal hands. There was certain to be a reaction to all this concentrated fire.

4. *Tanaka Strikes Back, 2320–2348*

The reaction came, not from American explosives as Wright and his men hoped, but from the well-aimed torpedoes of Tanaka's destroyer squadron. Picket *Takanami* claimed to have sighted the Americans a full eight minutes before the opening of the gun battle. If so, she was a tardy reporter, since Tanaka's first intimation of the foe was the appearance of two torpedo wakes directly ahead of his flagship. Winking flashes of gunfire on his port beam marked the source of the torpedoes.[11]

Taken by surprise, the Nipponese force was ripe for stampeding. But sound Japanese discipline and doctrine prevented a rout. Ever since the summer of 1941, Destroyer Squadron 2 under Tanaka's command had steamed together in peacetime exercises and wartime operations. Night tactics and adroit use of torpedoes were second nature to the Tanaka tars. On this occasion pre-battle orders to the destroyer captains had been simple: torpedoes would be employed liberally against the enemy, followed by retirement with no attempt to employ guns. Gunfire was specifically forbidden unless absolutely necessary. For point of torpedo aim, American gun flashes would serve very well.

Thus it needed but a spark to bring these ships into action. Chief of staff Toyama merely signaled for a mass torpedo attack that required a column movement by each of the three destroyer divisions at a speed of 24 knots. Easy enough, perhaps; but even among old teammates darkness and ambush can produce error. Let us compare what actually occurred with what was intended.

Upon execution of the attack order, destroyer *Takanami*, as an independent unit, acted correctly, firing torpedoes and reversing course to the right. But her position, nearest to the Americans, made her image stand out on radar screens like a ball of St. Elmo's

[11] There is reason to doubt that Tanaka's men saw actual torpedo wakes before the gun flashes, as Wright's guns opened fire only a minute after torpedoes started their long run.

fire. She began to collect hits from the American line and, in self-defense, replied with her own guns. It was a hopeless geometric progression: the more she fired, the more she was fired upon; the more flaming hits she received, the more she enticed. She managed desperately to squirt out some 70 shots before being stopped and silenced. *Takanami,* as the sacrificial offering, satisfied the gods of Dai Nippon.

Flagship *Naganami,* maneuvering individually to avoid torpedoes, swung violently right in countermarch, receiving a few minor shell fragments in the after stack. *Makinami,* next in column, led Sato's four-destroyer unit on a continuing southeasterly course, while the sailors struggled to release drums of supplies. As the Japanese later remarked, "Since the leading destroyer-transport units had to recover from a situation in which the lines lashing the drums together were being unsecured, standard speed was being maintained and debarkation was planned; thus a full display of offensive power could not be accomplished." [12] *Makinami* led the unit in a column turn to the right. *Kuroshio* got off two torpedoes at 2328; *Oyashio* took nearly twenty minutes to clear eight of hers. *Kagero,* embarrassed by her cargo, could not launch at all during the battle's first phase. There was further confusion during the turn; *Oyashio* and *Kuroshio* broke sharply away to the right from *Makinami's* lead, while *Kagero* closed in astern of the flagship. Captain Nakahara's unit, however, performed the maneuver exactly as prescribed; *Suzukaze* loosed a salvo of torpedoes almost as soon as Wright's force was sighted; *Kawakaze* held fire until a column left was completed, then dispatched eight torpedoes to the northward. Thus, despite their initial handicaps of surprise, cluttered decks and enemy gunfire, Tanaka's disciplined crews in the first moments of battle managed to counterattack with more than 20 fast-running torpedoes. [13] The Admiral's plan to fight defensively and retreat hurriedly was confirmed by the estimate of his staff that

[12] "Battle of Tassafaronga" ATIS 16086.
[13] Toyama stated that only *Takanami* used gunfire. This does not jibe with American observations of both gun flashes and enemy near-misses.

the opposition comprised one battleship, four cruisers and a dozen destroyers.

As the Japanese warheads were coming his way, Commander Cole, leader of the American van destroyers, ordered 25 knots' speed and stood along on his course of 300 degrees. At 2325 *Fletcher* lost track of her target and ceased firing. To the southward a "wall of splashes" [14] from American gunfire could be seen; but except for an occasional quick glimmer there was no sign of return fire — the enemy had flashless powder and we had not. At 2327 Cole led his four ships 50 degrees right to a retirement course west of Savo Island.

The spectacle of *Takanami* afire and exploding cheered the American cruiser sailors. *Minneapolis*, thinking she had destroyed a transport, shifted gunsights to another target sharp on her bow and blasted away. By 2327 nine 8-inch salvos had left her gun muzzles. *New Orleans* kept pace by getting off nine heavy salvos in less than four minutes. *Pensacola*, off to a late start because of her poor radar, slammed out 120 rounds of 8-inch at four different targets between 2324 and 2338, but lost time searching for targets against the dark background of Guadalcanal. Both *Honolulu* and *Northampton* engaged vessels sharp on their bows, their shells converging on *Takanami* like iron filings on a magnet. Rear-guard destroyers *Lamson* and *Lardner* wanted mightily to get into the action but saw little, either on their radar screens or in their telescopes.

At 2327 the Japanese collected first payment for the mauling *Takanami* had undergone. Just as flagship *Minneapolis* triggered her ninth salvo, two powerful warheads hurled themselves against her hull, releasing vast explosive energy. One torpedo exploded in the bow compartments forward of No. 1 turret, the other dealt death and destruction to No. 2 fireroom. Two gigantic mushrooms of sea water erupted on the port side, pausing momentarily at masthead height. Pinnacles of jagged flame on the forecastle, fed by burning aviation gasoline, reached up to the heavens; while amid-

[14] *Fletcher* Action Report.

ships, fuel oil burned no less dangerously. The heavy body of the cruiser shook, rolled and thrashed like a harpooned Moby Dick. Then the water descended on the deck and superstructure. Flames and moisture wrestled in dense clouds that swept aft to the fantail.

Minneapolis sailors topside, battered against steel bulkheads and stanchions by the initial blast, had no chance to recover before the descent of the watery avalanche buffeted them mercilessly, even sucking two men over the side. Yet the water that choked men quenched fires. On the bridge Captain Rosendahl,[15] sloshing in a foot of swirling water, noticed with relief that the forecastle fire was out and took stock of his ship's condition. Steering control was lost but only momentarily, speed fell off rapidly, a 4-degree port list canted the deck, some 60 feet of the bow dangled downward like an immense scoop, the forecastle deck was awash to the foundations of No. 1 turret. Then, to the Captain's astonishment and gratification, his 8-inch guns resumed firing, actually discharging three full salvos until power was lost in the two forward turrets. But could his ship survive the effects of two such devastating hits?

New Orleans, next astern, closed the crippled flagship so rapidly that Captain Roper was forced to throw his rudder hard right to avoid. This action averted a collision but put *New Orleans* in the track of a torpedo which hit her port bow abreast two magazines. These united with the torpedo blast to rip off the forward part of the ship as far back as No. 2 turret. Like a soldier seeing his leg blown off, horrified men watched the forward part of their ship, with turret guns pointing skyward, pass swiftly along their port side, gouging holes and tangling briefly with the propellers. So sudden was the catastrophe that one telephone talker near the ship's stern called a forward station to report that *New Orleans* had just passed over the "sinking *Minneapolis*."[16]

There was no question in the mind of her executive officer, Commander Riggs, that *New Orleans* had been fearfully dam-

[15] Charles E. Rosendahl, foremost expert and advocate of lighter-than-air craft, like all line officers, was serving a required tour of sea duty in order to qualify for flag rank.

[16] Cdr. J. C. Shaw conversation with a *Minneapolis* survivor in 1943.

aged. From his post in "Bat. II," the after control station, he had seen a geyser of flame and water spout up from the bow, felt the ship's convulsions and concluded that a magazine had exploded. Since communication with the bridge was severed, he took over the conn, trying to avoid further torpedoes by a reversal of course. While she was in the turn, the officer of the after turret reported that his guns were still fit to fight. Chief Gunner's Mate Sam Matulavich, in a 5-inch gun battery, also wanted to fight. The torpedo explosion and waist-deep rushing water stunned the secondary-battery gun crews and swept them off their feet, but Sam bellowed "Get back to your guns!" and they did. *New Orleans* slowed to five knots, spouting flame from her truncated bow.

At this disastrous juncture the tardy flare planes, skirting the coastline on a northwesterly course, arrived over the battle area. One of the pilots beheld three burning ships which he believed to be enemy transports. They were *Minneapolis, New Orleans* and *Takanami.* In the dark avenue between the beach and the row of short-ranged American star shells, the pilots discerned six enemy destroyers, even witnessed *Makinami* lead Sato's unit in the countermarch. The powerful flares that they carried would have helped shipmates below; but no orders came from the mutilated flagship and so no flares were dropped.

Pensacola caught it next. Captain Lowe was in the anti-aircraft control station, and his executive officer (Commander Keeler) in the pilothouse, when *New Orleans* slowed and sheered right. As it appeared that the two damaged cruisers ahead were through fighting, *Pensacola* turned left, a good choice to prevent collision, but unfortunate in that it silhouetted her between the enemy and the burning cruisers, right in the Japanese line of fire. A salvo from *Minneapolis* screamed over at masthead height. At 2339, after *Pensacola* returned to base course 300° and, as Commander Keeler was ordering a left turn to clear the south shore of Savo Island, one of 18 torpedoes launched by the foremost Japanese destroyers hit her directly below the mainmast on the port side, flooded the after engine room, put three turrets out of commission, knocked out gyros and communications, ruptured oil tanks and made an oil-soaked torch of the mast, where trapped sailors were roasted to death. So quickly did the after engine room flood that only one man got through the escape hatch, yelling wildly to keep hot gases from his lungs; a second would have made it, but he forgot to take off his telephone headset and the cord tripped him at the bottom of the hatch. The fire main in the after part of the ship was ruptured and handy-billys could not cope with the intense fires. A 13-degree list was corrected by jettisoning fuel oil, and 8-knot speed was maintained with the steam from one fireroom driving the turbines of one engine room. Captain Lowe set course for Tulagi.

So far, the American cruisers had been picked off like mechanical ducks in a carnival shooting gallery. *Honolulu*, the lucky "Blue Goose" of the Pacific Fleet, escaped by smart seamanship on the part of the officer of the deck, Lieutenant Commander George F. Davis. Instead of sheering to port behind *Pensacola*, he swung hard-a-starboard, which placed his ship on the disengaged side of the two burning cruisers, thus avoiding torpedo water and preventing her from being silhouetted. *Honolulu* fishtailed radically on westerly and northwesterly courses at 30 knots, her 6-inch guns continuing their rapid fire, and she never received one hit.

Northampton, last American cruiser in column, took the worst beating. Captain Kitts turned right with *Honolulu* to avoid the three damaged vessels; but his heavy cruiser could not fly or weave like the "Blue Goose" and after twelve minutes, during which *Northampton* fired eighteen 8-inch salvos at destroyer targets, Kitts made the mistake of bringing her back to a westerly heading. For at 2339 destroyer *Oyashio* had put the correct fire control solution on torpedo directors and sent off eight underwater missiles in her direction. Nine minutes later, Captain Kitts saw two wakes coming sharp on the port bow and swung his ship left, but not in time. Two warheads, each containing 660 pounds of high explosive, duplicated on a larger scale the havoc inflicted on *Pensacola*. The after engine room was opened to the sea, the ship listed sharply to port, huge black gobs of fuel oil drenched the main deck aft, fires roared over the entire after part of the ship with the main-mast acting as a gigantic wick. Damage control measures were promptly applied by pumping fuel oil and water overboard to correct the list, while strenuous efforts were made to subdue the fire. But she was too badly holed and too completely enveloped in flame. As the list increased, *Northampton* slowed and was finally brought to a complete stop, in the hope of checking the progressive flooding.

During this series of disasters, the rear destroyers *Lamson* and *Lardner* became separated from the task force. *Lamson* turned right to follow *Northampton*, but finding herself under fire from one of the damaged American cruisers increased speed and pulled clear. *Lardner* made a complete circle to the left, to avoid the damaged ship area and, like *Lamson*, was fired upon by friendly cripples, so hauled out with alacrity.

5. Saving Cripples

As time ran out in this bloody month of November, Admiral Tanaka commenced reorganizing his forces. *Kagero* and *Kuroshio* had another try at the flaming American ships, but this time failed to score. *Oyashio* and *Kuroshio* looped back into the battle zone in an effort to rescue abandoned *Takanami*. Some of the drummed cargo was tossed over the side in the excitement; how much of it reached the consignees is not known. By 0130 December 1 all Japanese destroyers except *Takanami* were clear of Ironbottom Sound. Before noon they were back in Shortland Harbor, claiming one battleship and two cruisers sunk and four more heavily damaged.

When *Northampton* suffered her twin torpedo hits, *Honolulu* sailors stood petrified, believing the big cruiser would go down without a trace. So terrific an explosion ripped taut nerves; brave bluejackets on *Honolulu*'s bridge actually burst into tears. But *Northampton* was quickly left behind. Captain Hayler steered *Honolulu* in the general direction of Savo Island and was taken under fire by sensitive American cripples who stopped shooting only when he flashed his recognition lights, green over white over white. At about this time the navigator, Commander Ringle, advised his Captain that a left turn was in order, to avoid Savo Island. Hayler offered to turn 10 degrees left, to which Ringle replied, "Captain, you'll turn 25 degrees or you'll have to take her over the mountain!" And the turn was made in the nick of time.[17]

As midnight passed, Rear Admiral Wright radioed from *Minneapolis*, relinquishing his tactical command to Rear Admiral Tisdale in *Honolulu*. The new O.T.C., rather than waste time gathering ships into formation, ordered *Honolulu* to round Savo Island in search of the enemy. The tardy flare planes now spoke up over the radio. While waiting for directions they had kept their eyes open; in addition to noting the Japanese countermarch, they had spotted enemy navigation lights off Cape Esperance, had seen the phosphorescent wake of a westward-speeding heavy ship — thought to be enemy but actually *Honolulu*. But it was not until Tisdale had brought *Honolulu* to a southerly course northeast of Savo that one of the pilots asked and was granted permission to illuminate a destroyer landing troops on the beach. Then Tisdale ordered *Honolulu* to stand toward the coast and bombard the enemy. Unfortunately this target proved to be a transport wrecked a fortnight before, in the Battle of Guadalcanal.[18]

Honolulu spent the second hour of the midwatch in an exploratory prowl of Ironbottom Sound. On her westward leg a high-pitched sound like the voices of birds arose from the water. She was steaming amid loaded life rafts and swimming men whose cheers and cries of "*Honolulu! Honolulu!*" made an ululation like that "unearthly wail" from the spirits of departed warriors which threw "pale fear" into the stout heart of Ulysses.[19] *Honolulu* could not help them, but she slowed and picked her way gingerly among the survivors, while Admiral Tisdale ordered *Fletcher* and *Dray-*

[17] *Honolulu's* dead reckoning track as shown on our chart does not confirm this, but DR tracers can be very inaccurate at high speeds.
[18] *Minneapolis* Action Report, Enclosure C.
[19] *Odyssey* xi 36–43.

ton to their rescue. *Honolulu* steamed once more around Savo Island and patrolled the Sound during the remaining hours of darkness.

Meanwhile the plight of flagship *Minneapolis* was improving in consequence of determined and intelligent damage control action. The Chief [20] fed sea water into the boilers of his one dry fireroom and succeeded in operating all engines for a time, some continuously. Brave watertenders and firemen of No. 4 fireroom stuck to their stations with flooded compartments not only around but above them; the ship had but a few feet of freeboard left. Damage control officers [21] directed repair parties in saving the slight margin of buoyancy by pumping oil over the side and jettisoning heavy weights such as projectiles and powder tanks from the forward turrets. Captain Rosendahl's immediate concern was to keep his ship from falling into Japanese hands. For aught he knew, *Minneapolis* was the one cruiser left afloat. By 0200, when word reached him that *Honolulu* and friendly destroyers were still around and that *Minneapolis* could turn up three knots, he set course for Tulagi, 18 miles distant. At 0445 motor torpedo boats and tug *Bobolink* met and escorted her in, the old "bird" boat steaming alongside with her salvage pump rigged into the flooded cruiser compartments. The same berth which had sheltered damaged *Portland* was now occupied by *Minneapolis*, and sailors at once turned to with foliage and nets to camouflage their ship from enemy observation. *Minneapolis* was safe but not yet out of trouble.

In some respects *New Orleans* was worse off than her sister ship. Her bow was gone for 120 feet — over one fifth of the ship's length; effects of the blast and flooding created hazards as far aft as No. 1 fireroom bulkhead. All men in the detached bow and in the fire-consumed No. 2 turret had been killed by the initial blast. In the central damage control station Lieutenant Commander Hayter sniffed a poisonous vapor seeping in, a by-product of the explosion. Aware that his post would soon be untenable, he ordered

[20] Lt. Cdr. Alton E. Parker.
[21] Lt. Cdrs. Hubert W. Chandler and Dewitt C. McIver.

everyone to don a gas mask, gave his own to a sailor who had none, and received permission by telephone to evacuate. Most of the men, assisted and directed by Hayter and two other officers,[22] reached safety; but Hayter and the officers with him were too weak from gas to climb the ladder when their turn came, and all three perished.

Damage control now became another task of the engineer officer — and what a task! The wardroom, flooded to a depth of four feet, marked the waterline which gave the ship twice her normal draft forward, a dangerous 40 feet. Even at a bare two knots, the water pressure so strained the forward fireroom bulkhead that this space had to be abandoned. But *New Orleans's* engineering plant was intact, power and lighting normal, fires under control. Captain Roper remained on the bridge whence he had a clear view ahead; his executive officer stayed aft to control steering and engines; the ship turned up five knots and course was set for harbor. *Maury* joined her at 0235 and the two vessels kept company to Tulagi where they tied up side by side at 0610 December 1.

Pensacola's troubles were amplified by the fire that swept over the main deck aft. Within nine minutes of her torpedoing, machine-gun ammunition began to "cook off" with terrifying pyrotechnics. Only the most strenuous and skillful damage control measures could save the ship. Captain Lowe and his damage control officer [23] directed and encouraged the crew in leading hoses aft, spreading CO_2 and foam-extinguishing compounds, and flooding magazines until the fire began a gradual retreat, interrupted by later flare-ups. At 0145 the frightening thud of exploding 8-inch projectiles in No. 3 turret created anxiety lest the entire batch of heavy shells detonate en masse; but all 150 of them popped singly, with low-order explosions, over a period of several hours. Meanwhile the ship was making steady progress toward Tulagi, arriving at the end of the midwatch still afire and in deadly peril. Destroyer *Perkins* closed to assist fire-fighting. Not until twelve hours after

[22] Lt. Richard A. Haines USNR, Ensign Andrew L. Forman USNR.
[23] Lt. Julian D. Venter.

the torpedo battle did the last fire flicker out. *Pensacola* had won her fight to live.

Northampton never joined her damaged friends in Tulagi. Captain Kitts's crew fought a losing battle handicapped by fire, which prevented the establishment of flooding boundaries to stop further salt-water infiltration. Her initial list increased to 23 degrees by 0115, when an orderly abandonment by all except the Captain and a salvage crew was begun. This operation was enlivened though not endangered by inaccurate enemy artillery fire from the beach four miles distant. At 0150 *Fletcher* and *Drayton* approached and commenced rescue of the *Northampton* men. Captain Kitts and the salvage party, clinging precariously to the ship until she heeled over 35 degrees, took to the water at 0240. Twenty-four minutes later the proud lady completed her long career, sliding stern-first through the dark waters to a final resting place 600 fathoms deep. The two destroyers, searching in the darkness, with the aid of their boats and stout swimmers, performed the remarkable feat of rescuing 773 men before first light. Only 58 of the original crew were lost.

Subsequent to the actual gunfire and torpedo action, the six destroyers were little troubled by the retiring enemy. At 2337 *Drayton* fired four torpedoes at *Kawakaze*, *Naganami* and *Suzukaze*, then north of Cape Esperance and headed west; but the range was too long and no hits are recorded. The leading American destroyers, after rounding Savo Island, busied themselves with salvage and rescue. *Fletcher* did a magnificent job, literally netting 700 survivors by dragging cork-floated nets through the water.

Commander Abercrombie, division commander of tag-along destroyers *Lamson* and *Lardner*, did not enjoy being fired on by "friendly" though crippled cruisers even after recognition lights were flashed. He correctly inferred that special fighting lights were in use by this force, and since he hadn't the right book he decided the best bet was to haul clear and stay clear. His two destroyers moved off to the eastward until ordered to escort *Minneapolis* into Tulagi Harbor.

The labor of preparing the three damaged cruisers for sea was a triumph of Yankee ingenuity and Rebel tenacity. Tulagi was a repair base only for motor torpedo boats; the best materials it could furnish were coconut logs. These were used as shoring, stanchions and even as buffer bulkheads for the jury-bows manufactured for *Minneapolis* and *New Orleans*. Artificers from tender *Vestal* and three fleet tugs helped loyally, but working conditions were of the worst. In order to conceal themselves from Japanese aviators, the cruisers moored to tree trunks in high-sided, jungle-rimmed coves of Tulagi Harbor where there was not a breath of air but plenty of flies, mosquitoes, malaria and dysentery. Living conditions in these jungle-muffled ships were bad enough; working in them taxed men's minds and bodies. *Minneapolis's* crew sweated for five days and nights, regaining buoyancy by inches, when a sudden bewildering gas explosion flooded several hitherto dry compartments, destroyed more equipment and caused the heartbreaking loss of seven feet in draft. The ship was now worse off than ever, but the crew worked so hard and fast that by 12 December she could venture to sea. After calling at Espiritu Santo, and Pearl Harbor twice, for more first aid, she was hospitalized at Mare Island. Finally, on 9 September 1943, she reported ready to sail and to fight, which well she did for the rest of the war.

New Orleans also was given a coconut-log false face for her return to civilization. She sailed from Tulagi on 12 December, fueled from *Guadalupe,* and, to the vast joy of her crew, managed to make Sydney on Christmas Eve. The 7th of March found her again at sea, bound Stateside with a jury bow. By the time she arrived at Puget Sound, or shortly after, the Bremerton Navy Yard had a completely new bow section all tailored and ready to be fitted. She too was in time for the Gilbert Islands campaign. *Pensacola* made Pearl on one propeller and, after extensive repairs, rejoined the Fleet in late October 1943.[24]

These vicissitudes illustrate the difficulty of waging war half a world away from major bases. The cruisers "With wandering steps

[24] Buships War Damage Reports.

and slow . . . took their solitary way" [25] back to the major repair bases, and a complete cycle of seasons passed before they were ready to fight again.

6. Post-mortem

It is a painful truth that the Battle of Tassafaronga was a sharp defeat inflicted on an alert and superior cruiser force by a partially surprised and inferior destroyer force.

Every flag officer concerned — Tisdale, Wright, Halsey and Nimitz — sought an explanation for the disaster to Task Force 67, but each was hard put to find a simple answer. Everyone agreed that the plan was sound, Admiral Wright took full responsibility for the torpedo damage [26] and nobody else except Commander Cole was blamed.[27]

A Japanese analyst made a very pertinent contribution to criticism of American tactics at Tassafaronga: —

The enemy had discovered our plans and movements, had put planes in the air beforehand for purposes of illumination, had got into formation for an artillery engagement, and cleverly gained the advantage of prior neutralization fire. But his fire was inaccurate, shells [im]properly set for deflection were especially numerous, and it is conjectured that either his marksmanship is not remarkable or else the illumination from his star shells was not sufficiently effective.[28]

True enough. The Navy's marksmanship that night was abominable.

[25] *Paradise Lost* xii 646.
[26] Admiral Spruance once remarked that, since Wright was a newcomer with little choice of route and dependent on somebody else's plan, his acceptance of responsibility indicated a "high military character."
[27] Admiral Halsey's endorsement on Wright's Action Report indicates extreme displeasure with the van destroyers on two accounts: (1) shooting torpedoes at excessive range; (2) retiring to the northwest without assisting the cruisers. My opinion, for what it's worth, is that Wright, not Cole, was responsible for the van destroyers' failure to cast off from the cruisers in time to surprise the enemy with a torpedo attack. After gunfire started, Cole had no alternative but to haul clear; *Honolulu* did exactly that, without criticism.
[28] "Battle of Tassafaronga" ATIS 16086.

Another Japanese officer remarked after the war: —

A more active use of destroyer divisions is necessary in night battles. Annihilation of our reinforcing units would not necessarily have been difficult even for a few destroyers, if they had chosen to penetrate our lines and carry on a decisive battle with the support of the main force.[29]

That was it! American commanders of cruiser-destroyer task forces had the bad practice of tying their destroyers to a cruiser column instead of sending them off on an independent torpedo shoot before gunfire was opened. As for the cruisers, might they not have evaded deadly "fish" if the O.T.C., by ordering successive simultaneous ships' turns, and other maneuvers, had avoided bringing them into torpedo water immediately after opening gunfire? That is what "Tip" Merrill did off Empress Augusta Bay in 1943.

Both sides made exaggerated claims of sinkings; those of the Americans were due to overconfidence in what the radar had seen. Even after several *Takanami* survivors had been interrogated, that unfortunate vessel was expanded into four "sunk" and three "damaged." Tokyo claimed one nonexistent battleship and a heavy cruiser sunk, three destroyers damaged. So the public on both sides were satisfied. Not so Admiral Nimitz, and a part of his comment written two months after the battle is still valid: —

The fortunes of war and the restricted waters in which we were forced to bring the enemy into action caused our ships to suffer greater loss than their leadership and action merited, and prevented them from inflicting heavier damage on the enemy.

The remedy, he concluded, was "training, *training* and MORE TRAINING." [30]

Fortunes of war, yes; but "in the reproof of chance lies the true proof of man." The heroes of Tassafaronga were the junior officers and bluejackets who fought fire and flood most valiantly. What an improvement in damage control methods since the Battle of Savo Island! *Minneapolis, New Orleans* and *Pensacola* would have

[29] Desron 2 Records (WDC No. 161,711).
[30] Cincpac Action Report 15 Feb. 1943.

been lost, had they received similar damage four months earlier.

Nimitz, ever magnanimous to the enemy as generous to his task force commanders, praised Japanese gunfire, torpedo technique, "energy, persistence, and courage." It is always some consolation to reflect that the enemy who defeats you is really good, and Rear Admiral Tanaka was better than that — he was superb. Without his trusted flagship *Jintsu*, his decks cluttered with supplies, he sank a heavy cruiser and put three others out of action for nearly a year, at the cost of one destroyer. In many actions of the war, mistakes on the American side were cancelled by those of the enemy; but despite the brief confusion of his destroyers, Tanaka made no mistakes at Tassafaronga.

It must be remembered that the United States force, though larger than the enemy's, had never before steamed together, even in daylight, and that it was strictly a "scratch team"; while Tanaka's force had been well trained and long practised under the same commander.

Tassafaronga, last major sea battle in the arena of the Southern Solomons, ended four months of vicious hull-to-hull slugging the like of which neither the Americans nor the Japanese had ever seen. No man who fought in those bloody waters can forget the apprehension, the exultation and the terror that he experienced, the hideous forms of death that he witnessed, or the self-sacrificing heroism that gave him a new respect for his fellow seamen. "Savo," "Guadalcanal," "Tassafaronga" and the rest are no mere battle names to the survivors; they are flaming banners of deathless deeds by ships and men whose bones forever rest in Ironbottom Sound.

So, reader, if this tale has seemed repetitious with shock and gore, exploding magazines, burning and sinking ships and plummeting planes — that is simply how it was.

CHAPTER XIV

Securing Guadalcanal

1 December 1942–29 January 1943

1. *The Emperor Is Troubled*

IT took the Japanese a long time to adjust themselves to their strategic defeat in the lower Solomons. An occasional tactical victory like Tassafaronga blinded them to the fact that the American hold on Guadalcanal was tight and permanent. Like exhausted salmon trying to ascend an impassable stream, the fanatic Nipponese continued to hurl themselves at the American barrier in suicidal frenzy. On 1 December the Cincpac analyst noted, "It is still indicated that a major attempt to recapture 'Cactus' is making up." He was right.

Up from Java in December came General Hitoshi Imamura, and by the year's end some 50,000 troops of his Eighth Area Army had joined him in Rabaul. Imamura was under orders from Imperial Headquarters to recapture Guadalcanal. He decided to throw two more divisions into the island on 1 February.[1] He issued an order: "We must by the most furious, swift and positive action deal the enemy annihilating blows to foil his plans completely. . . . It is necessary to arouse the officers and men to a fighting rage." That would be a tough job for his rabble-rousers, as some captured diaries of his troops attest: —

December 18: Rice long since eaten up, even coconuts running short. December 23: Haven't seen one of our planes for ages, but "every day enemy planes dance in the sky, fly low, strafe, bomb,

---

[1] Miyazaki's personal account in USSBS pub. "Allied Campaign against Rabaul."

and numerous officers and men fall," and there is no medicine for them. December 26: "We are about to welcome the New Year with no provisions; the sick are moaning within the dismal tents, and men are dying daily. We are in a completely miserable situation. . . . Why should we be subdued by these blue-eyed Americans? I intend to get onto the enemy airfield and let two or three of them have a taste of my sword. . . . O friendly planes! I beg that you come over soon and cheer us up!" [2]

Nor was the atmosphere much happier in Tokyo. The annual New Year's Day Imperial Rescript, issued the day after Christmas, sounded very different from that of 1941. "The Emperor is troubled by the great difficulties of the present war situation," announced Hirohito to his people. "The darkness is very deep but dawn is about to break in the Eastern Sky. Today the finest of the Japanese Army, Navy and Air units are gathering. Sooner or later they will head toward the Solomon Islands where a decisive battle is being fought between Japan and America." [3]

In Nouméa, Halsey's staff made plans to trouble the Emperor still further and break up this last serious effort of his subjects to recapture Guadalcanal. Replacement of depleted Marine regiments with Army infantry was given high priority. Henderson Field still suffered from effects of rainy weather and traffic congestion, so work was pushed forward to improve the original strips, to construct a new field at Koli Point and to build storage tanks for a million gallons of gasoline. Want of facilities and man power kept the local naval base a somewhat rickety affair manned partly by uninterested survivors from sunken ships. One expected to wake up some morning to see it disappearing into the mud. Not until the close of the year were base projects given adequate equipment and personnel. At Tulagi, where a miniature naval base was set up with *McFarland's* bluejackets and fuzzy-haired Melanesians from Malaita as the labor force, motor torpedo boat facilities ex-

---

[2] Cincpac–Cincpoa Intelligence translation ser. 4739.
[3] Same source, reprinted in "Reprint of Cincpac Reports Feb. 1942–Feb. 1943" Sec. 114.

panded from Sesape across the harbor to "Calvertville." Near-by
Purvis Bay, seat of the Right Reverend Bishop of Melanesia, was
designated a fleet anchorage for light forces, soon to be permanently on tap as foils to the "Tokyo Express." Bases such as
Espiritu Santo, Nouméa, Efate and Nandi were continually being
improved to fit them to handle larger numbers of ground troops,
sailors, planes, aviators and ships.[4]

American air and naval actions in early December were directed
largely toward thwarting the enemy's reinforcement. Tanaka's
scheduled 3 December dash into Ironbottom Sound with ten destroyers, duly reported by coastwatchers, was tracked by American
air scouts and raided by a striking force of 15 bombers and torpedo
planes with fighter cover from Henderson Field. But this "Tokyo
Express" had air protection, which fouled up the attack so that
only one damaging hit was made, on destroyer *Makinami*, and it
cost us two planes. Wright's task force was too much battered to
engage and, for some reason, the PTs were not ordered out; so
Tanaka discharged his drummed supplies and retired safely. On the
occasion of his next run, on 7 December, the PTs were brought
into play, but only after his eleven destroyer transports had been
subjected to blistering dusk attacks by fighters, bombers and torpedo planes. Destroyer *Nowaki* had her side blown in by a near-
miss which flooded an engine room and fireroom and killed 17
men; another received minor damage. But the Americans lost a
top-notch dive-bombing pilot, Major Joseph Sailer USMC, who
was hit by anti-aircraft fire, then winged by a "Zeke."

Next, eight motor torpedo boats out of Tulagi were deployed
to catch the enemy. A two-boat patrol was established between
Kokumbona and Cape Esperance, a similar patrol operated off the
northwest shore of Guadalcanal and a striking force of four boats
idled in the lee of Savo Island. Assisting the PTs as scouts were
several float planes belonging to the cruisers damaged at Tassafaronga. The first watch was nearly over when Tanaka's ships were

[4] Cincpac "Solomon Islands Campaign from Fourth Battle of Savo, 30 Nov. 1942
to Munda Bombardment, 4–5 Jan. 1943" 9 Mar. 1943.

sighted by two patrolling PTs. The engine of one broke down at this critical moment; the other covered her with a smoke screen and no torpedoes were fired; yet the mere presence of these two small craft caused the resolute Tanaka to reverse course, at 2330. Fifteen minutes later he changed his mind, entered the Sound again and this time was met by the four-boat striking force, which promptly uncorked twelve torpedoes. Swirling torpedo wakes and some fancy strafing by the PT machine guns persuaded Tanaka to abandon this reënforcement effort altogether. *PT–59*, Lieutenant (jg) John M. Searles, came within a hundred yards of *Oyashio* and was hit ten times, but inflicted as many casualties as she received hits, and got home; Tanaka's force retired without further damage. This fight on the first anniversary of Pearl Harbor is justly considered a victory for the PT men, nor was it their last.

On the night of 9 December, *PT–59* made a successful attack on a 2000-ton blockade-running Japanese submarine. Near Cape Esperance, Searles's boat, in company with another, was machine-gunning an enemy landing barge when she sighted *I–3* on the surface. Two torpedoes, promptly fired, tore the submarine to bits, leaving but one Nip ensign to swim ashore and report her fate.

The usual four-day interval followed before Tanaka again ventured down the Slot, this time with ten destroyer deckloads of provisions and arms. Off northern New Georgia on 11 December, P–38s and F4Fs escorted 14 SBDs into a striking position, from which the bombers hurtled down with 1000-pound eggs. Unfortunately no hits were registered and the airmen passed the ball to the PT skippers. The motor torpedo boats, always willing to oblige, came out in force and met Tanaka's ships on the happy hunting ground between Tassafaronga and Cape Esperance. The Japanese, wary as always of the mosquito fleet, used searchlights and bullets but still failed to drive off three boats commanded by Lieutenant (jg) Lester H. Gamble USNR. It was a clear night with good visibility under brilliant starlight. At 0100 December 12 two torpedoes from Gamble's boats rammed destroyer *Teruzuki*. She lost all headway and burst into brilliant flames, and Tanaka promptly headed for home. *PT-44* (Lieutenant Frank Freeland USNR), another boat then patrolling off Kamimbo Bay, received a radio report of this action and at once headed into the Sound. Passing burning *Teruzuki*, she picked up Tanaka's column steaming west and, at 8000 yards' distance, started a fast run at two of them. Silhouetted by the burning destroyer, she was driven off on her first attempt, but Freeland returned for more. A destroyer invisible to him, standing by *Teruzuki*, landed a shell in his engine room. Most of the crew were killed by the explosion of a gas tank when they went aft to launch a life ring; the rest, who dove overboard promptly, were stunned by the concussion of heavy gun salvos which crushed the PT like an eggshell. Only two out of eleven survived. Lieutenant (jg) Charles M. Melhorn USNR tells what happened to him: —

I dove deep and was still under water when the salvo struck. The concussion jarred me badly, but I kept swimming under water. There was a tremendous explosion, paralyzing me from the waist down. The water around me went red. The life jacket took control and pulled me to the surface. I came up in a sea of fire, the flaming embers of the boat cascading all about me. I tried to get free of the life jacket but couldn't, so I started swimming feebly. I thought the game was up, but the water which had shot sky-high in the explosion, rained down and put out the fires around me. From the first hit to this point took less than fifteen seconds.[5]

In the meantime, one of the PTs assigned to the Cape Esperance patrol ran aground on Pig Rock Reef; her escort stood by but was unable to get her off. At first light a patrol craft of the "Cactus Navy," *PC-476*, was sent to her rescue, towed her clear, and also picked up a deserted Japanese landing barge containing some useful charts.

The crew of *Teruzuki* worked all the midwatch trying to save her, but at 0440 flames entered the depth-charge magazine and she went with a bang to a permanent berth in the Savo boneyard.[6]

[5] Cdr. R. J. Bulkley Ms. "History of Motor Torpedo Boats"; Cdr. A. P. Calvert Report on "How to Abandon an MTB."
[6] "Battle Lessons Learned in the Greater East Asia War" (Jicpoa Item No. 5782–A).

This was the last surface engagement of the year. We shall leave it to the "Quiz Kids" to count up how many there had been in the Pacific in 1942, and how many of them were American victories.

2. *Munda Built, Bombed and Bombarded*

Loss of valuable destroyers was making the Japanese wince, and for the rest of the month, while the moon waxed full and then waned to last quarter, they refrained from sending anything but submarines to relieve the Guadalcanal garrison. But they were shoring up their crumbling foothold on New Guinea and at the same time building a launching platform in the central Solomons for later thrusts against Guadalcanal. This put the burden of the Solomons offensive on American land-based aircraft; the Japanese project gave them a new target within comfortable flying range, Munda Point airfield.

A hundred miles up the Slot from Guadalcanal starts the New Georgia group, composed of five large islands and myriad islets, extending northwesterly some 150 miles. Ringed by reefs and shoals and topped by low jumbled mountains, New Georgia has only a few cultivated spots of coconut plantations and presents a forbidding appearance to navigator and landsman alike. The Japanese had originally by-passed New Georgia in favor of Guadalcanal. That was one of their big mistakes, for Guadalcanal was beyond range of their fighter planes and a bomber unaccompanied by a fighter in those days was about ten times as vulnerable as a bomber-fighter team. Buin field in Southern Bougainville shortened the range so that "Zekes" could fly to Guadalcanal and back but had no time to linger. A new airfield on New Georgia was the answer.

On a few acres of flat land bordering the southern bight of New Georgia, ten miles south of Kula Gulf and ten miles north of Rendova, an Australian planter had grown long rows of coconut palms. Here was the ideal spot, only 175 miles from Henderson Field. "Zekes" based there could orbit over Lunga all day; big-bellied "Bettys" could stage through and carry double their previous bomb loads. So on 24 November 1942 a convoy put in at Munda Point, New Georgia island, and commenced work on the new "Munda Emergency Airfield." [7]

This convoy aroused American interest and there was much speculation as to its meaning. As early as 28 November Admiral Halsey suspected that airfield development was under way, but American pilots who swooped over Munda saw only a few new buildings and the disciplined rows of coconut palms. It remained for the prying lens of an airplane's camera to disclose the truth on 3 December. The Japanese, like termites, were building under the coconut grove; when it became necessary to remove a tree, palm fronds were laid on overhead wires in its exact position. The "Photo Joes" of the air force redoubled their efforts, and by the 5th the skilled photo interpreters on Admiral Fitch's staff at Espiritu Santo could see gun emplacements, a 2000-foot runway, and other nasty things under the rustling palms. Next day P–39s from Henderson Field fired the opening gun in what was to be a long campaign against that pesky airstrip. The busy Japs kept right on working; and when they were good and ready down came both real and false palm trees, holes were promptly filled up, and there was a nice airfield!

On 9 December the first major air strike against it was carried out by 18 B–17s, and from then on planes of all types made Munda a routine daytime bull's-eye. On the 13th a PBY inaugurated a series of night harassing runs on the strip. By mid-December the Japs were being pasted at all hours with heavy bombs, fragmentation bombs, incendiaries, strafing bullets and even empty beer bottles, whose banshee-like whistles when falling were presumed to be a prime sleep-robber. Even so, the field was finished and nesting "Zekes" by the second fortnight of December. This was all to the good, because it gave the Wildcats, P–38s and P–39s

[7] Japanese Naval War Diary.

accompanying the bombers something to fight. On the morning of 24 December, a fighter-escorted flight of dive-bombers caught the Nips with all their planes except eight grounded. Four were destroyed in mid-air, ten "Zekes" were met and shot down just after take-off, and a dozen more waiting to take off were splattered over the landscape by the SBDs. Returning for a second strike, the American planes made very nasty mincemeat out of ten landing barges filled with troops and supplies. Flying Forts also celebrated Christmas Eve by sowing the airstrip with bombs.

During this period the "Tokyo Express" ran a spur line to Munda, but soon discovered that overhead was eating up profits. On 16 December a pair of SBDs damaged destroyer *Kagero*. On Christmas Day supply ship *Nankai Maru*, after taking a torpedo from an American submarine, collided with destroyer *Uzuki*, two of whose firerooms were flooded. The day following, destroyer *Ariake*, under air attack, suffered a near-miss which killed 28, wounded 40 and set the ship on fire. Planes from Henderson Field sank a small transport and a freighter,[8] that were plying to Wickham Anchorage on Vangunu Island south of New Georgia where the enemy was setting up a protective outpost. But these attacks were no more to the Japs than fleas to a dog. Coastwatchers, airmen and natives also reported ship and troop movements into the northern islands of the New Georgia group. At Rekata Bay on Santa Isabel, the suspected destination of Admiral Mikawa on the fatal August 8, the Japanese had a flourishing barge-staging point and seaplane base which American air power could never seem to knock out. It seemed clear that only fast work could prevent New Georgia from becoming the Japanese answer to Guadalcanal.

In past experience, any concentration of Japanese shipping meant something. Consequently, when in late December the number of combat and supply ships at Rabaul rapidly increased to 70 or more, Admiral Halsey became intensely interested. Not only his but MacArthur's B–17s were assigned to this target. Attacks were made nightly for about a week. Considering that they were

[8] JANAC p. 37.

hit-or-miss affairs in waning moonlight,[9] and that bombs were released at 11,000 feet altitude, results were surprisingly good. One transport was sunk and three damaged while destroyer *Tachikaze* had her bow torn off. Yet, regardless of bombs, the Japanese kept coming and by New Year's Eve nearly a hundred ships swung at anchor in volcano-rimmed Simpson Harbor, Rabaul.

Several United States submarines were on hand during December to block the enemy's moves, but the usual impediment of calm water, high speed convoys and excellent air cover made each detonating warhead a signal accomplishment. On the 10th, *Wahoo* (Lieutenant Commander Dudley W. Morton) met a heavily loaded convoy en route to the Shortlands, blasted one 500-tonner with four torpedoes but missed a chance at two others because of countermeasures. A week later *Grouper* (Lieutenant Commander Rob R. McGregor) nosed into a convoy off Bougainville and fired two torpedoes at 4000-ton *Bandoeng Maru*. McGregor saw a lot of smoke and spray, heard explosions and reported correctly that any further movement of the target would be in a "vertical direction." *Albacore* (Lieutenant Commander Richard C. Lake) exacted another payment for Savo by a successful attack on light cruiser *Tenryu*. *Sea Dragon* (Lieutenant Commander William E. Ferrall) and *Grayback* (Lieutenant Commander Edward C. Stephan) got a Japanese submarine apiece.[10] *Greenling* (Lieutenant Commander Henry C. Bruton), operating in the vicinity of New Ireland, "sighted in" by sinking a small patrol boat on the night of 21–22 December. Eight nights later she hit and stopped two large ships of a Truk-bound convoy. After outdistancing the escorts in a surface chase, Bruton returned and made sure of his game with more torpedoes.

After Tanaka's battle with the motor torpedo boats on 11 December, three weeks passed without any Japanese reinforcements reaching Guadalcanal. The trickle of supplies sent in by submarines and barges was not enough even to keep the troops fed.

---

[9] Full moon 22 Dec., last quarter 30th.
[10] *I-4* (Dec. 20) and *I-18* (Jan. 2).

Captured Japanese diaries of this period reflect discomfort and discouragement; the one bright spot was a movie news reel shown on 11 December. Troops at the front eked out scanty rice and soybean rations with grass, roots, ferns and even, on occasion, human flesh. The malaria rate was practically 100 per cent; dysentery ditto, spread by flies feeding on unburied corpses and exposed refuse. The "indignity" of bombardment by American ships proved that Dai Nippon no longer ruled the Sound, even at night; air bombardment added injury. One soldier consoled himself by recording in his diary that when the Americans finally surrendered he would secure a prisoner and "abuse" (i.e., torture) him "to have revenge for our dead companions." [11]

The Japanese on Guadalcanal were relieved when the waning moon allowed resumption of "Tokyo Express" runs on 2 January 1943. Ten destroyers swept boldly down the Slot, ignoring a B–17 bombing attack from 20,000 feet. Just before dark, as the destroyer sailors were congratulating themselves on their luck, a flight of SBDs roared out of the darkening sky to plant a bomb alongside *Suzukaze*. A flooded living space slowed the ship to 12 knots. One destroyer remained behind to shepherd her while the remaining eight continued on their mission. Upon arrival off Cape Esperance they were greeted with 18 torpedoes from 11 motor torpedo boats. All were dodged successfully but the drummed stores jettisoned off the beaches were rounded up and destroyed with machine-gun fire by the American PTs on the following morning.

Now was the time for Halsey to try a night bombardment of the new Munda airstrip. The character selected for the conductor rôle on this new north-bound express was the ruddy, genial Rear Admiral Walden L. Ainsworth, better known as "Pug." [12] A for-

---

[11] Translation of captured Japanese document by Combat Intelligence Center Sopac, ser. 0370.

[12] Walden Lee Ainsworth, b. Minneapolis 1886, Naval Academy '10, served successively in *Idaho*, *Prairie* and *Florida* before 1917. During World War I gunnery officer on transports. Ordnance duty ashore for 3 years, "exec." *Hancock* and *Birmingham*, C.O. *Marcus*, ordnance and Navy Yard duties 1923–25. Asiatic Fleet for 2 years, instructor Naval Academy 3 years, navigator *Idaho* and *Pensacola* 1931–33. In Panama 1934–35; senior War College course; "exec." *Mississippi* 2 years;

mer destroyer squadron commander in the Atlantic Fleet, Ainsworth in July had been given flag rank and the administrative job of Commander Destroyers Pacific Fleet. In December, when on an inspection tour to Nouméa, he was willingly "shanghaied" by Halsey and placed in command of Task Force 67, the cruiser-destroyer force that had just taken a beating off Tassafaronga.

Ainsworth was new to the South Pacific but entered the arena as if he had been fighting Japs all his life.[13] His ships were a mixture of types with varied experience; Guadalcanal veterans such as *Honolulu, Helena, Fletcher* and *O'Bannon*; heavy cruiser *Louisville* sent down to avenge the loss of her sister *Northampton*; even a New Zealand light cruiser, H.M.N.Z.S. *Achilles*, hero of the Battle of the River Plate in 1939. Other light cruisers and destroyers with little or no battle experience were thrown in. Yet this scratch team pulled off a bombardment which would be long regarded as a model.

Since another U.S. infantry echelon was due to make Lunga Roads on the morning of 4 January 1943, Halsey decided to raid Munda the following night, and to make a triple play of bombardment, diversion and cover. Light cruisers *Nashville, St. Louis,* and *Helena* and destroyers *Fletcher* and *O'Bannon* were selected to deliver the bombardment, for which the rapid-firing 6-inch cruiser guns were well suited. As a distant support group, light cruisers *Honolulu, Achilles* and *Columbia* (first of the new *Cleveland* class to reach the South Pacific), heavy cruiser *Louisville* and destroyers *Drayton, Lamson* and *Nicholas,* under the command of Rear Admiral Tisdale, were to maneuver southeast of New Georgia. Ainsworth held conferences, studied charts and photographs and drew up an excellent detailed plan.

Night-fighting Catalinas, first of the famous "Black Cats," [14]

---

head of Tulane Univ. R.O.T.C.; Comdesron 2 1940–41; C.O. *Mississippi* first half of 1942.

[13] Some months later the writer overheard an old chief petty officer in *Honolulu* remark, "Admiral 'Pug' may be a 'sundowner' but when I fight Japs I choose to fight with him!" Sundowner is Navy for strict disciplinarian.

[14] See next section, 3.

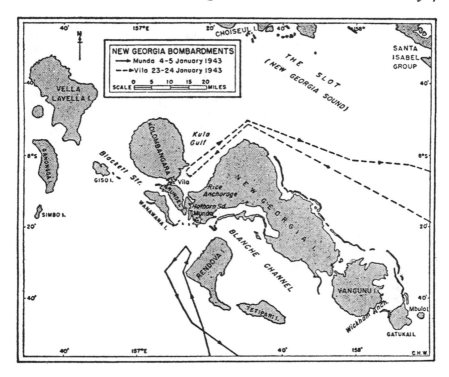

designated to carry gunfire spotters for the cruisers, flew over Munda field for two nights prior to the bombardment. The idea was to get the Japanese used to their presence so that they would not suspect anything unusual, and to enable spotters to study landmarks. And, as part of the show, submarine *Grayback* took station as a navigational beacon off the west coast of Rendova Island.

Ainsworth's Task Force 67 covered the transports on their passage from Espiritu Santo to Lunga Roads and split up on 4 January 1943, the bombardment group standing north toward Rendova Island at a 26-knot clip. After dark each cruiser launched a flare-laden scout plane with orders to stay clear unless required. The Black Cats sniffed ahead for possible enemy forces, then began orbiting over Munda air strip. It was a fine night for the business at hand; dark of the moon and a black rain cloud covering the sky in the direction of Munda. To the naked eye there was little to be seen but on radar scopes the ectoplasmic indications of land masses stood out clearly. Navigators plotted their courses as accurately as on a clear day in Chesapeake Bay. *Grayback* showed up as a separate pin-point on the scope shortly after midnight and radioed that she was in position, a good check for the navigators.

Fletcher led the column but flagship *Nashville* in second place was to shoot first. The approach on a northeast course paralleled the west coast of Rendova. Just before commencing fire the column slowed to 18 knots and in a few minutes changed course to NW to bring guns to bear. Shortly after 0100 January 5, with fire control radars using a prominent black rock as a reference point, the first salvo flew out. "No change!" radioed the spotter. A second and a third salvo followed, and then the gunners shifted to continuous rapid fire. It was a magnificent sight; each cruiser, continually wrapped in muzzle flashes, seemed a ball of fire. Spotting aviators aloft stared at the bridge of tracers arching onto the field and mushrooming like sheet lightning all over the target. They shook their heads in amazement — this was really the stuff! Occasionally a large and sustained flash would indicate that some of Tojo's ammunition or gasoline was afire.

Lookouts and gunners of destroyer *Fletcher* [15] suddenly saw, dead ahead, the awesome outline of a strange ship, surely enemy? The skipper swung hard left to bring his torpedo batteries to bear and shouted a warning over voice radio. Down in radar plot the executive officer searched in perspiring frenzy for indications of the unknown vessel. But the screen was completely clear. The operator beside him shook his fist at the radar and growled, "Oh, you bastard, if you let us down now!" Anxious lookouts, straining eyes and peering through night glasses, saw the unidentified "ship" turn to parallel *Fletcher's* course, and dart ahead at a fantastic rate. Must be making 40 knots! Suddenly the "ship" disappeared completely. She was merely a phantom shadow of *Fletcher* on the light haze.

[15] Lt. Cdr. Frank L. Johnson, with the squadron commander, Capt. Robert P. Briscoe, on board.

Return fire from enemy shore batteries was meager. Occasional tracers floated toward *St. Louis* as she took the ball, but dribbled short into the ocean. *Helena* socked the target vigorously in turn while the spotter aloft radioed "Beautiful, excellent!" Now it was the destroyers' innings. At 0150 they reached the end of the firing line and turned southeast to follow the cruisers who had commenced retirement.

During less than an hour Munda had been treated to nearly 3000 rounds of 6-inch projectiles and 1400 rounds of 5-inch. It had been a remarkable demonstration of the American Navy's favorite weapon, the naval gun. To this day it is not known how much damage the enemy suffered during this first trip of the "Ainsworth Express," but next morning scout planes reported the airfield and environs well chewed up and no anti-aircraft fire.

The bombardment group scrambled out of the New Georgia Islands at 28 knots and by 0900 January 6 was twenty miles south of Cape Hunter on the south coast of Guadalcanal. Everything was as smooth as silk bunting; a fair, bright morning, combat air patrol of Wildcats from Henderson Field circling overhead, an anti-submarine patrol ranging ahead of the ships, three more approaching from Tulagi, a scouting PBY loafing on the rim of the horizon, Admiral Tisdale's support group hull down and coming in fast.

Ainsworth slowed down to recover aircraft just as Tisdale's ships arrived within signal-hoist distance. Tisdale disposed his ships in column to the north of the Ainsworth group on a parallel easterly course, zigzagging at 15 knots. Suddenly came a bolt from the blue. Down the slanting rays of the sun rocketed four Japanese "Vals," their wingtips glittering malevolently. Hardly anyone saw them until too late, after three bombs had near-missed *Honolulu* and a fourth had hit *Achilles's* No. 3 turret. The Japanese were afforded a free throw; it was only during their pull-out and retirement that startled gunners and combat air patrol retaliated. A Wildcat knocked down one of the enemy quartet and ships' guns claimed another. *Helena* fired at this latter plane with a new weapon, the Mark 32 proximity-influence fuze, and claimed a hit.

If so, it was the first by a device which was to dispose of thousands of enemy planes, yet remain a secret until the end of the war.

The bomb that hit *Achilles* went right through the top of No. 3 turret and detonated against a gun. The turret was wrecked and 13 men were killed and 8 wounded, but the fire was quickly extinguished and *Achilles* held her station in formation. When she returned home for repairs, Captain C. A. L. Mansergh RN, transferred to the command of her relief, H.M.N.Z.S. *Leander*, put his men into long blue American dungarees and ruled out shorts as exposing sailors to unnecessary burns.

3. *"Black Cats"* and *"Dumbo"* [16]

A significant event in December was the formation of a "Black Cat" squadron at Guadalcanal. Throughout the war, from the sighting by a British Catalina that proved fatal to battleship *Bismarck*, the PBY had proved her worth. Scouting, anti-submarine patrol, rescue missions, bombing and torpedo attacks were all part of the day's work for the lumbering "Cats." But they had insufficient speed, armament or armor to cope with enemy fighters, or anti-aircraft fire in daylight. There was more truth than fun in that story of the PBY pilot who radioed "Sighted enemy carrier. Please notify next of kin." [17] Since it was impossible to give the flying boats fighter protection, the answer was to operate "Cats" under the mask of night. And with the advent of satisfactory aircraft radars this became possible.

Night flights were still few until Squadron VP–12, Commander Clarence O. Taff, appeared on the Guadalcanal scene. These planes were amphibians (PBY–5As) equipped with landing wheels as well as pontoon hulls, so they could operate directly from Henderson Field and it was decided to paint them black for night use

[16] Comsopacforce "The Old Black Cats" 29 June 1943 (microfilm).
[17] PBYs on patrol actually adopted as a radio sign-off call the letters NNK (Notify Next of Kin).

only. There was no doubt as to proper squadron insignia, but VP–12 had embellishments. For her first mission a basic cat symbol could be painted on the plane; after the second, eyes might be added; after the third the feline grew teeth and whiskers; and after the fourth he was allowed "anatomical insignia of a more personal nature."

On 15 December the first Black Cat was set down on Henderson Field, and by the end of the month there were nine. Their services were in great demand. Search, bombing and gunfire-spotting were their most frequent missions. Take-off time was generally scheduled for 2230, which was also the hour for "Washing Machine Charlie" to appear. Pilots and crew would tumble into foxholes when enemy bombs were dropped, man their planes between bombing runs, take off over the coconut palms, blinded by bright field lights, and be well out over the water before acquiring night vision.[18] Once safely airborne, the principal antagonist became weather. Flying in a turbulent weather front all night was only routine; thunderheads butted the Cats mercilessly and often the ghostly fires of St. Elmo danced up and down the wings and fuselage. Only radar saved the planes from becoming lost in the sightless void. Then came breathless moments over the target, a fast glide to drop a torpedo or a stick of bombs on a Japanese ship, or a run over a hostile airfield with searchlight wands weaving, probing and sometimes finding, flak explosions jolting, stabbing and sometimes hitting, hot-tempered "Zekes" darting and sometimes

[18] During the war, naval medical researchers devoted much time to the problem of visual acuity at night and their investigations were of inestimable value to both sailors and aviators. The retina of the eye has two sets of visual nerves, the cones and the rods. The cones are used for day vision, while the rods respond to low light intensities. The cones are sensitive to form and color; the rods have no color response and very little definition of form. Furthermore the rods, after being subjected to bright, white light, require an hour or more to reach their maximum effectiveness in the dark. But it was possible to employ red lights or red goggles in lighted spaces so that sudden emergence into darkness would not result in "dark blindness." By the wearing of polaroid goggles during sunlight the night visual perception was noticeably increased. Instrument panels in planes and standing lights in ships were all given red illumination to prevent loss of valuable night vision. But during the Guadalcanal campaign all this was little known and seldom practiced. Capt. John H. Korb "Night Vision" *U.S. Nav. Inst. Proc.* Oct. 1946.

spearing. After the attack, a long flight home with dwindling fuel supply and perhaps a damaged plane, to land on a bomb-pocked airstrip. This was no task for the faint of heart.

Like Uncle Wiggly of nursery fame, the Cats were always searching for adventure and frequently found it. One of their first missions was to rescue the crew of a B–17 that splashed only 35 miles from Munda. Cats played Santa to Japanese at Buin on Christmas Eve with a sockful of torpedoes. The holiday spirit was carried over to New Year's Eve, when Lieutenant Norman E. Pederson USNR, over Munda, sounded his plane's crew-warning horn exactly at midnight and released a bomb, a flare and two dozen empty beer bottles. On another occasion, a Cat unable to get back to Henderson because of foul weather, landed in the open sea with only a teacup of gasoline left. The crew paddled their rubber boats 30 miles in 36 hours to Buraku Island west of the Russells, where they lived on coconuts and raw fish until rescued by "Dumbo," of whom more anon. Trailing the "Tokyo Express," scouting for PT boats and supplying or transporting coast-watchers were common tasks of the flying boats.

In late December the Cats began to spot for night surface bombardments. These missions were highly successful, not only for making gunfire more accurate but for good feeling between airmen and bluejackets. Previously there had been occasions when Cats gave destroyer crews the jitters by their close-to inspections, and sometimes the destroyers, unable to identify their inquisitors, opened up with anti-aircraft shells. Now they started working together as a team.

First cousin to the Black Cat was "Dumbo," the rescue PBY. As a sideline to regular combat missions the orthodox Catalina had long made it a practice to fish downed aviators and sailors out of the "drink." These successful though incidental rescues led to the creation of a specially equipped PBY known throughout the Navy as "Dumbo" after Walt Disney's cartoon character, the flying elephant. The beginning of 1943 saw the first regularly assigned Dumbo operating from Guadalcanal. Equipped with a doctor and a pharmacist's mate, Dumbo would fly into troubled waters to pluck survivors from life rafts or enemy-held shores. Sometimes Dumbo was favored with fighter-plane protection, but more often not; in either case it was dangerous work. A landing in the open sea might damage the hull and put Dumbo's crew in the same position as the men they had set out to save. Enemy shore batteries found him an interesting and tantalizing target. Would-be Japanese fighter aces went after him as an easy kill. But Dumbo was not easily diverted, and from 1 January to 15 August 1943 he saved no fewer than 161 flight crewmen. By the war's end he had become an honored institution.[19]

4. *December Doings Ashore* [20]

Ever since losing the Naval Battle of Guadalcanal in November, the Japanese Navy had been in favor of abandoning the island. To this frank proposal the Army opposed a decided negative. Tojo, having switched his major South Pacific objective from New Guinea to the Solomons, would not change again if he could help it. But he could not help it. The attrition of men, planes and ships, especially of destroyers, finally convinced him at the turn of the year that the island could not be taken. Accordingly, on 4 January 1943 word went forth from Tokyo that Guadalcanal must be evacuated within a month.[21] The Japanese characteristically imparted this decision only to their top commanders, while their forces on the island had to fight as though victory were around the corner. Immediate necessities could be relieved to some extent

[19] Bupers Information Bulletin "The Catalina Kids" July 1944.

[20] John Miller *Guadalcanal: The First Offensive* (Historical Division, Dept. of the Army), a vol. in the Pacific series of K. R. Greenfield (ed.) *U.S. Army in World War II* becomes increasingly valuable toward the close of the campaign; the author kindly allowed us to use it in advance of printing.

[21] Salomon Tokyo Notes, confirmed by ATIS trans. of "Southeast Area Operations Part I (Navy)," and in 1949 by Capt. Ohmae, who informed Lt. Pineau that the Russells and Rendova were occupied to facilitate evacuation by small craft, that the Navy, although reluctant to risk its scarce destroyers, finally did use them as convinced that evacuation otherwise would fail.

by planes, submarines and "Tokyo Expresses" dropping rubberized metal bales and drums of food and ammunition, to be retrieved from the water next day.

As Allied Intelligence obtained no hint that evacuation was even being discussed, the new ground force commander at Guadalcanal, Major General Alexander M. Patch USA, prepared to push the enemy off the island by force. He had relieved General Vandegrift on 9 December 1942; and on that very day the 5th and 11th Regiments, 1st Marine Division, after completing a four months' tour of duty on the island, filed down to the beach, climbed on board transports and sailed for Australia and a well merited rest. The 1st and 7th Regiments followed on 22 December and 5 January, respectively. But virtually the entire 2nd Marine Division remained, to represent the leathernecks. Plenty of Army reinforcements were on their way,[22] but until they arrived General Patch was constrained to take it easy. The Japanese Seventeenth Army was reckoned to contain about 25,000 fighting men, and Imamura alone knew how many more would be injected into the campaign by way of the "Express." Patch figured that three divisions could defend the airfield and clean up the jungle, but as yet he had less than two, including many sick and weary men as well as those untested by combat. So he decided not to start a major offensive before the new year; merely to clean up sore spots.

His decision was sound. This letup in urgent calls for men and materiel allowed a critical supply tangle at Nouméa to be unsnarled. In November nearly a hundred incoming vessels jammed the harbor and there were not enough men or facilities to unload and transship their cargoes. The Army pitched in, so that an even flow of materiel to the 'Canal was assured before Christmas. But at Lunga there were no docks, insufficient lighterage, few trucks and always a paucity of stevedores. General Patch assigned combat

[22] During December the U.S. Army in Guadalcanal included two regiments (164th and 182nd) of the Americal Division and the 147th Infantry. The 25th Division was on its way from Hawaii direct to Guadalcanal, remaining units of the Americal were soon to arrive, and the 6th Marine Regiment of the 2nd Marine Division arrived 4 January.

troops and natives to unload but, as he wryly observed, combat troops were "apathetic toward labor." [23] Nevertheless, 7737 officers and men of the 25th Infantry Division were disembarked, and 180 vehicles and 7110 tons of cargo unloaded, from three transports at Lunga Point on 29–31 December, with "spirit, vigor and zeal." [24] Landing stores was not all, for Guadalcanal roads were hardly worthy of the name and on inland trails the versatile jeep, rugged Missouri mule and shanks' mare were prime movers of victuals and explosives.

One Japanese strongpoint demanded immediate removal. Observe on the map the American perimeter, shaped like a chicken drumstick with the narrow, bony shank extending west to Point Cruz, the meaty thigh containing the airfield territory. Look now at Mount Austen 3.2 miles southwest of Henderson Field. This commanding series of grass-covered ridges had been one of the first objectives in the August assault but the Japanese got there first, and from that vantage point, with excellent binoculars they could report every plane that landed on or took off from Henderson Field and compile a daily list of shipping in Lunga Roads. General Patch decided to take Mount Austen, both to wipe out the observation post and to start an enveloping movement.

While the 2nd and 8th Marine Regiments cleaned out resistance pockets in the lower Matanikau sector, the 132nd Regiment United States Army prepared to assault the mountains. This time the enemy got the jump. On the night of 12 December a raiding party stole through the American lines and wrecked a plane and a gasoline truck on Fighter Strip No. 2. On the 14th, American reconnaissance of Mount Austen's northwest slopes met enemy rifle, machine-gun and mortar fire. General Patch's Intelligence still underestimated enemy strength on the mountain. Colonel Oka had two infantry battalions and a mountain artillery regiment perched on the hilltop, and a ridge to the southwest contained a 1500-yard

[23] Army History p. 232.
[24] Capt. T. C. Peyton "Report on Reinforcement of Cactus 29 Dec. 1942." The transports were *Republic, President Grant* and *Holbrook*, escorted from Suva by DDs *Cummings, Case, Reid, Saufley* and *Lang*.

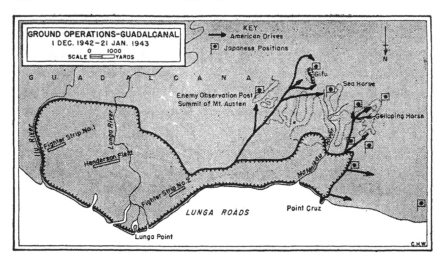

pillbox line manned by 500 men. The Japanese named this the Gifu, after a homeland prefecture.

Colonel John M. Arthur USMC, in command of the operation, slated Lieutenant Colonel Wright's 3rd Battalion to lead off. Both Marine and Army artillery were to lend support at the same instant. The bout began on 17 December with an advance which slowed as soon as the troops entered the jungle and became exposed to fire from cleverly placed machine guns and rifles, one of which killed Colonel Wright. The enemy's favorite infiltration tactics worked well; supply lines were cut, the battalion command post was brought under fire, and at night his noise-making ruses raised a general hullabaloo. Meanwhile most of the 1st Battalion 132nd Infantry was moving up to help. December 20–24 were spent in patrolling and sporadic jungle fighting, with the supply people and litter-bearers constantly under attack; but on Christmas Eve the Japanese observation post on Mount Austen's highest point fell to the 3rd Battalion. Further advance was halted when the soldiers ran into a withering fire from the Gifu strongpoint, but the enemy could no longer keep Henderson Field and Lunga Roads in his sights.

Frontal attacks against Gifu were launched on Christmas Day and the next, while destroyers *Mustin* and *Perkins* fired almost 2000 rounds of 5-inch ammunition in a diversionary bombardment of enemy supply columns and rear areas to prevent reinforcement. But the Gifu's dirt-covered pillboxes were hard to find and harder to stamp out; the clean-up had to be postponed. On the other side, General Sano assured his men that their patience under attack and starvation would soon be rewarded by all kinds of reinforcement.

On New Year's Day 1943, Colonel Ferry's fresh 2nd Battalion 132nd Regiment moved into a jump-off position to the southeast of the Gifu, and at daybreak 2 January the drive began. The 1st and 3rd Battalions plunged in from the east and north respectively, keeping the enemy occupied while the 2nd Battalion made a flanking climb from the southeast — a hot, grinding march through dense undergrowth and sawtooth kunai grass. Their efforts paid off handsomely. At 1100, two companies reached the summit of the Gifu ridge where they caught a Japanese artillery crew lolling in the shade. The gunners, completely surprised, were killed with looks of astonishment frozen on their features. But their fellows soon recovered and began a desperate series of counterattacks. Six times Colonel Oka's infuriated soldiers charged with blazing rifles; six times they were driven back. Only a welcome and accurate interdiction by artillery fire saved the 2nd Battalion from being completely surrounded.

As the Gifu was now menaced by American guns on every side except the west, Colonel George of the 132nd Regiment felt he could afford to wait. His soldiers dug in and held on until 9 January, when infantry men from the 25th Division climbed the hill and relieved them in preparation for greater doings.

5. PTs Heckle Tanaka, 5–15 January 1943

After the Munda bombardment there was a five-day interval of comparative quiet in the Slot and Ironbottom Sound. On 10 January everyone got up on his toes again when a New Georgia coastwatcher passed the word that an eight-ship "Tokyo Express" was highballing down the Slot. His report arrived too late for Henderson Field aircraft to take a crack at them, but the PT boats had plenty of warning and took early station for attack.

Four boats formed a barrier to the west of the Savo Island–Cape Esperance line, two covered the coast from Esperance to Doma Cove, and two more were stationed between Doma and Tassafaronga. At 0037 January 11, Lieutenant Rollin E. Westholm commanding the Esperance–Doma patrol in *PT–112* and slowly steaming only 450 yards from the Japanese-held coast, sighted four destroyers moving southeast less than a mile off shore. One peeled off and headed back toward Savo but the others stood on. Westholm radioed a deploy order, adding, "Make 'em good!" *PT–43*, commanded by Lieutenant (jg) Charles E. Tilden USNR, closed the leading destroyer to 400 yards before letting go two torpedoes. Both missed and, worse still, a defect in her port torpedo tube sparked a bright red flash which revealed her position. The destroyer immediately opened fire, caught *PT–43* with its second salvo, closed rapidly. Tilden ordered Abandon Ship; all hands dove deep, surfacing in time to see splashes of machine-gun bullets all around them and to hear excited Japanese talk on the destroyer's deck as she swept past. *PT–43* was towed ashore by Japanese next morning, but a New Zealand corvette destroyed her by gunfire before the enemy had a chance to find out what made motor torpedo boats tick. In the meantime *PT–40* (Lieutenant Clark W. Faulkner USNR), which had selected the second destroyer as target for four torpedoes, was rewarded by the sound of a fair hit, and streaked off to the east and safety. *PT–112*, which took on the third destroyer in column, also had the satisfaction of making a solid hit but shortly after found herself to be the object of crossfire. Two shells punctured the fragile craft, one striking the waterline and another near the engine room bulkhead. Lieutenant Westholm and the crew of eleven took to a life raft from which they sadly watched their boat go down.

Neither Westholm nor Faulkner knew how much damage their

hits had caused, but the enemy knew. A torpedo had exploded under the wardroom of *Hatsukaze* and, in the skipper's own words, "she was certainly in bad shape." He thought that he had been attacked by more than eight PTs.[25] The destroyer was still mobile and managed to sneak out to safety before morning. The other PTs on patrol that night fired twelve torpedoes but made no hits. Next morning they rescued survivors and held target practice on 250 packages of supplies and ammunition which the "Tokyo Express" had sloughed off.

On the night of 14–15 January Tanaka brought down the Slot in nine destroyers a 600-man rear guard destined to cover the Japanese evacuation. Sighted too late for a dusk air attack, this echelon still had to run a gauntlet of motor torpedo boats. Thirteen PTs put forth from Tulagi and patrolled the Guadalcanal coastline from Kamimbo on the northwest corner to Doma Cove seven miles east of Cape Esperance. It was a black night with rain; the enemy could be located only in brief flashes of lightning, and between flashes a PT helmsman could not see even the bow of his own boat. Yet it was not too dark for Japanese planes which dropped bombs hopefully and even strafed the PTs. Lieutenant Gamble in *PT–45*, accompanied by Clagett's *PT–37*, was engaging one of them with his machine gun when lightning revealed five destroyers between Savo Island and Cape Esperance. Both boats fired torpedoes and then tried to pull out; but the destroyers boxed them in to the westward of Savo. Clagett finally made Tulagi; but Gamble, with visibility zero, ran aground off Florida Island. A tug rescued his boat next day. Five other PTs were equally unsuccessful; not every night's hunting could be good.

Early in the morning of 15 January, Henderson Field fliers roared up the Slot to collect toll on the "Express." Fifteen SBDs squired by fighter planes attacked the retiring foe. A near-miss damaged *Arashi's* rudder, and strafing bullets holed *Urukaze*. But all destroyers had delivered their goods and all returned.

This was not the last, but one of the best field days of Marine

[25] Japanese "Torpedo School Battle Lessons."

Fighter Squadron 121, who helped their fellow airmen make a day's score of 30 planes. Major J. J. Foss USMC got three "Zekes" to bring his total score to 26; but his runner-up, Lieutenant Eugene Marontate, was shot down. VMF–121 was credited with 164 Japanese planes destroyed in 122 days' fighting ending 29 January, at the cost of less than 20 pilots.

A stupid and ineffective attempt at retaliation by the Japanese, to prevent sending plane reinforcements to Guadalcanal, was a series of five night bombardments of the Espiritu Santo base by big flying boats from Rekata Bay during the last ten days of January. No significant damage was inflicted. At the same time a heavy cruiser division made a feint out of Jaluit in the Marshalls, and a submarine shelled Canton Island on 23 January, hoping to divert United States naval forces.[26] Nobody fell for this ruse, although the implied threat to Samoa made some high-placed commanders very anxious.

6. *Patch's Push, 10–26 January*

The tenth of January was D-day for an American westward drive of unprecedented magnitude, all in ignorance of the Japanese decision to evacuate Guadalcanal. General Patch's command was now dignified by the title of XIV Corps; the 25th Army Division, arriving in late December and early January, was groomed for front-line fighting; and the 6th Marine Regiment, landing on 4 January, brought the 2nd Marine Division to full strength.[27] He now commanded nigh 50,000 men, including those in the air forces and the naval bases at Lunga and Tulagi. Objectives of the four-pronged attack were the Gifu, the "Sea Horse" series of hills one mile to the westward, "Galloping Horse" hill,[28] and the coast westward from Point Cruz. The coastal objective was given to the 2nd

[26] Trans. of "Southeast Area Operations Part I (Navy)" pp. 59–60.
[27] Brigadier General Alphonse DeCarre USMC was acting commander of the 2nd Marine Division; Major General John Marston USMC, the division commander, had to remain in New Zealand because he was senior to General Patch.
[28] So called from their rough resemblance to these animals in aërial photographs.

Marine Division; the other three to units of the 25th Division under Major General J. Lawton Collins USA.

Cracking the Gifu was a tough job. Assaults on 10, 11 and 12 January were stopped by Colonel Oka's 40 well-hidden machine guns. Destroyer *Reid* contributed a shore bombardment on 12 January, expending 360 rounds of 5-inch ammunition on Japanese shore positions between Kokumbona and Visale on Cape Esperance. An assault on the 15th netted only a hundred yards to angry Americans. Major Inagaki, out of rations, completely surrounded, hopelessly outnumbered and without artillery support, decided to fight it out despite his colonel's orders. A loud-speaker broadcast urging the Japs to surrender brought in only half a dozen starved soldiers. One enemy platoon, hearing the plea, talked the matter over but decided they were too ill and weak even to walk to the American lines. So the loud-speaker was replaced by Army 105-mm and 155-mm howitzers, which on the 17th dropped over 1700 rounds in the 1000 square yards of the strong point. The break came on the 21st when a Marine tank, manned by troopers and supported by infantry, snorted up the hillside. That night Major Inagaki, with a hundred followers, charged madly and hopelessly into the American lines. Every one was mowed down. Next day Colonel Larsen's battalion of the 35th Infantry Regiment overran the Gifu and ended a month-long campaign which had employed over five American battalions.

The drive to capture the Sea Horse also began on 10 January. Fortunately there was neither a fanatical major nor a Gifu to oppose the line of advance, but this group of ridged, wooded and gullied hills made an ideal terrain for Japanese-style defense. Two battalions of the 35th Infantry Regiment, assigned the job of lassoing the Sea Horse, made fair progress; the principal problem was to supply them. Three hundred native bearers, an impromptu barge line on the Mantanikau River (known as the "Pusha Maru"), and air drops by B–17s helped, and by the 16th the Sea Horse was safely corralled, together with 600 more dead Japanese. Galloping Horse, believed to be an enemy strong point, was taken by the 27th Infantry Regiment on the evening of 13 January.

General Patch now had enough elbowroom on his western front to undertake a further advance without fear of being flanked on the south or crowded on the west. The next step was to capture the Japanese base at Kokumbona, three miles west of Point Cruz. There were only two exits from Kokumbona: a jungle trail across the island to Beaufort Bay on the southwest coast, and the coastal road to Cape Esperance. Since Beaufort Bay was in friendly hands — the Dutch missionary had never evacuated — a contingent of the 147th Infantry Regiment was easily dispatched by water and landed there safely. Half of this amphibious group moved northward over the trail and set up a block the Japanese would have found difficult to rupture. But it so happened that the enemy never attempted to retreat by this trail. His other escape route along the coast was so easy that General Patch would have to move fast to trap the Kokumbona gang.

Two factors thwarted Patch's scheme to catch this sizable Japanese force. The lesser was the difficulty of supplying front-line troops; the greater and more significant was the decision of 4 January by the Imperial War Council at Tokyo to abandon Guadalcanal and let Imamura salvage what he could of the garrison. It was in preparation for this movement that Imamura dispatched his special "Tokyo Express" destroyer runs of the 10th and 14th. As we have seen, the first brought in ammunition, most of which the PTs destroyed, and the second successfully landed 600 fresh troops. But the Japanese retreat from Kokumbona toward embarkation points on Cape Esperance did not begin until the night of 22–23 January.

In the meantime Captain Briscoe's "Cactus Striking Force" of destroyers *Nicholas, O'Bannon, Radford* and *DeHaven*, sent up by Admiral Halsey to operate from Purvis Bay near Tulagi, bombarded enemy shore positions intermittently for eight hours on 19 January, each expending 500 to 600 rounds of 5-inch ammunition, while engineers were sweating out a road up to and beyond Galloping Horse. On 22 January the troops were sufficiently supplied with ammunition and food to resume their advance. A unit of the 25th Division under General Collins marched across the hills to the west of Galloping Horse; a composite Army–Marine outfit, newly formed under General DeCarre, pushed along the coastal road with the 6th Marine Regiment to seaward, the 147th Infantry in the center, and the 182nd Infantry on the left flank. Despite enthusiastic support by their own artillery, destroyer gunfire and aërial bombardment, the Marines ran into some very aggressive Nips and had to kill about 200 of them in order to reach Kokumbona late on 23 January. Occupation of that village won the Americans a new landing beach for staging supplies, as well as a radar station, trucks, artillery, landing craft, and about 400 dead Japanese for the burial detail. But the main enemy force had flown the coop.

The Americans took off in pursuit and, by 1 February, were at the Bonegi River just below Tassafaronga. Here the 600 newly arrived rear guard made a brave stand, covering Hyakutake's evacuation.

Since mid-October destroyers and occasionally cruisers had given gunfire support to ground operations when requested, but for lack of a liaison system it had not been very effective. The first group of trained naval gunfire liaison officers arrived at Guadalcanal 26 November and were assigned to various Marine and Army infantry units, some of which also placed liaison artillery officers on board gunfire ships. However, owing to the thick foliage on Guadalcanal, the crudely gridded air photographs with which the officers worked, and the slight use of aircraft spotters, naval gunfire support during the campaign never became very good. It was best when fighting took place near the coast, as now happened. During the Japanese stand at the Bonegi River, 29 January 1943, important gunfire assistance was furnished by destroyers *Anderson* and *Wilson*, taking station less than a mile from the river's mouth. A field artillery post ashore indicated the targets and spotted gunfire to liaison officers on board *Anderson*. Steaming only 1000 to 1500 yards off shore, and using a conspicuous tree as a point of aim for indirect fire, the ships slapped hundreds of 5-inch shells onto the enemy positions. Soldiers of the 147th and Marines of the 6th watched with delight as the salvos "changed the flora and the fauna — palm trees and Japs flying into the air" east of Tassafaronga. After witnessing this demonstration of what 1100 rounds of a naval 5-inch gun could do, the troops demanded more of the same, declaring their old 75-mm pack howitzers to be "no more good than talcum powder." Some front-line troops still distrusted naval gunfire, fearing it might hit them instead of the enemy; but one battalion commander, hearing the closeness of a 5-inch barrage complained of, bellowed, "Don't call me till it falls in your mess kits!" The proof of the pudding was a nasty mangle of enemy dead on Bonegi Ridge when the troops walked in. This little affair was a happy prelude to the complicated fire support missions of later campaigns.[29]

7. *Vila Bombardment, 23–24 January*

Our narrative has to progress much like the 2nd Marine Division along the coast; first the ground troops get ahead in the chronology and then the sea forces. It is now the Navy's turn.

Secretary Knox always wished to see things for himself, and it was time he had a good look at Guadalcanal. Accompanied by Admiral Nimitz, he met Admiral Halsey on board tender *Curtiss* at Espiritu Santo on 21 January. The enemy chose that night to start his series of bombing raids on Segond Channel; eight bombs were dropped but did no damage. The following night, when the distinguished trio had reached Guadalcanal, they were treated to a prolonged bombing raid. Whether or not their itinerary had leaked out, the coincidence put an idea into somebody's head which, come spring, was to cost Admiral Yamamoto his life.

[29] Letter of Lt. A. E. Moon, one of the first group, Jan. 1949; *Anderson* and *Wilson* Action Reports; writer's notes taken at 147th Infantry orientation conference, Apr. 1943. General Patch rode destroyer *Fletcher* in a bombardment of positions near Visale on 26 Jan. to see how it was done, and was completely converted to this form of artillery support.

Halsey's immediate idea, however, was to try a second "Ainsworth Express" run. For the enemy was becoming active in Kula Gulf north of New Georgia, owing to difficulties of supplying the Munda airstrip. Approaching Munda from the south meant sailing over foul ground and under dangerous skies. But a supply ship could enter Kula Gulf at night, discharge cargo ashore or into barges and forward the stuff to Munda by overland trail or through Hathorn Sound. The supply ship could then turn north, ring up full speed and be back at Faisi, Shortlands, in time for breakfast.

On the west side of Kula Gulf lies Kolombangara Island, an almost perfect volcanic cone. Along its edge is a narrow plain sprouting coconut plantations at two places, Vila and Stanmore. There the Japanese were staging supplies to Munda and also building an airstrip. By 22 January a 6000-foot runway was more than 90 per cent completed.

"Pug" Ainsworth's Task Force 67, this time made up of four light cruisers and seven destroyers, took departure from the New Hebrides so as to arrive south of the Russells in early evening on the 23rd. All day long enemy aircraft were snooping and trailing; Ainsworth, unable to get word to the fighter planes at Henderson Field to drive them off, did his best to mislead the enemy by making a feint toward Munda. After dark the task force divided; cruisers *Nashville* and *Helena* and destroyers *Nicholas*, *DeHaven*, *Radford* and *O'Bannon* continued up the Slot to conduct the bombardment while cruisers *Honolulu* and *St. Louis* and destroyers *Drayton*, *Lamson* and *Hughes* backtracked to the south of Guadalcanal, alert to support the bombardment group if invited. Ainsworth's well trained aërial spotters, who had already looked over the target area, now took off in two Black Cats while a third scouted ahead of the bombardment group.

This foray was fraught with more dangerous possibilities than the attack on Munda. A full moon sifted ample light through the overcast. A forewarned enemy might well try to cork up the bombardment ships in Kula Gulf. Shortly after midnight two frisky planes, displaying running lights, challenged the force with unintelligible blinker signals. "Pug" wisely ignored them and the enemy "Bettys" finally left under the impression that they had sighted friendly ships.

It was nearly 0100 January 24 when the six ships swung to a southwesterly course to enter Kula Gulf. *O'Bannon* probed well ahead, then turned to take picket station at the northwest entrance close by Kolombangara. Slitting the calm waters behind *O'Bannon* came destroyer *Nicholas* followed by flagship *Nashville*, cruiser *Helena*, destroyers *DeHaven* and *Radford*. Near the mouth of the Gulf *Nicholas* (flying Briscoe's pennant) turned west, then north to parallel the coast and scout for seaborne opposition. The two cruisers and the rear destroyers made a sweeping turn to course NNW, and then the fun began.

From 0200 until 0229 the 6-inch guns gave tongue. *Nashville* and *Helena*, varying their Munda procedure, fired simultaneously but at different targets so that the Black Cat spotters would have no difficulty identifying salvos. Captain Briscoe's destroyers, penetrating farther into the Gulf and steering close to the western shore, commenced firing when the cruisers had shot off their allowance. In about an hour's time the two light cruisers poured nearly 2000 rounds of 6-inch onto and around the new airstrip, and with the aid of the destroyer added some 1500 rounds of 5-inch. The 6-inch guns behaved magnificently — no check to the continuous rapid fire,[30] and spectacular fires were ignited ashore. A few short, puny and inaccurate salvos from the coastal batteries bothered the Americans not at all. Throughout the war, Japanese coast defense batteries were strangely ineffective.

Half an hour after the bombardment, the enemy reacted with an air attack, for which "Pug" had deployed his four destroyers in a box formation around the cruisers. Diffused moonlight and high-speed wakes attracted planes to the force, but Ainsworth's skillful steering into convenient rain squalls kept the enemy guessing, while radar-controlled anti-aircraft fire drove off eager

[30] Cdr. W. Kirten Jr., "Guns" of *Nashville*, wrote almost a prose poem on the 6-inch performance in his Action Report and sent his congratulations to the much-abused Bureau of Ordnance for providing the Navy with such fine weapons.

"Bettys." By radar alone, *Radford* directed 5-inch fire to a plane, then invisible; seconds later she had the satisfaction of seeing it fall in flames. On this occasion the Emperor's fliers for the first time exhibited their new pyrotechnic technique, suspending colored flares around the American ships and dropping float lights into the water, a display which aroused much curiosity. One destroyer even investigated a flare, thinking it might be a distress signal from a downed plane. But the Japanese had something here which they would presently demonstrate against *Chicago.*

Fighter planes from Henderson joined Ainsworth's force at dawn and escorted his ships safely out of the danger zone. But the Americans were not yet through with Vila, nor would be before fall. Carrier *Saratoga,* up from Nouméa for the occasion, had dispatched her air group to Guadalcanal on the 23rd. Next day 24 SBDs, 17 TBFs and 18 F4Fs left Henderson Field for Vila and by 0800 had dumped 23 tons of bombs on the unhappy Japanese and returned to their parent ship the same day.

Although Halsey expected little more from these operations than attrition and delay, the Munda and Vila bombardments raised an unwarranted hope in some quarters that by air and surface raids alone the Japanese could be prevented from completing air bases. As the year 1943 grew older and evidence accumulated that the enemy next day merely filled in the holes, replaced bomb damage and resumed air operations, it was realized that the only certain cure was to take the fields away from him. For that, Halsey must bide his time.

Admiral Kusaka no longer dared send naval guns to Guadalcanal, but in preparation for the troop evacuation he sent 73 fighters and 13 bombers on a raid down the Slot on 25 January.[31] The "Zekes," looking for easy kills, tried to lure American fliers into vulnerable positions beneath their main force. The Americans failed to bite and the whole enemy force, less four shot down, turned tail without finding Henderson Field. Two days later the enemy was back again in strength, and this time there was a mid-air tangle which net-

[31] Japanese Naval War Diary.

ted the United States pilots over a dozen "Zekes" at a cost of four American planes. Again no bombs fell on Henderson Field. What a difference the build-up and experience of two months can make!

8. *Submarines pro and con*

The last month of the campaign was the best for American submarines operating in Bismarck–Solomons waters. On 9 January *Nautilus* and her veteran skipper, Lieutenant Commander William H. Brockman, tried out her new-fangled SJ radar on a small freighter north of Bougainville. The night was dark, the *Maru* was hit twice and went down without a glimpse of her foe. *Guardfish* sustained her good reputation in southern latitudes as she had off Honshu, nailing a patrol boat, a 4000-ton *Maru* and destroyer *Hakaze*. As was his custom, Lieutenant Commander Klakring let the crew have a look at the destroyer's bright red bottom just before she blew up and sank. *Greenling*, operating in the Bismarcks, attacked *Kinposan Maru*, dove deep and heard her victim's ammunition blow up in a long, loud death rattle. *Growler* sank a 6000-tonner on the 16th, but she lost her gallant skipper within a month.[32] *Swordfish* on 19 January made a bold daylight attack on a convoy enjoying both plane and destroyer protection. From within the destroyer screen she pumped two into *Myoho Maru*. Then the shattered transport unintentionally, and the submarine intentionally, vied with each other in quick submergence. *Swordfish* surfaced after evading both bombs and depth charges. *Gato* during the last fortnight of January downed two *Marus* in separate daylight shots at escorted convoys.

On the other side, the Japanese were turning to the use of submarine transports for supply and evacuation. Kamimbo Bay, just around a bulge of land west of Cape Esperance, was a favorite

[32] It was on 7 Feb. 1943 that *Growler* collided with a Japanese ship and Cdr. Howard W. Gilmore issued his last, immortal order, "Take her down!" Details in Vol. IV of this History. Lt. Cdr. C. E. Smith was C.O. of *Swordfish;* Lt. Cdr. R. J. Foley of *Gato.*

terminus for the boats, some of which carried midgets. PTs and aircraft attacked them frequently with doubtful results, but not so with *Kiwi's* kill.

Since 14 December, Tulagi had been the home of two brace of Royal New Zealand corvettes named after Maori birds and trees: *Matai, Kiwi, Moa* and *Tui.* Of their spirited officers and crewmen none was better known than the colossal skipper of tiny *Kiwi,* Lieutenant Commander G. Bridson RNZNVR. One dark night, when Lieutenant Gamble was out looking for game in his motor torpedo boat, he mistook *Kiwi* for one of the "Tokyo Express." Fortunately his torpedoes missed, but Bridson saw them and rumbled over the voice radio, "Are you little bastards shooting at us?" Gamble was forced to reply "Affirmative!" but next day he met Bridson and the two became fast friends.[33] And no ship was more appropriately named, for of the kiwi it is written that his absence of wings is compensated by fleetness of foot, and that in the twilight he "moves about cautiously and noiselessly as a rat."

On the night of 29 January *Kiwi* and *Moa* are on patrol near Kamimbo Bay when at 2105 *Kiwi* makes sound contact on submarine *I–1,* carrying a load of troops and supplies, and sights the wake. Bridson rings up full speed to ram. Engineer officer asks "Why?" and is told to "Shut up" because "There's a week end's leave in Auckland ahead of us!" Although the sub is bigger and more heavily manned than *Kiwi,* the corvette piles in with all batteries, from 20-mm to 4-inch, banging lustily. Her bow hits the I-boat on the port side abaft the conning tower; startled soldiers jump overboard with full packs. *Kiwi* backs off, and at pistol range fires on landing barges lashed to the sub's afterdeck. The barges catch fire and *Kiwi* follows up with a devastating 4-inch barrage. Bridson rams again, this time "for a week's leave," and strikes the hydroplanes a glancing blow while a 20-mm gunner picks off an officer on the conning tower. With range never exceeding 150 yards, *Kiwi's* crew pour out a steady stream of bullets mixed with imprecations. Now Bridson conns his ship

[33] Naval Records and Library interview with Lt. Gamble.

for a third ram and a "fortnight's leave." *Kiwi* walks right up
on the submarine's deck; backs off, leaving *I–1* gushing great
gouts of oil. His guns now being too hot to operate, Bridson turns
over the job to Lieutenant Commander Peter Phipps of sister ship
Moa who, owing to *Kiwi's* close and repeated clinches has as yet
been unable to enter the fight. *Moa* promptly pummels the boat
with heavy and light-caliber shot. At 2320 the battle ends when
the boat runs aground. Both corvettes stand by until dawn and
rescue the submarine's wounded gunnery officer. *I–1* remained on
the reef and later yielded enemy documents of great value.[34]

[34] *Kiwi* and *Moa* Action Reports; *Admiral Halsey's Story*.

CHAPTER XV

The Battle of Rennell Island[1]

29–30 January 1943

1. Big Reinforcement

ADMIRAL NIMITZ flew down to Nouméa to discuss the situation with Admiral Halsey and staff on 23 January. Over two months had passed since the Naval Battle of Guadalcanal, but nobody could see that the Japanese were on their way out, and 1 April was the earliest date at which General Patch expected to eliminate their military power on the disputed island and commence the long-postponed second phase of Operation "Watchtower." Commanding officers, respecting the enemy's proved ability to bounce back into the arena after a defeat, made conservative estimates of the situation. This attitude of reasoned caution was very marked in the last week of January, when aërial reconnaissance reported an ever increasing number of Japanese transports, freighters and destroyers at Rabaul and Buin, while carriers and battleships milled around Ontong Java, north of Guadalcanal. It looked as if something tremendous were in the wind. Something was — the evacuation of Guadalcanal — but to staff officers at Pearl Harbor and Nouméa the signs pointed to another major effort to reinforce Guadalcanal, as in mid-November.

---

[1] Comsopac Op Plans 3–43 and 4–43, 27 Jan. 1943; Action Reports of American ships and commands involved; Cincpac "Solomon Islands Campaign — Fall of Guadalcanal, period 25 Jan. to 10 Feb. 1943"; O.N.I. Combat Narrative No. 8, *Japanese Evacuation of Guadalcanal*; "War Diary of Japanese Naval Operations" ATIS 16268; conversations with Admiral Halsey's operations officer and Admiral Giffen's chief of staff. A story which has had considerable circulation, to the effect that Halsey in this operation was trying to bait Yamamoto into a big surface engagement south of the Solomons, is apocryphal.

In any case, Halsey could meet the threat with the greatest aggregation of sea power yet collected in the South Pacific. And, since relief of the last Marine elements on Guadalcanal required the movement of four loaded transports up to Guadalcanal at the close of January,[2] Halsey decided to send them up in style — covered and protected by five separate task forces comprising two fleet carriers, two escort carriers, three new battleships, twelve cruisers and twenty-five destroyers. These should have been able to take care of anything Yamamoto might send south, as well as to give the soldiers a peaceful passage north and a safe landing. Halsey rather hoped that Yamamoto would challenge. He might have done so if the Imperial War Council had not tightened up on his fuel supply. But he did put on a spectacular and successful night air attack which cost the United States Navy a valuable heavy cruiser.

Because the several task forces had to be assembled in different harbors, Halsey's ships moved north in six separate groups. Three which never got into the fight were Rear Admiral Ainsworth's force of four light cruisers and four destroyers; Rear Admiral Lee's battleship force, in which *North Carolina* and *Indiana* had replaced *South Dakota;* and Rear Admiral DeWitt Ramsey's carrier group, built around *Saratoga.* There was also the *Enterprise* group, under Rear Admiral "Ted" Sherman, which did see action — "Big E" never missed one! These four steamed from 250 to 400 miles behind the two forward groups, one composed of three *President* transports and *Crescent City;* the other a close support group of cruisers, escort carriers and destroyers, commanded by Rear Admiral Robert C. Giffen. This last, Task Force 18, was the one that took the rap.

Colorful "Ike" Giffen had just brought heavy cruiser *Wichita* and two escort carriers more than halfway around the world from Casablanca, where they had had things rather easy in the air but had learned to be very wary of submarines.[3] His orders were to

---

[2] King sent Nimitz and Halsey a rather sharp dispatch about the relief of the 2nd Marine Division, suggesting that "wait, delay and linger" had become the watchwords of the Guadalcanal campaign.

[3] See Vol. II of this History.

cross courses with the transport group which left Nouméa 27 January 1943, the same day that he departed Efate. Details of formations in case of air attack were left to his judgment, as Admiral Halsey wanted "Ike" to "get his feet wet in the Pacific." He had definite orders, however, to rendezvous at a point 15 miles off Cape Hunter, on the southwest coast of Guadalcanal, at 2100 January 30, with Captain Briscoe's Desron 21, the four-destroyer "Cactus Striking Force." [4] These two would then make a daylight sweep up the Slot, while the transports, which would enter Ironbottom Sound via Lengo Channel, were discharging at Lunga Point.

Task Force 18 was constituted as follows, under Admiral Giffen's command: —

Heavy Cruisers, Rear Admiral Giffen (CTF 18)

WICHITA	Capt. Francis S. Low
CHICAGO	Capt. Ralph O. Davis
LOUISVILLE	Capt. Charles T. Joy

Light Cruisers, Rear Admiral A. Stanton Merrill (Comcrudiv 12)

MONTPELIER	Capt. Leighton Wood
CLEVELAND	Capt. Edmund W. Burrough
COLUMBIA	Capt. William A. Heard

Air Support Group, Captain Ben H. Wyatt

CHENANGO	Capt. Wyatt	
VGF–28:	11 F4F–4	Lt. Cdr. Jack I. Bandy
VGS–28:	8 SBD–3, 9 TBF–1	Lt. Cdr. W. S. Butts

SUWANNEE	Capt. Frederick W. McMahon	
VGF–27:	18 F4F–4	Lt. Joseph F. Fitzpatrick
VGS–27:	15 TBF–1	Lt. Cdr. Robert E. C. Jones

Destroyer Screen, Captain Harold F. Pullen

LA VALLETTE	Cdr. Harry H. Henderson
WALLER	Cdr. Laurence H. Frost
CONWAY	Lt. Cdr. Nathaniel S. Prime
FRAZIER	Lt. Cdr. Frank Virden

Desdiv 41, Cdr. Alvin D. Chandler

CHEVALIER	Cdr. Ephraim R. McLean
EDWARDS	Lt. Cdr. Paul G. Osler
MEADE	Cdr. Raymond S. Lamb
TAYLOR	Lt. Cdr. Benjamin Katz

[4] Lat. 10° S, long. 159°40′ E. This does not appear in either Op Plan, but orders to that effect were issued before sailing.

The expedient of taking along two escort carriers for close air support, was not well managed. They should have been sent well ahead to await the cruisers just outside Japanese land-based air range; but they were closely attached to the task force, where their low speed (18 knots), and necessity of heading into the light southeast tradewind to launch and recover planes, slowed down the speed of advance. Giffen called them his "ball-and-chain." A simple calculation having shown that otherwise he could never make the designated rendezvous with Briscoe on time, he dropped off *Chenango* and *Suwannee* with two destroyers at 1400 January 29 and pushed on at 24 knots. Captain Wyatt of the escort carrier group agreed to furnish combat air patrol during daylight hours and also to scout for flying snoopers; but Admiral Giffen was mainly concerned with the submarine menace. During the afternoon he received a warning to look out for Japanese submarines advancing through the passage between San Cristobal and Guadalcanal. That naturally made him all the more anxious to make time toward his rendezvous with Briscoe, where he would be protected by planes based on Henderson Field.

2. *Twilight Torpedo Attack*

Some time during that afternoon radar screens in the cruisers began to show indications of strange aircraft hovering on the northwestern horizon. Nobody could be certain whether these were friendly or enemy, since the radar identification system (IFF) on American planes was notoriously erratic. Stringent radio silence — an article of faith with Admiral Giffen — prevented his fighter-director team in *Chicago* from vectoring out combat air patrol to check up on aircraft indications shown on radar screens. The Japanese, however, were getting firsthand information of Giffen's movements from their submarines, stationed for that purpose. At the new Munda field, at Buka and probably in Rabaul, too, mechanics and ordnance men made final checks on the engines and torpedoes of 31 twin-engined bombers; and in the course of the afternoon these "Bettys" took off for the reported position of Task Force 18.

At 1850 the sun set into a calm sea scarcely ruffled by light airs from the eastward. Low clouds covering four fifths of a moonless sky promised a black night. The last combat air patrol retired with the sun — although unidentified planes were still indicated on radar screens — leaving the six cruisers without air protection in the twilight.

Task Force 18 was now about 50 miles north of Rennell Island, steaming northwesterly toward the rendezvous point at 24 knots in a rivet-shaped formation, destroyers in a semicircle two miles ahead of the flagship, cruisers in two columns 2500 yards apart. This disposition, designed for a rapid transition from cruising to surface battle, was well enough, because of the high speed, for meeting submarines; but ineffective against air attack because huge, unprotected gaps lay astern and on both quarters. Before sunset the flagship's and other ships' radars recorded "bogies" 60 miles to the westward; but Admiral Giffen neither ordered a change of course, nor alerted his force for plane attack, nor gave orders what the ships were to do if attacked. *Chicago* and some of the others had secured from dusk General Quarters before the attack developed, and were unprepared to meet it.

These mysterious aircraft were Japanese torpedo-bombers. They had a keen, intelligent attack group commander who, instead of silhouetting his planes by rushing in from the direction of the twilight glow, circled to the south of Giffen, rounded up some 14 miles on his starboard quarter and split his force into two equal parts. Now the high-tailed, big-bosomed "Bettys" begin their low, fast approach. The leading plane drops a torpedo at destroyer *Waller*, then strafes her and *Wichita* too. A second plane passes between *Chicago* and *Wichita*, launching a torpedo which *Louisville* avoids only by a hard left turn. All ships whack away at the intruders, tracers pencil the slate-gray sky with darting lines of fire, and at least one "Betty" splashes in a sphere of flame astern of *Chicago*.

As the gunfire died away, sailors looked from ship to ship but observed no damage; nor was there any. Admiral Giffen, thinking the worst was over, continued doggedly on the same course, 305°, in the same formation, and at 1930 even ceased zigzagging in accordance with previous routine. His one idea was to make the rendezvous on time, and for that he hadn't a minute to spare.

The enemy, however, had just begun to fight. As twilight faded he opened a bag of pyrotechnic tricks that was to be standard for the next two years. On both sides of the formation flickering white flares suddenly appeared on the water, so disposed as to make a lighted lane indicating the ships' course. Dim yellow-white flares hung overhead from slowly descending parachutes, lighting up the decks. Red and green float lights glowed mysteriously on the surface, inciting overenthusiastic gunners to action. What sort of Oriental trickery was this? Some regarded the lights as a mere diversion, others thought they marked a rendezvous, and a few guessed the correct answer — these were beacons, spotted by scout planes, to indicate to the Japanese bombers the location, course and composition of the American force.

At 1931 another, or the same, flight of "Bettys" appeared from the eastward. One released a torpedo which passed slightly ahead of *Chicago*. Another torpedo hit *Louisville* but failed to detonate. The attackers did not escape with whole hides; smoking fuselages and bright surface bonfires attested the accuracy of anti-aircraft batteries and the efficiency of the super-secret Mark-32 shell fuze which here had one of its first combat tests.[5]

Regardless of losses, including that of their group commander,[6] the Japanese planes continued to press their attack and at 1938 several made a concerted run against the right-hand cruiser column. Anti-aircraft fire splashed one "Betty" explosively astern of

---

[5] This proximity influence fuze required no clockwork time setting. If the shell passed close to the target, a small radio-like device was activated by electrical waves bouncing off the target's surface, detonating the shell. Tiny and complicated as it was, this fuze was to be the death of hundreds of enemy fliers in actions to come.

[6] Japanese Communiqué 2 Feb. 1943.

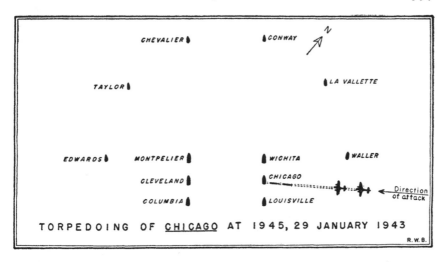

CHEVALIER ▮   ▮CONWAY

TAYLOR ▮   ▮ LA VALLETTE

EDWARDS ▮   MONTPELIER ▮   ▮ WICHITA   ▮ WALLER

CLEVELAND ▮   ▮ CHICAGO

COLUMBIA ▮   ▮ LOUISVILLE   ← Direction of attack

TORPEDOING OF <u>CHICAGO</u> AT 1945, 29 JANUARY 1943

R. W. B.

Waller and lit up a second, which dove off *Chicago's* port bow, illuminating her brightly and searing her deck with the intense flame from burning aviation gasoline. Other planes winged in for a kill on the now obvious target, and at 1945 one fateful torpedo stabbed *Chicago's* starboard side.[7] Two large compartments were immediately flooded. The aftermost fireroom commenced slowly to fill. Three shafts stopped revolving. Bridge control of rudder was lost. Before the damage control officer could take stock, a second torpedo holed and flooded No. 3 fireroom, swamped the forward engine room and abruptly halted the one remaining drive shaft. With two such wounds the prospect of saving the ship was exceedingly doubtful. But Captain Ralph O. Davis's repair parties were well trained and most determined; they had pulled *Chicago* through the Savo Island battle and they had no intention of giving her up now.

Louisville, following *Chicago,* sheered to avoid her stricken sister and the wreckage of two shot-down "Bettys." Clearing *Chicago* at 30 knots, she slowed and took station astern of the flagship. Shortly thereafter, a dud warhead smacked *Wichita.* The strange air-sea battle continued, one side trying to entice ships into re-

[7] Position then, lat. 10°26′ S, long. 160°7′ E.

vealing gunfire, the other blinded by the flash of their own 5-inch powder whenever they let go. Radar gun control was performing better than it had ever done in the mountain-ringed waters of Ironbottom Sound; but it was difficult to track targets when, as Admiral Giffen observed, the radar plot looked like a "disturbed hornet's nest." And nobody thought of making protective smoke because the task force had neither doctrine nor orders to that effect.

At 2000, when the last glimmer of twilight had faded, Giffen ordered a countermarch to course 120 degrees, slowed to reduce the phosphorescent wake, and forbade shooting except at definite targets. The Japanese pilots could not locate him, even by such provocative measures as turning on running lights and firing bursts of machine-gun tracer, so at 2015 most of the remaining bombers lit out for home. But for hours afterward individual search planes were on the radar screens, and occasionally they heckled the force with parachute flares.

On board *Chicago* two small fires were quickly quenched and the damage control parties turned their attention to counterflooding. Bulkheads were shored and bucket brigades sluiced water out of living compartments. Fortunately the ship's emergency diesel generators were in operation, supplying light and power. An eleven-degree starboard list and a deep trim by the stern were an added handicap. The only way to save the stricken cruiser was to tow her clear of plane range. At 2030 *Louisville* left the formation for this purpose, while the remaining cruisers operated to the westward to anticipate the possible approach of enemy air or surface forces.

The feat of taking *Chicago* in tow in sepulchral darkness was a remarkable exhibition of masterful seamanship. Captain Joy of *Louisville* placed his cruiser's stern about 1000 yards on *Chicago's* weather bow and lowered a whaleboat containing a manila messenger, the end of which was delivered on board *Chicago*. Sweating sailors groping in the dark managed to rig the complicated towing tackle. On *Chicago's* forecastle the thick steel hawser was brought on board by manual heave-ho, its bitter end shackled to the anchor cable and 60 fathom of chain tenderly paid out. By midnight this back-breaking job was accomplished and Captain Joy ordered *Louisville's* engines slow ahead. It was then discovered that *Chicago's* rudder was jammed left; fast work freed it, and in the early midwatch of 30 January course was set for Espiritu Santo at a speed of about 4 knots. Below decks, fires had been lighted under a boiler, pumps started, and the list corrected by pumping oil.

3. *Loss of* CHICAGO

When Admiral Halsey in Nouméa was apprised of Giffen's woes, he took immediate action to protect *Chicago*. Escort carriers *Chenango* and *Suwannee*, already ordered to provide combat air patrol at dawn, moved up to a suitable position. Admiral Fitch was ordered to send a Black Cat from Espiritu Santo; it arrived on station shortly after midnight. Rear Admiral Frederick C. Sherman, commanding the *Enterprise* group, was directed to close and provide additional dawn combat air patrol, which he did. Tug *Navajo* and destroyer-transport *Sands*, diverted from other tasks, set a course for the cripple. But the Japanese were still interested in Task Force 18. Right after breakfast an *Enterprise* combat air patrol sighted and chased a reconnaissance plane 20 miles west of the big carrier. It looked as though more trouble were on the menu.

At the start of the forenoon watch, *Louisville* transferred her tow to *Navajo* and rejoined the other cruisers covering *Chicago*. Progress was made, but another snooper appeared at noon and escaped with a whole hide.

Admiral Halsey had earlier directed that the able-bodied cruisers proceed independently to Efate; so at 1500 January 30 Giffen signaled Adieu and Good Luck to *Chicago*. The crippled cruiser was now screened by six destroyers (including *Sands*) and towed by *Navajo* at 4 knots. The destroyers formed a moving circle around tug and tow, chasing each other round and round as in a maypole dance. But nobody made arrangements for using *Chicago's* fighter-director team to vector out combat air patrol.

Lest the quarry escape them by sundown, the eager Japanese attacked in broad daylight. At 1445 a dozen "Bettys" were reported south of New Georgia heading for Rennell Island. Radio Guadalcanal put a warning message on the air at 1505 which reached both *Chicago* and *Enterprise* in sufficient time for them to prepare a reception. In the big carrier a plot of the enemy's probable speed along his reported track indicated that he would arrive shortly after 1600. At this time *Chicago* was 43 miles NNW of *Enterprise;* Giffen's cruisers were off to the north. A combat air patrol of ten fighters was over *Chicago.* The escort carrier group, uninformed and so unaware that Giffen's force had parted company with *Chicago,* also planned to put a ten-plane combat air patrol over the retiring cruisers in late afternoon.

At 1540 four planes of the combat air patrol over *Chicago* sighted and gave chase to a snooping "Betty," which headed toward Rennell Island. After a 40-mile chase it was overtaken, slowed by hits on the engines and finally knocked down.

The 12-plane enemy flight registered at 1554 on an *Enterprise* radar scope, 67 miles away, bearing 300 degrees. "Big E" swung her bow into the gentle wind and launched a supplementary ten-plane combat air patrol. But the escort carrier airmen had difficulty in rendezvousing and got off to a late start.

Enterprise fighter-directors now vectored Lieutenant MacGregor Kilpatrick's six-plane combat air patrol from Giffen's force to an intercepting position about 17 miles southwest of the carrier, where the dozen torpedo-carrying "Bettys" were loping along at an easy 160 knots in line abreast. They were gunning for *Enterprise;* but with a gauntlet of Wildcats between them and her, the Japanese leader quickly changed his target to *Chicago,* which he had sighted a few minutes earlier north of him. The "Bettys" reversed course, increased speed and went into a long power glide toward the crippled cruiser.

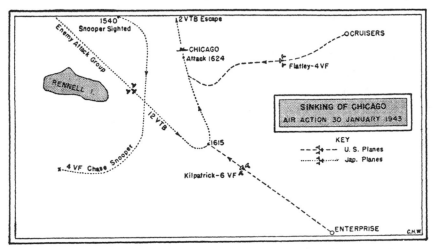

This move placed Kilpatrick and his wingman in a good spot for attacking, and they neatly splashed three bombers. But there were still nine left, and the remaining fighter planes at full throttle were too slow to overtake the enemy, now making 300 knots. Meanwhile, Lieutenant Commander James H. Flatley, leading a four-plane fighter division from *Enterprise*, saw the Nips from his position over Giffen's group and made every effort to head them off before they could reach *Chicago*.

He was too late. The nine "Bettys" tore out of a cloud cluster south of the cruiser and fanned out to launch torpedoes. There was no time to lay a smoke screen even if anyone had thought of it; anti-aircraft fire was the only possible defense. *Navajo* made a gallant but futile effort to pull *Chicago's* bow into line with the planes. Every gun in the group that could be brought to bear woofed at the whale-sized "Bettys." It was a rowdy fight, filled with the usual paraphernalia of fast-moving and splashing planes, falling torpedoes, fire and smoke. Destroyer *La Vallette*, the only screening ship which happened to be in the direct line of the Japanese attack, enjoyed a period of uninterrupted shooting at the big bombers; but this also put her in the line of torpedo fire. Nobody who saw the action, whether from a fighter plane cockpit or from a ship's bridge, told the same story; each man thought his own ship or fighter group was doing all the damage. Flatley's and Kilpatrick's fighter planes buzzed right into the anti-aircraft fire after the "Bettys," and, miraculously, not one of them was hit. Wisps of flame, charred bits of shattered planes and the mangled, green-clad bodies of Yamamoto's fliers fouled the water in the vicinity of the battle. The Japanese lost seven of their remaining nine planes, but at 1624 four torpedoes cracked into *Chicago's* tender starboard side. One, hitting well forward, showered bridge and forecastle with debris. Three others exploded in the already damaged engineering spaces. Captain Davis passed the word Abandon Ship. On board *Navajo* a sailor burned the towing cable with an acetylene torch and the tug reversed course to pick up survivors.

Recall now that *La Vallette* was out ahead between the enemy planes and *Chicago*. In sailors' parlance, she was in torpedo water and caught a "fish," the torpedo plopping fairly into the forward engine room. Both that and the forward fireroom were flooded, and the after fireroom was threatened with flooding through a ruptured bulkhead. Despite the fact that Lieutenant Eli Roth, damage control and engineer officer, and 21 of his men were killed, the rest of his well-drilled crew plugged the rupture, shored the bulkhead and started the pumps. M. W. Tollberg, Watertender Second Class, horribly and fatally burned by superheated steam, grasped the rungs of the forward fireroom ladder with his fleshless hands, painfully lifted his flayed feet and climbed topside. Groping blindly, he desperately tried to close the oil control valve to his fireroom. Then he collapsed. Within two minutes, Commander Harry Henderson had his ship moving again at slow speed on the after engine.

Captain Davis had about 20 minutes to clear *Chicago* of all hands including the wounded. The evacuation was carried out with efficiency and dispatch. From the water the Captain saw his ship go down stern-first with colors flying.[8] *Navajo, Edwards, Waller* and *Sands* collected 1049 survivors of her crew.

---

[8] *Chicago* sank in 2000 fathoms at lat. 11°25′30″ S, long. 160°56′ E.

Now another warning of more enemy aircraft en route came through from Guadalcanal. This time the Nip fliers failed to connect or to hinder the American retirement. *La Vallette* was forced to take a tow from *Navajo* when her feed-water failed, *Waller* chased down a submarine contact; otherwise the passage to Espiritu Santo was uneventful.

The Battle of Rennell Island was over. Japan made extravagant claims of sinking one battleship (*Chicago*, as usual) and three cruisers and damaging others. The official propaganda, snatching eagerly at something to divert the people's attention from the imminent evacuation of Guadalcanal, even predicted that this would be considered the decisive battle of the war. Actually it placed the seal of success on the new Japanese night air attack technique. Even so, the gunners of Task Force 18 and the Wildcats of the carriers gave a good account of themselves. This defeat was due not only to a combination of bad luck and bad judgment, as at Tassafaronga, but to Admiral Giffen's inexperience and his determination to make the rendezvous with Briscoe on time. Halsey's endorsement on Giffen's Action Report was a scathing indictment of mistakes in judgment; that of Nimitz was more tolerant.

Japanese flares and float lights soon became familiar to American sailors, but it was not until the Pacific Fleet developed carrier-based night fighter technique that the menace of twilight and moonlight air attacks was effectively met.

There was one consolation; owing to Giffen's diversion of Japanese air forces, the American transports unloaded their troops and materiel at Lunga Point without molestation, as did a second convoy of five transports which left Espiritu Santo 31 January and arrived 4 February 1943. The other task forces that had been sent forward to support them remained operating in the Coral Sea south of the Solomons for almost a week, because of information that Admiral Kondo, with a good part of the Combined Fleet, was still milling around Ontong Java. But Kondo, as we have seen, was covering the secret evacuation of Guadalcanal.

CHAPTER XVI

Guadalcanal Evacuated[1]

1–9 February 1943

1. *Operation "KE"*

BACK in December, General Patch wished to land a regimental combat team on the southwest coast of Guadalcanal to plug the enemy's reinforcement channel near Cape Esperance and, at the same time, pinch him in the stern. That plan fell through because the Navy was unable to furnish either troop lift or support. But six LCTs (landing craft, tank)[2] that arrived at Tulagi in January were sufficient for a shore-to-shore amphibious operation, and Captain Briscoe's "Cactus Striking Force," the four Tulagi-based destroyers, were deemed adequate support.

General Patch selected the 2nd Battalion 132nd Infantry for this interesting task. Since very little was known about that part of Guadalcanal, a reconnaissance party marched across the island by the Kokumbona trail and at Beaufort Bay embarked in *Kocorana*, a small Solomon Islands schooner, in the early hours of 1 February, to set up an observation post at Verahue. At the same time, destroyer transport *Stringham* and 5 LCTs were being loaded with troops, trucks, artillery, ammunition and rations at Kukum. At 0400 February 1, they shoved off for the seven-hour trip around Cape Esperance. Well screened by destroyers *Fletcher*, *Radford*, *Nicholas* and *DeHaven*, and by Henderson Field fighter planes, the

[1] Cincpac "Solomon Islands Campaign – Fall of Guadalcanal" 17 Apr. 1943; Action Reports of ships and commands involved; Records of 2nd Destroyer Squadron (WDC No. 161,711); "Japanese Naval War Diary" ATIS 16268; Cdr. R. J. Bulkley's PT History.
[2] See Vol. II of this History p. 269.

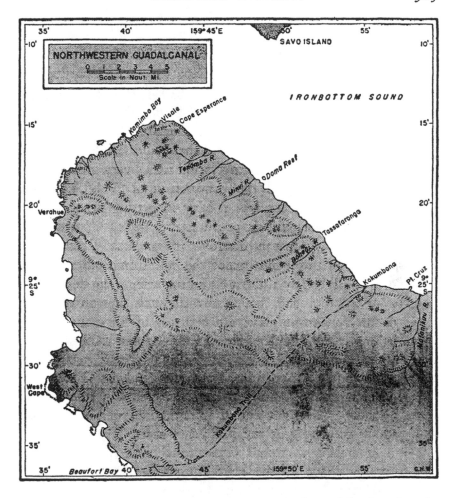

troops and their gear were safely deposited on Verahue beach. Japanese bombers on the "milk run" to Henderson Field never even fluttered an aileron at the sight, but one of them was shot down by the destroyers.

Unknown to the Americans, the enemy had chosen the night of 1–2 February to begin his big evacuation, and his aviators were instructed to prevent any interference with the sea lane of retreat. It doubtless looked to them as if the secret of Operation "KE" had leaked out, and that Briscoe was trying to break it up.

Destroyers *DeHaven* and *Nicholas*, escorting back to Iron-bottom Sound three LCTs which had completed unloading, had reached a point about three miles south of Savo Island. *Radford* and *Fletcher* were still t'other side Cape Esperance escorting the other two landing craft and, by some unexplained mismanagement, they had all the fighter escort, leaving *DeHaven* and *Nicholas* bare. Enemy dive-bombers winged in over Florida Island at 1450 and turned toward Savo Island. Guadalcanal radio hastily broadcast a warning which put both destroyers and LCTs very much on the alert. Within a few minutes the formation of 14 "Vals" appeared. On board *DeHaven* there was a delay in getting permission to shoot, and it was not until six of the enemy peeled off from low altitude — 5000 feet — that the destroyer fought back. Three bombs hit *DeHaven* and a near-miss mined the hull. Commander Charles E. Tolman was killed by a direct hit on the bridge; the ship settled quickly by the bow and, within two minutes, was on her way down to the Ironbottom graveyard with 167 of her crew. During this brief action the machine guns of *LCT-63* and *LCT-181* shot down a plane, and after it was over, the landing craft rescued 146 survivors including 38 wounded. Destroyer *Nicholas* (Lieutenant Commander Andrew J. Hill), which attracted the attention of eight Japanese planes, got out of it with only near-misses that damaged the steering gear and killed two men.

Naval commanders around Guadalcanal soon had something else to worry about. In the early afternoon, coastwatchers and scouting aircraft reported a score of enemy destroyers, north of Vella Lavella, coming down the Slot at high speed. This was the first echelon of Operation "KE." It looked like another drive to land troops; it must be stopped. At 1820, 17 SBDs and 7 TBFs covered by 17 F4Fs swooped down on the destroyers when passing Vangunu Island and met a hot reception from a combat patrol of 30 "Zekes." At a cost of four American planes, destroyer *Makinami* was stopped by a bomb hit; but the other nineteen, after some adroit dodging, continued toward Guadalcanal.

At the coming of darkness, four different weapons were readied by four separate forces to greet the "Express" — mines, destroyers, PTs and aircraft. The first were carried by the converted four-stack destroyers *Tracy, Montgomery* and *Preble,* which started dropping some 300 of them, beginning at Doma Reef and continuing halfway to Cape Esperance. This offensive mine field was a bitter surprise to the Japanese. Destroyer *Makigumo,* maneuvering to avoid PT warheads, ran afoul of it and had to be scuttled.

The second instrument of opposition was Captain Briscoe's team, now reduced to three ships. Briscoe knew that his only chance of success lay in a surprise assault; unfortunately that is what the enemy expected. Night-flying aircraft protecting the Japanese destroyers so heckled *Fletcher, Radford* and *Nicholas* that they were unable to deliver an attack.

Meantime the third American weapon, a force of eleven PT boats, was brought into action.[3] Clagett's *PT-111* and Gamble's *PT-48,* stationed two miles southwest of Savo, were the first to find an enemy. Clagett took after a destroyer three miles east of Cape Esperance while Gamble set course for two others a couple of miles west of Savo. At 2315 Clagett, within a quarter of a mile of his target, and already under fire, loosed all four torpedoes, then hightailed for safety. An enemy shell, probably from destroyer *Kawakaze,* erupted within the paper-thin hull, battered the crew badly and set the boat afire.[4] The men quickly and painfully went over the side. Schools of sharks which attacked the wounded were fought off by able-bodied survivors until morning and *PT-111* lost but one officer and one man.

Gamble's *PT-48* closed her target to 900 yards, fired two torpedoes, followed by the second pair, but she made no hits. Gamble, after attempting to flee through heavy enemy salvos, beached her on Savo Island where all hands piled ashore and next day were rescued along with their boat. *PT-115,* patrolling north of Cape Esperance about 2300, had an experience similar to that of her team-

[3] Cdr. MTB Flot. One "Report of PT Activities Night of 1–2 Feb. 1943."
[4] Trans. of "Battle Lessons Learned in Greater East Asia War (Torpedoes)," Jicpoa Item No. 5782-A.

mate. *PT–37* (Ensign James J. Kelly USNR) had just got off her last torpedo when a direct hit in the gasoline tanks blew her to smithereens. The accompanying fire cast brilliant sky and water reflections around Cape Esperance, giving rise to the erroneous belief of other PT crews that torpedo hits were being scored. Only one man, badly wounded, survived the wreck of *PT–37*. A third boat caught in the Cape Esperance trap, *PT–47*, escaped by retiring under cover of a heavy rain squall.

Two more boats had run a gauntlet of plane strafing and bombing to reach station. They waited until 2249 before the loom of a Japanese hull appeared. *PT–124* (Lieutenant Clark W. Faulkner USNR) led off with three torpedoes which appeared to hit, then beat a hasty retreat to Tulagi. *PT–123* (Ensign Ralph L. Richards USNR), following her, approached to within 500 yards of the target before a strange and unprecedented disaster overtook her. An enemy plane glided in and released a lucky bomb which landed with a fatal "wham" on the torpedo boat's stern. The boat disintegrated into flaming splinters and four of her men were lost.

The fourth American weapon was also ineffectual. About midnight six SBDs from Henderson Field made an indecisive attack on "two burning destroyers," probably only *Makigumo*. That finished the evening's performance for the Americans.

It is to their credit that the Japanese destroyers, in the face of this varied opposition, managed to carry out their evacuation mission. Bright and early on 2 February the indefatigable Dauntless and Avenger aircraft found the retiring destroyers, but their bombs did little or no damage. A last look at the enemy by a search plane revealed 19 destroyers, including *Makinami* under tow, making for Faisi.

This was the last and most violent PT boat action in the Guadalcanal campaign. As on other occasions, their valiant officers and men accomplished less than they had intended, or thought they had done; but they would have been pleased to have read Tokyo's lament in a special report devoted to the doings of such men as Clagett and Kelly. "The enemy has used PT boats aggressively

. . . on their account our naval ships have had many a bitter pill to swallow — there are many examples of their having rendered the transport of supplies exceptionally difficult." [5] The writer, urging Japan to develop a motor torpedo boat force, wisely observed, "It is necessary to assign to the boats young men who are both robust and vigorous."

Not long after that, this writer accompanied General Patch to "Calvertville," the PT base on Tulagi Harbor, when he presented the medals awarded to some of these robust and vigorous youths of our side. "A wonderful and touching sight," said the General — "all these fine young men, ready to go anywhere and do anything. Makes you feel humble."

Even after the start of Operation "KE" the Japanese kept it secret. The only indication of a retreat was our capture of an abandoned base near Tassafaronga on 2 February. A powerful radio station, a large undamaged machine shop and ten pieces of artillery fell to the Americans. But this might still have indicated consolidation for a renewed offensive. The hectic events of 1-2 February only increased the apprehension that another reinforcement similar to that of mid-November was under way. The fact that enemy carrier air groups were flying from Bougainville fields was an unhealthy sign. The constant shuttle of evacuation barges between Guadalcanal and the Russells looked like a southbound reinforcement instead of a northbound evacuation. Admiral Halsey's concern prompted American carriers to edge closer to the island, General MacArthur's aircraft were asked to help out, Mitscher's land-based planes sowed bombs up and down the Solomons chain and even the old battleships moved up from their base in the Fijis.

The second Japanese evacuation echelon was scheduled for 4 February, but this time there was little excitement off Cape Esperance. Early in the afternoon one cruiser and 22 destroyers weighed anchor at Faisi and commenced a rugged run down the Slot. Again Henderson Field airmen went halfway to meet them

[5] "Battle Lessons Learned in Greater East Asia War (Torpedoes)."

with bombs. Thirty-three SBDs and TBFs covered by 31 fighters were met by swarms of "Zekes" and seasoned ships' gunners. In the resulting mêlée 10 American and 17 Japanese planes were lost. *Maikaze* was disabled by flooding from near-misses; *Shiranuhi* took a bomb on an after gun mount, and two other destroyers were slightly damaged by near-misses.

The PTs made no contact that night and Briscoe's exhausted destroyers had departed. So the heckling was left to Black Cats and dive-bombers. One Cat illuminated the enemy with flares while five SBDs vainly tried to make hits. Japanese bombers and flare planes were over Henderson Field most of the night.

When the sun rose over Florida Island on 5 February, American patrol craft were puzzled by the presence of 30 abandoned barges drifting west of Cape Esperance. An air strike launched to catch the retiring destroyers never found them. And search planes reported 4 battleships, 6 cruisers and 12 destroyers 200 miles north of Choiseul. Did Yamamoto still intend to capture Guadalcanal? One could only guess.

On 7 February the third evacuation echelon comprising 18 destroyers was sighted on its way down the Slot. Because of rain squalls only 15 dive-bombers got through. They made two hits on *Isokaze* and one on *Hamakaze* but neither destroyer fell out of formation. Compared with the night of 1–2 February, the rest of that run was a lark for the Nips. Japanese troops at Cape Esperance and the Russells ferried themselves to the waiting destroyers in landing barges. When the last barge was unloaded and cut adrift, this final run of the "Tokyo Express" hastened up the Slot crowded with high-ranking officers, rear-echelon soldiers and sailors. And the Rising Sun never rose again over Ironbottom Sound.

During these three nights of evacuation, 11,706 men were pulled out of Guadalcanal; an amazing performance which elicited praise from Admiral Nimitz: "Only skill in keeping their plans disguised and bold celerity in carrying them out enabled the Japanese to withdraw the remnants of the Guadalcanal garrison." [6] Never in

6 Cincpac "Fall of Guadalcanal." Withdrawal figures from Japanese Naval War Diary.

the history of naval warfare have there been such clever evacuations as those by the Japanese from Kiska and Guadalcanal. But evacuation does not win wars, and a large proportion of the troops here withdrawn were starved, wounded, disease-racked and of no further use to the Emperor. According to a reliable coastwatcher on northeastern Bougainville, some 3000 evacuees in bad shape were set ashore there from destroyers and told to shift for themselves. From the Japanese point of view, that was more honorable than leaving them to be captured by the enemy.

General Patch's ground forces, slogging along jungle trails during the first week of February, were bemused. What were the Japanese up to? By 7 February Colonel George's western pincer, operating from Verahue, was about three miles from Cape Esperance, organizing for a decisive thrust.[7] His eastern tentacle, composed of the 161st Infantry and the 10th Marines as supporting artillery, was already a mile west of Tassafaronga and going strong. On the morning of 8 February, nothing could be found on the Cape Esperance beaches but empty boats and abandoned supplies. And that was the General's first certain knowledge of an evacuation.

The troops now redoubled their efforts to close the gap. At 1625 February 9, in a village on the Tenamba River, the 2nd Battalion of the 132nd Infantry coming from the west met the 2nd Battalion of the 161st Infantry coming from the east.

General Patch radioed to Admiral Halsey: "Total and complete defeat of Japanese forces on Guadalcanal effected 1625 today. . . . Am happy to report this kind of compliance with your orders. . . . 'Tokyo Express' no longer has terminus on Guadalcanal."

2. *The Cost and the Return*

There it was — 2500 square miles of miasmic plain, thick jungle and savage mountains in American hands, after exactly six months

[7] Colonel George was wounded 7 Feb. and was relieved by Col. Ferry.

of toil, suffering and terror. What had it cost? What was the return? Where were we going next?

In war's brutal scale of lives lost against lives risked, the bloodletting from 60,000 Army and Marine Corps troops committed to Guadalcanal, had not been excessive; 1592 killed in action. Navy losses, never to this day compiled, were certainly in excess of that figure, and several score fliers of all three air forces had given their lives. But the Japanese had lost about two thirds of the 36,000 men who fought on Guadalcanal — 14,800 killed or missing, 9000 dead of disease and 1000 taken prisoner. Many thousand more soldiers went down in blasted transports or barges, and the number of Japanese sailors lost in the vicious sea battles will never be known, because such matters do not interest the Japanese.

On the material side the tallies of combat ships lost by each side in the Guadalcanal campaign [8] are surprisingly even: —

| | Allied | | Japanese | |
	number	tonnage	number	tonnage
Battleships	0		2	62,000
Aircraft Carriers	2	34,500	0	
Light Carriers	0		1	8,500
Heavy Cruisers	6	56,925	3	26,400
Light Cruisers	2	12,000	1	5,700
Destroyers	14	22,815	11	20,930
Submarines	0		6	11,309
Total	24	126,240	24	134,839

Tactically — in the sense of coming to grips with the enemy — Guadalcanal was a profitable lesson book. The recommendations of Guadalcanal commanders became doctrine for Allied fighting men the world over. And it was the veteran from "the 'Canal" who went back to man the new ship or form the cornerstone for the new regiment. On top level, mark well the names of Halsey, Turner, Vandegrift, Patch, Geiger, Collins, Lee, Kinkaid, Ainsworth, Merrill. They would be heard from again.

[8] Table compiled by Mr. W. L. Robinson. It does not include transports (AP, AK or APD) of which the Japanese had far the heavier loss, or auxiliaries such as *Seminole*, or patrol craft.

Strategically, as seen from Pearl Harbor or Constitution Avenue, Guadalcanal was worth every ship, plane and life that it cost. The enemy was stopped in his many-taloned reach for the antipodes. Task One in the arduous climb to Rabaul was neatly if tardily packaged and filed away.

There were more subtle implications to Guadalcanal. The lordly Samurai, with his nose rubbed in the mud and his sword rusted by the salt of Ironbottom Sound, was forced to revise his theory of invincibility. A month previously Hirohito had issued an imperial rescript stating that in the Solomon Islands "a decisive battle is being fought between Japan and America." Radio Tokyo gave out that the Imperial forces, "after pinning down the Americans to a corner of the island," had accomplished their mission and so departed to fight elsewhere. There was a laugh for Americans in that; but Guadalcanal never inspired much laughter.

For us who were there, or whose friends were there, Guadalcanal is not a name but an emotion, recalling desperate fights in the air, furious night naval battles, frantic work at supply or construction, savage fighting in the sodden jungle, nights broken by screaming bombs and deafening explosions of naval shells. Sometimes I dream of a great battle monument on Guadalcanal; a granite monolith on which the names of all who fell and of all ships that rest in Ironbottom Sound may be carved. At other times I feel that the jagged cone of Savo Island, forever brooding over the blood-thickened waters of the Sound, is the best monument to the men and ships who here rolled back the enemy tide.

APPENDIX

Allied Air Squadrons at Henderson Field, Guadalcanal[1]

20 August 1942–2 February 1943

Dates following C.O.'s are of death in action when asterisked; otherwise, of relief. Numbers of planes in a squadron fluctuated from 1 to 19. *E.* means an Echelon or Detachment only.

Commander Air South Pacific (Comairsopac)
Vice Admiral John S. McCain, *20 Sept.*
Rear Admiral Aubrey W. Fitch

Commander Air Solomons (Comaircactus)
Brigadier General Roy S. Geiger USMC, *Nov.*
Brigadier General Louis E. Woods USMC, *Nov.*
Brigadier General Francis P. Mulcahy USMC

UNITED STATES MARINE CORPS

Squadron	Type	Arrived	Commanding Officer
VMSB–232	SBD–1	20 Aug. 1942	Lt. Col. Richard C. Mangrum
VMSB–231	SBD–1	30 Aug. 1942	Maj. Leo R. Smith *20 Sept.*
			* Capt. Ruben Iden *20 Sept.*
			Capt. Elmer G. Glidden
VMSB–141	SBD–3	23 Sept. 1942	* Capt. Gordon A. Bell *14 Oct.*
			* 1st Lt. W. S. Ashcroft USMCR *8 Nov.*
			1st Lt. R. M. Patterson *13 Nov.*
			Major Joseph Sailer *2 Dec.*
			Maj. L. B. Robertshaw *24 Dec.*
			2nd Lt. J. E. Kepke USMCR *25 Dec.*
			Capt. C. A. Carlson *1 Jan. 1943*
VMSB–131	TBF–1	12 Nov. 1942	Capt. Jens C. Aggerbeck
VMSB–132	SBD–3	29 Oct. 1942	* Maj. Joseph Sailer *7 Dec.*
			Maj. L. B. Robertshaw
VMSB–142	SBD–3	12 Nov. 1942	Maj. Robert H. Richard
VMSB–233	SBD–4	12 Dec. 1942	Maj. Clyde T. Madison *26 Dec.*
			Capt. Elmer L. Gilbert
VMSB–234	SBD–4	28 Jan. 1943	Maj. Otis B. Calhoun
VMF–223	F4F–4	20 Aug. 1942	Maj. John L. Smith
VMF–224	F4F–4	30 Aug. 1942	Capt. Robert E. Galer *31 Dec.*
			Maj. Darrell D. Irwin USMCR
VMF–121	F4F–4	25 Sept. 1942	Maj. Leonard K. Davis *16 Dec.*
			2nd Lt. William F. Wilson *31 Dec.*
			Maj. Donald K. Yost

[1] The PBY and B–17 squadrons were based on various tenders or at Espiritu Santo.

Squadron	Type	Arrived	Commanding Officer
VMF-212	F4F-4	3–16 Oct. 1942	* Lt. Col. Harold W. Bauer *14 Nov.* Capt. J. K. Little USMCR *20 Jan. 1943* Capt. R. F. Stout USMCR
VMF-112	F4F-4	2 Nov. 1942	Maj. Paul J. Fontana
VMF-122	F4F-4	13 Nov. 1942	Capt. Elmer E. Brackett
VMD-154[1]	PB4Y-1	2 Dec. 1942	Lt. Col. Elliott E. Bard
VMF-123	F4F-4	2 Feb. 1943	Maj. Richard M. Baker

UNITED STATES ARMY AIR FORCE

Squadron	Type	Arrived	Commanding Officer
67th Fighter, E.	P-400, P-38	22 Aug. 1942	Capt. Dale D. Brannon *3 Oct.*
68th Fighter	P-40	8 Dec. 1942	Maj. Robert M. Caldwell *8 Nov.* Lt. Stanley A. Palmer *31 Dec.* Capt. Robert B. Hubbell *27 Jan. 1943*
339th Fighter, E.	P-38	3 Oct. 1942	Lt. Fred V. Purnell Maj. D. D. Brannon, *25 Nov.* Capt. J. W. Mitchell
44th Fighter, E.	P-40	22 Dec. 1942	Maj. Kermit A. Taylor
12th Fighter, E.	P-39	3 Jan. 1943	Maj. Paul S. Bechtel *27 Jan. 1943* Capt. Theron J. Graves
70th Fighter, E.	P-39, P-38	21 Dec. 1942	Maj. Waldon Williams
17th Photo Recon.	F-5 [3]	17 Jan. 1943	Capt. John E. Murray
69th Bombdt.	B-25, B-26	31 Dec. 1942	Maj. James F. Collins
31st Bombdt.	B-24	14 Jan. 1943	Maj. George E. Glober

UNITED STATES NAVAL AIR ARM

VS-5 from ENTERPRISE, E.	SBD-3	24 Aug. 1942	Lt. Turner F. Caldwell
VB-6 from ENTERPRISE, E.	SBD-3	24 Aug. 1942	Lt. Cdr. Ray Davis
VT-8 from SARATOGA, E.	TBF-1	13 Sept. 1942	Lt. Harold H. Larsen
VS-71 from WASP	SBD-3	28 Sept 1942	Lt. Porter W. Maxwell
VS-5-D14	OS2U-3	15 Oct. 1942	Lt. Charles H. Franklin USNR
VS-4-D14	OS2U-3	17 Dec. 1942	Lt. John S. Farrington USNR
VP-12 (Black Cats)	PBY-5A	15 Dec. 1942	Lt. Cdr. J. P. Fitzsimmons, *Dec.* Cdr. C. O. Taff
VGS-11 [4]	F4F-4, TBF	1 Feb. 1943	Lt. Cdr. Charles H. Ostrom
VGS-12	F4F-4, TBF	1 Feb. 1943	Lt. Cdr. John Hulme
VGS-16	F4F-4, TBF	1 Feb. 1943	Lt. Cdr. Charles E. Brunton

ROYAL NEW ZEALAND AIR FORCE

Squadron	Type	Arrived	Commanding Officer
9th Bomb Recon., E.	Ventura	14 Nov. 1942	Sq. Ldr. H. M. MacFarlane
3rd Recon.	Hudson	24 Nov. 1942	Wing Cdr. G. H. Fisher

[2] One photo plane of this squadron arrived 11 Nov. It — or another so equipped — discovered Munda Airfield 5 Dec. 1942.

[3] P-38s equipped as photo planes.

[4] Escort Scouting Squadrons; Avenger torpedo planes with fighter escort.

Index

Index

Names of Combat Ships in SMALL CAPITALS
Names of Merchant Ships, and lettered Combat Ships like
I-boats and PTs, in *Italics*

In the following Task Organizations, only the names of Flag Officers are indexed:
Battle of the Eastern Solomons, pp. 84–7; Battle of the Santa Cruz Islands,
pp. 204–7; Naval Battle of Guadalcanal, pp. 231–5; Battle of Tassafaronga, pp. 296–7;
Battle of Rennell Island, p. 353; Allied Air Squadrons at Henderson Field, pp. 374–5.
As references to Air Attacks, Aircraft and Marines would include almost every
page in this volume, only principal operations of the Marines and types of planes
are indexed.

A

AARON WARD, 166, 182, 226, 237, 248–9, 253–5
Abe, Vice Adm. Hiroaki, 82, 85, 200, 206, 208, 222, 233; Guadal. battle, 238, 241–2, 246; retires, 251, 258*n*
Abe, Vice Adm. Koso, 258*n*
Abercrombie, Cdr. L. A., 296, 311
ACHILLES, 184, 326–30
Adams, Lt. Cdr. R. L., 47
Agnew, Lt. Cdr. D. M., 194–5
Ainsworth, Rear Adm. W. L., biog. 325; bombardment missions, 326–9, 345–7, 352
Air search, Savo I., 23–7, 32; chart, 24; E. Sols., 80, 82; Sta. Cruz, 202–3, 224; Guadal., 264; Tassaf., 295–6, 298, 305
Aircraft, Australian, 19–20, 25
Aircraft, carrier-based, see *under names of carriers*
Aircraft, Japanese, float planes, 20, 22, 34, 36, 40–1, 44, 91, 104, 139; "Emily," 87; Kawanishi, 121, 131; losses and new tactics, 139
Aircraft, Marines', see Marine Corps, Aviation
Aircraft, New Zealand, 290, 375
Aircraft, squadrons at Henderson Field, list of, 374–5
Aircraft, U.S. Army, B–17s, 19, 23–5, 70, 105, 117, 121, 138–9, 150, 177, 184, 197, 257, 260–1, 267, 290, 322–3, 325, 341; P–400s, 74, 122; other types, 375

Aircraft, U.S. Navy, float planes, 152, 277, 295, 305, 318; Catalina, 23, 81–8, 118, 122, 177, 200, 202–4, 222–3, 322, 330; SBD, 113; Skytrooper, 179; see "Black Cats"
AKATSUKI, 194–6, 242, 254
AKIGUMO, 223
AKITSUSHIMA, 20, 117–18
AKIZUKI, 151, 197
ALBACORE, 324
ALCHIBA, 57, 179, 292–3
Alderman, Lt. Cdr. J. C., 23, 180
Aleutian situation, 184
ALHENA, 81
ALTAMAHA, 291
AMATSUKAZE, 254
AMBERJACK, 179, 196
ANDERSON, 222–3, 343
Andrew, Lt. Cdr. J. D., 44, 46
Andrews, Ens. F. A., 167
AOBA, at Savo I., 22, 34, 37, 44, 59–61; at E. Sols., 105; at Cape Esperance, 150–1, 158–63, 168–9
Aola Bay, 145
ARASHI, 220*n*, 339
ARIAKE, 323
Army, U.S., XIV Corps, 340; Divisions: Americal, 12, 147, 172, 288, 289*n*, 334–7, 340–3, 371; 25th, 183, 335, 340, 371; 43rd, 181*n*; 101st Med. Regt., 289
Army Air Force, list of squadrons, 375; see Aircraft, Army
Arnold, General H. H., 115–17, 185
Arthur, Col. J. M., 336